upon this rock

upon this rock

The Popes
and their
Changing Role

paul collins

A Crossroad Book
The Crossroad Publishing Company
New York

#49317680

THE CROSSROAD PUBLISHING COMPANY
481 Eighth Avenue, New York, NY 10001

Text © Paul Collins 2000
Design and typography © Melbourne University Press 2000

Text Designed by Lauren Statham, Alice Graphics, Melbourne
Typeset by Syarikat Seng Teik Sdn. Bhd., Malaysia in Perpetua 12.5 point
Printed in the United States of America

Library of Congress Cataloging-in-Publication Data is available.

ISBN 0-8245-1939-6

The scripture quotations contained herein are from the *New Revised Standard Version of the Bible: Catholic
Edition*, copyright 1993 and 1989 by the Division of Christian Education of the National Council of
Churches of Christ in the USA, and are used by permission. All rights reserved.

1 2 3 4 5 6 7 8 9 10   07 06 05 04 03 02

contents

preface

BOTH THE CATHOLIC CHURCH and the papacy seem to hold an extraordinary fascination for the Western mind. The reasons are probably three-fold. Firstly, because the church predates European culture by centuries, it is the matrix from which it emerged. Secondly, the church was the primary vehicle through which the cultural values of Greece and Rome were communicated to the barbaric *volk* who lived beyond the Roman frontiers and eventually occupied Western Europe. And thirdly, it was the church that brought together the disparate cultural elements that underpinned the formation of European civilisation. As Christopher Dawson argued in his perceptive *The Making of Europe*, Western culture, upon which the whole of the Continental, Latin and Anglo-American world is now built, is a product of Christian faith and the Western Catholic church.[1] And the papacy is central to that church.

Further, Catholicism has not simply been fundamental in the for-mation of our culture. The fact is that, despite extraordinary vicissitudes, the church has survived to see in our time the emergence of a new, global culture. In other words, we are now witnessing the reasonably quick mutation of a church rooted in the European cultural tradition into a genuine world church. Part of the essential genius of Catholicism is its ability to change, grow and develop. The majority of Catholics now live in the non-European, emerging world. Despite many setbacks, the church is already slowly learning to speak to them in their own terms, to translate its essential message into new cultural forms, as it did centuries ago for the new European peoples.

That is why now is a significant moment in which to reflect on one of the institutions that are pivotal to Catholicism: the papacy. But here I hasten to add that I do not want to equate the papacy with the church, or vice versa, as some Catholics are inclined to do. While the pope is the most visible sign of Catholicism in the world, particularly in our time, I do not consider this a healthy development for the church. On the contrary, I think we need a much more modest, less dominant model of papal governance. We need popes who are servants, like Jesus himself, not lords of the world, as some of the mediaeval popes thought they were. We need popes who see themselves as a focus of the church's unity, not the sole theological oracles, legal owners and administrators of the ecclesial institution. We need a new way of modelling the papacy for a new cultural and ecclesiastical situation.

When we look back through church history, the extraordinary thing is that the church and the papacy have survived at all. The historian attributes this to the church's remarkable ability to adapt to new cultural circumstances, to respond to new challenges. Yet, paradoxically, the church is the most conservative of institutions, hanging on to outdated ideas and political forms of the past with amazing tenacity. In contrast to the historian, the Christian believer attributes the church's longevity to the promise made by Christ to his apostles that he would send a Spirit who would remain with them until the end of time.

Here I should declare my hand: while I try to take the stance of the detached historian, I also confess that I belong to the group of believers, and at heart I do think that the church has made its way through two thousand years of history because of the delicate, sensitive and pervasive presence of God's Spirit. But, as I argued in an earlier book, *God's Earth* (1995), God takes the world and human affairs seriously. God respects human freedom. Church history is not predetermined, as though God had some detailed master plan that is expressed through the 'divine will', or whatever cliche is used for a manipulative deity who never ceases to interfere in the minutiae of our personal lives in order to diminish our responsibility. Such a view is primitivist, fundamentalist nonsense.

The Spirit's presence in church history is subtle, liberal and gentle. God grants us responsibility and freedom to determine not only our personal lives, but also to participate in our culture and in the great institutions that shape that culture. So the historian who is a believer approaches the history of the church knowing full well that it was the interaction of complex circumstances and people that led to the decisions that for good or ill have determined the history of the Catholic Church. At the same time the historian recognises the subtle and pervasive presence of God in and through those events. While allowing that God writes straight with our crooked lines, the historian tries to understand and delineate the ideas and forces that shaped church history. He or she comes with a critical, slightly cynical eye, trying to clarify, describe and make sense of the events of the past. The post-modernists are right in that we will never be able to do this with finality and completion, and we will always infuse into the lives and affairs of the people of the past our own cultural and personal agendas. But they are wrong to make this an absolute principle. We can comprehend many elements of the past, understand motivations and cultural contexts, discern the connective threads that run through human and societal action, and eventually come to some overall conclusion. This is especially true when we actually 'belong' to the organisation about which we write.

The papacy is an integral part of the church and its history. It is not some sort of free-floating institution that exists above or beyond the community of the faithful. While no serious scholar actually expresses such a view, many historians approach the papacy as though it did have some form of independent existence. Perhaps the reason for this is that the emphasis in many papal histories is political. They examine the papacy's interaction with the social institutions that over the centuries have provided government for the peoples of Europe and the wider world. While not neglecting the political and social role of the popes, my emphasis in this book is more on theology and ecclesiology, on examining the place and role of the papacy in the context of the church, and within that context, the popes' relationships to the world. Many modern historians have neglected this dimension.

Yet this is not to claim for one moment that this book is a complete, detailed history of the theology of ecclesial governance. It is a *popular* history and, as such, aims at providing an accessible, overall survey of the papal institution for the intelligent reader. Part of my inspiration was Monsignor Philip Hughes' *A Popular History of the Catholic Church* (first published in 1939).[2]

In some ways this book is a by-product of or, perhaps more accurately, the broader context for my previous book, *Papal Power* (1997). In writing *Papal Power* I had to look at church history in some detail. I ended up with much more material than I could possibly use in a book that was primarily proposing change in Catholicism's third millennium. And so a second book gradually took shape.

My book *Papal Power* has gained some notoriety due to the fact that soon after its publication it was anonymously reported (the technical term is 'delated') to the Congregation for the Doctrine of the Faith (CDF) in Rome. The CDF had the book 'assessed' by an equally anonymous consultor. *Papal Power* drew on the history of Catholicism to propose a new way of viewing papal authority in the church. Naturally enough, this historical approach would cause problems for those whose theological position is that faith is lived out in a static, normative way as though it were outside and untouched by the realities of history. The historical approach would cause even more problems for those whose personal power would be lessened or otherwise affected by the changes I suggested. My position is that change and development, inspired and guided by the Holy Spirit, are an essential and integral part of the process of belief. I hold that there is an organic and continuous development that occurs in, through—and often enough, despite—the vagaries of church history. *Upon This Rock* is quite different from *Papal Power*. The reader will be the judge of my success or otherwise.

In dealing with such a wide-ranging topic, my indebtedness to others is great. Firstly, to my colleague and friend, Fr Edmund Campion of the Catholic Institute of Sydney, who read the entire manuscript and made many helpful suggestions. Secondly, to the librarians and to those who sponsor the Joint Theological Library at Ormond College in the University of Melbourne, the Chifley Library at the Australian National

University, and the library of Saint Mark's National Theological Centre in Canberra.

Anyone writing history on such a broad canvas is indebted to many other scholars and authors. I have endeavoured to acknowledge them in the notes and bibliography. But several books must be particularly mentioned: Canon J. N. D. Kelly's indispensable *Oxford Dictionary of Popes* sat beside me on my desk throughout the writing of both *Papal Power* and *Upon This Rock*. Constant use is the only real test for a reference book, and Kelly's *Dictionary* stands up to every challenge. Also very useful was F. L. Cross' *The Oxford Dictionary of the Christian Church*. Again, it is a reference source of great reliability. Fr Norman P. Tanner, SJ, has done scholarship a great service with his *Decrees of the Ecumenical Councils*. Richard McBrien's *HarperCollins Encyclopedia of Catholicism* was also useful.

I owe real gratitude to the friends who have supported me while this book was being written. They know who they are, but there are three I want to especially mention. Firstly, Doctor Joy Damousi. We learned to write history together in the Research School of Social Sciences at the Australian National University in Canberra. She is a fine historian and writer, and we have remained friends ever since. Secondly, Doctor Judith Champ and I first met in London more than a decade ago with a common interest in Archbishop William Ullathorne; he was centrally important in both Australian and English nineteenth-century Catholic history. Judith has supported me not only through friendship but also in practical ways by checking books and references both in the United Kingdom and Rome. Finally, and most importantly, thanks are due to Sister Mary Pescott, RSM, who really launched me as a writer by suggesting back in 1985 the topic of my first book. A fine historian and teacher, she is always a dear friend and an honest critic. Such people are rare.

In a book this size, covering two thousand years of history, there will be errors; they are hard to avoid when working on such a large field. For any such errors I take full responsibility.

Paul Collins
Canberra, November 1999

1

From the New Testament to constantine the great

Who is Peter?

WE ACTUALLY HAVE a lot of information in the New Testament about the man whom the Roman church regards as the first pope. The one whom today we call St Peter began life with a Hebrew name: Simeon. The Greek version of his name was Simon. In the New Testament the Greek surname *Petros* is often attached to the forename Simon. The word *petros* is a masculine version of the feminine noun *petra*, which means 'rock'. The original word for rock in Aramaic was *kepha*, and in several passages in the later New Testament Peter is referred to as Cephas. The origin of this confusion of names and titles for the man we call Peter is an Aramaic pun devised by Jesus and reported in the sixteenth chapter of St Matthew's gospel. But before discussing the significance of his names and titles, who was Simon Peter?

The gospels tell us that he was a fisherman, the son of Jonah or John, and that he originated in Bethsaida, a small village below the Golan Heights near the east bank of the Jordan, where it enters the Sea of Galilee. The gospels also tell us that he had a house in Capernaum on the north-western shore of the same sea. The town became a base for Jesus during his ministry in Galilee. Peter was a fisherman in partnership with his brother Andrew. The brothers obviously had some form of business relationship with James and John, the sons of Zebedee. So Peter does not seem to have been a pauper; in fact, he may have been reasonably comfortable. All four men had been disciples of John the Baptist and they had probably known Jesus for some time. Jesus must have impressed them because 'as he walked by the Sea of Galilee' he called them to minister with him and 'immediately they left their nets and followed him' (Matthew 4:18–22).

The gospels reveal Peter as an impetuous and passionate man, often lacking judgement and misunderstanding the whole point of Jesus' teaching and ministry. In this he probably reflects his origins. In the Acts of the Apostles he is bluntly described as an 'uneducated and ordinary' man (Acts 4:13).

Yet right from the start Peter is clearly given an important leadership role in the immediate group of disciples and apostles around Jesus, and he often acts as their spokesman. At the last supper Jesus tells him to 'strengthen your brothers' (Luke 22:32) and after the resurrection he is given charge of 'shepherding' the flock (John 21:15–17). Nevertheless, he is severely rebuked by Jesus for his impetuosity and lack of judgement. We now know that the gospels reflect something of the situation in the early churches where such stories were part of an oral tradition before being written down. From this we can confidently deduce that Peter was recognised as having an important leadership role in the early Christian communities. He is mentioned much more often than any of the other apostles in the gospels, and is always mentioned first in the lists of the Twelve.

In the period after the ascension of Jesus, Peter assumes an unchallenged leadership role (see Acts 1–12). It is he who assumes the responsibility to preach the first sermon to the Jewish people proclaiming the messianic role of the resurrected Jesus: 'This Jesus God raised up and of that all of us are witnesses . . . Therefore let the entire house of Israel know with certainty that God has made him both Lord and Messiah, this Jesus whom you crucified' (Acts 2:32, 36).

It is also Peter who takes the leadership of the earliest Christian community in Jerusalem, and he is miraculously rescued from prison when Herod tries to kill him (Acts 12:1–17). However, from about this period onwards it is more difficult to discern the biography and role of

Peter. At the Council of Jerusalem, which debated the issue of whether non-Jewish converts to Christianity had to undergo the initiation processes required of converts to Judaism, such as circumcision, he seems to have played a mediating role between Paul and James (Acts 15:14). From this point onwards it is Paul who takes most of the New Testament limelight. James, 'the brother of the Lord', seems to have taken over as 'bishop' in Jerusalem, and Peter seems to have left the city because of continuing threats from Herod.

However, before examining the latter period of Peter's life, we need to take a more detailed look at the key gospel texts that delineate his role. But first, one other aspect of Peter's life is worth briefly noting. Paul makes it clear that at the time of writing the First Letter to the Corinthians (around AD 56–57), Peter was a married man: he refers to 'the believing wife' of Cephas (I Corinthians 9:5). That is reinforced by the reference in Matthew's gospel to Peter's mother-in-law, whom Jesus cured of fever (Matthew 8:15).

'Get behind me, Satan!'—Peter as leader

NOWADAYS THERE IS a consensus that the remote origins of the papacy can be discerned in the New Testament and the sub-apostolic church— the period immediately after the death of the apostles. But there is also equal recognition that the institution as we know it only begins to take a shape that is recognisable to us today in the mid-fourth century, after the age of the Emperor Constantine the Great (306–37). When looking for the origins of the papacy in the New Testament, Catholics usually go straight to the famous Petrine text in Matthew's gospel (16:13–20) where Peter is called the 'rock' upon which the church is built. This text has been the subject of many debates, but there is a consensus today that in the text Jesus confers the leadership of the apostles upon Peter.

Yet this passage should not be seen in isolation from the broader New Testament depiction of Peter. The role of Peter as leader of the early community needs to be placed in the general context of Jesus' teaching about church leadership, and in the specific context of the Gospels' emphasis on Peter's betrayal of Jesus. The New Testament is very realistic about leadership in the church: the person who leads is fundamentally a servant whose imperfections and sinfulness are known to the community. In the New Testament Peter emerges as a failed man who has betrayed his Lord and this betrayal is well known to the whole church.

So to understand the so-called 'Petrine text' in Matthew we need to place it in its broader context, especially the verses that describe the events that immediately follow it (Matthew 16:21–3). It is this passage that I want to consider first, for it gives us a further clue as to the type of man that Peter was.

Jesus tells the disciples that he 'must go to Jerusalem and undergo great suffering at the hands of the elders and chief priests and scribes, and be killed, and on the third day be raised' (Matthew 16:21). This is unacceptable to Peter, who tells him that 'this must never happen' (16:22). The fact that Peter was insensitive to the pain and fear contained in this remark is shown when Jesus turns on him and responds with a sudden, chilling rebuke: 'Get behind me, Satan! You are a stumbling block [the Greek word used here is *skandalon*, from which our word 'scandal' is derived] to me; for you are setting your mind not on divine things but on human things' (16:23). In intertestamental Judaism, the figure of Satan, whose remote origins are found in the Hebrew Scriptures, becomes associated with illness and evil and comes to be seen as the direct rival of God. In Jesus' own life Satan tempts him in the desert (Matthew 4:1–11, Mark 1:12–13, Luke 4:1–13); he is the adversary who tries to divert Jesus from the work assigned to him by God. He later enters into the heart of Judas Iscariot so that he betrays Jesus (Luke 22:3). In the incident in Matthew 16, Jesus identifies Peter with Satan. The proximity of this text to the appointment of Peter as head of the apostles is not accidental, for the gospels are carefully constructed. Peter is also a *scandalon*, a 'stumbling block', an obstacle over which one trips. The text is meant to be humiliating. So Jesus is bluntly saying that Peter is more than a nagging and obtuse follower. He is an adversary, an enemy, a fool whose mind is 'not on divine things but on human'. Implicit in the text is the sense that Peter is symbolic of all of Jesus' disciples and followers: people caught between faith and doubt, unwilling to embrace the cross that Jesus again emphasises in the very next verse: 'If any want to become my followers, let them deny themselves and take up their cross and follow me' (Matthew 16:24).

This portrait of Peter as failed disciple is strongly reinforced by his betrayal of Jesus at the time of his passion and death. Again Jesus forewarns him at the last supper: 'Truly I tell you, this very night, before the cock crows, you will deny me three times' (Matthew 26:34). Peter replies adamantly: 'Even though I must die with you I will not deny you'. Yet within a few hours Peter denies even knowing Jesus. It is significant that his denial is not the result of real pressure. He is challenged by two mere 'servant-girls'—nobodies without any social or political influence. Yet 'he denied it with an oath: "I do not know the man"' (see Matthew 26:69–75).

John P. Meier, a Catholic expert on Matthew's gospel, says that Peter's failures and Jesus' rebukes are warnings directed specifically to church leaders.[1] This highlights the importance of reading the gospels within the context of the early church communities from which the texts originally emerged. These references to Peter's betrayal and the rebukes of Jesus have a broader context, for Matthew's gospel particularly seems to emphasise Peter's failures. The original provenance of this gospel was a Jewish-Christian community, probably in Syrian Antioch (now Antakya in Turkey) in the years after AD 70.[2] This community obviously recognised Peter's leadership in the early church, but there is a probable reason for the emphasis on his failures: even in the early church there is evidence that forms of 'clericalism' were already beginning to emerge.[3] The references to Peter's failures stressed that the leadership of the church was all too human and in need of constant reform. The texts may also have contained the ironic implication that Peter was an appropriate leader precisely because he had failed so badly. He had committed the worst and most frightening sin, especially in times of persecution: apostasy. He had buckled under pressure and denied his Lord.

The New Testament model of leadership

THE QUESTION OF Christian leadership is basic to everything that follows in this book. That is why it is important to examine the New Testament vision of it in some detail. There is a profound sense in which the New Testament presents Peter as the fundamental paradigm for later popes. Through his personality and experience, the New Testament spells out unequivocally the model of leadership that is appropriate for the Christian community.

In Matthew's gospel Jesus contrasts the exercise of secular power with the kind of authority that must be found in the church. The church is a unique institution and the way it operates must reflect this. In the Christian understanding the co-relative of authority and power is humble service:

> But Jesus called [the disciples] to him and said, 'You know that the rulers of the Gentiles lord it over them, and their great ones are tyrants over them. It will not be so among you; but whoever wishes to be great among you must be your servant, and whoever wishes to be first among you must be your slave; just as the Son of Man came not to be served but to serve, and to give his life as a ransom for many'. [Matthew 20:25–28]

Here Jesus presents a stark contrast between the secular exercise of tyrannical power through force and the Christian emphasis on slave-like service. Jesus models this himself when he washes his disciples' feet at the last supper (John 13:3–11). It is ironic that, once again, it is Peter who, in his embarrassment, misunderstands Jesus' action, and protests, 'You will never wash my feet'. Jesus responds bluntly: 'Unless I wash you, you have no share with me'.

In Matthew's gospel Jesus also stresses that leadership is not about the perks and symbols of office. He specifically accused the religious leaders of his own day of making

> their phylacteries broad and their fringes long. They love to have the place of honour at banquets and the best seats in the synagogues, and to be greeted with respect in the marketplaces, and to have people call them rabbi. But you are not to be called rabbi, for you have one teacher and you are all students. And call no one your father . . . Nor are you to be called instructors . . . The greatest among you will be your servant. All who exalt themselves will be humbled, and all who humble themselves will be exalted. [Matthew 23:5–12]

Here the emphasis is on the contrast between the attitude and titles adopted by the religious establishment who have rejected Matthew's community of Christians as 'heretics', and the humility required of the leaders of the community by the teaching of Jesus.[4] The clear implication here is that some Christians are already abrogating to themselves titles such as 'rabbi', 'father' and 'instructor' that are totally alien to the followers of Christ. It is in texts like these that the strong sense of equality operative in the early Christian communities emerges: titles and distinctions of rank were anathema and there was a willingness to act against them. In this context the person who led the church was both disciple and servant.

The theme of humility and leadership is taken up also in the First Letter of Peter, but here it is developed in a broader context. This letter was universally attributed to Peter himself until the nineteenth century, but since then various arguments have been proposed against his authorship. In a sensible compromise between these two views, Raymond E. Brown suggested that the Letter expresses what he termed the heritage of Peter.[5] Brown thought it was written by a disciple of Peter in Rome in either the 80s or the 90s. It emphasises that the church leader should not 'lord it over' church members (I Peter 5:3). The letter tells all the members of the community that they 'must clothe [themselves] with humility in [their] dealings with one another, for "God opposes the proud but gives grace to the humble"' (5:5). It also points to the fact that all church leadership will be judged in the light of Peter's humility.

However, it is also clear that even in New Testament times Christians did not achieve their own ideals, and that power, politics, clericalism and manipulation were part of church life. The attainment of humility will always be a struggle. This is precisely why Matthew emphasises the failures of Peter as the primal leader of the New Testament church.

The Petrine text

THE TEXT THAT has become the authoritative passage to demonstrate the origins of the papacy in the New Testament is Matthew 16:17–19. Interestingly, it was not until the time of Pope Damasus I (366–84) that the popes really appealed to this passage of Matthew's gospel as the New Testament source for papal primacy. Certainly, the text gives great authority to the leader of the apostles. Jesus says:

> Blessed are you Simon, son of Jonah! . . . And I tell you, you are Peter and on this rock I will build my church, and the gates of Hades will not prevail against it. I will give you the keys of the kingdom of heaven, and whatever you bind on earth will be bound in heaven, and whatever you loose on earth will be loosed in heaven.

Despite its apparent clarity, there has been much debate about this text. Some writers feel it belongs much more appropriately among the post-resurrection narratives.[6] For instance, the Orthodox scholar Veselin Kesich argues that placing it after the resurrection actually strengthens the claim to Petrine primacy by distancing it from Jesus' harsh rebuke of Peter as a *skandalon*.[7] Because these verses are found only in Matthew and not in Mark and Luke, some nineteenth-century Protestant scholars, such as Adolf von Harnack, argued that the text was an interpolation to support the fact of papal primacy. Others held it was added later, possibly by Matthew's own community. While no final conclusion has yet been reached about these debates, the text of Matthew 16 indicates a strong Palestinian, Aramaic background.

What is the meaning of the text?[8] Speaking for the apostolic group, Peter confesses that Jesus is 'the Messiah [or the Christ], the Son of the living God' (Matthew 16:16). As Meier points out, this sounds like a confessional formula from Matthew's community.[9] This elicits from Jesus an elaborate play on words that is only really clear in Aramaic, the language Jesus actually spoke. In response to the question 'Who do people say the Son of Man is?', Peter has given Jesus a title: he is the son of the living God. Jesus reciprocates by giving Peter a title. The original name of the leader of the apostles was Simon Bar-Jonah (Simon, son of John). In this text Jesus calls him in Aramaic, *kepha*. As we saw previously, this word is translated into Greek as *petros* or *petra*. Both the Greek words and the Aramaic word mean 'rock'. This is not a proper name; it is a title that Jesus is conferring on Simon—he is 'the rock'.[10] It was not until the end of the second century AD in the writings of Tertullian that 'Peter' was actually used as a proper name.

In the light of the earlier discussion about the word *scandalon* (stumbling stone) the reference here to Peter as 'rock' is significant; there are clear connections between the two. There are also strong Old Testament overtones in the use of the word 'rock' in this context: Abraham was the 'rock' from which the chosen people was hewn, and 'the quarry from which [they] were dug' (Isaiah 51:1). God also is a 'rock': 'Trust in the Lord forever, for in the Lord God you have an ever-lasting rock' (Isaiah 26:4). Peter has now become the bedrock upon which the new church or people of God will be built. The term 'church' is only used twice in the gospels; its real home is in the letters of Paul.[11] Meier thinks that the phrase 'gates of Hades (hell)' probably refers to death rather than to the forces of Satan and evil.[12] Thus the church will survive the end of the world, for it is already the community of those who have experienced the salvation that has now been realised in Christ.

The reference to 'the keys of the kingdom of heaven' clearly grants to Peter the power of Jesus' vice-regent. The phrase also draws on an in-cident described in Isaiah (22:15–25) where God instructs the prophet to remove Shebna, the steward or prime minister of King Hezekiah. The keys to the palace, the symbols of office, are taken from Shebna. The Matthean text draws on contemporary Judaism and refers to the rabbinic authority to 'bind' (that is, to impose a kind of excommuni-cation) and to 'loose' (to absolve from excommunication). It also refers to the permission to hold certain opinions or to forbid those opinions to be held, or to allow or prohibit specific works on the Sabbath day.

The tendency of some Roman Catholic scholars is to focus on the Petrine text almost exclusively. In contrast, Kesich rightly argues that the Petrine text makes full sense only within a wider New Testament context.[13] Firstly, he refers to the role of the other apostles in the process of binding and loosing. Two chapters after the Petrine text in Matthew 16, Jesus extends to all the disciples the power of binding and loosing: 'Truly I tell you, whatever you bind on earth will be bound in heaven, and whatever you loose on earth will be loosed loosed in heaven' (Matthew 18:18). In this context, Kesich also refers to the Council of Jerusalem, described in chapter 15 of the Acts of the Apostles, as a para-digm of how collegial authority should be exercised in the church. Here the whole leadership cadre of the church participates in the process of making a decision about what gentile converts are bound to observe. Secondly, Kesich emphasises the role of the believers, especially in the Pauline communities, in mediating and proclaiming Christ to the world. It is upon them and their ministry that the church is also built. Finally, Kesich emphasises the central role of the Holy Spirit in the life of the church and its leadership. It is 'the Advocate, the Holy Spirit, whom the Father will send in my name [who] will teach you everything and remind you of all that I have said to you' (John 14:26). In other words the Petrine text must be viewed within the broader context of the New Testament teaching about the other apostles and the Christian community.

One of the most important studies of the Petrine text is that of the Protestant Reformed scholar Oscar Cullmann.[14] He accepts unequivocally that leadership in the apostolic church is conferred on Peter. But he argues that this Petrine leadership is unique, as is the role of the apostle. The primary function of the apostle is to witness to the resurrection of Jesus and to lay the foundation of church. Cullmann maintains that this function cannot survive the apostolic period; in fact, he tends to limit this even further to the earliest foundation period in Jerusalem, when Peter's primacy was clear. This is not to suggest that Cullmann does not allow for the ministry of leadership to be exercised right down through church history. However, while Peter might be the example and pattern of church leadership, Cullmann says he and his ministry cannot be expected to 'arise' through every period of church history.[15] In other words, he denies that there can be successors to Peter in the sense that he is the unique apostolic rock upon which the foundations of the church are laid.

Nowadays the discussion has moved on since Cullmann's book. Catholics have conceded that the apostolic period is non-repeatable in the sense that the founding members of the church are the primary witnesses to the resurrection. As the unique bedrock upon which the church is built, there is a sense in which Peter and the apostles cannot have successors. However, the French Canadian Catholic theologian J. M. R. Tillard argues that, although it is impossible to speak of an unqualified Petrine succession, there is a profound sense in which the apostle lives on in the bishops of Rome.[16] Peter, as a founder (with Paul) of the Roman church, has continuators rather than strict replacements. Tillard says that Peter is followed by a line of papal 'vicars' who come after him as bishops in the see of Rome. Their task is to continue the mission given once-for-all to Peter and Paul. Orthodox theologians also correctly point out that Rome is not the only see in which Peter exercised his apostolic role: Antioch would also have to be seen as one of the churches that has a claim to Petrine succession.

But does this mean that there was no continuation of the ministry of leadership? The answer is clearly negative: the work of Paul, for instance, was continued by Timothy, Titus and others, as can be seen in the pastoral epistles.[17] The mission of Christ was obviously unique, yet he tells the apostles 'As the Father has sent me, so I send you' (John 20:21). Certainly, in the early church there was a strong expectation that the end of the world would come soon, so the question of the continuation of the church was not in the forefront of early Christian consciousness. But as this expectation faded, so the question of what was permanent in the New Testament pattern of church life had to be faced. There was a realisation that the community needed basic structural forms, and slowly the notion dawned that the work of the apostles continued in the ministry of bishops who, at this stage, were not clearly differentiated from priests. A monarchical episcopate (that is, rule by a single presiding bishop, as distinct from some type of presbyterial leadership group) first emerged in the sub-apostolic age, probably primarily in Syrian Antioch, and it is clear that the church only gradually sorted out various roles and functions. An important element in this evolution was the slow emergence of the bishop of Rome.

Peter and the long journey to Rome

WHILE PETER'S LEADERSHIP in the Jerusalem church is clear in Acts 1–12, the details of his life become difficult to sort out after that. Paul attests in the Letter to the Galatians 2:1–14 to the emergence of the influence of James in Jerusalem. James seems to have eclipsed Peter, who, Paul suggests, became an 'apostle to the circumcised [Jews]' of the diaspora (Galatians 2:8). Certainly, Peter came to Antioch, for it was there that Paul 'opposed him to his face' over the disputes about the decisions of the Council of Jerusalem (Galatians 2:11–14). Obviously Paul saw Peter as weak and reneging on the logical consequences of agreements hammered out in Jerusalem. However, Peter saw his role as preventing schism and moderating the divisions between the different groups of Christians. This certainly implies that Paul assumed some form of equality with Peter.

All this seems to suggest that Peter felt that his role of 'tending the [expanding] flock' required a roving ministry, leaving James to look after headquarters in Jerusalem until the destruction of the city in AD 70. Certainly, the structures of the apostolic period were understandably fluid and Peter did not assume the role of a monarchical bishop in the sense understood in Antioch, for instance, fifty years later. As mentioned earlier, Matthew's gospel was most probably written in Antioch, which was most likely the first city of the empire to become a Christian centre. The strong emphasis in Matthew on the role of Peter indicates that the apostle must have spent time in the city and that he probably was somehow pivotal in the life of the Christian community there.

Peter and Paul were presumably not to meet again until they both came to Rome and were martyred there in the 60s. Paul set out on his missionary journeys to fresh fields in Asia Minor (present-day Turkey) and Greece for, he said, he did not want to 'build on someone else's foundation' (Romans 15:20). We can more or less work out the detailed progression of Paul's travels and roughly assign dates to the key events in his life. No such chronology can be reconstructed for Peter. Acts 12:17 simply states: 'Then he left [Jerusalem] and went to another place'.

There is good evidence that he was martyred in Rome, like Paul, between 64 and 66, during the persecution of the Emperor Nero (54–68).[18] Certainly, the tradition of Peter's presence in the city is both strong and ancient. Raymond Brown thinks that Peter probably did not come to the capital before 58 and possibly not until just before his martyrdom. He was not the original missionary to Rome, and there is no proof that he was the first bishop of Rome in the monarchical sense.[19] This claim was not made until the third century.

The evidence is strong that the Christian community in Rome dates back to the early or mid-40s. It may have even been begun by 'the visitors from Rome, both Jews and proselytes' who were converted on the day of Pentecost (Acts 2:10). We know that there was a thriving Jewish community of up to 50 000 people in the capital during the first century. (The total population at the time was probably a little less than a million.) So it would be natural for a Jewish-Christian group to form a synagogue within this larger context. Early Roman Christianity appears to have been strongly Jewish in orientation and, according to Suetonius' *Life of Claudius*, its presence in the Jewish community led to 'disturbances at the instigation of Chrestus' and to large-scale expulsions of the Jews from Rome.[20] It may well be that there was a gentile Christian group also in the capital, but it is difficult to work out the relative sizes of these Christian communities.[21]

One of the key documents that gives us some insight into the Christian community in Rome in the mid-50s is Paul's Letter to the Romans, which was probably written from Corinth in the winter of 57–58. Frederick Cwiekowski proposes an interesting theory: at the time of the writing of Romans, the gentile Christians in the city were using Paul's polemics against the 'Judaisers' in his letters to the Galatians, Philippians and II Corinthians, to browbeat the conservative sensitivities of the Jewish Christians.[22] If this is true, the Letter to the Romans would constitute an appeal to the gentile Christians to appreciate the pivotal function of the Jewish tradition in the origins and theology of Christian life. In other words, it was an older, more mature Paul asking more progressive Christians to be sensitive to the peculiarities of their conservative Jewish fellow Christians.

Many attempts have been made to clarify Peter's relationship to the Roman Christian community. While it is now largely accepted it that Peter died in Rome with Paul during the persecution of the Emperor Nero, it is impossible to exactly date the arrival of Peter in Rome. Paul's arrival, however, can be dated almost exactly. It is clear from Acts 20 that Paul was not unanimously welcomed by the Jewish Christians when he returned to Jerusalem in 58, despite his generosity in arranging a collection to support them. His arrival in the Temple led to a riot and, for his own safety, Paul was held in prison by the Roman authorities for two years. As a Roman citizen he eventually 'appealed to Caesar' (Acts 25:11) and after various adventures and a shipwreck on Malta, he arrived in Rome in mid-61 (Acts 27:1, 28:14).

The Emperor Nero, whose appalling behaviour led to the alienation of the contemporary Roman elite and to condemnation by later writers, blamed the Christians for the massive fire that broke out near the Circus Maximus on the night of 18 July 64. By the time it was extinguished, ten of the fourteen *regiones* of the city were utterly destroyed, or virtually reduced to ruins. The Roman historian Tacitus says that the origins of the fire were uncertain, although the tendency of the populace of Rome was to blame the increasingly unpopular Nero. He, in turn, apparently tried to shift the blame to the Christians. Tacitus' account of the events is well known:

> Consequently, to get rid of the report [of his own responsibility], Nero fastened the guilt and inflicted the most exquisite tortures on a class hated for their abominations, called Christians by the populace . . .
>
> Accordingly, an arrest was made of all who confessed; then, upon their information, an immense multitude was convicted, not so much of the crime of arson, as of hatred of the human race.[23]

Possibly Nero attempted to blame the Roman Jews who, at the time were popularly suspected of having incendiary tendencies, and they in turn were able to shift blame to the Christian synagogue.[24] Clement's *First Letter to the Corinthians*, which was written around the year 100, says that it was through 'jealousy and envy [that] the greatest and most righteous pillars [Peter and Paul] of the church were persecuted'.[25] The apparent implication here is that it was non-Christian Jews who were envious. Following the theory of the complex composition of the Roman Christian community, Cwiekowski makes the further interesting suggestion that it was actually ultraconservative Jewish Christian missionaries who denounced Peter and Paul to the imperial authorities.[26] Whatever the truth of this matter, there is no doubt that a vicious persecution occurred in Rome between 64 and 66, and there is good evidence that Peter and Paul were both victims of it.

The tradition of Peter's residence and martyrdom in Rome is certainly strong and ancient. However, it has never been proved conclusively, although it has been popularly supposed that the archaeological evidence of Peter's martyrdom in Rome has now sealed the argument. This confidence arises from the evidence that has been discovered in the *scarvi*—the fascinating archaeological excavations under St Peter's Basilica in Rome. This work began in 1939 in secret, and was made public a decade later.[27] However, this whole issue is complicated by the claim that there was also a supposed tomb of the apostles beneath the church now called St Sebastian on the Via Appia, which in the fourth century was known as the *ecclesia apostolorum* (church of the apostles). There is archaeological evidence here of a mid-third-century shrine to Peter and Paul. Thus we actually have two Roman shrines of the apostles.

Although the weight of evidence still points to the excavations below St Peter's Basilica as the place of the burial of Peter, nothing final can be said. What we know is that the present Petrine basilica was built on the remnants of the early-fourth-century basilica of the Emperor Constantine (died 337). This church fell into disrepair in the Middle Ages and was demolished in the late fifteenth century to be replaced by the present basilica. From archaeological research under St Peter's we know that the church built by Constantine had been deliberately built above a Roman cemetery that was on the lower side of the Vatican hill. Just below the cemetery on level ground was the Circus of Nero; this covered about half the area of the present-day piazza of St Peter's and extended along the left side of the contemporary basilica and beyond. It was about 650 yards long and 100 yards wide.[28]

Tacitus reports that the persecuted Christians were killed in the Circus of Nero.[29] So the assumption is that this is where St Peter was martyred some time during Nero's persecution. It is reasonable to suppose that, if he had been martyred there and if Christians managed to recover his body, it would have been buried in the nearby cemetery. By the late second century the Circus was no longer in use, and the archaeological evidence is that there was a modest Christian monument built in the cemetery between the years 160 and 170. This is reinforced by the comment of an early-third-century Christian, Gaius. He is quoted by Eusebius in his *History of the Church*: 'I can point out the monuments of the victorious apostles. If you will go as far as the Vatican or the Ostian Way [for the tomb of Paul], you will find the monuments of those who founded this church'.[30] Despite the unequivocal comment of Gaius, there was still obviously doubt in the third century as to the actual burial place of Peter. Christians could choose between the Vatican and the shrine under St Sebastian on the Via Appia.

In the early fourth century, however, Constantine was apparently sure of the site because he chose the cemetery close to the Vatican hill and the disused Circus of Nero. It was here that he built his basilica right in the middle of the cemetery, which he had to close. In doing this he broke Roman law, and offended Roman sensibility, by destroying many of the graves. Roman graves, like Italian graves today, were often mausoleums built above the ground. Constantine also had to excavate to build the basilica right into the side of the Vatican hill. All of this indicates that the emperor wanted to place his church on a quite specific site: clearly, the place where he thought the tomb of St Peter was situated.

However, not all of the graves were destroyed because Constantine filled in some of the area with rubble. When this was cleared in the 1940s a street of mausoleums was discovered, and most of them date from the years AD 130 to 200. However, this is only part of a much larger cemetery and it is probable that many of the unexcavated graves are much older. For the remains of Peter the key area in the excavations is a rather plain *aedicula* (tomb) abutting a second-century red wall dating from about AD 160. In a niche in the red wall, some of the bones of an old man were found. Claims have been made that these are actually those of Peter. Despite considerable technical difficulties, Constantine's fourth-century church is oriented to this tomb. The tomb is still almost directly below the *confessio* (the lower-level shrine immediately in front of the high altar) in the present-day basilica.

The early optimistic assessments that the actual grave of Peter had been found, such as those of John Walsh in *The Bones of Saint Peter*, are now widely questioned.[31] The most that can be said is that all of the evidence points to Peter's coming to Rome some time toward the latter part of Nero's reign, and that he was most probably martyred there between 64 and 66. Given his prominence in the early church, it is not surprising that a simple monument was erected in the cemetery close to the Circus of Nero where he was probably killed. We have no way of knowing whether his body was recovered, but we do know that a cult developed around the supposed place of his burial in the latter part of the second century when the cult of relics became important.[32] This minimalist assessment, however, must be placed within the context of the constant and very early tradition that Peter and Paul were in Rome at the end of their lives and that they were seen as the foundations upon which the Roman church was built.

The question of Peter's actual presence in Rome is significant for, as church history progressed, Peter's residence lent a unique importance to the Roman church. This was the apostolic church *par excellence*. But it was especially his martyrdom that gave to the capital city of the Roman Empire a dignity and significance that no other church had. The 'rock' upon which the apostolic group was founded had finally died for his Lord in the city that was the foundation of the Roman Empire.

Peter's successors in the see of Rome[33]

ACCORDING TO THE list of Roman bishops in the *Liber Pontificalis* and reproduced in the *Annuario Pontificio*, the official Vatican Year Book, St Peter died somewhere between 64 and 67 and he was succeeded as bishop of Rome by St Linus (67–76), St Anacletus (76–88) and St Clement (88–97). The *Liber Pontificalis* is a series of brief biographies of the popes, the first redaction of which comes from the papal chancery in the Lateran around 530 to 540; it was then resumed about 625 and continued through to 870.[34] It is probably reliable only after the late fourth century. The reality of the immediate sub-apostolic church in Rome is much more complex than the *Liber Pontificalis* and the *Annuario Pontificio* suggest. The earliest succession list of Roman bishops was drawn up by a Jewish Christian, St Hegesippus, who visited Rome about 160; it was contained in a larger set of five books of *Memoirs* directed against the Gnostics. Fragments of these *Memoirs* can be found in Eusebius' *Ecclesiastical History*, although complete copies of Hegesippus were thought to be in European libraries as late as the sixteenth century. In Eusebius, Hegesippus is quoted as saying: 'On arrival in Rome I pieced together the succession list down to Anicetus, whose deacon was Eleutherius, Anicetus being succeeded by Soter and he by Eleutherius'.[35] No copy of this list is extant today. A second list was drawn up by St Irenaeus around 180, its purpose also being to demonstrate the importance attributed by Irenaeus to apostolic tradition.

It is impossible now to authenticate these lists. The problem is that all of the evidence that we have indicates that the monarchical episcopate was a late development in Rome, emerging only in the mid-second century, even though it arose much earlier in Antioch and other places in the East.

The fact is that we know nothing of the two immediate successors of Peter. Both Tertullian (died *c*.225) and St Jerome (*c*.342–420) say that Peter ordained Clement as his successor. If that is the case, where does it leave Linus and Anacletus? J. N. D. Kelly gives estimated dates for their papacies, but he is clear that these cannot be taken as accurate.[36] Later cataloguers, like Hegesippus, tend to read back a monarchical episcopate into the early Roman community when we now know that it did not exist there. We know who Clement was, but the dates of his two successors Evaristus and Alexander I are complete guesswork. Some historians have even suggested that the whole list prior to Sixtus I (Kelly gives his dates as *c*.116–*c*.125) is a pious fiction.

Until the emergence of modern biblical and historical studies in the last two centuries, it was assumed that the ministerial model of monarchical bishop, surrounded by priests and deacons, could be discerned in the later writings of the New Testament. Nowadays it is clear that the reality was much more complex. In the New Testament and in the sub-apostolic period up to about 150, the structural situation of the church was actually quite fluid. Different forms of church leadership developed in different places. Some cities, such as Antioch, seemingly developed a monarchical episcopate much earlier than others. Even in the earliest period of the church, as we have seen, there was real tension between a stable local community, like that under the control of James in Jerusalem, and travelling apostles and missionaries working principally with gentiles, along the lines set up by Paul, Barnabas and others.

Christianity suffered persecution at varying levels of intensity in many places where it was established. The persecution of Nero, which was confined to Rome, was particularly vicious. But this did not seem to have halted the growth of the community in the capital. Although it is impossible to nominate precise numbers, it is clear that in the first century the Roman civil population was growing and there is every reason to think that the Christian population was increasing also. In the first century most residents in Rome dwelt in apartments. The Christian community was obviously too large to meet in one place. As a result, they naturally looked to the more powerful and wealthy members of the community to provide meeting places. This led to the growth of 'house churches'—large houses that could accommodate regular communal gatherings.

In fact, we have an example of a partially excavated house church in Rome: ongoing works since the nineteenth century below the present eleventh-century basilica of San Clemente, which is near the Colosseum, have revealed not only a fourth-century church, but also two adjoining buildings.[37] One is a Roman house from the last decade of the first century, which from about 200 onwards was devoted to the worship of the Persian cult of Mithra. It is separated by an alleyway from a large warehouse which had a series of rooms off a courtyard. The theory is that this is the original house of Clement and that the fourth-century church was built over the courtyard of the first-century house by a Christian also named Clement.[38] Thus there is a ongoing connection between the house and the two subsequent churches above it—this has been a place of Christian worship since the first century.

In the Letter to the Romans, Paul also speaks of a house church, in this instance administered by women: 'Greet Prisca and Aquila, who work with me in Christ Jesus and who risked their necks for my life . . . Greet also the church in their house' (Romans 16:3–5). Not only did the householders provide the place for worship; they often also provided all the necessities for the community gathering. These householders were not always men: wealthy women were often the patrons of these gatherings. Prisca and Aquila are obvious examples.

The evidence is that by the end of the first century the Roman community was made up of a number of these house churches. Some of them, no doubt, would have been based on nationality. As the capital of an international empire, Rome had many foreign groups resident.

Each of the house churches was led by a presbyter/*episkopos*. It is clear
that the owner of the house as patron sometimes served in the role of
leader; it is on the basis of this that feminist historians have plausibly
argued for a leadership role for women in the early church.[39] Possibly
Linus, Anacletus and Clement (and others) were more or less contemporary with each other and were leaders of different house churches in
Rome. However, we have no way of knowing the actual nature of their
relationships.

The basilica of San Clemente is usually identified with Clement of
Rome, who was possibly either the first or third bishop after Peter. It is
unlikely that he can be identified with the consul, Titus Flavius Clemens,
the cousin of the Emperor Domitian (81–96), although he may have been
a relation, or a freed ex-slave of the family. The house indicates that he
was a wealthy man. He was also probably the author of the famous *Letter
to the Corinthians*, which was almost included in the New Testament and
is a centrally important document.[40] It is dated around 96. Although we
know little about the author, reading the letter, you have the sense of a
man who admires Roman order and wants it applied to the church.
Clement addresses the fierce conflict that was then raging in the church
in Corinth. The Corinthian Christians were apparently given to internal
strife: Paul himself had had to deal with similar strife some forty years
earlier in the First Letter to the Corinthians. The problem in 96 was
that some of the presbyters had been dismissed by the local community.

Clement apparently writes on behalf of the Roman church. He
begins with an apology for the delay in writing that sounds rather imperial: 'We consider we have been somewhat tardy in giving heed to the
matters of dispute that have arisen among you, dearly beloved'. This is
reinforced by the statement addressed to those in revolt: 'Ye therefore
that laid the foundation of the sedition, submit yourselves unto the presbyters and receive chastisement unto repentance, bending the knees of
your heart'.[41] Clement nowhere says that he is the 'bishop' of Rome,
and the feel of the letter is that it is really one church exercising fraternal correction of another. The letter seems to suggest a sense of Roman
responsibility for the other churches.

The Roman church may have felt itself in a position to do this, but we do not know the consequences of the letter or whether the Corinthian church took it particularly seriously. The most that can be said is that Clement was a presbyter/*episkopos* of a Roman community speaking on behalf of all the Roman communities. We are unable to sort out his precise 'constitutional role'.[42] He certainly distinguishes the leaders of worship from the *laikos*—the laity, the first time this distinction appears in Christian writing.[43] He emphasises church unity, order, and the apostolic succession of bishops and deacons.[44]

Rome's role is reinforced by a second major source coming from the first decade of the second century. This is Ignatius of Antioch's *Letter to the Romans*. He was possibly either the second or third bishop of Antioch after Peter. This is very important: Antioch, like Rome, can claim to be 'apostolic' in the proper sense, for Peter had been resident there before going on to the capital of the empire. As we have seen, a monarchical episcopate emerged in Antioch very early. Despite the clarity of his see's apostolic origins, Ignatius shows considerable deference to Rome, and this might well be more significant than the vaguer claims of Clement to authority over the Corinthians. We know nothing about the life of Ignatius except that he journeyed to Rome for martyrdom during the reign of Trajan (98–117) and that he wrote seven extant letters.[45] What is of particular interest to us about them is that they offer evidence that Ignatius, like Clement, thought that his responsibility was wider than the territory of his own church of Antioch. As a successor of the apostles he felt he was part of a collegiality that comprises all bishops.

His *Letter to the Romans* has a slightly different feel from that of the other letters. He wrote to Rome from Smyrna (now Izmir in Turkey), begging them not to intercede for him with the imperial authorities and thus take from him the dignity of martyrdom.[46] In the letter there are passages that indicate that the Roman church (which he speaks of as though it were one church, despite the fact that it consisted of several communities, as we have previously noted) had a special role among all the Christian communities. The opening passage, for instance, is quite

deferential in contrast to the openings of his other letters: 'Ignatius . . .
to the church . . . that hath the presidency in . . . the region of the
Romans, being worthy of God, worthy of honour, worthy of felici-
tation, worthy of praise, worthy of success, worthy in purity and having
the presidency of love . . . which church I salute'.[47] He twice uses the
term 'presidency' to refer to the Roman church. He writes that Rome
has 'the presidency in the country of the region of the Romans' (meaning
that the Roman church presides in the immediate vicinity of the city)
and that it has 'the presidency of love [*agape*]'. Here Ignatius is probably
referring to the way in which the local church expresses itself most truly
and most perfectly through the Eucharist.[48] This was to evolve into the
notion that the Roman church held the presidency of charity, the presidency of the communion of the whole church united in concord. For
Ignatius the image was that, just as a local bishop sits in first place in the
Eucharistic assembly, so the Roman church (and eventually its bishop)
sits in the first place in the eucharistic concord of all the local churches
throughout the world.

Ignatius also tells the Roman church: 'Ye were the instructors of
others'.[49] Again this is a brief, passing reference to the potential emergence of the church of Rome as a latter-day norm of orthodoxy, and it
must be read within its specific historical context. Located in the capital
city of the empire and as the place of martyrdom of Peter and Paul, the
Roman church would inevitably emerge with a degree of pre-eminence.
However, there were other churches in the East that could also claim
apostolic foundation. Later, this was to become a focus of division between the eastern (Orthodox) and western (Catholic) churches.

Clement's prestige in the early church is undoubted, but his successors were far more shadowy characters. We can guess that Evaristus,
Alexander I, Sixtus I, Telesphorus and Hyginus all probably had important roles in the Roman church, but we are unable to specify their exact
ecclesiastical and constitutional position, given that the monarchical
episcopate only emerged at the earliest in Rome around the time of
Hyginus (*c*.138–*c*.142). Certainly, from about 150 onwards the monarchical episcopate prevailed throughout the church and the word *episkopos* (bishop) was reserved for that office.

The development of the structures of the church

THE EVIDENCE IS that Rome was one of the last communities to develop a structure centred on a solo bishop. Pius I (*c*.145–*c*.155) was possibly the first bishop of Rome in our sense. However, the dates for these early bishops are doubtful until about the time of Popes Eleutherius (*c*.174–89) or Victor I (189–98). It seems that the monarchical episcopate only emerged in Rome after a struggle. The core of this struggle apparently centred on the attempt to draw the various house churches, some of them based on nationality, into a unified church under a single bishop. For instance, the strong-minded Pope Victor I's attempt to force the churches of the East to observe the same date for Easter as that held in Rome might well have actually been motivated by an attempt to impose a common date on the Asiatic communities in Rome itself.[50] This led to a storm of protest, which included complaints from Irenaeus about the Roman bishop's severity, but it also illustrates Victor's assumption that he had the right to interfere in the affairs of other churches. There is no doubt that the Roman church was held in respect. Throughout the latter part of the second century a number of important Christian thinkers, both orthodox and heretical, visited Rome. Among them was Irenaeus himself, Polycarp from Smyrna, Justin Martyr and Hegesippus from Palestine. They came not because the city was an intellectual or theological centre, but more likely because of the influence of the Roman church and its reputation for orthodoxy.

Certainly the monarchical episcopate seems to have been in existence in Rome when Irenaeus (*c*.130–*c*.200) made his famous reference to the Roman church in his book *Adversus Haereses* (Against the Heresies). But Denis Minns cautions that there are clear hints in Irenaeus' writings that he also knew the collegial style of leadership evident in the New Testament and other sources.[51] Minns says that the monarchical model of bishop may not have been established in every church with which Irenaeus was familiar, but that it was not long in coming. Irenaeus' preoccupation in the *Adversus Haereses* was Gnosticism. This religious philosophy pre-dated Christianity and it emphasised a kind of special *gnosis* (knowledge) granted to the initiate that gave access to a deeper spiritual wisdom not granted to the ordinary believer. It had seriously infected the Christian community. Irenaeus' interest in bishops was that the genuine apostolic tradition could only be objectively traced through the episcopate to the apostles, and that apostolic tradition was the one sure litmus text of orthodox doctrine. This was in contrast to the Gnostics' notion of a secret *paradosis* (historical tradition)—they claimed that true doctrine was handed down secretly. Thus in order to sort out the apostolic tradition, lists of bishops back to the apostles were important. But Irenaeus admitted that it would take too long to canvass every local church, so he satisfied himself with the Roman succession list. This begins with Linus. Interestingly, Irenaeus does not say that Peter was first bishop, but rather that Peter and Paul as equals provided the apostolic foundation upon which Linus and his successors built. Pope Elutherius (died 189) is the last Roman bishop in the list of Irenaeus. With him we enter into a historical succession of bishops.

It can be safely said that by the latter half of the second century some level of common structure had appeared across all of the churches. Structure was linked to doctrinal orthodoxy. From this time it was no longer a question of what each individual bishop and community believed and passed on, but whether the community was in synchronisation with what gradually came to be called the 'apostolic tradition'.

All of this has to be seen within the larger religious context in which Christianity found itself in the culture of the second and third centuries. There was an extraordinary medley of beliefs and sects, mainly originating in the East, which constantly tempted the religious enthusiast with promises of saviours and salvation. Among Christians there were strong centrifugal forces, such as Docetism and Gnosticism, that could have easily torn early Christian communities apart. Docetism was a tendency within the early church that overemphasised the spiritual and downplayed the physicality of the sufferings and death of Christ. So it was natural that mainstream Christians, for whom the continuity of the church was important, would move toward the evolution of a centralised tradition that was accepted by all, a doctrinal foundation that defined specifically which beliefs were orthodox Christian and those that were not. The definition of this foundational tradition came more and more under the influence of 'elders', or community presiders. As a result the question of the succession of these elders became important. So the church began to compile lists of bishops in order to trace apostolic authority. We have already seen this in the lists of Roman bishops drawn up by Hegissipus and Irenaeus. The tendency toward uniformity in the early church was not just an example of the usual sociological tendency to institutionalise the founding charism. It was above all directed at the ever present reality of the danger of heresy in the church. The German Protestant scholar Ernst Käsemann calls this consolidation of church structure 'primitive Catholicism'. The suggestion here is that a hierarchical 'Catholicising' tendency slowly emerged after 150 that replaced the eschatological expectation among early Christians that Christ would return soon in judgement and glory.[52]

The papacy in the third century

BY THE LATTER half of the second century we can confidently say that the outline of church order familiar to us today had gradually emerged in the church. The bishop was the principal celebrant of the liturgy, and his participation in the apostolic succession—the line of bishops reaching back to the apostles—ensured the local church's doctrinal orthodoxy. The practical affairs of the church were in the hands of deacons, and the presbyterate, or college of elders, was the body that advised the bishop. The presbyters had begun the process of evolution that would eventually lead in the fourth century to the emergence of priesthood as we know it.[53]

Victor I was certainly the most important pope of the late second century. In this period we can discern something of the variety of the underbelly of Roman Christianity. What we now know as 'heretical' groups were present in force: there were Christians from Asia Minor who kept Easter on a different date to Rome whom Victor tried to suppress. There were the followers of Theodotus who held that Christ was a kind of super Jewish prophet. The apocalyptic and charismatic rigorism of Montanus was promoted in Rome by Proclus; it influenced many, including the North African theologian Tertullian, who went over to the sect. The Montanists refused absolution for any serious sin committed after baptism. The monotheistic modalism of Sabellius was also present: this held that the three persons of the trinity were only temporary operative modes, or aspects adopted by the one divine person in the process of redemption.

The Roman persecutions were, of course, always a threat to the church, but during the second century they were not as constant or as widespread as is popularly thought.[54] For most of Victor's papacy the church did not suffer any significant persecution and, in fact, it was during this period that Marcia, the pro-Christian concubine of the Emperor Commodus (180–92), intervened on behalf of those Christians previously condemned to slavery in the mines of Sardinia. Although the church was never legally recognised by the Roman imperial state until the time of Constantine the Great, mainstream Christianity struggled against the sectarianism of the heretical groups, and during the second century Christians were never shy of playing a part in public life when they were given the opportunity.

However, persecution was always a potential threat. There had been persecution for the last four years of Nero's reign (54–68) and the last two years of Domitian's (81–96). It also occurred intermittently under Trajan (98–117), Antoninus Pius (138–61), and Marcus Aurelius (161–80). Between the Antonine emperors and Decius (249–51) there was again intermittent persecution, but in the second half of the third century things changed. Persecution became official and the whole church was targeted. The persecution by Decius, for instance, was conducted throughout the whole empire according to a unified plan, but because the persecutions tended to be short-lived, they were not all that successful. Valerian (253–60) became a persecutor in the last three years of his reign and then there was a period of relative peace leading up to the traumatic persecution by Diocletian the Great (284–305) from 303 to 305. This sense of looming persecution has always to be kept in mind as a broader civil backdrop for the development of the papacy.

Pope Victor was succeeded by the rather weak Zephyrinus (198–217), who was much influenced by his deacon Callistus, who succeeded him as bishop of Rome (217–22). Callistus had a colourful background as a Christian slave-banker who lost his depositors' money and then ran away and attempted suicide, and was punished with a period in the Sardinian mines. He apparently bribed his way out, and soon became principal deacon under Zephyrinus, and then pope. His whole ecclesiastical career was dogged by the leading intellectual presbyter of the Roman church, the Greek-speaking Hippolytus, who was probably born in Egypt. Hippolytus' scholarship was considerable and had been engaged in attacking all of the heretical sects among the Roman Christians, especially the continuing influence of the Gnostics.

Given his background, Callistus understandably had a tolerant policy on penance and reconciliation, whereas the rigorist Hippolytus wanted the Roman church to be a community of saints. He attacked Callistus during his papacy and especially after his death. Until recently it had been thought that this dispute led to an open break between the two men and that Hippolytus formed his own community and had himself consecrated as the first antipope.[55] This is now being seriously questioned. The dispute over church discipline was deepened by theological disagreements. Hippolytus held a very high view of ecclesiastical office and its important link with the preservation of apostolic tradition. To maintain traditional sacramental forms he drew together a church order. The *Traditio Apostolica* (Apostolic Tradition), a liturgical book that sets out several parts of the sacramental worship of the church, presumably of Rome in the third century, no longer survives in its original language; it has come down to us as *The Egyptian Church Order*.[56] It is the earliest detailed text we have of the church's worship. But Hippolytus' views of the high dignity of ecclesiastical office did not stop him accusing both Popes Zerhyrinus and Callistus of being theological modalists, despite the fact that Callistus had excommunicated the Roman priest Sabellius for the modalist heresy. He, in turn, accused Hippolytus of so emphasising Christ's divinity as to create two Gods. Hippolytus died in 235, well after Callistus.

Two things emerge from the dispute between the two men that are significant for later history. First, Callistus is willing to accept lapsed members from other heretical and separated Christian communities.

Their sins are forgiven simply after the laying on of hands; extreme penances were not required. No doubt some of these people would have been from Hippolytus' own community, which indicates that Callistus recognised the baptism of other Christian groups. Second, he held that a bishop who sins seriously need not necessarily be deposed. It is part of the Roman tradition not to allow the deposition of clergy lightly. Both of these actions are coherent with the continuing tradition of the mainstream Roman church. We will see this again just over thirty years later in the dispute between Pope Stephen and Cyprian of Carthage.

Pope Fabian (236–50) was also a significant pope of the third century. He was a good administrator who probably reorganised the structure of the Roman church into seven communities under deacons and sub-deacons. He was one of the first to die in the persecution by Decius. After the martyrdom of Fabian there was a fourteen-month break before the election of Pope Cornelius (251–53), caused by the Decian persecution. Within the next half-century there were two similar breaks: one of two years between Sixtus II (257–58) and Dionysius (260–68), and then a probable three and a half year break between Marcellinus (296–*c*.304) and Marcellus I (306–08). Each of these breaks was caused by hesitation to elect someone during a period of persecution.

During the break between Fabian and Cornelius, the priest-theologian Novatian acted as a kind of vicar for the collegial administration of priests that governed the Roman church. His brilliant treatise on the trinity resolved most of the issues that had been debated in the time of Callistus. Novatian, like Hippolytus, was a rigorist and he had expected to be elected bishop of Rome. Thus he was bitterly disappointed when he did not become pope in March 251, possibly because of his rigorism. In less than a year, he was in schism.

The persecution of Decius had been probably the worst and most extensive of all the persecutions to that point. Its purpose was to establish religious and civic unity and common prayer to the gods in order to unite the state against the threat of barbarian invasion.[57] There was no universal proscription of Christians as such, but the process was that everyone had to offer sacrifice and obtain a *libellus*—a certificate of sacrifice.[58] Christians were exposed by their refusal. It was a new technique and it caught many unprepared. The persecution was especially violent in North Africa. Although some Christians made a stand and died as martyrs, the majority knuckled under and lapsed. Others went into hiding. The persecution was brief, for Decius was killed in June 251 in a campaign against the Goths. The persecution was continued in a milder form by the Emperor Gallus (251–53).

In the intensity of the Decian persecution many Christians lapsed and sacrificed to the gods. Like others in the early church, such as Hippolytus, Novatian opposed the readmission to the community of those who had apostatised, and he used this as a way of attacking Pope Cornelius, who favoured the readmission of *lapsi* (the fallen) after due penance. In some ways the centre of conservative rigorism in the Roman church was the presbyterate, which probably reflected the fact that it was made up largely of old men. It was the deacons who tended to be younger and certainly more pastorally practical. Cornelius did not hesitate to defame Novatian, whom he had had condemned in 251 by a Roman synod comprised of bishops from all over Italy. Novatian then had himself ordained to the episcopate by three southern Italian rigorist bishops and set himself up with a small community. His schism spread quickly as a kind of parallel church in both the East and the West. They held the strict view that there was no forgiveness for any serious sin committed after baptism. The Novatianist church persisted until the fifth century.

Roman influence was strong in central and southern Italy at this time through the fact that the pope ordained bishops after local election. But by the fourth century Italy had become more regionalised and there was less deference to Rome on the question of ordination. In fact it is difficult to assess the actual influence of Rome in the third century. Certainly the Bishop of the capital was held in high regard and Rome was seen as the apostolic see founded by Peter and Paul that was the touchstone of orthodoxy. But the greatest number of Christians was centred in the East and there were other dioceses of apostolic origin, such as Antioch and Alexandria (the provincial capital of Roman Egypt). In contrast, the north African churches looked to Rome for leadership, but there were limitations to their tolerance of Roman interference.

In the West, where the bishop of Rome's influence would have been strong, large concentrations of Christians were few and far between: Rome, central Italy, Naples, Lyons, the area around Marseilles, and south Italy had reasonable numbers of Christians. Central and northern Gaul, Britain, Germany and Pannonia (present-day central Balkans) were hardly touched by Christianity at all.

One of those who was forced to flee during the Decian persecution was the convert rhetorician Cyprian, who had become bishop of Carthage in 258. He wrote to the Roman church about his decamping from Carthage (capital of Africa Proconsularis, close to present-day Tunis) saying that his action had 'been reported in a somewhat garbled and untruthful manner'. He argued that the reason for his departure was 'the general quiet of the brethren' lest his presence provoke the imperial authorities further.[59] Large numbers of Christians had lapsed, Cyprian maintained, because 'it pleased the Lord to prove His family; and as a long period of peace had corrupted the discipline which had come to us from Him, the divine judgement awakened our faith from a declining and . . . almost slumbering state'.[60]

Because of his wide influence Cyprian became a major figure in the discussions as to what to do with the *lapsi*. He held the view that they ought to be received back into the church after due penance. But, as we have seen, this was not universally acceptable, especially to rigorists like Novatian, who wrote to Carthage accusing Cyprian of being a hireling who had abandoned the flock, unlike Pope Fabian (236–50) in Rome, who had been martyred. This led to a correspondence between Cyprian and Pope Cornelius. Given that Cyprian had already discussed this issue with Novatian before Cornelius' election, the Carthiginian bishop was at first suspicious of the pope. Although his instincts were probably with Novatian, he accepted Cornelius' canonical priority as bishop. So eventually both pope and bishop agreed on a moderate policy in receiving the *lapsi* back into the church.

The focus of Cyprian's theology was the unity of the local church. His major work on this is his *De Catholicae ecclesiae unitate*, written in 251 within the context of the dispute between Novatian and Cornelius.[61] Fundamentally, he supported Pope Cornelius and opposed Novatian.

Cornelius, as the heir of Peter, inherited the promise made to Peter: *primatus Petro datur*—'the primacy is given to Peter', says Cyprian.[62] For the Carthaginian bishop, Cornelius, as successor of Peter, inherits a genuine disciplinary power from the apostle. However, this does not exhaust the full meaning of Cyprian's theory of the role of the bishop.

One of Cyprian's most complex (and perhaps, from our perspective, convoluted) images is that of the *cathedra Petri*, the 'chair of Peter'. At first sight this image would seem to refer clearly to the Roman bishop. He says: 'God is one and Christ is one: there is one church and one chair founded, by the Lord's authority, upon Peter. It is not possible that another altar can be set up, or that a new priesthood can be appointed, over and above this one altar and this one priesthood.'[63] The extraordinary thing is that this phrase does not refer primarily to Rome, but actually to the local church. For in Cyprian's view the local bishop sits as much in the *cathedra Petri* as the Roman bishop. While admitting that Rome is the primordial church, Cyprian also emphasised the unity of the bishops throughout the world. He said that the way to achieve this was by frequent episcopal meetings in councils and synods.

This agreement between Rome and Carthage did not last into the papacy of Stephen I (254–57) when there was considerable tension between the two—which illustrates Cyprian's theology of the episcopate. Kelly says that Pope Stephen 'emerges as an imperious and uncompromising prelate'.[64] Nevertheless, he continued the established Roman tradition of tolerance. The first series of disputes between Rome and Carthage centred around deposition of bishops in Gaul and Spain. But more important than this was the controversy over baptism or, more specifically, over rebaptism. Stephen followed the Roman, Antiochian and Palestinian custom that Christian baptism was Christian baptism as long as Jesus Christ was named, even if it was administered by a heretic. Cyprian followed the North African and Asiatic custom that regarded heretical church ceremonies as the devil's mockery. For them only the sacraments of the one, true Catholic church were effective. Thus heretics seeking reconciliation needed to be rebaptised. Two Carthiginian synods in 255 and 256 supported Cyprian. Somewhat impetuously, Stephen demanded that everyone everywhere accept the Roman view;

the liberal view was to be imposed! It looked as though much of the church could be out of communion with Rome. Bishop Dionysius of Alexandria begged Stephen to compromise. Fortunately, the problem was solved by Stephen's death in August 257 and Cyprian's martyrdom in the persecution of later years of the Emperor Valerian's reign in September 258. Before his death Cyprian seems to have been reconciled with Pope Sixtus II (257–58) who had held to the Roman View on rebaptism but who adopted a much more conciliatory approach. The pope himself was martyred with four deacons while celebrating Mass.

However, the issue of rebaptism did not go away: it resurfaced in North Africa in the next century in the Donatist crisis. What is interesting in all of this is that fundamentally the Roman church stood for a more generous and more truly 'catholic' community, in contrast to the strict legalistic limits of communion proposed by Cyprian and Novatian and before them, Hippolytus. After his disputes with Rome there is a real sense in which Cyprian's theology changes and the emphasis moves decisively in the direction of the unity of the local church.

From the death of the Emperor Valerian (260) until the outbreak of the persecution by the Emperor Diocletian the Great in 303, there is something of a gap in historical sources. Pope Dionysius (260–68) was not elected for two years because the Valerian persecution focused especially on the clergy. Again the Roman church was governed by the presbyters. This pope reorganised the church both structurally and in terms of practical charity. He also participated in theological discussion with his namesake, Bishop Dionysius of Alexandria. The popes who followed him—Felix I (269–74), Eutychian (275–83) and Gaius (283–96)—remain shrouded in obscurity. Possibly the reason for this is the severity of Diocletian's persecution and the successful attempts by this emperor to destroy the books and records of the church.

From the time of Emperor Gallienus (260–68) there had been religious peace focused basically on a kind of solar syncretism. Christians were willing to use the solar symbolism even to the extent of seeing Christ as *Sol Justitiae* (the Sun of Justice). Diocletian reacted against this and reinstated the ancient gods. The number of Christians grew during this period, especially in the East, and they permeated all classes of society, including the army and even the imperial household itself (Diocletian's wife Prisca and his daughter Valeria were probably Christians); this development clearly frightened the pagans, especially traditionalists like Diocletian's co-emperor, Galerius. Marta Sordi thinks that Diocletian held back from persecution of the Christians because of the serious political consequences of tackling a large and well-entrenched minority.[65] However, the emperor began a purgation of the army between 297 and 301.[66] The persecution became general in 303.

It was applied in stages: firstly churches and Christian books were destroyed. Secondly, a capital sentence for bishops was introduced. Finally, everyone, everywhere had to participate publicly in the civil cult and offer sacrifice to the gods. The persecution was particularly severe in the East. We know that the archives of the Roman church were taken and destroyed. Diocletian abdicated in May 305, and by 306 the persecution had ceased in Italy and the West. It had never even occurred in Gaul and Britain under Constantius Chlorus. It continued intermittently in the East until as late as 313.

Right at the beginning of the persecution, in May 303, Pope Marcellinus (296–c.304) handed over the Bible and the sacred books, and also apparently, with several of his presbyters, offered incense to the gods. There was some debate about his behaviour in the following centuries. However, Kelly says that despite the claim of the *Liber Pontificalis* that he repented a few days later and was martyred, there is no doubt no about the fact of his apostasy.[67] He was probably forced, or volunteered, to abdicate the papacy soon afterward. As a result the Roman church was left for three and a half years without an acknowledged head. His successor, Marcellus I (306–08) was elected after peace for Christians was restored by the Emperor Maxentius (306–12). A tough-minded rigorist, he expunged Marcellinus' name from the papal lists and adopted a hard-line penitential discipline against *lapsi*. This led to disputes in the community, which flowed over into the papacy of Eusebius (310).

But peace for the church was on the horizon, and Pope Miltiades (311–14) was the first to begin to enjoy it. The source of security, Constantine, came from the least Christian part of the empire. He was born in Moesia Superior (present-day Serbia) sometime between 274 and

288. His parents were Constantius Chlorus, one of the tetrarchy (four Caesars) set up by Diocletian, and Flavia Helena, a woman of humble origin, who was put aside by her husband in 292 for political reasons. Growing up almost as a hostage in the court of Diocletian, he was trained as a soldier and returned to join his father who had crossed to Britain to repel an invasion of Picts and Scots. His father died in Eburacum (York), the capital of Britannia Inferior, in July 306. Following his father's death, Constantine was proclaimed emperor there by the troops.

A new stage of church history was about to begin.

2 The consolidation of the papacy

Constantine and the church

ON 27 OCTOBER 312 Maxentius, ruler of Italy and Africa, was defeated in battle by Constantine near Rome at Saxa Rubra on the Tiber, just to the north of the present-day Porta del Popolo. Escaping from the battle, he drowned in the river near the Ponte Milvio. A whole new era was beginning for both the late Roman world and the Christian church. Maxentius had already granted toleration to Christianity earlier in the year and had restored church property. Imperial tolerance and patronage were extended to the church by Constantine, who had never been a persecutor. The Edict of Milan (313) granted toleration to all religions and legally recognised the Christian church.

A clear symbol of imperial favour was the presentation of the Empress Fausta's Lateran palace to Pope Miltiades. Constantine's wife had brought it to her marriage as part of her dowry, and in the fourth century it was known as the *domus Faustae* (house of Fausta). It remained the papal residence until 1309; it was eventually pulled down by Sixtus V (1585–90) in what Georgina Masson calls 'an unpardonable act of vandalism'.[1] For a thousand years the Lateran was the administrative centre of the Roman church and the residence of the pope, just as the

Vatican is now. A church dedicated to the Saviour was built beside the palace in Constantine's time, and the successor of this church nowadays is the Lateran basilica, the cathedral church of Rome.[2] Until 326, when he turned decisively to building his own city on the Bosporus, Constantine carried on a church building programme in Rome but as a result of senatorial opposition most of the grand church buildings were on the outskirts of the city rather than in its civil core.[3]

So within a few months, Christianity suddenly confronted the second historical mutation in its history. The first had occurred when the church emerged in the late first and early second centuries from the matrix of Judaism into the broader Graeco-Roman world, with its religious pluralism and ever-present threat of heresy. The second occurred when the church ceased being a legally proscribed and sometimes persecuted minority—albeit a numerically large one in the Eastern part of the empire, especially in Egypt and Palestine—to become, in a sudden about-face, the most powerful and significant religion in late Roman culture.[4] For the first time in its history the Christian church was directly confronted with the task of sorting out its relationship with the secular world of late Roman culture and politics. Given the church's history, and the violence and extent of Diocletian's persecution, as well as the radical nature of the change that Christianity faced under Constantine, it is understandable that the leadership of the church took a couple of decades to get its breath back and to begin to respond to changed circumstances. The kind of church that emerged from this process still affects the way in which Christianity views the world today.

During its previous 280 years the church had lived in a state of intermittent persecution as it strove to maintain and develop the meaning of Christ's teaching in the context of the late Roman world. To a greater or lesser extent, early Christian attitudes were shaped by the possibility of persecution, although this varied both in different periods and in different places. But in 312–13 the question of church–state relationships arose for the first time and this occurred within the specific religious-social context of the late empire, and in interaction with the priorities and personality of the Emperor Constantine the Great (306–37) and his successors.

Soon after the final defeat of his co-emperor Licinius, in 324, Constantine began to shift the centre of the empire from Rome to Byzantium on the Bosporus, which, as a result of his massive and rapid building programme, quickly emerged as the 'new Rome'—Constantinople.[5] The church came to reflect this political division, but the gradual drift toward separation between East and West went deeper. There were clear differences of language (Greek versus Latin), culture and attitude. The relatively quick collapse of the empire in the West at the beginning of the fifth century created something of a vacuum into which the church and the papacy were able to move. In contrast, the church in the East became increasingly intertwined with Byzantine culture and imperial power structures.

Constantine had been proclaimed emperor by the troops in York, Britain, in 306. After defeating Maxentius at the Milvian Bridge he became the ruler of the city of Rome and the Western empire. After the eventual defeat of Licinius in 324, he ruled as sole emperor. It was before his battle with Maxentius that Constantine had his famous vision of a cross in the sky, followed by a dream in which Christ explained to him the meaning of the vision. As a result he ascribed his victory to the Christian God. He did this for profoundly Roman reasons: he wanted an alliance with the strongest deity and, after the vision, he became convinced that the Christian God was both his protector in battle and the guardian of his state.[6] The traditional Roman belief was that the world was maintained by the goodwill of the gods who needed to be appeased by the collective worship of the whole community. This notion continued into the Christian era. It needs to be recalled that religious toleration was coming into fashion at the beginning of the fourth century. Thus it is open to debate as to whether Constantine underwent a Christian 'conversion' in the strict sense, but his religious attitude had far-reaching consequences for both the church and the late Roman state. We can certainly say that the Christian God was Constantine's protective deity; as such, he was probably converted in the Roman rather than in the strictly theological sense. In the Eastern church he is seen as a saint.

While the Edict of Milan granted full toleration to all faiths, the Emperor bestowed special imperial favour on the church. We saw this in

the donation of the Lateran palace and the building of the basilica over
the grave of St Peter. Christian bishops now became official Roman dig-
nitaries with civil status. For instance, Constantine instructed his proconsul in Africa that Christian clerics were exempted from all public
offices so that they could worship the God who had brought good for-
tune to the empire. Sunday became a public holiday in 321. Churches
became legal personalities and thus legacies and resources could be built
up through inheritance. But the Emperor remained the *pontifex maximus*
(chief pagan priest of the Roman state) and paganism retained its official
status. His actions reflect his own dual religiosity that combined the
notions of the sun as a symbol of the all-powerful God with Christ as a
representative of that God who threw his weight behind the emperor. It
is a reminder of the earlier Christian notion of Christ as *Sol Justitiae*.

Several courses were open to the church after state patronage was
bestowed upon it. It could entertain political ambitions and try to dominate the state and its rulers—as the popes tried to do in the Middle
Ages. In the late Roman world this was probably not a real option.
Or the church could become an instrument of the state—the so-called
erastian, or caesaro-papist, solution. Or it could try to maintain its own
Christian identity and keep some distance between itself and the state.
Given the attitudes of Constantine and his successors regarding the role
of religion in the service of the state, a compromise between church and
state was probably out of the question. The caesaro-papist solution was
to be the predominant way the relationship developed, especially in the
Byzantine East after the establishment of Constantinople and the evolution of a separate Eastern church tradition. For Constantine was very
conscious of his own 'divine mission', and much of his relationship with
the church was governed by this sense of mission.

Although Constantine obviously respected the Petrine role of the
bishop of Rome, the attitude of the popes was actually irrelevant to
the politico-religious decisions of the emperor. This was reinforced by
the popes of the time: Pope Miltiades was short-lived, and Sylvester I
(314–35) was not a strong personality. He did not attend the councils
called by the emperor, although he sent representatives. At Nicaea, for
instance, Sylvester's two priest-delegates signed the acts of the council

immediately after the imperial legate, Bishop Hosius of Cordova, in recognition of Sylvester's position.[7]

Church controversies: the Donatists and Arius

ALTHOUGH CONSTANTINE WAS tolerantly prepared to let paganism either survive or decline, he certainly did demand doctrinal conformity from his Christian subjects. He considered it his duty to maintain the unity of the church and to make sure that everyone professed the true faith. For where there was right belief and true worship, the state would continue to enjoy divine protection.

Pope Miltiades would have been in Rome when Constantine entered the city as victor in late October 312. Within a year both pope and emperor faced the recurrent problem of Christian moral rigorism. Not unexpectedly this had re-emerged in North Africa. The African form of severity also spread to the church in Spain, as the Council of Elvira (303) shows with its profusion of threats of lifelong excommunication for a range of sins, with no hope of reconciliation, even on one's deathbed.[8] In North Africa the rigorists denied the validity of the sacraments of bishops and priests who had been *lapsi* during the persecution by Diocletian. They claimed that one of the bishops who ordained Caecilian, the then bishop of Carthage, had been a *traditor* (apostate) during the persecution. In the place of Caecilian they eventually elected one Donatus, who then appealed to the emperor for support and protection.[9]

Constantine asked Pope Miltiades to judge the case. Shrewdly, Miltiades called a synod in Rome (October 313) that quickly excommunicated Donatus, but at the same time the pope made sure the other rigorist African bishops were kept in communion. Donatus then appealed directly to the emperor, who eventually called a synod for Arles in southern Gaul (August 314). Constantine's patience was being tried as he complained about 'different persons who often petitioned me [vehemently]' about Caecilian.[10] This was the first synod in the West after the granting of toleration, and it is significant that it was called by the emperor, not the pope. Forty-four bishops attended, plus representatives of Pope Sylvester; Miltiades had just died.

The Synod of Arles considered Donatus' appeal to the emperor and the question of heretical baptism; the bishops reaffirmed the decision of Pope Miltiades and the Roman synod. The other major issue was a decision about the date for the celebration of Easter. The synod decided to follow the Roman date. Historians have tended to see this debate about the date of Easter as a disciplinary question, but the early church saw it as a genuine theological issue. It did not differentiate as clearly as we do between disciplinary and doctrinal issues. The question of the date of Easter was part of sacramental and symbolic theology, and was therefore doctrinally important; it is for this reason that it recurs so often in the first millennium. The bishops simply informed Sylvester that they were confirming the Roman date. However, there was a clear recognition at Arles that the Roman date was normative. The synod also granted Christians permission to hold public office, and it encouraged their participation in the imperial military service. Finally, the synod requested Sylvester as the primate of the West to send the decisions to all the churches. The synod said that the Roman Bishop *majores dioceses tenet*, an obscure expression that seems to mean that it was the task of the pope to ensure the unity of the discipline of the Western church and maintain regular contact.[11] This is a recognition of Roman primacy, even if in a somewhat backhanded way.

The irrepressible Donatus appealed again. Constantine's patience was almost exhausted with this seemingly endless dispute. He told the proconsul of Africa:

> It is our will that . . . it may be made quite clear, in the presence and hearing of those who are concerned with this affair, [who] for some time past have been incessantly appealing to me, that it is to no purpose that they show their malice against Caecilian the bishop. [They] have been pleased to bestir themselves against him with violence.[12]

The proconsul obviously failed, for Constantine decided on 10 November 316 in favour of Caecilian. The condemnation of the Donatists was reiterated. They refused to submit, and a brief persecution resulted. Constantine clearly never really understood the historical depth of feeling behind the rigorist issue that had come to the surface in the

Donatist crisis. The Donatist church survived for several centuries in North Africa.

The emphasis on correct belief was manifested even more clearly when Constantine intervened directly in a new crisis, the Arian dispute, and called the Council of Nicaea (325). It met in early summer of that year in the imperial palace of Nicaea about 90 kilometres south-east of Constantinople.[13] The emperor presided at the opening session and probably appointed his ecclesiastical adviser, Hosius of Cordova, as president. Constantine certainly made his intervention felt. His assent to the canons of the council gave them the force of public law, and the church found itself very much in the debt of the state.

The Arian crisis centred on Arius (*c*.250–336), a presbyter of Alexandria. He was a popular preacher who held that Christ was actually subordinate to God, with the net result that the Son was reduced to a demigod.[14] According to the church historian Socrates, the dispute began when Bishop Alexander of Alexandria attempted 'in the presence of the presbyters and the rest of the clergy, too ambitious a discourse about the Holy Trinity'. He continues:

> Arius, one of the presbyters under his jurisdiction, a man possessed of no inconsiderable logical acumen, thinking that the Bishop was introducing the doctrine of Sabellius the Libyan, from love of controversy advanced another view diametrically opposed . . . 'If', he said, 'the Father begat the Son, he that was begotten has a beginning of existence; and from this it is evident, that there was when the Son was not'.[15]

The theological issue at stake was the exact nature of the relationship between Christ and God: how could Christ be both man and God? Arius' whole point was to protect the personal unity and unique transcendence of God. In doing this he had unavoidably raised the question of the status of Christ—was he fully divine, or merely a creature? Arius' position was that, because God is the transcendent and unique source of all reality, Christ must be a creature, non-self-existent, contingent, and produced by God's will. Thus there was a time when Christ was non-existent. In Arianism Christ becomes at most a demigod.

Arius was bringing into focus, for the new world of the fourth century, questions that had simmered in Eastern theology for upwards of a
century and a half. For his pains he was excommunicated by a synod
(*c*.320) called by Bishop Alexander of Alexandria. A party quickly
formed around Arius, a leading member of which was Bishop Eusebius
of Nicomedia (present-day Ismit in Turkey) (died *c*.342), who was to
become very influential on Constantine and to baptise him on his deathbed.[16] The teaching continued to spread. There is a kind of theological
straight-forwardness about Arianism that seems to make it uniquely
attractive to common people. It certainly spread quickly among the
ordinary Christians of Egypt and was a cause of considerable civil
tension. We will see the success of Arianism again in the missionary
movements of the fifth century. The Western church was poorly represented at Nicaea: only seven or eight Western bishops were present,
including Constantine's ecclesiastical adviser, Hosius. Sylvester I declined
to attend, but he did send two priests who, as we have seen, signed the
acts of the council immediately after Hosius. The leader of the anti-
Arian party at the council was Athanasius (*c*.296–373), then deacon and
later bishop of Alexandria from 328 to 373. The council defined the
Catholic faith in terms of the Nicene creed: the co-equality and co-
eternity of Father and Son were proclaimed in terms of the Greek word
homoousios meaning 'of the same substance'.[17] Thus Christ is 'God from
God, light from light, true God from true God'. He is pre-existent,
of the same substance as the Father. Both Arius and Eusebius were
banished for a brief period.

Although it found against Arius, the council was not the end of
Arianism. At first Constantine was a supporter of conciliar orthodoxy,
but after 328 he began to waver and the Arian party grew in strength.
Battle lines were quickly drawn between Bishop Athanasius of Alexandria, the champion of Nicene orthodoxy, and the Arian party,
especially after the return of Eusebius of Nicomedia and the other pro-
Arian bishops from exile in 328. Even though the West supported
Nicene orthodoxy, Arianism became a recurrent theme in the history of
the papacy for the rest of the century.

The fourth-century popes

THE ANGLICAN SCHOLAR Henry Chadwick makes the point that the second half of the fourth century saw the rapid emergence of the Roman see as a major centre of both leadership and juridical authority.[18] But the first popes of the fourth century seemed to show little initiative, and their practical power was severely limited. They were overshadowed by the towering figure of Constantine and by the power of his successors. Little is known of the short-lived Pope Mark (336) who succeeded Sylvester I. Julius I (337–52) was a strong supporter of Athanasius of Alexandria (who was exiled in the West at Trier from 336 to 339) and Nicene orthodoxy. The Alexandrian bishop was in Rome in 339 and again in 345, and he maintained close contacts with the Western bishops, especially Julius I. Thus the empire itself was split: the Western church and the emperor of the West, Constans (337–50), were supporters of Catholic orthodoxy; but Constans' brother, Constantius II (337–61), the Eastern emperor, openly embraced Arianism, which was very much in the ascendant in the East. To try to deal with this split, and especially with the role and position of Athanasius, the emperors asked Pope Julius to call a council of East and West at Sardica (present-day Sofia in Bulgaria) in 342. The Eastern bishops arrived at Sardica but refused to attend the council because of the presence of Athanasius. They bluntly blamed Pope Julius and withdrew, excommunicating the entire Western episcopate. So with total Western dominance, it is understandable that the deposed Athanasius was restored to his see and that the council voted to support episcopal appeals to Rome. Increasingly the real issue became the position of Athanasius. It was an impasse.

Things only got worse during the papacy of Liberius (352–66). With the death of Constans, Constantius II, a capricious despot, became sole ruler of East and West in 350, and he put enormous pressure on the Western bishops, especially on Liberius, to accept Arianism and disown Athanasius. At first Liberius stood against this, but during a two-year exile in Thrace (northern Greece) he capitulated to the emperor and excommunicated Athanasius. He was then allowed to return to

Rome, where he found an Arianising antipope in occupation, Felix
(355–65). The Roman mob supported Liberius, and Felix was forced to
withdraw to the suburbs. After Constantius II died late in 361, Liberius
'rediscovered' Nicene orthodoxy and contributed somewhat to the re-
establishment of unity between East and West. After his death there
were riots in Rome; these were to have a significant bearing on the beginning of the next papacy.

Underpinning the approach of Emperor Constantius II was the
notion that he was *episcopus episcoporum*—the bishop of bishops. The
Arians were inclined to accede to imperial pretensions, as were many of
the Western bishops during the period of his eleven years of sole rule
from 350 to 361. After a brief flirtation with restored paganism under
the Emperor Julian (361–63), the Emperor Valentinian I (364–75) was
nominated. He appointed his brother Valens (364–78) to rule the East.
Valens adopted the same approach to church affairs as Constantius II
and supported Arianism.

As early as the latter part of Constantine's reign, the church historian Eusebius of Caesarea in his *Ecclesiastical History* had glorified imperial pretensions and power. This kind of caesaro-papist ideology,
combined with constant interference by the emperors in church affairs,
led to a reaction by some of the best theological minds in the church:
for instance, Gregory of Nyssa (*c.*330–95) was worried about the way
the church–state system was developing in the East; and later in the
West, Ambrose of Milan (*c.*339–97) was prepared to confront both
Valentinian II (375–92) and Theodosius I (379–95).

Something of a revival also occurred in the papacy. If it had reached a
low point in the dismal surrender of Pope Liberius to imperial pressure,
during the last four decades of the century things changed and the popes
attained real influence in Italy and to a lesser degree in the broader
church, mainly in the West. To an extent this reflected the increasing
political centralisation of the fourth century. As a result of regular
military coups, especially during the third century, the empire prior
to Diocletian's reforms was actually quite decentralised. The church
tended to follow this model. However, Diocletian achieved a real centralisation of administrative power, even if it was split between co-

emperors. Constantine and his successors reinforced this centralisation. The popes began to follow this centralised model and, according to the *Liber Pontificalis*, Julius I partially reorganised the papal chancery, probably on the imperial model.[19]

But if papal influence began to increase in the second part of the fourth century, the actual acceptance of this varied considerably from region to region. The key issue in this acceptance was what the historian Pierre Batiffol calls pre-existing 'zones of ecclesiastical influence'.[20] These were centred on the major churches of apostolic origin and they had been gradually developing for several centuries. Batiffol maintains that these zones help us to make sense out of the complex situation that evolved in the fourth and fifth centuries. He cites canon six of the Council of Nicaea, which distinguished three zones of influence centring on three apostolic churches—Rome, Antioch and Alexandria. This canon states:

> The ancient customs of Egypt, Libya and Pentapolis shall be maintained, according to which the bishop of Alexandria has authority over all these places, since a similar custom exists with reference to the bishop of Rome. Similarly in Antioch and the other provinces the prerogatives of the churches are to be preserved . . . If anyone is made a bishop without the consent of the metropolitan, this great synod determines that such a one shall not be a bishop.[21]

The council added Constantinople to these churches of apostolic foundation. The patriarch of Constantinople became increasingly important as the bishop of the new capital.

An essential element of this metropolitan form of church government was the regular meeting of the provincial synod. It considered disciplinary issues, episcopal elections, and the formation and division of dioceses. This synodal form of administration tended to be used more in the East than the West.

In the Italian zone the bishop of Rome clearly had a role of special supervision and exercised considerable influence over the bishops of the *regiones suburbicariae* (the suburbicarian regions, that is, the dioceses immediately around Rome). The influence of the papacy also extended

to the whole of the present-day Italian peninsula south and east of the
northern borders of Tuscany and Umbria, as well as Sardinia, Corsica
and Sicily. In the many small dioceses of this region, bishops were either
consecrated or confirmed by the pope. The Roman Synod, which was
made up of the bishop of Rome and the bishops of the surrounding area,
was unique in that it dealt not only with local ecclesiastical events, but
also with wider issues that had impact beyond the geographical area of
central Italy. The popes used the Roman Synod as a forum for discussion
and decision-making on issues that had a wider application and impact
than the pope's own metropolitan sphere.

Thus papal influence extended beyond central Italy to the Western
empire generally—northern Italy, Gaul, Spain, Germany, Britain,
western North Africa and Illyricum (the large territory on the Danube
frontier). In the West papal influence and power gradually grew. However, ecclesiastical power was still very localised; Rome was simply recognised as the only diocese of apostolic origin in the Western empire.
In the Eastern empire, however, the activities of the bishop of Constantinople were constantly scrutinised and limited by the imperial palace.
If the popes of the early fourth century were men of modest pretensions
and achievements, the situation changed after 366. A series of strong
and assertive popes from Damasus I (366–84) onwards led to an increase in the extent of the claims made by the Roman bishops.

After the death of Liberius in September 366, ecclesiastical and civil
confusion reigned in Rome. The antipope Felix had died nine months
previously. The sources on the disputed election are confusing and reflect the views of one or other party.[22] What probably happened is that,
almost immediately after the death of Liberius on 24 September 366, a
group of deacons and presbyters elected the deacon Ursinus as pope
and had him quickly consecrated. It is possible that the ambitious deacon
Damasus was elected around the same time, or slightly afterwards by
the majority of the clergy, but he carefully fulfilled the legal require-
ments and waited for consecration by the bishop of Ostia, who tradi-
tionally carried out the ceremony. This occurred on 1 October 366.
Damasus also made sure that he had the support of the civil authorities.
Born in Rome, Damasus had been briefly in exile with Liberius, had

abandoned him and had served under Felix, and was then reconciled with the forgiving Liberius. After his consecration, Damasus tried to have Ursinus and his clerical supporters banished. But they were protected by many among the Roman laity and sought asylum in the Liberian basilica. Damasus then called in the emperor and city prefect to support him, thus setting a precedent that was to become an unfortunate characteristic of many papal elections over the centuries. According to the *Gesta inter Liberium et Felicem*—which was compiled by the pro-Ursinus party—Ursinus could count on considerable sympathy among the Roman laity, and the civil intervention against his supporters led to a dreadful massacre and continuing civil unrest. This outbreak of violence weakened Damasus' reputation among his fellow Italian bishops and led the pagan philosopher Ammianus Marcellinus (who was city prefect from 367 to 368) to comment that these Christians had an odd way of showing charity to each other!

Throughout his episcopate Damasus was challenged by the supporters of Ursinus, who virtually waged continuous guerilla war against him. According to the *Liber Pontificalis*, it was Ursinus and his faction who, seemingly maliciously, brought a charge of adultery against the Pope in the 370s.[23] He was exonerated by an imperial court and the intervention of the emperor. Certainly before his election he had been seen as something of a ladies' man; he had been dubbed a *matronarum auriscalpius*, a ladies' ear-scratcher! No doubt his confrontational style earned him a lot of possibly untruthful and certainly unscrupulous enemies. The entry in the *Liber Pontificalis* on Damasus is brief, even though the first of the many compilers of the book actually incorrectly attributed the composition of the chronicle to him, probably because he was the reorganiser of the papal archives.[24] Damasus had considerable literary pretensions and had the reputation of being something of a wit and a writer of what many of his contemporaries judged to be obscure and commonplace poetry.

Throughout the fourth century the Roman aristocracy had generally remained staunchly pagan.[25] Damasus was the first pope to begin to penetrate their anti-Christian prejudices. Previously, they had studiously ignored the new religion. Throughout the fourth century the classical

Roman cityscape remained intact, and pagan apologists could point to
the glories of Roman history embodied in beautiful public buildings.
The historian Ammianus Marcellinus (*c*.330–95) was fascinated by a
transfigured and probably unreal vision of the past. Although he recognised the existence of Christianity, he was seemingly oblivious to its
penetration of late Roman society and of the radical change in external
circumstances, especially in the Western empire with the ever-increasing
pressure of the barbarians on the frontiers. For a brief period under the
Emperor Julian (361–63), paganism had enjoyed a short revival, but it
was in general decline throughout the fourth century. The evidence is
that in those noble Roman families who had adopted Christianity, it was
the women of the clan who took the initiative.

Damasus was a strong and assertive pope. He was particularly active
in attacking heresy. To achieve this he used both synods and imperial
authority. He was also active in the West against Arianism, although
he considered it unwise to move against the Arian bishop of Milan,
Auxentius, because of the support he enjoyed from the emperor. Valentinian I was mildly Catholic in his attitude, but he was unwilling to see
the bishop of his capital city condemned. He was strongly committed to
the defence of the empire.[26] He ruled from either Trier or Milan and
was the best emperor-general of the century. As we have seen, his
brother Valens who ruled the East was pro-Arian.

Damasus, although he was anti-Arian, played no part in the eventual
resolution of the Arian crisis. Various theological compromises had
been proposed and slowly the Nicene doctrine gained ground in the
East, especially after the death of Constantius in 361. The three great
Cappadocian theologians, Basil (*c*.330–79), Gregory of Nyssa (*c*.330–
c.395) and Gregory Nazianzus (329–89) supported Nicaea, and the
final blow to Arianism came after the defeat and death of Valens at the
Battle of Adrianople in 381. The rock-solid persistence of Athanasius
was eventually rewarded eight years after his death. The new emperor,
Theodosius I (378–95), called a council for Constantinople in 381.
Neither papal legates nor Western bishops were present at the council,
which finally settled the Arian crisis by restating the orthodoxy of
Nicaea. At its conclusion the council did write a letter to the Western

bishops mentioning Pope Damasus first.[27] As well as settling the Arian dispute the council granted the church of Constantinople honorary precedence over all churches, except Rome: 'Because it is new Rome, the bishop of Constantinople is to enjoy the privileges of honour after the bishop of Rome'.[28] This disciplinary decision was to lead directly into the next series of divisions, debates and councils.

No doubt this claim to precedence for Constantinople would have stirred Damasus, for he was very concerned about the enhancement of Roman primacy. He appealed directly to the Petrine text in Matthew (16:18–19) to support his position, and he claimed that his power came not from the church, but from the fact that he was St Peter's successor. Damasus held, like Julius I before him, that Peter continued to work in and through the Roman bishop and that when he ruled from the *cathedra Petri*, it was Peter who was acting in him. The Petrine text had been used previously to support the claims of the Roman bishop, but it was Damasus who began to exploit it fully. He claimed the power to bind and loose in ecclesiastical matters, and Rome became a court of appeal for the entire Western episcopate. In other words, what Walter Ullmann calls a 'juristic' interpretation was now applied to the Matthean text.[29] One of the problems with the Matthean text is that, although it clearly bestows authority on Peter, at best it only implies that that authority was passed on to his successors. It was at this time that the so-called *Clementine Homilies* became popular. These are supposedly letters sent by Clement to James of Jerusalem telling him that, among other things, Peter on his deathbed, passed on the power to bind and loose to Clement —and by implication to his successors. This juristic power was recognised in the Western church, for around the year 374 a group of Gallic bishops sent to Rome a series of questions about ecclesiastical discipline. The letter certainly shows that the Western church looked to Rome and valued the views of its bishop. The Gallic bishops had taken the initiative and Damasus' reply, *Ad Gallos Episcopos*, has something of the feel of a papal decretal about it. (A decretal is a papal letter that is legally binding.) But in answering their questions he appeals not to his own position, but to the authority of previous councils and the practice of the Roman church.

The great biblical translator St Jerome (331–420) was in Rome for a brief period in the latter years of Damasus' papacy, between 382 and 385. While there he worked on biblical issues and translation work in the papal chancery and acted as a kind of 'papal secretary'.[30] He describes the see of Peter in a series of biblical images: 'On that rock [the see of Peter] I know the church is built. Whoever shall eat the lamb outside this house is profane. If any be not with Noah in the ark, he shall perish in the flood'.[31] As well as being a consummate biblical translator, later much admired by Erasmus, Jerome was an unstable, violent character, a trait that was demonstrated especially in his vicious intellectual attacks upon opponents. No doubt Jerome's considerable rhetorical skills would have appealed to Damasus, who carried on a considerable correspondence with him. He encouraged him to translate the third-century Alexandrian theologian Origen into Latin, and also asked him to revise the defective Latin translation of the gospels then in liturgical use in Rome.[32] The liturgical language in the city was now Latin rather than Greek, although a Greek-speaking colony continued to exist in the city. Ullmann here makes the interesting point that Jerome's Vulgate translation uses much of the legal terminology of the late Roman world, and that this not only 'buttressed' the legalistic aspects of the papacy, but also acted as a vehicle for transmitting Roman legalism to the medieval period.[33] In his spare time, Jerome pontificated on the education of women, and taught a group of rich Roman matrons biblical exegesis and introduced them to the virginal and monastic life.

At the time of Damasus' death (11 December 384) Jerome believed he might be elected pope himself. But he had attacked the pretensions and wealth of the Roman deacons and he was bitterly disappointed. The deacon who was quickly elected, Siricius, was understandably not one of his friends. Eventually Jerome was forced to leave the city due to recriminations with some of the Roman clergy.[34] He commented bitterly: 'Pray for me now that I have escaped from Babylon'.[35]

The year of Jerome's arrival in Rome saw the Emperor Gratian (376–83)—persuaded by Ambrose, bishop of Milan—take the momentous step of finally separating the Roman state from paganism.[36] Ambrose was an old-style Roman nobleman, tall and thin, with classical features and enormous presence. Born in Trier in 339, the son of the Praetorian Prefect of Gaul, he trained as a lawyer and became a civil administrator. Only a catechumen (an adult candidate for baptism) when elected by the Catholics of Milan to the bishopric in 374, he replaced the Arian Auxentius. He quickly emerged as the greatest Western bishop of the century. During his episcopate Milan was the capital of the Western empire and it became a metropolitan see.[37]

Ambrose's level-headedness and experience in the civil service meant that he could put his political skills to work in the service of the church. He strongly argued for the independence of the spiritual power from the temporal, a theory which was to be developed in the next century, especially by Pope Gelasius I, and taken up as normative in the Middle Ages. In a local struggle in Milan over a basilica for the Arian community, Ambrose bluntly told the young Emperor Valentinian II:

> When did your gracious Majesty ever hear of laymen judging bishops in a matter of faith? . . . In the view of the holy Scriptures and the precedents of antiquity, it is impossible to deny that in a matter of faith . . . it is the practise for bishops to judge Christian emperors, and not emperors bishops.[38]

This is reinforced by Ambrose's blunt statement: 'The emperor is part of the church, not someone above it'.[39] His excommunication of the Emperor Theodosius I, because of the massacre of several thousand people in the circus at Thessalonica in 390, showed Ambrose's willingness to speak out against the civil power. Theodosius' repentance speaks well for the authority of the Milanese bishop. This and other incidents indicate that Ambrose and Western ecclesiology had developed beyond the caesaro-papism of the Constantinian era to assert the autonomy of the church and its right to offer a critique of the actions even of the emperor.

Ambrose was a poet who wrote fine Latin verse. He was also well trained in theological literature and was famous as a preacher. His influence on the conversion of Augustine was pivotal. There is a real sense in which he overshadowed both Popes Damasus and Siricius. However, he saw the Roman church as *totius orbis Romani caput* (the head of the whole Roman world), that is, the senior church that forms the bond of ecclesial

communion.[40] He had a high regard for the Roman church as the touchstone of true belief. Yet, somewhat confusedly, he did not have a highly
developed concept of Roman primacy and he even sometimes says that
Peter was given the keys of the kingdom as a representative of the other
apostles and of all subsequent bishops.[41]

From the time of Gratian's decree disestablishing paganism in 382,
the Christian church became the state church. The emperor withdrew
financial subsidies, disestablished the priestly colleges and vestal virgins,
and removed the altar of victory from the senate. The days of the power
of the pagan nobility in Rome were numbered and the toleration granted
to all religions was fast disappearing. The last stronghold of paganism
in Rome, the conservative senatorial class, was finally losing the long
battle against Christianity.

Although the ecclesiastical authority of the Roman church was built
up slowly in the West, there is a sense in which the evolution of the
Petrine ideology of the papacy was a response to the pagan argument
that *Roma aeterna* (eternal Rome) was safe as long as the gods were
worshipped properly. As the empire in the West disintegrated, the
papacy slowly emerged as a major focus of cultural stability. But at the
end of the fourth century the surviving pagan aristocrats still saw Christianity as an upstart and radical religion that endangered the state. The
sack of Rome by Alaric's Visigoths in August 410 seemed to confirm
their worst fears and had enormous emotional impact, even if its strategic importance was minimal.

After the death of Damasus, as we have seen, the deacon Siricius
(394–99) was quickly elected, perhaps because Ursinus again put himself forward as a candidate. An unhappy Jerome dismissed Siricius'
simplicitas (simple-mindedness), and Bishop Paulinus of Nola (in present-
day Italy, near Naples) found him haughty. The Anglican scholar T. G.
Jalland says that Siricius continued the Roman see's sense of consciousness of responsibility for the welfare of the church, and he argues that it
was this pope who began the process of issuing decretals.[42] This may
or may not be correct; certainly his are the first extant decretals. It was
Siricius' view that his responses to specific questions from bishops had
the force of law, in the same sense that the emperor's responses to provincial governors were legally binding. He was also profoundly aware of

his call to care for all the churches, and of the presence of the apostle Peter speaking in him: 'We bear the burdens of all who are heavy laden; nay more, the Blessed Apostle Peter bears them in us, he who, as we hope, protects and guards us as the sole heirs of his office'.[43] Jalland refers to the 'semi-mystical identification' of the pope with Peter, and says that it is one of the secrets of papal influence.[44] This is illustrated in a series of questions from Bishop Himerius of Tarragona (Spain). The responses of Siricius constitute a series of 'apostolic statutes', and he tells Himerius that the apostle Peter guards and protects the bishops of Rome as the ones who inherit his office. He instruct Himerius to pass on his rulings to other bishops. A number of other letters survive from this pope to the North African bishops, the bishops of central and southern Italy, and the bishops of Gaul. However, the influence of Siricius was probably overshadowed by that of Ambrose, and the powerful and attractive personality of the Milanese bishop meant that Pope Siricius' influence would have to be weighed up within this context.

The first three decades of the fifth century

ON 24 AUGUST 410 someone inside the city of Rome opened the Salerian Gate, and the besieging Visigothic army led by Alaric took the city. It was the first time Rome had been in enemy hands in eight hundred years. Alaric had actually laid siege to the city on and off from the end of 408.[45] Although they only remained for three days, the Visigoths did considerable damage: they killed and raped many, they burnt buildings and stripped palaces and temples of valuables. The pope of the time, Innocent I (401–17), was absent in Ravenna trying to negotiate a truce. Both Jerome and Saint Augustine were almost in despair when they heard of the fall of the city.

The event shocked the whole Roman world; it seemed like the arrival of the apocalypse. It was thought that if Rome fell, the end of the world would follow. For the Roman pagans it was the last straw. Their view was that the city had fallen because the gods had not been appeased. It was all the result of the advent of the upstart Christian religion. Unappeased, the gods wreaked revenge on civilised humankind by handing them over to the barbarians. But, in a way, this was the last gasp of upper-class Roman paganism. From this point onward the focus of stabilisation in the West in the unsettled and violent centuries that followed would be the Christian church and, especially in Italy, the papacy.

In the obscure North African town of Hippo, the local bishop, Augustine (354–430), the greatest mind of the age, began the composition of the *City of God* in response to the apparent collapse of civilisation. He strongly repudiated the pagan argument that the sack of Rome had occurred because the gods were no longer worshipped.[46] Augustine held that those who belonged to the city of God had set their hearts on a transcendent purpose and would find their final home in heaven; those who set their heart on worldly things belonged to the city of the world. The two cities were not co-terminus with church and state, but this notion did set the pattern for the eventual separation of the *causa ecclesiae* (the agenda of the church) from the *causa imperii* (the function of the state). True Christians were never totally at home in the world; they were pilgrims on the journey to the ultimate heavenly city of God.

The sack of Rome was a symbolic moment in a long process, rather than a significant strategic event in itself. For most of the fourth century the Romans had been able to hold their extended frontiers. The first sign of real trouble was the defeat of the Emperor Julian in Mesopotamia in the Persian campaign of 363 against Shapur II. This defeat in turn encouraged barbarian threats on both the Danube and Rhine frontiers, but these defence lines were shored up by the efforts of the very effective soldier-emperor, Valentinian I. But after his sudden death in a fit of anger in 375, the most vivid and frightening sign of Roman weakness was the disastrous defeat of the Emperor Valens at Adrianople (Edirne in European Turkey) in 378 by the Visigoths led by Fritigern.[47] The Visigoths had revolted because of mistreatment by agents of the empire, and the defeat had occurred because Valens had not taken the barbarian people seriously. Adrianople was just 200 kilometres from Constantinople.

The Visigoths, who had converted to Arian Christianity, had been pushed up hard against the Roman frontier by a new force in south-eastern Europe, the Huns. After Adrianople the Huns threatened both the East and particularly the West. Jerome had called the Huns the 'wolves of the north' and he prayed that Jesus would 'protect the world from such beasts'.[48] They provided the impetus for a vast movement of people within northern Europe. The pressure on the frontiers, especially along the Rhine and the Danube, increased, but after the death of Theodosius I in January 395 no one within the imperial administrations of either East or West had either the will or the ability to do much about it.[49] The most competent general of the period, Stilicho, had a series of skirmishes with Alaric's Visigoths, but he never succeeded in dealing decisively with them. The pressure on the frontier from other tribes continued to grow.

Finally, a barbarian tribal alliance of Vandals, Suebi and Alans crossed the ice-bound Rhine near Mainz on the last day of 406.[50] The Roman river fleet was disabled in the frozen conditions and, in an amazingly quick invasion, northern Gaul was overrun. The Vandals pushed on through Gaul and Spain, crossing the Straits of Gibraltar in 429, eventually reaching Carthage in North Africa. They were besieging the city of Hippo when Augustine died in August 430. Britain had been abandoned by Roman troops in 407 and the Emperor Honorius had bluntly told the Britons that they were on their own in 410. This was not the first time the Roman frontiers had collapsed, but the crossing of the Rhine led to a general invasion of Gaul, Spain and northern Italy. The break in the defence line was now permanent, and a long period of military, social and political instability was to follow.

To some extent the barbarian invasions were more migrations than planned incursions. Peter Brown has described them as a '"gold rush" of immigrants' into the imperial territories.[51] Because of long contact and trade with the empire, the barbarians were, to some extent, Romanised. Some of them, like the Goths, were already Christian. But we should not underestimate the dreadful fear, suffering and dislocation that these events caused in the lives of ordinary people throughout the Western section of the empire. From this point onward civil, political and military insecurity was to be the order of the day for most people. In response to the invasions, most Christians tended to identify strongly with the idea of imperial Rome. By now there was a conviction among many Christians that the empire was a providential vehicle for the spread of the Catholic faith.

Others, especially in the West, showed a more positive attitude to the barbarians, and the idea emerged that the migrations were an opportunity for the conversion of the barbarian tribes. Some of them were already Christian, even if they were Arians. Those Romans who suffered from very destructive groups, such as the Vandals, did begin to doubt that God was still guiding the world as civilisation was destroyed around them. But more open and creative churchmen like St Martin, bishop of Tours from 372 to 397, began to take a more proactive line toward the barbarians. They set about converting them and, in the process brought the new people of Europe within the ambit of Roman culture, custom and language.

The early-fifth-century popes

THE FIFTH CENTURY brought the Roman church the usual mixed bag of popes, but it was fortunate in that a couple of truly significant men were elected in this period, the most important of them, of course, being Leo the Great. These popes acted according to the precedents set by their fourth-century predecessors and they unequivocally asserted papal primacy.

The first of these able popes was Anastasius I (399–401). His brief papacy was caught up in the controversy raging around the question of the orthodoxy of the theologian Origen (c.185–c.254), the great biblical scholar, theologian and spiritual writer of Alexandria. Perhaps the attitude of the fifth-century Roman bishops can be best summed up in the words of Innocent I (402–17), a forceful personality whom Kelly describes as 'one of the outstanding popes of the early centuries'.[52] Innocent asserted that he was the *caput atque apex episcopatus*—the head and summit of the episcopate.[53] This high notion of papal primacy was generally recognised in the pope's own metropolitan zone, central and southern Italy, but Innocent wanted to extend it to the whole of the West and North Africa. He was determined to bring about uniformity by making the Roman customs in liturgy and ecclesiastical order normative for the Western church. He saw Rome as the final court of appeal in major cases.

Innocent unsuccessfully tested his right to intervene throughout the church when he attempted to call a synod to hear the case of the dismissal of St John Chrysostom (*c.*347–407) from the Patriarchate of Constantinople. In 398, Chrysostom, a monk and a presbyter of Antioch, was elected bishop of Constantinople despite the strong opposition and continuing enmity of the bishop of Alexandria, Theophilus, who had hoped to be elected himself. On arrival in Constantinople, Chrysostom encountered corruption in both court and church. With a combination of honesty and tactlessness he made many enemies. He did not help his cause by referring to the Empress Eudoxia as 'Jezebel', and his insistence on the clergy and monks living moral lives. His relationship with Bishop Theophilus of Alexandria declined even further when he supported the monks of Nitra (in the Egyptian desert) against their bishop, and he further offended the empress by referring to her as 'Herodias'. John was exiled by the court in 404, despite the support of the people of the capital and the Western church, especially Pope Innocent I. The Emperor Arcadius (395–408) and the bishops of Alexandria and Antioch resented papal interference and ignored Innocent, who remained faithful to Chrysostom to the end of his life in 407. In fact, a technical state of schism existed for several years between Rome and the Eastern churches of Antioch, Alexandria and Constantinople.

Rome was also to discover the limitations of its authority in its intervention in the Pelagian controversy. Pelagianism was an ascetical movement that emphasised both the call of all Christians to holiness, and the element of the human will in the process of sanctification. It played down the role of original sin. Pelagius (*c.*360–*c.*420), a British theologian and monk, had taught a doctrine along these lines in Rome at the turn of the century and then, as an *émigré* after the sack of Rome by Alaric, in North Africa. He seems to have held that Christians can reach the state of *apatheia* —the control of passion—by their own willpower. The North Africans took exception to his teaching: two synods and a third group of bishops, including Augustine, who had written against Pelagius' doctrine of grace, sent letters to Rome in 417 emphasising the *potior principalitas* (pre-eminence) of the see of Peter and asking the pope to confirm their verdict of condemnation of Pelagius' teaching. Innocent was happy to do so and in the process declared that

> You decided that your verdict should be referred to our judgement, with the knowledge of your duty to the apostolic see, since all of us who are placed in this position desire to follow none other than the Apostle, who is the source of both our episcopate and of the prestige of our name.[54]

Rome, Innocent said, could definitively settle questions because it possessed the highest teaching authority in the church.[55]

Despite Augustine's comment in a sermon that 'the dispute is at an end'—from which comes the apocryphal saying *Roma locuta est, causa finita est* (Rome has spoken; the case is closed)—this was not the end of the matter.[56] Pelagius' colleague Celestius came to Rome and persuaded the impulsive and arrogant Greek Pope Zosimus (417–18) to reverse Innocent's decision. This led to a stand-off with the North Africans until the Emperor Honorius banished the adherents of Pelagianism, and the pope and the Roman Synod condemned the Pelagian doctrines. Zosimus also clashed with the Africans over the excommunicated priest Apiarius, who had appealed to Rome; he also managed to offend the Gallic episcopate by imposing Bishop Protroclus of Arles as a kind of papal vicar and metropolitan in southern Gaul. In fact, the impulsive, short-lived Greek had squandered much of the respect that had been built up by his predecessors.[57]

A disputed papal election followed the death of Zosimus, with one faction electing the deacon Eulalius and the other the elderly presbyter Boniface. After decreeing that a synod of bishops from Gaul and Africa decide between the two candidates, the Emperor Honorius finally ruled that Boniface should assume the office after non-cooperative behaviour from Eulalius. In a rescript the emperor prescribed that in any future double election the government would disqualify both candidates and only recognise someone the entire Roman community had chosen as pope in a new election.

Sensibly, Boniface (418–22) withdrew the scheme for making Arles a papal vicariate and made peace with the Gallic bishops. However, the case of the North African presbyter Apiarius continued right through Boniface's papacy and into that of Celestine I (422–32). North African relations with Rome were further complicated by the deposition of Antony, bishop of Fussala. In both cases the African bishops reminded the popes of their traditional autonomy and they requested that Rome respect their decisions about excommunication.

An area of continuing dispute between East and West was the papal vicariate of Thessalonica. To maintain papal influence in the area of eastern Illyricum and Dacia (the present-day south-eastern Balkans), Pope Siricius had appointed the bishop of Thessalonica as papal vicar in 385. This was challenged under Boniface I because the area was part of the Eastern empire. The papacy successfully maintained its position through the intervention of both the Western and Eastern emperors, and the position of Thessalonica was confirmed by Celestine I. But the tension between East and West pointed to deeper differences, especially in theology and ecclesiology.

It is to the East and its doctrinal disputes that we must now turn.

Doctrinal disputes

THE GENIUS OF the Eastern church was mainly speculative, while the West tended to be more practical. As a result the East was late in developing an ecclesiology (a theology of how the church operates) and it tended to accept the prevailing imperial caesaro-papism. The Roman church, at the same time, was developing a more focused ecclesiology —focused, that is, on metropolitans and especially on the primatial metropolitan of the West, the bishop of Rome. The separation between East and West was also deepened by the growing claims of the bishops of Constantinople. Apart from Leo I and Gelasius I, none of the popes of this period were speculative theologians, and the papacy was not strongly represented at any of the ecumenical councils of the period except at Chalcedon (451).

Closely connected with the theological disputes that led to the councils of Ephesus (431) and Chalcedon was deepening political and ecclesiastical antagonism between the bishops of Antioch, Alexandria and Constantinople. Given that Antioch and Alexandria were both apostolic in origin, there was real resentment against the upstart see of Constantinople. But even deeper was the bad feeling between the sees of Antioch and Alexandria themselves. In some ways this rivalry was as much theological as it was ecclesiastical.

The resolution of the Arian dispute had clarified the fact of Christ's divinity and the nature of the relationship between the Father and the Son. But that led directly to the question of how the divine and human natures in Christ are related in the one unitary person.[58] The difference between Antioch and Alexandria on this issue was largely one of emphasis. Antioch emphasised the human and historical nature of Christ; its approach was more empirical. Alexandrian theology was more abstract and mystical, with a strong stress on the divinity of Christ. The tragedy is that all of the passionate theological energy of Eastern Christianity was to be thrown into this dispute, with disastrous, long-term consequences. Louis Duchesne states the results bluntly:

> The unleashing of religious passions, conflicts between metropolitan sees, rivalries between ecclesiastical potentates, noisy councils, imperial laws, depravations, sentences of exile, tumults, schisms—such were the conditions under which Greek theologians studied the dogma of the incarnation. And if we look to the result of their quarrels, we see at the end of the vista, the Eastern church irreparably divided, the Christian Empire dismembered, the lieutenants of Mahomet trampling under foot Syria and Egypt. Such was the price of these exercises in metaphysics.[59]

We have already seen Pope Innocent's unsuccessful intervention in the affair of John Chrysostom. Innocent refused to recognise his successor and broke off communion with the bishops who had sided with the imperial court. Among them was Theophilus of Alexandria. Theophilus died in 412 and was succeeded by his nephew Cyril, a saint and theologian, also an unscrupulous and power-hungry man, who carried on the destructive rivalry between Antioch and Alexandria with energy and passion. The whole dispute blew up again with the election in 428 of the monk and presbyter of Antioch, Nestorius, to the bishopric of Constantinople. He was much like John Chrysostom, able, diligent, and a great pulpit orator. He was also something of a zealot, and he had been in the capital less than six months when he began a campaign against 'heretical' opinions. On Christmas Day 428 he attacked the suitability of applying the title *Theotokos* (literally, God-bearer) to Mary, the mother of Jesus. True to the theology of Antioch, Nestorius claimed that this title was incompatible with full humanity of Christ. He proposed that the titles *Christotokos* (Christ-bearer) or *Anthropotokos* (man-bearer) would be far more appropriate. This was a mistake, for the title *Theotokos* had a long tradition of devotion in the Eastern church, especially among the monks.

The popular reaction to Nestorius' criticism was that he was saying that Christ was an ordinary man, inspired, but not really God. Nestorius was rather cavalier in his attitude to Rome, and his letters and sermons were sent with 'great humility and great adroitness', as Duchesne says, by the Alexandrian party to Pope Celestine I.[60] In the letter war that broke out between Cyril and Nestorius, the bishop of Constantinople conceded that Mary could be called *Christokos* but not *Theotokos*. Celestine, who claimed throughout the controversy that he had oversight of the whole church, intervened and condemned the views of Nestorius outright at the Roman Synod in 430. Rather stupidly, he entrusted to Cyril the execution of the condemnation! Cyril used his delegation to try to impose on Nestorius a document that enshrined the extreme Alexandrine theological view—the 'twelve anathemas'. Nestorius, correctly, rejected this and appealed to the Eastern emperor, Theodosius II (408–50). The emperor called an ecumenical council to meet in Ephesus (on the Aegean coast of Turkey) in June 431.

Nestorius was already there when Cyril, with typical impetuosity, decided to open the council on 21 June before the papal delegates, John, the bishop of Antioch, and other bishops sympathetic to Nestorius arrived. Cyril had come with a bevy of bishops and fanatical monks who were quite prepared to fight physically for his cause. This led to riots in the city between rival groups of supporters. Within two days Cyril had jackbooted a condemnation of Nestorius through the gathering and had his own views adopted as the faith of the church. Nestorius was declared deposed without ceremony. When John and his supporting bishops arrived, they proceeded to excommunicate and depose Cyril and appealed to the emperor. The Roman delegates (two bishops and a priest) arrived on 10 July and ratified Cyril's views and excommunicated Bishop John. It was at this stage that the Roman priest Philip made a speech lauding papal authority. Since he spoke in Latin we do not know the response of the Eastern bishops, but it was translated and included in the Greek text of the council.

By August the imperial legate had arrested both Nestorius and Cyril. In the following months all the bishops drifted home except Nestorius, who was forcefully retired to a monastery in Antioch for four years, and was then exiled to the edge of the desert at the oasis of El-Kharga in upper Egypt. The date of his death is unknown. Peace was restored, at least temporarily, when, in 433, John of Antioch wrote to Cyril proposing that they jointly declare their faith that Mary is *Theotokos* and that in the one person there are united two natures without confusion. John also disowned the tragic Nestorius. It was a generous offer to Alexandria, and Cyril gladly accepted the proffered reunion. Pope Sixtus III (432–40) had been a major actor in bringing the two together.

Like most compromises this reunion did not settle the matter, even though it was a finely balanced attempt to express the church's faith. However, before the whole problem broke out again most of the main actors in the conflict at Ephesus were dead.[61] The old disputes exploded again as a result of the opinions of the Archimandrite Eutyches (c. 378–451), abbot of a monastery in Constantinople. This rather stupid monk had influence at court and his main aim was opposition to Nestorianism, no doubt recalling Nestorius' opposition to the monks of the capital. Strongly Alexandrian in his theology, Eutyches maintained that there were two natures in Christ prior to the incarnation but only one after it, the human being absorbed by the divine. His position was fundamentally monophysite, the notion that there is only one nature in Christ, the divine nature. Eutyches was condemned by the Synod of Constantinople (448) and deposed by Bishop Flavian. Eutyches appealed to Pope Leo I and then to the Emperor Theodosius II, who held the so-called *Latrocinium* (Robber Synod) of Ephesus (449). Eutyches was acquitted and restored as abbot. Bishop Flavian of Constantinople was deposed and died in exile. The delegates sent by Pope Leo I to the *Latrocinium* were insulted. As soon as he heard of the results of the synod, Leo wrote repudiating its acts and stating the true faith in his famous *Tome* or *Epistola ad Flavianum*, which he sent to Bishop Flavian in 449.[62] In it he outlined the doctrine of two natures in the one person of Christ.

Leo the Great (440–461)

I HAVE ALREADY mentioned Pope Leo I several times. He is one of only two popes accorded the title 'the great'. According to the *Liber Pontificalis*, he was born in Tuscany.[63] Little is known about his early life, but he was a deacon in Rome from about 422. His life and papacy span some of the worst years of the collapse of the Roman Empire in the West. He had been elected bishop of Rome in September 440 by the Roman clergy and people while he was in Gaul. In outlook and attitude he was conservatively Roman and did not really understand the new barbarian world that was emerging around him. But he did see the papacy as a stabilising element in the chaos facing the Western church, and he certainly had a high view of its role in the wider church.

We do not know if Leo was in the city at the time of the Visigothic sacking, but he certainly was present as pope in 452 when he confronted Attila and the Huns, who had invaded Italy. They had moved across Europe from the steppes north of the Caspian Sea, invaded the Eastern empire, and then had crossed the Rhine in 451.[64] As the representative of the city he went out to meet them and persuaded them to withdraw with a bribe and promises of an imperial grant. Leo's leadership of the delegation to pacify and deflect Attila indicates that the papacy was playing an increasingly important role in the government of the city. Rome was again sacked in 455, this time by the Vandals under Gaiseric; they invaded the city from their stronghold in North Africa. Again Leo I intervened and saved the city from worse destruction. The stabilising role of the pope inevitably increased with the complete collapse of the Western empire and the abdication in 476 of the last emperor, Romulus, nicknamed 'Augustulus' (Little Augustus), in Ravenna.

Leo envisaged the bishop of Rome as having authority over and responsibility for the whole church. He argued that it was through the continuing semi-sacramental presence of Peter and Paul that Rome had truly become the *caput mundi*, the head of the world. He claimed that the fidelity of Christ's commitment to Peter was eternal and that this found its contemporary realisation in the actions of the bishop of Rome: 'Blessed Peter maintained rock-like fortitude and he has not surrendered the government of the church bestowed on him . . . Everything pertaining to his office and his pastoral care he carries out in and through the successor in whom he is honoured.'[65] This notion of Peter living on almost sacramentally in his diocese has been largely lost in the contemporary theology of the papacy.[66] But it was an essential element of papal theology in the first millennium. The succession of vicars of Peter gave the papacy a stability that had major practical consequences in a world that was falling apart.

Leo's greatness is most vividly seen in his intervention in the seemingly neverending disputes that troubled the Eastern church. As so often happens, the solution to the impasse created by the *Latrocinium* synod came through the death of one of the principal protagonists: Theodosius II. After negotiations with the new Emperor Marcian (450–58) and the Empress Pulcheria, a council was called for 451 at Chalcedon (very close to Constantinople). Chalcedon was the largest council of antiquity: there were about 360 or more bishops present, and they were accompanied by the usual bevy of clergy and monks.

Chalcedon was the only early council at which the papacy played a major role. Leo I had a good knowledge of Western views on the Christological controversies (he was well advised by Prosper of Aquitaine, a disciple of Augustine), and his knowledge of Eastern theology was considerable. Leo was actually opposed to holding the council of Chalcedon; as Duchesne says, the bishops of the West 'were more disturbed about Attila than about Eutyches [and] had every possible reason for staying at home'.[67] However, the pope was prepared to fall in with the imperial government, and the leader of Leo's legates at the council was Paschasinus, bishop of Lilybaeum on the west coast of Sicily (present-day Marsala). The papal legates did not preside, but they were given a place of honour to the right of the imperial delegates.[68] Both the Emperor Marcian and his delegates played an important role.

After the posthumous rehabilitation of Bishop Flavian and some debate about the suitability of Leo's *Tome*, the council eventually declared that the 'orthodox doctrines' have come down to the church through 'Blessed Cyril' (of Alexandria), as well as in 'the Letter of the primate of greatest and older Rome, the most blessed and most saintly archbishop Leo written to the sainted archbishop Flavian to put down Eutyches' evilmindedness, because it is in agreement with great Peter's confession'.[69] The council simply restated the faith of Nicaea and the First Council of Constantinople that in Christ there is one divine person with two natures. Thus the council substantially accepted Leo's *Tome* with respectful approval, and Leo's teaching clearly emerges in the council's *Definitio*. Tragically, in the East the council was to lead not to peace but to another whole series of destructive debates about its interpretation. But that is another story.

The council was also concerned with disciplinary measures regulating clerical, monastic and lay life. In this there was no mere rubber-stamping of Roman views; in fact, the contrary was true. From Pope Leo's perspective, the most obnoxious disciplinary canon was Canon 28. This established the pre-eminence of the see of Constantinople over Alexandria and Antioch on the grounds that the capital, like Rome, was an imperial city. Leo at first refused to sign the council's proceedings; even when he did sign, in March 453, he declared Canon 28 invalid because he claimed that it contradicted the teaching of the Council of Nicaea on patriarchal sees.

Leo died on 10 November 461. The next three popes—Hilarius (461–68), Simplicius (468–83) and Felix III (483–92)[70]—followed in his footsteps, but they were confronted with the ongoing disintegration of the Western Roman world. In 476 the Roman empire in the West effectively ended with the abdication of the emperor Romulus Augustulus.[71] The effective ruler of Italy was the barbarian Odoacer, who, although he never adopted the title King of Italy, was now the effective ruler of the peninsula. He ruled from 476 to 493; after his murder he was replaced in Ravenna by the Ostrogothic kingdom ruled by Theodoric (493–526). There was a brief period of stability under this cultured ruler, but following his death Italy quickly descended again into chaos.

This whole new world of instability that was emerging in the West faced the papacy with the challenge to find a new way to respond to it.

3

The popes in the early middle ages

The context: the first 'dark age'[1]

THE POPES HAD COME a long way in the 175 years since Constantine. By the time of Gelasius I (492–96) they had defeated the powerful pagan senatorial class and they had Christianised Rome. The classical basilica style was now the model for church buildings.[2] The popes had expelled the heretical communities and their bishops from the city. The Latin language had brought standardisation in church worship. Throughout this period their control of the city and central Italy increased. In fact, one of the most remarkable achievements, given the instability of the times, was the ongoing development and expansion of the papal central government, especially in the sixth and seventh centuries.[3] The influence of the late imperial administration on the development of the papal chancery was considerable. The Lateran palace was slowly becoming the centre of stable government in Italy.[4]

The popes also faced a succession of Eastern heresies, and they conceived of their task as maintaining the agreed faith against novelty. Given that much of this was sponsored by the Byzantine government, the papacy gradually emerged as a real centre of opposition to caesaro-papism, and in the latter part of the period to the brutal, unpopular and colonialist Byzantine exarchs (governors) in Ravenna. This is not to say that the popes abandoned their support for the imperial ideal; rather, the papacy was simply the only real point of stability in the Italian peninsula.

This period has posthumously been called a 'dark age', with good reason. During these two centuries Italy faced a trinity of terror: barbarian invasions, recurrent plague, and Byzantine neo-colonialism. Increasingly the popes found themselves responding to immediate issues, and it was within this practical context that the reality of papal primacy was worked out. In fact, in this period the papacy, as the only consistent force in Italy, was very popular in the peninsula. That is why papal elections became more and more intense and passionate affairs, for the ability and opinions of the pope were issues of real importance for Italians.

Plague, invasion and war resulted in political, social and economic dislocation in Italy. The popes emerged as defenders and negotiators with the barbarian invaders. More importantly, they interceded with God through prayer and worship for divine mercy on suffering people. They also offered forms of social security and practical charity, and were often the sole source of food for the city and central Italy. They supported refugees, ransomed captives, and continued to build and maintain Rome itself. All of this required both an expansion of the papal government and a regular source of revenue.[5] The latter came from two sources: bequests and donations to the pope, and the papal estates in central Italy, Sicily, Gaul and North Africa.[6] These estates came to be collectively called the *Patrimonium Petri*, the Patrimony of St Peter. The profits from them not only supported the papal social service and charities, but it also paid clerical salaries and supported church building and maintenance.

Clearly the popes had considerable influence in suburbicarian Italy, especially through the Roman Synod. It is also evident that their primatial authority was generally recognised throughout Italy. In fact, the papacy was fundamentally an Italian-centred institution throughout this period. In the rest of the West real papal influence is hard to assess, and was probably slight. Often enough the reason for this was mundane: external circumstances, such as the collapse of centralised power, meant that Rome was out of contact, or could only make sporadic contact with difficulty, with many regions in Western Europe. The Roman communications structure had largely collapsed. Certainly, papal primacy was theoretically recognised; it was just that practical problems of communication inhibited its exercise. In an interesting analysis of papal letters and decretals for the period of Gelasius I, the German historian Bernhard Schimmelpfenning shows that the pope's main area of influence was suburbicarian Italy. Beyond that there was only intermittent correspondence.[7] This decreased even more under Gelasius' successors. Schimmelpfenning also points out that the 'mental horizon' of the Roman bishops was limited. This is revealed in that product of the papal curia, the *Liber Pontificalis*. Its focus is relatively parochial, although relationships with the Eastern empire receive some emphasis. This may also reflect the fact that the writers of the *Liber* were not men of broad education, but were probably clerks in the papal chancery. Each biography was usually, but not always, written after the death of the pope.

If there was a theoretical recognition of primacy, Rome's authority in disciplinary matters was less likely to be accepted as normative. Unless there was some major dispute, almost all of these decisions were taken at the local level. Despite the demand of several popes that major issues be referred to the Lateran, Rome's actual remit in the judgement of disciplinary matters was largely limited to suburbicarian Italy and, to a much lesser extent, the West. The authority and influence of the Eastern patriarchates—Antioch, Alexandria, Constantinople and, to a lesser extent, Jerusalem—were pretty much normative in their own areas. Even on as important a point as the date of Easter, the East did not accept Rome's position: Easter is still celebrated on different dates in the Eastern and Western churches.

Gelasius I (492–496) to the end of the Acacian Schism (518)

Pope Gelasius I was second only to Leo as the great pope of the fifth century. From the beginning of his short papacy he had to deal with all the consequences of another barbarian incursion into Italy led by the Ostrogoth Theodoric, who conquered Odoacer in Ravenna in 493. As a

result of the war, Rome was filled with refugees. Gelasius was successful in dealing with Theodoric, a moderate Arian and a humane and just
ruler, who went on to establish a cultured and civilised kingdom in Italy
with Ravenna as his capital. Theodoric respected the Catholic church
and the papacy. Jeffrey Richards says that the importance of Gelasius as
pope lay in his 'fierce conservatism', his administrative reforms, his
opposition to heresy, and his theological ability.[8]

Gelasius is important in three areas of church life: his high pretensions regarding papal primacy; his theory of the relationship between
church and state (both of these are linked to his defence of Chalcedonian
orthodoxy); and his extensive pastoral work.

Gelasius inherited the Acacian Schism between East and West. As
far as many in the East were concerned, the Council of Chalcedon had
not settled the dispute about the relationship of nature and person in
Christ: the monophysite theory (that there is only a single divine nature
in Christ) continued to be taught and it enjoyed imperial patronage. Both
Antioch and Alexandria soon had monophysite bishops. Pope Simplicius
(468–83) had tried to intervene in these episcopal appointments but
was ignored, and Felix III (483–92) excommunicated Acacius, the patriarch of Constantinople, because of his support for the pro-monophysite
bishops of Antioch and Alexandria. Felix bluntly told the Emperor Zeno
(474–91), who tried to abandon the Chalcedonian two-nature teaching:

> The Emperor is a son of the Church, not a bishop of the Church. In
> matters of faith he must learn, not teach . . . By God's will the direc-
> tion of the church belongs to the bishops, not to the civil power . . .
> God intends it to be subject to the church.[9]

This forthright language was typical also of Gelasius, who at this
time was Felix's deacon. It was the beginning of a schism between Rome
and Constantinople that lasted until 519.

After his election as pope, Gelasius rejected the overtures of both
the Eastern Emperor Anastasius I (491–518) and the Constantinople
Patriarch Euphemius. In his relations with the Eastern church Gelasius
consistently took a hard line. He asserted the rights and prerogatives
of the Roman see to approve and enforce the decisions of councils and

synods. He saw himself as the true defender of Chalcedon, and his bluntness did nothing to win friends and influence people! Ecclesiastical subservience to the state was a major reason why Chalcedonian orthodoxy was not accepted. So Gelasius was determined to make the church independent of both the emperor and the new leaders of the Western barbarian kingdoms.

In a famous passage that has caused much debate among historians, Gelasius appears to hold that there are two separate spheres: *auctoritas sacrata pontificium* (the sacred pontifical authority) and *regalis potestas* (regal power), roughly corresponding to what we would call church and state.[10] The church is superior to the state, and the pope to the emperor, because the church is responsible for the emperor's eternal salvation. Gelasius enunciates his position in his famous letter *Duo quippe sunt* to the Emperor Anastasius I in 494:

> For there are two powers, august emperor, by which this world is principally ruled: the sacred authority [*auctoritas*] of the pontiff and the regal power [*potestas*]. Of these, the power of the priests is more important for they have to answer for the kings of men in the divine tribunal.[11]

Contained in this passage are the seeds of later conflict, especially in the Middle Ages, for the pope is seemingly claiming to be responsible for the behaviour of kings. The claim is based on the premise that the spiritual is superior to the temporal. And the supreme spiritual authority is that of the bishop of Rome. Gelasius seems to be trying to use his 'Gelasian theory' to enforce papal supremacy even over the emperor. He apparently asserts the superiority of the priesthood over the faithful and emphasises the particular power granted by God to the Roman see. But behind all this is his deep concern with orthodoxy, for so often it was the imperial power that promoted doctrinal novelty, as was vividly illustrated in the case of monophysitism.

If Gelasius is asserting the superiority of the priesthood, it is the most far-reaching assertion that any pope had made to this point. For he would be claiming that he held the same position in the church as the emperor in the state, and that the church was superior to the state. However, Richards argues that Gelasius' letter of 494 was not advocating the supremacy of the spiritual over the temporal at all and must be seen within the broad context of his thought. He shows that two years later Gelasius held that the two orders of church and state were equal, 'neither being exalted by the subservience of the other', and that each was fitted for its own appropriate functions.[12]

Some historians, such as Walter Ullmann, have argued that Leo the Great and Gelasius, following Ambrose and Augustine, are major early articulators of a theory of papal monarchy that was to find its apogee in the Middle Ages.[13] According to this theory the popes progressively and systematically elaborated the idea of a papal monarch. Other historians, such as Richards, argue that this is a misreading, that there was never an ideology of papal monarchy. For them the growth of the papacy represents a much more *ad hoc* development. The popes simply responded as creatively as they could to the needs of the time. Personally, I lean to this pragmatic interpretation, but I would favour a theological interpretation of papal actions rather than an ideological one. The notion of Petrine (and Pauline) primacy—the apostle(s) living on almost 'sacramentally' in the Roman see—is a basic clue to papal attitudes in this period. In the first millennium there was much more a sense of papal leadership and *diaconia* (service) through acting as a focus for the unity of the church. The monarchical ideology of power and dominance came much later.

Gelasius is often seen as a liturgical reformer, but the *Gelasian Sacramentary* (which dates from eighth-century Gaul) is incorrectly named after him. The liturgical historian Kenneth Stevenson describes the liturgical compositions of Leo, Gelasius and Gregory the Great as 'subtle and dry'.[14] However, the general framework of the Roman Mass was settled by the fifth century, and both Popes Leo and Gelasius played a major part in the evolution of that liturgical form. Both were interested in the reform of church music. Gelasius was also deeply pastoral in his care for the poor, his generosity in the relief of famine, and his support for the church's social service. He also faced an acute shortage of clergy; he recruited many and was interested in their training.

Pope Anastasius II (496–98) took a more conciliatory attitude toward the East and worked hard to restore unity. But this led to trouble and a split within the Roman church itself, and the pope died before anything could be achieved. The split was realised three days later when two popes were elected simultaneously: Symmachus (498–514), who represented the hard-line position toward the East; and Lawrence (498–99), who stood for *détente*. Symmachus was eventually given the nod by Theodoric and on return to Rome issued an extraordinary decree on papal elections, which virtually gave the pope the power to appoint his successor. The laity were to be totally excluded.

At first peace prevailed, but in late 501 Lawrence emerged again to accuse the pope of unchastity and celebrating Easter on the wrong date. Theodoric suspended Symmachus, and for a brief time a visitator was appointed to rule the papacy, a most unusual step. Symmachus won his case on the grounds that no one, except God, could judge the pope, but the Roman church split and mob violence reigned for several years between the two factions. The Roman mob was to become a recurring theme in papal history for hundreds of years. Even when peace was restored, many were not reconciled with the abusive Symmachus. Due largely to papal intransigence, the Acacian Schism continued. Kelly notes that it was this pope who introduced the hymn *Gloria in Excelsis* into Masses celebrated by bishops.[15] He was succeeded the day after his death by Pope Hormisdas (514–23).

Even though he had been a close collaborator of Symmachus, Hormisdas pursued reconciliation with the East with both caution and flexibility. After two abortive attempts (largely forestalled by the emperor) before 518, he eventually achieved success. This was due largely to the ascent of the Emperor Justin I (518–27), to be followed by his nephew Justinian I (527–65). Both these monarchs wanted peace with the Western church, and Justin supported Chalcedon. The papal legates in Constantinople obtained agreement on a *Formula* proposed by Hormisdas, which the patriarch John signed in March 519. The *Formula* included the acceptance of Chalcedonian christology and an acknowledgement of Rome as the consistent upholder of orthodoxy. The 35-year-old schism was over. There was resistance in Egypt, and ultimately this reconciliation was only a brief reprieve in the tortured relationship between the Eastern and Western churches.

It is hard for us to comprehend how seriously the minutiae of theological debate were taken in the East, even among ordinary people. Monophysitism itself had split in varying forms, all implacably opposed to the Chalcedonian doctrine. Much of this debate was seemingly about words and not about reality. However, monophysitism was to be a continuing problem for the Eastern emperors, and much of their religious policy was concerned with winning monophysites over by finding formulas that were acceptable both to orthodox Chalcedonians and to them. By the sixth century the monosphysites had consolidated themselves in Egypt (the present-day Copts are their descendants), and also among the Syrian Jacobites and the Armenian Christians.

Hormisdas was succeeded by a series of weak and short-lived popes. The situation in Italy became progressively worse as the civilised Ostrogothic kingdom was gradually weakened and eventually overthrown by the forces of Byzantine neo-colonialism. It was truly a 'dark age', especially for Italy.

The papacy before Gregory the Great (590–604)[16]

ALTHOUGH HE DID NOT realise it himself, Gregory the Great was really the first of the medieval popes. No other writer was more widely read in the Middle Ages, especially in monastic circles, and none was more influential. Yet, simultaneously, Gregory was the last prominent product of the culture of imperial Rome, and it was in this context that he truly belonged.[17]

Gregory was one of the great transitional historical figures whose creative conservatism provided the foundation for the Western Christian tradition to begin the final and decisive stage of the process of separation from the antique world. But, on a conscious level, Gregory and his papal successors were still part of the Christian Roman empire centered on Constantinople.[18] They never contemplated withdrawal from it. Yet it was Gregory who, perhaps unconsciously, began to reorient the papacy from the old imperial values of the Byzantine empire and directed it toward the newly emerging peoples of the northern part of Western Europe. He pushed ahead with the process of linking the papacy closely with the new barbarian rulers and their priorities.

From about the time of Gelasius I the popes had increasingly felt a tension between their *Romanitas* (Romanness) and their *Christianitas* (Christianness). This was eventually brought to a head by the tendency of the Byzantine emperors to presuppose that it was their right to alter christological doctrine without any reference to church councils, synods or Rome. They acted simply by imperial edict. It was the popes who were conservative: they tried to persuade the imperial government to return to the established Chalcedonian settlement. These tensions increased the subtle but growing sense of alienation between Constantinople and Rome.

When Gregory was born about 540, the process of actually baptising the main West European peoples was close to completion. However, the process of conversion and cultural transformation was to take much longer, and was really only gradually achieved by expressing the faith in terms of the mores, culture and social structures of the Germanic peoples and integrating them into Christianity from their pre-Christian tribal culture. There was a sense in which the peasant society of Europe was never totally transformed; its pagan roots coexisted with its Christianity for many centuries.[19] In fact, the French historian Jean Delumeau has argued that there was no such a thing as medieval 'Christendom', and that it was not until the seventeenth century that the peasant masses of Europe were fully converted as a result of response to the conscious spiritual needs of the laity.[20] Anton Wessels has developed this interpretation further and asked whether the mass of the European population was ever really Christianised in any real theological sense.[21]

The Western European world after 540 was one of plague, war and unmitigated disaster. The tolerant and cultured Ostrogothic kingdom of Italy was finally overthrown after a long war in 554 by two Byzantine generals, Belisarios and Narses.[22] Direct imperial control was reimposed and Italy was again ruled by the Byzantine exarchs from Ravenna. Despite the fact that the people of Rome generally welcomed the return of the Byzantine government and still thought of themselves as Roman, a period of terrible suffering had begun in Italy. Byzantine rule was alien and Greek, and Italy was treated as a side-show to the real action in Constantinople.

Throughout the latter period of the Ostrogothic kingdom, the popes were caught up in the struggle of the emperors Justin I and Justinian I to reconquer the West, especially Italy. Generally the popes were pro-

Byzantine, although there was a clear recognition of the tolerance and civilising influence of Theodoric. Several of the popes—John I (523–26), Felix IV (526–30), Boniface II (530–32), who was the first pope of German stock, and Silverius (536–37)—were actually very sympathetic to Gothic rule. However, Justinian's policy of the reconquest of Italy drew the popes willy-nilly into the theological and ecclesio-political morass of the Byzantine empire.

After the end of the Acacian Schism, Justin required the Eastern bishops to accept Chalcedonian orthodoxy and to acknowledge Rome as the apostolic see which had always preserved the Catholic faith. But the formula used was as much political as it was theological, for the Emperor wanted the Pope's support for his invasion of Italy. Justinian referred to Rome as the 'head of all the churches', but this was also motivated by his policy of keeping the papacy politically on-side in Italy. In his attempts to reconcile as many Eastern monophysites as possible, Justinian persuaded Pope John II (533–35) to accept the formula 'one of the trinity suffered in the flesh', which had already been questioned by Pope Hormisdas as quasi-monophysite. This created a possible theological disagreement between a pope and his predecessor. John's successor, Agapitus I (535–36), went to Constantinople to try to persuade Justinian not to invade Italy, and while there he had the patriarch of the capital deposed as a monophysite. Agapitus died in Constantinople and his pro-Gothic successor, Silverius (536–37), was deposed in turn by his pro-Eastern and pro-monophysite successor, Vigilius (537–55). What we are seeing here is a struggle within the Roman church itself for and against the caesaro-papist ideology.

The Byzantine invasion of Italy reinvolved Rome in the affairs of the Eastern church, but inhibited its relations with the episcopate of the West. Direct papal power was limited again largely to suburbicarian Italy, which now comprised the six dioceses within a 160 kilometre radius around Rome. Contacts with several of the major Gaulish bishops were maintained, but whole areas such as Ireland and the Celtic parts of Britain had limited contact with Rome. St Columbanus, who died in Bobbio in northern Italy in 615, typified the Irish attitude to Rome: respect without subservience. Both Pope Vigilius and his successor

Pelagius I (556–61) were willing to toe the imperial line; the freedom the papacy had experienced under Ostrogothic rule was now lost.

Both these popes had troubled papacies. Vigilius was an ambitious man who had been part of the circle in Constantinople around the pro-monophysite Empress Theodora. He had acted as *apocrisiarius* (ambassador or nuncio) of the pope in the capital. This permanent post had been created after the Acacian Schism and was normally occupied by a deacon of the Roman church, many of whom became popes.[23] Theodora had secretly promised Vigilius the papacy if he would disown Chalcedon. He acquiesced, and on the death of Agapitus I he returned to Rome, only to find Silverius already elected. With Byzantine support, he seized the papacy by force. However, given Western support for Chalcedon, Vigilius could not openly attack the council. In the lead-up to the Second Council of Constantinople (553) Vigilius' theological vacillations came to a head. He refused to attend the council because there were no Western bishops present and he feared for his own life. He eventually accepted the council's decisions, although both Milan and Aquileia broke off communion with Rome. Vigilius' deviousness led to a fall-out with his patron Justinian, and his theological compromises were rejected in both East and West.

His successor, Pelagius I, was forced on the Roman church by the emperor and his orthodoxy was questioned in Gaul and northern Italy, especially again in Milan and Aquileia, where the popes remained excommunicated. The basic problem was the support of both these popes for Justinian's condemnation of the 'Three Chapters'. The 'Three Chapters' (or subjects) were said to be sympathetic to Nestorianism and thus anti-monophysite. Justinian hoped that a dash of anti-Nestorian zeal would help reconcile monophysites to the orthodox. But because the condemnation of the 'Three Chapters' compromised Chalcedon, this was not acceptable to the Western church. The question of the orthodoxy of popes Vigilius and Pelagius I arises from this complex debate. It hangs there, unresolved, due largely to the intricacy of the issues involved.

During the papacy of John III (561–74) the Arian Lombards invaded Italy and the Byzantines withdrew to Ravenna and to several coastal enclaves. By 574 the Lombards had broken up into separate groups; an eyewitness, Gregory of Tours, reported that murder, robbery, rape and

the destruction of churches had become endemic in the areas they conquered.[24] Rome was constantly threatened by them during the papacy
of Pelagius II (579–90). The Lombards were both preceded and followed by the plague. Over one-third of the population of Italy died in
the fifty years between 550 and 600. Between 589 and 591 there were
terrible floods in Italy (the Tiber inundated much of Rome) and after
591 there was a drought. In 599 the plague hit Rome again. It was a
dreadful time and it seemed like the end of the world. Many turned to
monasticism, or to primitive superstition.

Symptomatic of the troubles of the time was the decline in the
population of Rome. From about 100 000 at the beginning of the sixth
century, it had fallen to about 30 000 in 550.[25] It rose again to about
90 000 in Gregory's time with a flood of refugees fleeing from the
Lombards. Food supplies were inadequate. The Byzantine government
was hated. Much of the classical centre of the city around the forum was
deserted, and from the 580s onwards the senate ceased to operate.[26]

Pope Pelagius II was seen as a Byzantine stooge, even though he
worked hard to restore order to Italy and food supplies to Rome.
Throughout this period the popes had to assume more and more of the
civil administration of the city. Rome was physically isolated from the
exarch in Ravenna by Lombard territories to its north, west and south.
A corridor ran from Rome to Ravenna through the Lombard lands, but
this offered Rome little protection. A small Byzantine garrison was
eventually established in the city, but the popes were left with the bulk
of the civil administration. This was the situation when Gregory was
elected on 3 September 590. He was to become one of the greatest of
the popes.

Gregory I the Great (590–604)

GREGORY WAS BORN in Rome of a wealthy noble family who were devout
Catholics.[27] After a classical education and experience as a senior civil
administrator, he turned his house into a monastery in 574. Because
Gregory achieved so much as pope, it is easy to forget that he was essentially a monk and a contemplative, and one of the major spiritual writers
of the Western tradition. It was in this sense that he described himself as

servus servorum Dei—the servant of God's servants, a title still used by
the papacy. He was a deeply sensitive man who was able to analyse his
own inner experience with precision and subtlety. He also knew the
reality of suffering and illness (he had ruined his digestion with excess-
ive fasting) and, at the end of his life, he was crippled with gout. His
spirituality, which is centred on the radical human desire for God, has a
dynamic quality that many today find appealing. His belief in the near
proximity of the end of the world, understandable given the social and
political conditions of his time in Italy, further stimulated the yearning
for the transcendent. Gregory's spiritual teaching is to be found in the
Moralia in Job (his major theological work), the *Homilies on Ezechiel* and
in his handbook for bishops, the *Pastoral Rule*.[28]

He was appointed *apocrisiarius* in Constantinople in 579 by Pelagius
II. During his six years in the Eastern capital he lived as a monk. Despite
his residence there he never learned Greek, but he had a warm circle of
friends and he became something of an expert on Eastern affairs. It was
there that he saw caesaro-papism in action. When he returned to Rome
he acted as adviser to Pelagius and succeeded him when the pope died
of the plague in February 590.

His election was welcomed in the East but, in the long term,
Gregory acted independently of the imperial administration. Almost
immediately he faced a food shortage in Rome and he had to supply the
city from church estates in Sicily. He was as much Rome's temporal
ruler as its spiritual leader. He reorganised the *Patrimonium Petri* in order
to feed the city more efficiently. The imperial exarch remained holed up
in Ravenna, so Gregory negotiated a series of truces with the Lombard
King Agilulf (who remained an Arian) and his Queen Theodelinda (who
was already a Catholic), and set in train the conversion of the Lombards
from Arianism to Catholicism. The Lombards made peace with the
Byzantine exarch in Ravenna in 599. Although he was one of a couple of
truly great popes, Gregory's actual ecclesiastical control did not really
extend outside a narrow circle around Rome, and even there it was precarious. He certainly strengthened the primacy and laid foundations for
Rome's later dominance in the church, but it needs to be remembered
that his own ecclesiastical power was very limited. This did not prevent

him from attempting to project Rome's authority through his letters and legates, but beyond the city the pope had little real power. He was geographically isolated and he had great difficulty getting accurate information from many parts of the Christian world. He used legates with success in Constantinople and the Balkans, but they were generally a failure in north Africa and Gaul. Churches at the margins, such as the Celtic, more or less ignored Rome in that they retained their own practices.

St Columbanus is an example of this. He was an Irish monk who established a series of continental monasteries, the most important of which were Luxeuil (in eastern Merovingian Gaul) and Bobbio (in the Italian mountains south of the Lombard plain). The Irish monks set up the pattern of the Celtic church in these areas, despite protests from local bishops and to some extent from Gregory himself.[29] Columbanus was instrumental in the final conversion of the Lombards to Catholicism, and Gregory's papal successors Boniface IV (608–15) and Honorius I (625–38) became closely allied with the Lombard monarchy.[30] Gregory was tolerant of local culture and was prepared to encourage integration of it with Catholicism. Although he was a great believer in miracles, he was deeply opposed to magic and sorcery. This respect for local culture and its integration into Christianity became a characteristic of some of the popes who followed him.

This is seen especially in the conversion of the Anglo-Saxons to Catholicism. Bede's *Ecclesiastical History* records that on seeing some fair-skinned slaves in Rome and being told that they were Angles, Gregory commented, *Non Angli, sed angeli sunt* (They are not Angles, but angels). A variation on the saying is *Angli sunt, angeli fiunt* (They are Angles; they will become angels).[31] This led the pope to organise a mission of forty monks to England under the leadership of Augustine in 596. As Bede shows, Gregory had a continuing interest in the English church which remained strongly attached to Rome. In England the Celtic and Roman versions of the church also met each other; they were to settle their differences at the Synod of Whitby in 664. Gregory was deeply conscious of Rome's primatial position and took appeals to the papacy very seriously. His *Register* contains over 800 surviving letters.

At this period the vast majority of European people were rural. Cities, like Rome, were in decline. Many rural people were slaves or serfs. But church structures were still very urban, with the bishops living in the remnants of the Roman centres. So Gregory drew up a guide for bishops—the *Pastoral Rule*. It was practical and missionary in outlook, and it demanded that the bishop himself provide a model of Christian living for the faithful. The monastic virtues of celibacy, humility and obedience were emphasised. The bishop was not to stand above the church, but at its heart, and his task was to provide his ill-educated and superstitious flock with genuine leadership. The *Pastoral Rule* became the handbook of the entire Western medieval episcopate. At this stage most rural Christians were new converts and they had little sense of their connection with the ongoing history and experience of the church. What the *Pastoral Rule* did was to provide a stable tradition that could be handed on from bishop to bishop. Although Gregory remained very much attached to Roman culture and he still looked to Constantinople as the centre of the empire, he stood, albeit unknowingly, at the brink of the Middle Ages. His papacy was rooted, like himself, in the glory of the Roman cultural idea, but he looked outward, beyond his own age, to what was to come. The future of the papacy now lay with the northern European peoples, and it is to their conversion that we must now turn.

Missionary work among European peoples[32]

FROM THE LAST DAY of 406, what was to become Western Europe had been convulsed with the migrations and incursions of barbarian tribes. The sack of Rome by Alaric in 410 made it clear that the Western Roman Empire was in deep trouble: by 450 most of it had fallen to the barbarians. Many Roman Christians despaired of the survival of civilisation. But creative people were already at work trying to convert the tribes. In general terms the conversion of Europe can be divided into two stages: the first, up to 600; the second, from 600 to 1000. It is with the first period that I am concerned here.

One of the earliest missions was that of Wulfila (*c.*311–83), the missionary to the Gothic people. Because they ultimately occupied Italy, the

Goths are especially important in the context of the papacy. Consecrated a bishop by Eusebius of Nicomedia, Wulfila began work among
the Goths about 341.[33] For over forty years he worked both beyond the
Roman frontier and later within it. He was Arian in outlook, and this
simplification of the idea of the godhead helped him in his missionary
work. His most important achievement was that he reduced the Gothic
language to writing and translated the Bible. Parallel to the Goths on the
other side of Europe was the rapid conversion of the Vandals to Arian
Christianity in Spain after 406. Between 429 and 455 they established a
kingdom in North Africa under Geiseric. It is clear that the appeal of
modified Arianism was that it fitted in well with the traditional beliefs
of these tribal peoples.

In Roman Gaul prior to 406 there had been a lot of missionary work
in the pagan countryside (the very word 'pagan' comes from *paganus*,
meaning 'country bumpkin') by people like Martin, Bishop of Tours
(*c*.316–97). Roman civilisation survived after 406 in pockets in Gaul
right up to the establishment of the Frankish Merovingian kingdom at
the beginning of the sixth century. Missionary work had been going on
among the tribes, and the most significant event in this process was the
conversion of Clovis, king of the Franks, in 496. His wife, Clothilda,
was already a Catholic. The Catholic Franks were to establish the foundations upon which medieval civilisation was built.

The conversion of Ireland was entirely different.[34] Ireland had never
been part of the Roman empire, although there were small Catholic
communities in the south before St Patrick. The Gallic monk and theologian Prosper of Aquitaine (*c*.390–*c*.463), who was a secretary of Pope
Leo I, noted that Palladius was sent as the first bishop to the Irish by Pope
Celestine I (422–32).[35] He makes no mention of Patrick. Nowadays it is
agreed that Patrick came as a missionary to Ireland somewhere between
430 and 450. He had been born into a Christian community somewhere
in Britain around 390. It is fairly clear that he trained for his missionary
work in Britain. During his period as a slave in the west of Ireland he was
converted, escaped and returned to Britain. He may have visited Gaul,
but there now is little doubt that he was sent from Britain as a missionary bishop to Ireland. His work was mainly in the north and he seems

to have concentrated on converting the nobles and building up a local clergy. The old *toutha* (states) seemingly became his dioceses, which were arranged on a quasi-monastic pattern. After Patrick's death there was an enormous flowering of monasticism. Eventually the church became based on a monastic system and abbots became more important than bishops; episcopal sees were often centered on great monasteries, which were centres of learning. The emphasis on study led to the rapid growth of Irish Christian culture. By the eighth century this culture had reached its height and had itself become a source of missionaries, such as Columbanus.

Part of the penitential discipline of Irish monasticism was the notion of *perigrinatio*—exile.[36] The result was that the Irish became the great missionaries of their age. This began when Columba founded the monastery of Iona in 563; it became a base for the conversion of Northumbria, the English midlands and the Picts of Scotland. Celtic and Roman Catholicism (brought by Augustine) were soon in contact with each other in England. There were important differences between them— such as the date of Easter as the Irish followed the Jewish calendar. These issues were discussed at the Synod of Whitby (664) and, largely under the influence of Bishop Wilfred of York, the Roman view prevailed. However, many of the independent Irish continued to use their own date. In 668 Theodore of Tarsus arrived as archbishop of Canterbury and primate, and it was he who organised the diocesan and parochial system of England. The English church maintained strong bonds with Rome.

The Irish travelled further afield than England, more as monks than as missionaries. St Brendan possibly reached the Orkneys and the Hebrides, and by the mid-eighth century the Irish monks were settled in Iceland, well before the Vikings. There is a possibility that they reached North America. So the journey of St Columbanus (*c.*543–615) from Bangor in Ulster, to Luxeuil in eastern Gaul and then on to Bobbio in Lombardy, via Switzerland and southern Germany, is not at all surprising. His companion, St Gall (*c.*550–645), became the apostle of northeastern Switzerland. The Irish were generally erudite and cultured men, but their contacts were with people from across the whole social spectrum. The Irish brought with them their austerity and asceticism. While recognising Rome's position, the Irish firmly maintained their own practices and customs.

The Anglo-Saxons, meanwhile, had begun their very successful missionary work in Germany. These English missionaries were closely attached to Rome and constantly consulted the popes on ecclesiastical and pastoral issues. Willibrord (658–739), a monk of Ripon, worked in the Low Countries. To convert the Frisians, Willibrord was consecrated as archbishop of Utrecht by Pope Sergius I in 695, and the monastery of Echternach (in present-day Luxembourg) was established. The greatest of the English missionaries was Boniface (or Wynfrith) (c.680–754) from Crediton, just near Exeter in Devon. He had been trained from childhood in the Benedictine monastic tradition. He joined Willibrord in 716, but soon went on to Rome where he was commissioned as a missionary by Pope Gregory II (715–31). He taught himself Germanic customs and languages, spent several years in Utrecht, baptised many in Hesse and Thuringia, and was consecrated a bishop in 722 in Rome by the pope. In recommending Boniface to the Frankish ruler, Charles Martel, Pope Gregory sent him 'to preach the faith to the peoples of Germany who dwell on the eastern bank of the Rhine'.[37] Boniface's correspondence continued with Popes Gregory III (731–41) and Zacharias (741–52). After his missionary work Boniface reformed the Frankish church, which had been corrupted by the ignorance of bishops and clergy. Raised to the rank of archbishop in 732, Boniface, in true Roman fashion, set up an efficient and organised church with the ongoing support of the Frankish monarchs. In 754 he was killed by a group of heathen at Dokkum in Frisia.

C. H. Talbot notes the importance of women in this missionary movement and the sheer pastoral breadth and toleration of both the papacy and the missionaries. One sees this especially in the famous reply of Gregory II to Boniface concerning the question of the validity of second marriages. The pope is replying to a series of questions put to him by Boniface and in the process spells out a reliable pastoral norm: 'Moderation weighs more with these savage people than strict legal duties'. In the light of this he advises Boniface:

As to what a man shall do if his wife is unable through illness to allow him his marital rights, it would be better if he remained apart and practised continence. But since this is practicable only in the case of men of high ideals, the best course if he is unable to be continent would be for him to marry. Nevertheless, he should continue to support the woman who is sick.[38]

Talbot says that the Anglo-Saxon missionaries instilled into the Frankish and German churchmen a strong attachment to Rome and the notion of the unity of the universal church.[39] The foundations of a great church had been laid.

The papacy in the seventh and eighth centuries

WE LEFT THE PAPACY at the death of Gregory the Great (604). The popes who followed him were practical men and many were relatively short-lived. One result of Gregory's favour toward the monastic life was that rivalry between the secular clergy and the monks was experienced in these papacies. This was to become a significant part of ecclesiastical life in later centuries. Three of these popes—Boniface IV (608–15), Boniface V (619–25) and Honorius I (625–38)—were supportive of the struggling English mission.

In the seventh century a fundamental question facing the popes was whether they should turn from the Byzantine empire to Western Europe to find new patrons. Not that this question was articulated explicitly, but we can discern a hesitant process (it took almost 150 years) of turning from Byzantine to Frankish patronage. Here it needs to be recalled that until the mid-eighth century the popes still sought an imperial mandate from either Constantinople or the exarch before they were consecrated. There are several reasons why the popes turned towards the West and the Franks: firstly, the growing Islamic conquests increasingly separated Rome from the church in the East and North Africa and forced the popes to look westward and northward. Secondly, there was deepening alienation from the Eastern empire over a number of issues, not the least of which were the heresies of monothelitism and iconoclasm.[40] Thirdly, the position of the empire was progressively weakened in Italy, although the emperors still wanted a right of approval over papal elections. Fourthly, the papacy needed to find a counter-balance in Italy to the Lombards; the Franks offered this. We will look at these factors in more detail.

After the year 600 the whole perspective of European history changes. A totally new element enters the Mediterranean world—Islam. In less than a century Islam had overrun the Persian empire (637), Palestine and Syria (638–40), Egypt (642), Cyprus (649), North Africa and Carthage (697). In 711 the Moors crossed the Straits of Gibraltar and had conquered the weakened Visigothic kingdom of Spain by 715.[41] It was not until they were defeated by Charles Martel and his Franks at the decisive battle of Tours in 732 that their incursion into Europe was finally stopped. Meanwhile Arabic pressure on the Byzantine empire was relentless. Crete fell to the Arabs in 823, Malta in 870, Sicily in 878. But the tolerant Arabs were not anti-Christian; they did not indulge in forced conversion but slowly Islamised the societies they conquered. Nevertheless, the result was, as the Belgian historian Henri Pirenne argued in the 1920s, that the spread of Islam from the Middle East via North Africa to Spain ensured that Catholicism became and remained an essentially Western European reality. The Muslim invasions had closed off much of the eastern and southern Mediterranean, and large numbers of Christian refugees came to Rome through the seventh and eighth centuries.

Secondly, the popes turned north because of continuing schisms with the East. In the mid-seventh century they became increasingly caught up in the Eastern debates surrounding monothelitism. This is the theory that there is only one will in Christ. The theological problem posed by this view was that if there were two natures in Christ, divine and human, how did they act in unison? Supported by the Emperor Heraclius (610–42), Patriarch Sergius I of Constantinople proposed to Pope Honorius I the formula that in Christ there were 'two distinct natures but only one mode of operation', or will. This formula was more political than theological and was used as a way of winning over monophysites and finding an attempted compromise between Chalcedonian orthodoxy and monophysitism. The aim was to bring religious unity to the empire in the face of mounting external threats.

Honorius apparently happily embraced this formula. There is some debate about whether he really understood the question posed by Patriarch Sergius, and one view is that he interpreted it to mean that Christ's human nature was immune from sin. This seems to be supported by the fact that the actual reply to the patriarch's proposal was written by the Archpriest John who later, as Pope John IV (640–42), rejected monothelitism. This rejection was reinforced by subsequent popes, especially the heroic Pope Martin I (649–55). He was treated with appalling brutality by the Emperor Constans II (641–68) and neglected by the Roman church, which elected a successor, Eugene I (654–57), before Martin died in exile.[42]

The formula accepted by Honorius was condemned as heretical at the Third Council of Constantinople (680–81), which the Emperor Constantine IV Pogonatus (668–85) convoked to settle the monothelite question. The council accepted the teaching of Pope Agatho (678–81), who had obtained the support of the Western bishops and the Roman Synod in repudiating monothelitism. The council, acknowledging that Peter had spoken through Agatho, repeated the Chalcedonian doctrine on the two natures, to which it added that in Christ there were two wills and two modes of operation. Monothelites like Bishop Macarius of Antioch as well as Pope Honorius I were condemned. Agatho's successor, Leo II (682–83), said bluntly that Honorius, 'So far from quenching the flames of heretical doctrine, as befitted apostolic authority . . . actually fed them by sheer negligence'.[43] A temporary period of cooperation began between Rome and Constantinople, although there was a nasty incident when the army intervened in Rome in the election after the death of John V (685–86). The years 686 to 687 saw two antipopes elected despite the compromise candidate Conon (686–87).[44] Peace came with the election of Sergius I (687–701). The schism with the East was to be renewed by the iconoclastic controversy which began about 725.[45]

An iconoclast is literally an image breaker; this issue deeply divided the Eastern church for over a century. Judith Herrin argues that iconoclasm resulted from the anxiety that arose as a result of Muslim victories.[46] In fact, the first iconoclast emperor, Leo III (717–41), maintained that icons were an obstacle to the conversion of Muslims. It was the Eastern monks, such as St John of Damascus (*c*.675–*c*.749), who defened the legitimacy of icons, while the ordinary clergy simply surrendered to the caesaro-papism of the emperors. The details of the controversy are not important here, but the results are. The question of iconoclasm did not arise in the West, but the popes of the period were concerned with the seeming surrender of the Byzantine church to the imperial government. It added to the ever-growing rift between East and West and played a role in further alienating the popes from the Byzantine empire.

We have already seen something of the Arian Lombard invasion of Italy beginning in the late 560s. The Lombards' rule was harsh, but they were very gradually converted to Catholicism. However, they continued to be a real threat to the papacy, which first looked to the Byzantine exarchs for protection. These became increasingly unreliable and it was this unreliability that eventually led to the formation of the Papal States, and to the fact that in the eighth century the popes looked more and more to the Franks for protection.

The term 'Papal States' was first used in the late medieval period.[47] Their origin is usually attributed to the so-called 'Donation of Pepin' in 754–56. Recently, Thomas F. X. Noble has argued that the process of formation of the Papal States actually began seventy years earlier, in the 680s. He says that in the last years of the seventh century a succession of tough-minded popes, supported by the Roman nobility, liberated central Italy from the Byzantine empire and transformed it into a real state, the Petrine Republic.[48] The *respublica* of St Peter was governed from the Lateran palace and was independent of remnants of the Byzantine administration in Ravenna. Throughout the late seventh and the early eighth centuries the position of the Byzantine exarchate in Italy became ever more precarious, due to increasing pressure from the Lombards. Ravenna finally surrendered in 751. The Lombards remained a threat to Rome and the popes.

Noble's point is that a series of able popes—Sergius I (687–701), Gregory II (715–31), Gregory III (731–41) and Zacharias (741–52)— led an independence movement in Italy against the Byzantines and, at the same time, achieved a defensive Italian alliance against the Lombards. The outstanding Roman-born Pope, Gregory II, led the resistance to imperial tax demands on Italy and the Emperor Leo III (717–41) attempted to have him assassinated.[49] Gregory also opposed Leo's policy of iconoclasm and this drove a further wedge between Byzantium and the Italians. The pope also worked to contain the expansion of the Lombards. His successor, Gregory III, was the last pope to seek the mandate of the Byzantine exarch after his election. He firmly opposed the Emperor Leo's iconoclasm and entered into defensive alliances in Italy against the Lombards.

The position of the popes had became particularly difficult when the Lombard King Liutprand (712–44) captured most of northern and central Italy, and even more so when King Aistulf (749–56) captured Ravenna in 751. As early as 738 Gregory III felt very vulnerable to the Lombards, and he sent an embassy to Charles Martel (716–41), the *de facto* ruler of Franks, asking for help to defend the pope's *peculiarem populum* (unique people). This request fell on courteous, if deaf, ears. Peace with Liutprand had not been achieved when Pope Gregory III died in 741. Noble argues that by this time an independent state already existed in central Italy governed by the pope.[50] It was this Petrine republic that was now under threat from the Lombards.

Pope Zacharias negotiated peace with Liutprand, and contact with Constantinople was maintained, but the eighth-century popes increasingly felt the need for a powerful Western protector. As we have seen, papal attention had already been turned northward toward Western Europe and the dynamic missionary work going on there. Although Charles Martel had refused Gregory III's request for protection, the eighth-century popes saw the Franks as their new allies. The Merovingian Frankish dynasty was in complete decline; Pope Zacharias agreed to the removal of the last Merovingian king in 743, and the mayor of the palace, Pepin III (751–68), was crowned 'king of all the Franks' by St Boniface, as papal legate.

In 754 Pope Stephen II (752–57) crossed the Alps and asked for Pepin's help against the Lombard King Aistulf. There is some evidence that Stephen II partially based his claims on the so-called 'Donation

of Constantine'. Whether this is correct or not, Pepin did commit himself to the defence of the Roman church, and he was anointed by the
pope and given the title *Patricius Romanorum*—Patrician of the Romans.
The king kept his word and defeated the Lombards in 754 and 756;
he gave the pope Ravenna and confirmed his possession of what was
to become the Papal States. Pepin was succeeded in 768 by his son
Charlemagne.[51]

The Byzantines made various attempts to make treaties with both
the Lombards and the Franks against the popes, especially during the
time of Popes Paul I (757–67) and Stephen III (768–72). In 773–74
Charlemagne seized the Lombard kingdom and united it into his
Frankish domain. He reaffirmed the Donation of Pepin and placed the
papacy under Frankish protection.

The 'Donation of Constantine'[52]

HERE A COMMENT needs to be made on that enterprising forgery, the
Constitutum Constantini—the 'Donation of Constantine'. This was the
supposed grant made by Constantine to Pope Sylvester 1 in the fourth
century. The *Donation* says that Constantine, having been miraculously
cured of leprosy by the pope, decided to exalt the papacy above his own
'earthly throne' and conceded that the bishop of Rome

> should have primacy over the four principal sees of Antioch, Alex-
> andria, Constantinople and Jerusalem as well as over all the churches
> of God throughout the world . . . We give to the . . . Pontiff the city
> of Rome and all the provinces, districts and cities of Italy and the
> Western regions, relinquishing them to the authority of himself and
> his successors.[53]

Constantine is said to have made the pope supreme judge of the
clergy, and senior clergy were elevated to the rank of senator. The pope
was granted the right to wear a range of imperial insignia, including
the 'sparklingly bright tiara depicting the Lord's resurrection'. The
Donation was revealed as a forgery in the fifteenth century by Cardinal
Nicholas of Cusa and the humanist Lorenzo Valla.

The *Donation* is embedded in Book Two of the False or Pseudo-Isidorian Decretals. These decretals were attributed to St Isidore of Seville (died 636), but were actually compiled in France about 850. They are a complex mixture of genuine documents and many forgeries. Their ultimate purpose was to protect the privileges of bishops against the interference of metropolitan archbishops.[54] One of the unexpected forgeries included in the False Decretals is the *Donation of Constantine*. Reginald L. Poole comments:

> Most of these [Pseudo-Isidorian Decretals] were fabricated at one time for a definite political object, but some of them are traceable to an earlier date. In an uncritical age the Pseudo-Isidorian collection was soon accepted without question, though there are reasons for thinking that the Roman court was not so easily deceived as were the clergy of . . . Gaul.[55]

This would be especially true if a member of the Roman chancery was responsible for forging the *Donation* in the first place! Nowadays it is generally agreed that the papal chancery is its place of origin, and that its purpose was to create a legal context for the papacy to assert its emancipation from the Eastern empire. In other words, the pope's right to rule his republic comes from the greatest of the emperors—Constantine himself. Although it is still impossible to date the *Donation* accurately, for the document carefully omits any internal reference, the genesis of it may well be in the period of Popes Stephen II (752–57), Paul I (757–67) and Stephen III (768–72). The most likely period is that of Paul I.[56] It was also in this period that the iconoclastic Emperor Constantine V (741–75) attempted to negotiate a treaty behind the back of the pope with Pepin III, which the Frankish king rejected. Paul I also had a very high view of his office. Throughout this period the new Lombard King Desiderius (757–74) was also scheming to control the papacy. So a document forged in this period purporting to support papal claims would make eminent sense.

Judith Herrin points out that these popes also strengthened their link with the Frankish monarchy through the spiritual bond of *compaternitas* (godparent or sponsor). For just as Sylvester had supposedly baptised Constantine (he was actually baptised on his deathbed by the Arian bishop, Eusebius of Nicomedia), so the popes either baptised Frankish princes and princesses, or adopted them as their spiritual godchildren.[57] This spiritual relationship provided a model for the anointing and coronation of Charlemagne. What was clear in the eighth century was that the papacy had decisively moved away from the Byzantine milieu and looked more and more towards the Franks. In the process it committed Catholicism to Western Europe and deepened the already wide breach between the churches of the East and the West. This was to become permanent two centuries later, and it still remains.

Charlemagne and the popes

CHARLEMAGNE DESERVES HIS REPUTATION as the best-known figure of the medieval world.[58] When he became sole Frankish ruler in 771, he began a series of campaigns aimed at extending the Frankish realm: he added Saxony, the Lombard kingdom of Italy, Bavaria and, after an initial setback, southern France and northern Spain to his kingdom, and mounted attacks against the Avars in present-day eastern Austria and western Hungary. But Charlemagne was as much an administrator as a soldier. He was responsible for creating the conditions for the Carolingian renaissance, which was able to flourish because he also carried out a massive reform of the Frankish kingdom and church, establishing a strong central administration by using educated churchmen as key figures in his government.

The men who influenced Charlemagne were not the popes but his immediate ecclesiastical advisers, of whom the most important was Alcuin of York (*c*.735–804), the man who inspired the Carolingian renaissance, and his chief adviser in religious and educational matters. He was especially important historically for his influence on the liturgy. Among these advisers the Carolingian dynasty was seen as especially chosen by God to bring about a pan-Western European Christian *imperium* in contrast to the Byzantine claim to universal dominion.[59] This included all Christians; the unbaptised pagans were outside the pale. In real political terms this gave the Frankish monarch a working definition of friend and foe. Part of the Carolingian reform was a monastic revival led by an ascetic, St Benedict of Aniane (*c.*750–821), who systematised the Benedictine rule, which in many ways was given literary expression by the monastic poet, Notker of St Gall (*c.*840–912).[60]

Charlemagne's conquest of the Lombard kingdom of Italy in 774 was a turning-point for the papacy. It relieved the popes of the constant threat from the north, and on a visit to Pope Hadrian I (772–95) in 774, Charlemagne promised the pope three-quarters of Italy. The extent of what was actually given to the papacy was considerably less, but Hadrian is seen as the second founder of the Papal States. This distinguished pope supported Charlemagne's reform of the Frankish church along the lines laid down by the Roman church. Hadrian's dealings with the Eastern church regarding iconoclasm at the Second Council of Nicaea (787) led to tension with Charlemagne (he had not been invited to the council and was justifiably piqued by the adulatory tone adopted by the pope towards the Eastern emperor), but the relationship quickly settled down. The pope was represented at the Second Council of Nicaea, and his legates may have even presided. There was a fortunate coincidence between papal and imperial policy on icons: in many ways the council simply confirmed the policy of the Emperor Constantine VI (780–97) and his mother the Empress Irene. After the ravages of iconoclasm, it was now the Eastern monks who were beginning to question the prevailing caesaro-papism of Byzantine imperialism.

Hadrian was succeeded by Leo III (795–816), who informed Charlemagne as *Patricius Romanorum* of his election. Although Roman by birth, his background was southern Italian and modest, and his attitude to Charlemagne was almost abject. In 799 Pope Leo was violently attacked by disgruntled aristocratic elements in Rome who unsuccessfully attempted to cut out his eyes and tongue. The purpose of this attempted mutilation was to force him to give up all priestly offices, and it was certainly an effective way of disabling a rival! Pope Leo was then deposed on charges of perjury and adultery, but after some hesitation Charlemagne refused to recognise the deposition. The Frankish king came to Rome in November 800, and in a specially convoked council the pope was cleared of all charges. The principle enunciated at the time of Pope

Symmachus—*apostolica sedes a nemine iudicatur* (the apostolic see is to be judged by no one) was applied, and Pope Leo purged himself with an oath of innocence.

At Mass on Christmas Day 800, Leo crowned Charlemagne as 'Emperor and Augustus' in St Peter's. It was a momentous event in both papal and European history. In his *Life of Charlemagne* Einhard says it came as an unexpected and unwelcome surprise to Charlemagne, but this seems most unlikely. The significance of the act for both Charlemagne and the pope in relation to the Byzantines should not be missed. In accepting the title of *Augustus*, Charlemagne was in fact repudiating the authority of the Empress Irene (792–802) in Constantinople, and at the same time the pope was providing himself with a powerful protector against the Lombards in north and central Italy, the Greeks in the south, and the disorderly aristocratic elements in Rome itself. The impact on the Byzantine government is easy to underestimate from a Western perspective. For them it was a monstrous, almost idolatrous act, a pretence that somehow a barbarian upstart could assume the role of emperor. There is no doubt that Constantinople was very angry with the coronation, but this was just as much motivated by international tensions between the two empires as it was by the Frankish king's imperial pretensions. As a result, the Empress Irene's positive response to Charlemagne's marriage proposal led directly to her being dethroned in a coup, although her poor record in government was also well recognised in the Eastern capital.

Leo's successor Stephen IV (816–17) crowned and anointed Charlemagne's son, Louis the Pious (814–40), in Rheims. The ceremony had significance in that it suggested that the emperor needed coronation by the pope for the full exercise of his imperial position. It was also Pope Stephen who negotiated with Louis the *Pactum Ludovicianum*, in which the emperor gave the Papal States to the pope, pledged that he would not interfere, and guaranteed free papal elections. The new pope was simply obliged to notify the emperor of his election. In the papacy of Paschal I (817–24) the right of the pope to crown the emperor was established. During the time of Eugene II (824–27) Frankish influence in Rome and the Papal States was strengthened with the connivance of the pope.

But the Carolingian empire disintegrated as quickly as it had formed. According to the *Ordinatio imperii* (817), Louis the Pious' eldest son Lothar became co-emperor and his other sons were given parts of the empire. It was the Frankish custom to divide the inheritance between the sons. The Treaty of Verdun (843) confirmed the division of the empire into three parts. It was a recipe for disaster for the whole of Western Europe, which was not long in coming. For the latter part of the ninth and for the whole of the tenth century, the papacy faced a similar period of decline and disaster.

4 Through the *saeculum obscurum*—The Dark Age

Europe in the ninth and tenth centuries[1]

SEVERAL FACTORS COMBINED to make the second half of the ninth and most of the tenth centuries a second 'dark age'. The first of these was the division of the Carolingian empire. Charlemagne died in 814, and his successor was the feeble and incompetent Louis the Pious (814–40). His interests were ecclesiastical rather than militaristic. After his death the Treaty of Verdun (843) divided the empire into three parts: the German territories were to be given to Ludwig the German; Charles the Bald received the French territories—French historians list him as *le premier roi de France* (the first king of France); and the emperor, Lothar (840–55), gained the central Frankish territories west of Aachen (today the Benelux countries), plus Burgundy and Italy, including Rome. This division meant that centralised power was completely dissipated. It was not to emerge again until the advent of the Emperor Otto I (936–73).

The population of Europe at this time reached its lowest point between the Roman empire and the contemporary world. Less and less land was under cultivation; economic stagnation resulted, and people were often starving. The French part of the Carolingian empire disintegrated after 887, and people in France increasingly looked to local strong men to protect them. This, in its turn, led to almost constant internecine strife. In Germany the situation was far less diversified, and the period saw the rise of five great duchies.[2] A century and a half of savagery and chaos in both church and state began. Both Germany and France saw the re-emergence of feudalism as a system of socio-economic survival on the local level.[3] This localism was heightened as the Vikings threatened and invaded most of the coastal, and some of the inland, areas of Europe.[4] A Magyar incursion from the east (between 862 and 920 they threatened and invaded Bavaria and the Lombard plain), and a Saracen invasion of Byzantine Sicily added to the confusion. Syracuse was lost to the Muslims in 878, and the final stronghold there fell in 907.[5] The Muslims also advanced in Spain.

It was in this period of the collapse of centralised government that feudalism reached its zenith. While feudalism was a primitive form of government, it did represent the needs of the times. Feudalism should not be seen as a generalised 'system', as though it were uniform across Europe. It was highly localised, and in one sense its twin poles were land and armed protection. Wealth was dependent on the possession of land, and the armed protection provided by local lords maintained this possession. Thus the power of the local lord became increasingly paramount. It was within this context that the nobility gradually seized more and more control of church lands and offices. The spiritual duties of ecclesiastical office came to be disregarded, simony (the buying and selling of ecclesiastical offices) became widespread, and the practice of clerical marriage and concubinage became so common that later reformers normally imposed clerical celibacy as the symbol of the need for reform.

However, the titles and forms of central government survived intact, and they were to be reinjected with real meaning and power from the late tenth century onwards by the German Emperor Otto I and his successors. The notion of kingship as a sacred office was not lost, and these theocratic notions justified the use of bishops and clerics as civil functionaries in what survived of royal administrations. It seemed that there might be a brief revival of the empire under Charles III, the Fat (881–87), but he was deposed and died in poverty and disgrace.[6] The chronicler Regino of Prum describes what then happened: 'Now the kingdoms which had been subject to Charles, holding themselves bereft of lawful rulers, cut loose into separate realms. Now they looked for no prince of heredity descent; each divided part elected a king for itself from itself.'[7] The division of Western Europe originated in the late ninth century. In our time Europe is only beginning to transcend these divisions.

The papacy in the ninth century

THE UNPOPULAR (in Rome) Leo III outlived his imperial patron Charlemagne by two years, and was followed by the popular but short-lived Stephen IV (816–17). Paschal I (817–24) negotiated with Louis the Pious the *Pactum Ludovicianum*, confirming the pope's control of the Papal States under Carolingian protection and supervision. But friendly relations turned sour under Lothar, who had himself crowned as co-emperor in 817, and Rome itself was wracked by vicious divisions between the pro-Frankish party and the arrogant Paschal. Imperial control was reasserted by the so-called 'Roman Constitution' during the papacy of Eugene II (824–27), which included reimposition of the emperor's supervision of the Papal States and the restoration of the right of the clergy and people of Rome to participate in papal elections. Both groups had been marginalised by Stephen III in 769. Papal elections required imperial confirmation.

The longer-lived Gregory IV (827–44) was badly duped when he became involved by supporting Lothar in the revolt of Louis the Pious' sons against their father in 833; he was virtually excommunicated by the Frankish bishops who, of course, were more closely tied to the monarch than to the pope. Gregory responded by telling the bishops that he was not their 'brother' but their 'father'. Relations with Louis were patched up by the time of the emperor's death, but Frankish power quicky declined after Lothar became sole, but ineffective, emperor from 840 to 855. In reality, the empire was split among the sons. The next three popes were the corrupt Sergius II (844–47), who was elected and forced on the Roman church by the local clans after the populace had elected the antipope John; the unattractive Leo IV (847–55); and the insignificant Benedict III (855–58). All spent most of their time dealing with the interfering Frankish rulers who tended to see the Papal States as a fief of their Italian territories. The increasing influence of the great Roman clans in papal elections made the papacy increasingly the preserve of the central Italian elite. Throughout the second half of the ninth, the whole of the tenth and into the early eleventh century, a number of powerful families from the city and the surrounding areas—the Theophylacts and their relatives, the Tuscolani, the Crescentii, the Frangipani, the Colonna, the Tebaldi, the Orsini and others—dominated the *rione* (districts) of the city with their large fortified mansions. The papacy of the period was their plaything, and the only force that limited their ability to manipulate popes and papal elections was the German emperors. These were largely absent, but their irregular incursions were often accompanied with much violence.

In August 846 the Saracens from Sicily sacked Porto and Ostia and those parts of Rome, including St Peter's and St Paul's, that were outside the walls. As a result, the Roman leadership and populace became convinced of the need for self-defence. Leo IV began a programme of fortification. It was at this stage that the Leonine wall was built.[8]

While most papal energy was directed to relationships with the Frankish rulers, it was during the papacy of Eugene II that the problem of iconoclasm reappeared. It is easy to forget that relationships between the Eastern and Western churches continued right through the first Christian millennium; they were only finally ruptured at the beginning of the thirteenth century by the effects of the Crusades and those ruthlessly manipulative traders, the Venetians. At the beginning of the ninth century, it was the monks who had opposed Byzantine imperial policy on icons. The Emperor Leo V (813–20) had reimposed iconoclasm for practical reasons: to preserve domestic peace. Leo's assassin and successor, Michael II (820–29), was theologically illiterate, but he could not ignore the pro-papalist (and thus anti-caesaro-papist) stance of the monks and iconodules (those who supported the use of icons). For instance the monk St Theodore of Studios (759–826) wrote to Paschal I requesting his help against the iconoclasts in glowing terms: 'Listen to us, O Apostolic Head, charged by God with the guidance of Christ's sheep, porter of the heavenly kingdom, rock of faith on which the Catholic church is built'.[9] However, this does not mean that Theodore recognised an exclusive papal primacy. He actually extended this re-sponsibility to the whole episcopate. In repudiating caesaro-papism, he wrote to Michael II in terms reminiscent of Pope Gelasius I. Conceding that kings have power to judge earthly things, he continued:

> But . . . divine and heavenly dogmas . . . have been entrusted to those only to whom God has said: 'Whatsoever thou shalt bind on earth shall be bound also in heaven, and whatsoever thou shalt loose on earth shall be loosed in heaven'. Who are they who have received this power? The apostles and their successors.[10]

The Emperor Theophilius (829–42) renewed the persecution of iconodules, but peace came eventually with the empress Theodora on the first Sunday of Lent, 843, nowadays celebrated as the festival of Orthodoxy. In the West the Frankish bishops had intermittently opposed the teaching on icons of the Second Council of Nicaea (787), but under the influence of the popes and the more distinguished Western theo-logians, such as Hincmar of Rheims (c.806–82), the whole Western epis-copate gradually accepted icons.

Pope Nicholas I (858–67) was the only ninth-century pope strong enough to stand against the feudal conflation of the secular and the sacred. Jalland says that he was the real creator of the medieval papacy.[11] He held the Gelasian view of the papacy and strictly separated the secular sphere from the sacred. He saw himself as superior to rulers, especially in moral matters. He was very harsh to bishops who com-promised the sacred nature of their offices, and was a determined pro-ponent of papal power in both East and West. He was particularly concerned about reining in the authority of metropolitans, and, citing the False Decretals, he ordered the powerful Archbishop Hincmar of Rheims to reinstate a deposed suffragan bishop. He also confronted John, the archbishop of Ravenna, over the same issue.

It seemed that after the end of the iconoclast controversy a *modus vivendi* between East and West had emerged. But the deeply rooted breach had never really been healed, and relationships were disturbed again by the schism over the Patriarch Photius of Constantinople (858–c.895). The consequences of this tragic event are still with us in the division between the Eastern Orthodox and Western Catholic churches.

In many ways the blame for this lies with the stupidity and violence of the Patriarch Ignatius and the arrogance of Pope Nicholas. The origin of the schism lay in the complex of issues and relationships between Ignatius, the Emperor Michael III (842–67), and the imperial nominee to the patriarchate, the layman Photius. In December 858 Ignatius was summarily dismissed by the emperor and Photius appointed. Ignatius wrote to Rome to inform the pope of this. Nicholas I demanded that a commission of inquiry be set up; when that failed to restore Ignatius, Nicholas wrote to the patriarchs of Alexandria, Antioch and Jerusalem, and to Photius himself and the emperor, stating bluntly that Ignatius had been uncanonically and unjustly deposed and that he, as pope, could alone deprive the patriarch of office. This was confirmed by the Roman Synod in April 863, which proceeded to excommunicate Photius. The effect of all this in Constantinople was minimal.

There was nothing new about excommunication, but it was the cultural and psychological fall-out that was important in the long term. At heart the schism illustrated different understandings of the church and its relationship to the state. The whole affair was compounded by the understandable Byzantine annoyance over the activities of Latin missionaries in Bulgaria, encouraged as they were by Pope Nicholas. Photius, whom Francis Dvornik describes as an 'extraordinary man', saw himself as the guardian of classical and Hellenistic traditions.[12] He clearly lacked understanding of the tenuous position of the popes. While he recognised papal primacy, he felt the papacy had adopted a policy that was destructive of the Byzantine empire.[13] The tragedy is that both pope and patriarch exchanged mutual excommunications, and the Photian Schism, as it is now called, is seen as the beginning of the end of communion between the two branches of the church.

Pope Nicholas was the exception in the ninth century; after his death the papacy lost most of the ground it had gained. His successor, Hadrian II (867–72), renewed the excommunication of Photius and failed in his attempts to bring the Frankish bishops, including Hincmar of Rheims, to heel. The Byzantine Empeor Basil (867–86) called a council for Constantinople in 869 to solve the issue of who was the legitimate patriarch: Photius or Ignatius? The council was attended by papal legates, who did not preside. Photius was condemned and Ignatius reinstated. An order of precedence for the great patriarchates was worked out: Rome, Constantinople, Alexandria, Antioch and Jerusalem. Despite Roman opposition, Bulgaria was declared part of Constantinople's jurisdiction, not Rome's. While this council is recognised in the West as the Eighth General Council, it is not recognised as such in the East. Another council was held in Constantinople in 879–80, which restored Photius and annulled the acts of the 869–70 council; it is this that is now recognised as an Ecumenical Council by the Eastern church and was subsequently acknowledged as such by Pope John VIII (872–82).

Of Pope Hadrian's successors, John VIII was reasonably able, although he was the first pope assassinated, having been first poisoned and then beaten to death. Marinus I (882–84), Hadrian III (884–85) and Stephen V (885–91) had difficult papacies as a result of intrigues in the city itself, the vagaries of late Carolingian dynastic struggles, and the general feeling of independence among the powerful Frankish bishops. Externally, Rome was constantly threatened by the Saracens. As John VIII wrote, almost desperately, to Emperor Charles the Fat:

> We have sought to elect you above all men as defender and protector of the Holy See, as one deeply aware of its distress. It is for us a sheer necessity that our friends give us their help, not only against wicked Christians but against the Saracens, those brigands swarming over our country, robbing and plundering without cease.[14]

Generally speaking, all of these popes tried to maintain good relations with the East, which were reciprocated by Patriarch Photius.

The descent into the dark age[15]

MOST CHURCH HISTORIANS have tended to see the tenth-century papacy as a period of corruption, sacrilege and lechery. Nowadays the century is being reassessed. Modern historians point out that our sources for the period are both scarce and biassed; as a result a major new study of the period is needed. Often this period is completely neglected in papal history, which tends to leap from Charlemagne to the period of the reform of the church before Gregory VII. But it is part of the history of the papacy and must be acknowledged. The positive side of this period is that the papacy survived it. The negative is that for 140 years or more the papal office was the plaything of the powerful Roman families.

Also the tenth century was the last period of European history that faced the reality of major external invasion. The Saracens were always a threat from their bases in Sicily and North Africa. The Magyars threatened Western Europe for most of the first part of the century, and they were only decisively defeated at Augsburg in 955. The German rulers tried to set up protective shields of castles, especially near the frontiers. In Italy people moved inland from the coastal plains towards the hilltop towns and fortresses. As the Vikings, the terror of the previous century, settled down, there was increasing missionary activity in the Scandinavian territories. But even allowing for the historical context, it still has to be said that this was the lowest point in papal and European history.

The situation that was to trigger the descent into the mass of corruption was the election of Pope Formosus (891–96). Formosus was active, intelligent and ambitious. Prior to his election, as bishop of Porto he had represented the Roman church in Bulgaria where, because of his diplomatic success with King Boris I, there was pressure to make him archbishop (which was resisted on the grounds that he was already bishop in an Italian diocese). He had also carried out diplomatic missions for John VIII in Germany, but the pope suddenly turned on him and excommunicated him, reducing him to the lay state. Formosus had to flee Rome. In the papacies following the violent death of John VIII, he was gradually restored to his previous position.

As pope, Formosus became caught up in the inextricable political tangle of Italy and made many enemies. Personally, he was a kind and ascetic man, but with the particular fault of ambition. Except for strengthening mission work in Germany and England, he did not achieve a lot during his papacy. He was succeeded by the popularly elected and short-lived Boniface VI (896), who had also been deposed from orders for immoral behaviour by John VIII. A fortnight later the bishop of Anagni, Stephen VI (896–97), was elected.

Nothing is known of this pope except for his appalling mock 'trial' of Formosus. This was the macabre Cadaver Synod (January 897), in which Formosus' corpse (which had been buried for eight months) was tried for violations of the canons. The motivating forces behind this were internal Roman factional animosity and the vengeful determination of Guy of Spoleto and his mother Agiltrude (who Louis Duchesne says was the real instigator of the trial) for Formosus' perceived betrayal of them.[16] All of the popes of this period were under pressure to crown various Italian pretenders as emperor, and Formosus had managed to get caught between several pretenders, not least of whom was Guy of Spoleto.[17] The decaying corpse was propped up on a throne in papal vestments and spoken for by a terrified deacon. The issue for which Formosus was tried was the long-established canonical prohibition against the translation of a bishop from one diocese to another; in Formosus' case from bishop of Porto to bishop of Rome. The tradition was that the bishop was seen as 'married' to his diocese. The accounts of the trial were destroyed the next year, but Duchesne has pieced together what happened:

> The whole history of his past, his quarrels with John VIII, his oaths, his conspiracies, the perjuries imputed to him, were all brought up to his disadvantage. They revived old ecclesiastical canons . . . and ended by proclaiming the unworthiness of the accused, the irregularity of his promotion, the invalidity of his acts, especially his ordinations.[18]

His body was stripped of papal insignia, and a mob flung it into the Tiber. Having been consecrated bishop by Formosus, Stephen could now claim that his ordination was invalid. Thus, helped by hypocritical casuistry, he was now free to be bishop of Rome! The Roman clergy ordained by Formosus were deposed. Formosus' supporters among the clergy and laity responded by deposing Pope Stephen six months later and strangling him in jail.

For several years the pro-Formosan party was in control. Under Theodore II (897) the body of Formosus was recovered from the river and reburied in its original tomb, and his ordinations (and reputation) were restored. (The macabre facts seem to be that the body was washed up on the Tiber bank, recovered, then reburied by a monk, and then exhumed and finally reburied in its original tomb by the pro-Formosan faction). But the anti-Formosans were still present in strength in the city, and after Theodore's death they quickly elected Sergius III; but he was just as quickly deposed and exiled, to be replaced by the pro-Formosan John IX (898–900). This pope held a series of three synods, the last of which was well-attended in Ravenna, at which the ordinations and decisions of Formosus were held to be valid. The influence of the king of Italy, Lambert of Spoleto, is clear in all of this. This pope also patched up the relationship with the East and the patriarch of Constantinople.

Two pro-Formosan popes and a pro-Formosan antipope followed in quick succession—Benedict IV (900–03), Leo V (903–04) and the antipope Christopher (903–04). The pro-Formosan factions seem to have split in 903, and this left the way open for Sergius III to reassert his claim on the papacy. Supported by Alberic of Spoleto, he seized the city and the papacy from Leo V and Christopher, imprisoned them, and was made pope again in January 904. Duchesne describes him as 'spiteful, brutal and a scoundrel'.[19] He was a virulent anti-Formosan and he declared all popes since his abortive election in December 897 to have been intruders. All priestly and episcopal orders conferred in the meantime were declared null and void. The result was chaos. But Sergius had the support of the Roman nobility, especially the clan of Theophylact.

The worst feature of the Cadaver Synod was that it created two parties among the Roman clergy and people, and these two factions contributed to the disorders of the following generations. The volatility of the Roman mob and the power of the Roman clans now became a *de facto* part of the papal election process and the exercise of ecclesiastical power in Rome. It was into this bitter and divided context that Theophylact of Tusculum and his clan moved. He quickly became the *magister militum* (military governor) of Rome, senator, consul, financial adviser of the popes, and effective civil ruler of the city. The Theophylact family came from Tusculum (now Frascati) just outside Rome, although the name is clearly Greek. About 890 the original Theophylact established himself in Rome and gained power in the city. But it was his wife Theodora and their daughters, Marozia and Theodora, whose reputations survive with clarity, even if the chronicler who preserved their deeds, Bishop Liutprand of Cremona (*c*.922–*c*.972), was so bitterly hostile to them and their family that he did not hesitate to defame them. Theophylact was a strong supporter of the ambitious Sergius, who was probably responsible for the strangulation in prison in 904 of his two predecessors, Leo V and Christopher. There is good evidence that the then fifty-year-old Pope Sergius got the adolescent Marozia (she was between twelve and fourteen at the time) pregnant, and the resulting offspring was to become John XI (931–35).[20]

Here something needs to be said about Liutprand, bishop of Cremona from 961 to *c*.972, who is our major source for this whole period.[21] Liutprand, who could not resist recounting a clerical scandal, and who is writing a generation after the original Theophylacts, worked as chancellor for Berengar II (950–61), an immoral reprobate who had attained the kingship of Italy by the usual means of murder and treachery. Liutprand then moved into the service of the German emperors Otto I and Otto II. He was frequently employed by both king and emperor in negotiations with the papal and the Byzantine courts. Liutprand's bias towards the people whom he—or more importantly, his royal patrons—opposed has to be taken into account, and it should be noted that much of the subsequent Western European attitude towards Byzantium was formed by the jaundiced attitudes of Liutprand towards the Easterners. He hated the Theophylacts, especially the women. Theophylact's wife, Theodora the elder, was a powerful woman who seems to have taken control of the family and the papacy some time in the early 900s. Liutprand describes her as *meretrix satis impudentissima, veneris calore succensa* (an utterly impudent public prostitute, consumed by the fire of lust).[22] Other observers thought that she was a paragon of holiness and virtue. Liutprand considered that Marozia was abominable, probably because she, like her mother, was an independent woman who was politically active, a relatively common phenomenon in the tenth century.

The control of the Theophylact family continued with Popes Anastasius III (911–13) and Lando (913–14). Lando's successor, Pope John X (914–28), had been archbishop of Ravenna and was brought to Rome by the family because of the need for strong and experienced leadership.

However, Liutprand's probably accurate scuttlebutt was that he was the elder Theodora's lover and that she wanted him near her. But his later independence from Marozia, who had taken over from her dead parents as head of the family early in the 920s, led to his deposition and imprisonment in the Castel Sant'Angelo and his suffocation there in 929. John had been created by the mother and destroyed by the daughter. Marozia's power increased: the two short papacies of Leo VI (928) and Stephen VII (928–31) were followed by the election of Marozia's own son by Pope Sergius, now in his early twenties, as John XI (931–35). One of the first acts of his chancery was to enter into correspondence with Odo, abbot of Cluny, whence the later monastic reform movement was to draw its ablest men. Papal support for monastic reform was to continue throughout this period.

Morozia was now supreme in Rome. She was the *Senatrix* (the female senator) of Rome between 926 and 932 and the mother of the pope. She was to become the grandmother of John XII and possibly the great-grandmother of John XIX and Benedict VIII. She disposed of her second husband, Guy of Tuscany, who died in 932, and married the king of Italy, her half-brother, Hugh of Provence. He was already married and she was technically related to him, but all of this was swept aside with her son as pope. But it all ended in disaster, for her son by her first marriage to Alberic of Camerino, Alberic II, stormed the Castel Sant'Angelo, supported by the Roman mob, where Marozia and Hugh were in residence. Alberic imprisoned his mother for the rest of her life in the fortress. It is said that she became a nun. John XI was reduced to impotence and died in 935.

The myth of Pope Joan (a corruption of Johannes - John) probably originally emerged from Liutprand's history of the Theophylact women. The story is that around 850 a woman from Mainz, of English parentage, disguised herself as a man in order to follow her lover into a life of scholarship. A brilliant scholar herself, she went to Rome, rose through the curial hierarchy, and was eventually elected pope. The truth only emerged when she gave birth during a papal procession near the church of San Clemente. The story was first written down by the Polish Dominican, Martin of Troppau, in his late thirteenth century *Chronicle of the Popes of Rome and the Emperors*. In a recent study Alain Boureau maintains that the myth was fabricated in the thirteenth century, and it has been used for a number of different purposes since then:

misogynist clerics have used it as a moral tale to denigrate women and justify their exclusion from the priesthood, and in the Reformation it was used as a form of anti-Catholic propaganda.[23]

From 932 to 954, Alberic ruled Rome and restored order to the *Patrimonium Petri*. He made Rome the leading power in central Italy. He appealed to the glories of the city's past, and throughout the Middle Ages this notion of Rome's greatness was as important psychologically, both to its inhabitants and to medieval people generally, as its actual economic and political clout. Alberic's separation of temporal and spiritual power meant that the papacy had no attraction for the avaricious and ambitious, and the popes appointed under him were generally scholars and monks. It was he who invited monks from Cluny to come to Rome to reorganise monastic life in the city. The separation was to last until Alberic died in 954.

He was succeeded by his depraved, bastard son, Octavian, who had himself elected pope the next year as John XII (955–64). Octavian was only the second pope to change his name. He was about eighteen when elected. The spiritual and temporal had been fused again. There is no doubt that John XII's behaviour was utterly deplorable. Although Liutprand was a propagandist for the Emperor Otto I, he is probably substantially right, but possibly exaggerating, when he says that the young pope turned the Lateran palace into a brothel and that he and his companions raped pilgrims within St Peter's itself.[24] In politics John XII was not particularly talented, and he quickly became immured in internecine strife in Italy and fell foul of Berengar II. To shore up his position in the Papal States, which by then had been reduced to the *Patrimonium Petri*, a narrow stretch of land extending just to the west of Tivoli and bordered on the north by Orvieto and in the south by Terracina, John invited Otto I to come to Rome to be crowned as emperor. Anxious to gain the imperial title, the German ruler quickly responded and arrived in Rome in January 962.

Otto the Great (936–973) and the possibility of reform

OTTO AND HIS GERMAN KINGDOM were fast emerging as the focal point of stability in tenth-century Western Europe. Using ecclesiastics as his civil servants along the lines of Charlemagne, he was able to build up a reasonably strong, centralised administration. In 962 he went to

Rome for his imperial coronation, and on 2 February knelt in St Peter's, wisely surrounded by bodyguards, to receive the crown of the Holy Roman Empire from the deplorable pope. Otto promised to exalt the pope, to protect him, and to defend the property and borders of the Holy See. One-third of Italy—including Rome, Ravenna, Tuscany, much of central and northern Italy, as well as Naples and Sicily—was to be returned to the pope. This was a confirmation of the Donations of Pepin and Charlemagne. In return, John XII was forced to take an oath to be loyal to Otto. The *Priveligium Ottonis* was imposed on the pope: the Romans were not to instal anyone as pope until he had taken an oath before the *missi imperatoris* (the emperor's representatives).

The papacy consistently shows a remarkable ability to recover, even from its own worst excesses. John XII was a debauched, immature scoundrel, but it was the coronation of Otto in Rome that, in the long term, turned the tide in the direction of reform. It was to be a long-drawn-out process, but it had begun. It is also important to note that the papal government never broke down entirely during the Theophylact period. The chancery continued to function, and the papal archives were maintained. The records of Leo, Gelasius and Gregory were there to inspire later reforming popes.

Paradoxically, overlapping this low point in papal history was the establishment of the reformed Benedictine monastery of Cluny in Burgundy in 909. The monastery followed the strict Benedictine rule as interpreted by the Carolingian monastic reformer St Benedict of Aniane. The emphasis of the reform was on personal spirituality, the choir office, and the liturgy. Cluniac houses were independent of lay control and exempt from episcopal supervision; they placed themselves directly under the papacy. The reform spread right across eastern and southern France and over the Alps into Italy. These monasteries provided a spiritual impetus and trained personnel for the reform of the church.

The coronation of Otto led to a German domination of the papacy but, as we shall see, the clan of Theophylact was by no means defeated. As soon as Otto turned his back, John XII and the Romans began playing politics again. Otto returned to Rome, John fled, and in December 963 the pope was deposed with due decorum by a reasonably representative Roman Synod presided over by Luitprand. The synod had requested John to appear, but he refused and in turn excommunicated the participants. At the synod a parade of cardinals came forward to give evidence against the immoral pope.

> Then Peter, the cardinal priest arose to testify that he had seen the pope celebrate Mass without actually communicating himself. John the bishop of Narni and John, the cardinal deacon said that they had seen him ordain a deacon in a horse's stable . . . Benedict, the cardinal deacon, with the rest of the deacons and priests said that they knew that he ordained bishops for money . . . They said there was no necessity to investigate the pope's sacrilege because their knowledge came from seeing rather than hearing. They said that they had not seen him commit adultery but they certainly knew that the widow of Rainier and Stephana, his father's concubine, and the widow Anna and his own niece, all had been abused and that he had made the sacred [Lateran] palace a brothel. They said that he had publicly gone hunting, and that he blinded his spiritual father Benedict, and that the cardinal sub-deacon John had died after being castrated.[25]

Liutprand also reported that the pope was a heavy drinker and gambler and that he even worshipped the pagan gods. Naturally enough, the Roman Synod condemned John and deposed him. Otto made it clear that he considered himself ruler of Rome. The Romans deeply resented this.

John's successor, Leo VIII (963–65), endured a period of exile when John was invited back to Rome and inflicted savage reprisals on his enemies, but the pope-philanderer abandoned the city again when Otto returned. Liutprand blames 'the women, with whom the so-called Pope John was accustomed to carry on his voluptuous sports, being many in numbers and noble in rank' for the Roman revolt against Pope Leo. The ex-Pope John died, so the scuttlebutt said, as a result of a stroke suffered while in bed with a married woman. Another version of the story—recounted by Liutprand—was that the young Holy Father had been caught red-handed in bed by the devil (perhaps represented by the cuckolded husband?), who bashed him so severely that he died within the week, having refused the last sacraments.[26] Whatever the facts are, John was still in his mid-twenties when he died.

The German emperors were no longer prepared to allow the papacy to remain in the hands of the Roman families. It was too important an office for that. And there were increasing numbers of senior clerics willing to support imperial intervention in papal affairs. The unpredictable element in all of this was the Roman sense of proprietorship of the papacy; the office was seen by the local feudal families as their personal fiefdom, and by the Roman mob as essential for their economic support. For those who lived there, Rome was an independent principality; this notion would later reappear in the republican and commune movements in the later Middle Ages. These ideas were combined with local resentment of foreign interference in the affairs of their city and diocese. While in theory the popes claimed a universal jurisdiction, in practice the Romans wanted to possess it as their own. This is understandable, since it was the pilgrims who came to the shrines of Sts Peter and Paul and the kudos associated with the papal office that were the main economic support of the city. Rome continued to be faction-ridden throughout this period (the dominant family in the last part of the tenth century were the Crescentii, who were probably related to the Theophylacts). Intermittent intervention by the German emperors—Otto II (973–83), Otto III (983–1002) and Henry II (1002–24)—at best produced brief periods of reform. The *Patrimonium Petri* was little more than a series of hilltop strongholds and the city was still dominated by fortified mansions, and the main activity of the Roman clans seemed to be to render the papacy unstable. So the popes were under the control of either the Ottonian dynasty or the Roman families.

In a sense, a longlasting three-cornered struggle emerged in this period. The first element in this struggle was the German emperors, who saw the historical city of Rome with its imperial traditions, and the papacy with its sacral overtones, as a source of legitimacy and support for an emerging imperial theocracy. The second element was ecclesiastical, which saw Rome as the traditional place of the martyrdom of Peter and Paul and as the diocese with a long tradition of governing the whole church. The third element was the Roman nobility and people, who revolted against both imperial and papal pretensions to assert their right to a kind of independent principality or city state. All three elements saw Rome as the *caput mundi*, the centre of the world, and each of the three elements was to operate in interaction with each other with varying success over the next 450 years. In that period none ever gained complete control.

In the tenth century it was the clans who led Roman independence movements; one of their hilltop forts was Tusculum, the power-base of the Theophylacts, who in the late tenth century were far from a spent force. They were now led by Count Gregory. The extremely ugly period of Boniface VII (974–85), classified by the Vatican as an antipope in 1904, demonstrated that the old instability was still dominant. In exile for much of his papacy, Boniface nevertheless had two popes murdered: Benedict VI (973–74) was strangled in the Castel Sant'Angelo by a priest; and John XIV (983–84), who was imposed on Rome by Otto II, was either starved to death or poisoned. In this same period a cardinal was blinded, and Boniface himself was probably assassinated. Yet during the unstable period of Boniface's exile, Benedict VII (974–83), a man of deep spirituality with strong reforming tendencies, managed to encourage Cluniac influence and monastic reform and carry on a papal administration that was active throughout Europe.

After another period of instability, the brilliant and highly educated French-born archbishop of Ravenna, Gerbert of Aurillac, the most distinguished scholar of the age, was elected as Sylvester II (999–1003).[27] He was a statesman and a classical scholar who spent much of his time collecting and preserving secular Latin literature. He was also an astronomer, musician and mathematician. Early in his career Gerbert had seriously questioned the role of a papacy that had lost all moral and spiritual credibility. On election he became a proponent of papal authority, although much of his actual power depended on his relationship with the young Emperor Otto III, who had succeeded to the imperial throne in 983 at the age of three and had only assumed his majority in 996. Sylvester, who had been Otto's tutor, was a reformer of both clerical and monastic life and the organiser of the church in the newly converted territories of Poland and Hungary. Inspired by Sylvester, the young emperor dreamed of a *renovatio imperii Romanorum*, a restoration of the stability and culture of the Roman empire. Young Otto's vision was almost Byzantine in its scope (his mother was the Byzantine princess Theophano), and he set up his capital in Rome, probably among the ruined palaces on the Palatine. But he died of malaria in 1002, and the last year of Sylvester's papacy was spent under the dominance of the Crescentii family.

The old instability returned after Sylvester's death. The power of the Crescentii was broken with the death of Sergius IV (1009–12), and Gregory of Tusculum installed his second son, Theophylact, as Benedict VIII (1012–24). He was more a feudal baron than a priest. The Theophylacts were to control the Holy See through Benedict, John XIX (1024–32) and the appalling Benedict IX, who had three periods as pope: 1032–44, 1045, 1047–48. He was as immoral as his predecessor John XII, but less able. He was the last of the Tusculum family and appropriately named Theophylact before election. His adoption of the style Benedict led the gossipy monk-chronicler Rodulfus Glaber to comment:

> The Romans have found a singular means to palliate their insolent traffic in the election of popes. When they have made a choice of a pontiff which it pleases them to raise to the holy seat, they strip him of his own name and give him the name of some great pope so that his want of merit will be obscured by the glory of his title.[28]

Benedict's first stint in the papacy was for twelve years from 1032. Although he was the son of the ruler of Rome, various attempts were made on his life, the first of which occurred, according to Glaber, at Mass in St Peter's at the time of a frightening eclipse of the sun in April 1033, the year of the millennium of Christ's death. Throughout his papacy Benedict was anxious to assert his independence from the Germans. Despite this, in September 1044 he was expelled from the city in one of the regular uprisings. The cause, it was said, was his immoral life and violent actions, but the real cause was the plotting of the Crescentii clan, who immediately proceeded to elect their own man, Sylvester III (1045). The egregious Benedict regained the papacy in mid-1045, but within two months he had abdicated in favour of his godfather, Giovanni Gratiano, Pope Gregory VI (1045–46). The reasons for the abdication seemed to be that Benedict needed the money that Gregory was willing to pay and that he wanted to marry.[29]

Public order in Rome and the surrounding areas collapsed completely. Both Benedict (possibly disappointed in love) and Sylvester returned to establish armed enclaves in the city. Encouraged by a group of Roman clergy and citizens, in late 1046 the German King Henry III (1017–56) arrived in Italy determined to reform the papacy. Not only was he unwilling to accept the imperial crown from sullied papal hands; he also suffered from the German fascination with intervention in the morass of Italian political life. On 20 December 1046 the king held a synod at Sutri, which deposed both Sylvester and Gregory; the Roman Synod deposed Benedict on Christmas Eve. Henry then appointed Clement II (1046–47), who lived less than a year. However, he crowned Henry emperor on Christmas Day 1046. It was Henry who finally destroyed the power of the barons and families of the *Patrimonium Petri* and set in train conditions for a thorough-going reform of the papacy.

But there were two more years of chaos before the reform began in earnest. Clement actually began the process, but he died suddenly, probably of lead poisoning, in October 1047. Benedict IX resurfaced for his third papal stint between 1047 and 1048. After he was expelled again on imperial orders, his successor Damasus II lasted three weeks in office (1048). Excommunicated by Damasus and Leo IX, Benedict did not die until 1056. With his third choice Henry was more fortunate: Leo IX (1048–54) succeeded in transforming the papacy. The power of the clans of the *Patrimonium Petri* was finally broken.

But before looking at Leo's papacy and the reform of the church, some comments need to be made about this disastrous period in papal history. From the papacy of John XII onwards there were often two, and occasionally three, claimants to the papacy. This creates some real theological problems for apostolic succession. Because of a lack of clear criteria for legitimacy, how can apostolic succession be traced through the morass of different papal claimants? Virtually all of these popes were the creatures of one or other political master—or mistress, as in the early tenth century. What is the relationship of this to the claim that the bishop of Rome is the head of the church? What is the relationship between the two? There are no clear answers to these questions. During this period also the pope was almost exclusively the bishop of Rome rather than the head of the church.

But this does not mean that the popes did not look outward into the wider world. We have already seen the support given by even the most depraved of them to the monastic reforms that were emanating from Cluny. Cluny remained exempt from episcopal and local control and was responsible only to Rome. This became a model for later assertions of papal primacy over episcopal and regal jurisdiction in the cases of monastic establishments. These popes also intervened in disputes involving bishops in France and Spain. In southern Italy, there were problematic relationships with the Byzantine empire that became even more complicated with the partial defeat of the Saracens and the conquest of southern Italy by the Normans. In fact, Benedict VIII in the early eleventh century supported the Normans against the Byzantines.

In many ways the period sees the reversal of what was happening in the eighth century, when the German church was formed by the practices, liturgy and beliefs of the Roman church. In the tenth century the influence of the German church on Rome was considerable. Not only was the papal chancery modelled on that of the imperial German administration, but the liturgy and worship forms of the German church were imported into Rome. Byzantine influences also continued: the Lateran was increasingly referred to as a *palatium* (palace) and, with the reorganisation of the Roman church into twelve districts, the senior Roman clergy—deacons and priests—began to assume the title of 'cardinal'.

Mention of southern Italy reminds us of the difficult relationship between the Eastern and Western churches. Here we need to turn to events leading to the tragic and final divorce between the two.

The schism between East and West[30]

THE FINAL DIVORCE between the churches of the East and the West was the product more of cultural and political factors than of theological differences. The advent of the Lombards in Italy had slowly turned the papacy away from the Byzantine emperors toward the emerging power of the Frankish monarchs. The decisive moment came, as we have seen, when the popes asked Pepin the Short for help. Even after the break resulting from the coronation of Charlemagne, the links with Constantinople were maintained, although according to Francis Dvornik it was the coronation of Charlemagne that was the key turning-point.[31] The Easterners regarded this as treachery and insurrection by the pope, but Charlemagne was victorious in 812 over the Byzantines; in the Treaty of Aachen he was greeted by the Byzantine envoys as *basileus*—co-emperor. Eastern control of southern Italy and Dalmatia was confirmed, but East and West continued to drift apart. The decisive psychological break had now occurred. The new imperial protectors of the papacy were no longer Byzantine, but Frankish and German.

The Carolingian empire had virtually collapsed at the end of the ninth century, and papal elections were increasingly dominated by the Roman clans who tended to be pro-Byzantine (we have already seen that Theophylact is a Greek name). In this situation a kind of *modus vivendi* evolved between the Roman church and the East, which was strengthened by ongoing contact. An example is Liutprand of Cremona, who went as the ambassador of Berengar of Ivria to the Byzantine court in 949–50, and then as an envoy of Otto I in 968 in an attempt to arrange a marriage between a Byzantine princess and Otto's son. He was kept waiting in the pouring rain outside the city gates by the Emperor Nicephorus II Phocas (963–69). In Constantinople Liutprand had both success and failure, as he reports in the *Antapodosis* and the *Legatio*. The tragic irony is that the break in communion was to come right at the time when the Western church and the reformed papacy were on the edge of initiating real reform.

Dvornik stresses that the Byzantines continued to recognise Roman primacy, at least in theory, but they deeply resented German control of the papacy; Eastern emperors saw themselves alone as those with divine appointment to lead the Christian world.[32] If the south of Italy had become a political flashpoint between East and West, the so-called *Filioque* became the theologically divisive issue. The term is embedded in trinitarian theology and concerns the relationship of the Holy

Spirit to the Father and the Son. The Latin term simply means 'and from the Son'. Both Byzantines and Latins believed that the Holy Spirit proceeded from both Father and Son, but the debate was over the interpolation of the phrase into the Nicene Creed. It was not there originally, and the East regarded any change to the creed as unacceptable. Until the time of Pope Sergius IV (1009–12) the popes were careful not to use the term in their credal formulas. However, Sergius IV used the term *Filioque* in a letter to Constantinople; this annoyed the Easterners, but it did not lead to an immediate break.

The actual rupture was precipitated by two reforming synods established by Pope Leo IX. They were held at Salerno and Siponto in 1050. Both these towns were in Byzantine southern Italy, where Latin and Eastern Christians intermingled. Some of the decrees of these synods were seemingly directed at the Byzantines; in response, the patriarch of Constantinople, the ambitious and tough Michael Cerularius (1043–58), determined to strengthen his position in Italy.[33] He was very anti-Western in attitude, and unfortunately Pope Leo had just appointed Cardinal Humbert of Silva Candida as 'archbishop of all Sicily'. This title was based on the claim that the *Donation of Constantine* had given the island to the papacy. The whole affair was complicated by the involved ecclesiastical politics of southern Italy.

Despite the provocative appointment of Humbert, Patriarch Michael made conciliatory overtures to Rome. The pope sent an embassy to the emperor in Constantinople led by Humbert. This appointment was foolish, for the cardinal was diplomatically inept and theologically rigid. He had already written 'a bitter and biassed treatise' against the Byzantines, but Leo had not allowed it to be published.[34] In Constantinople the cardinal attacked the position of the patriarch, and Cerularius understandably refused to receive him. The cardinal published his bitter tract attacking the Byzantine church. He accused the Easterners of suppressing the *Filioque*, and he excommunicated the patriarch and deposited the bull on the high altar of Hagia Sophia. The Byzantines, in turn, excommunicated the legate, but not the pope. Dvornik says that this led to a break that was more 'fateful' than any previous one.[35]

The final separation between the two churches came a century later with the Crusades and the establishment of Latin patriarchates in the East, even though there were futile attempts in the fifteenth century at the Council of Florence to heal the breach. But it was already far too late; the damage was done, and Constantinople itself was on the edge of falling to the Turks.

Today the excommunications have been lifted, but the fear of Latin and papal hegemony is as great as it ever has been in Greece and the East. The ecumenical task ahead is daunting; there is so much bitter history to undo.

5

The Medieval papacy at its Height

The beginning of the reform of the papacy and the church[1]

IN THE EARLY eleventh century, reform and change were in the air. European society was beginning the process that would lead to 'the twelfth-century Renaissance', as the American medievalist Charles Homer Haskins and the English historian Christopher Brooke have correctly named it.[2] This is the age of the building of the great cathedrals and the revival of art and literature. A profound change in the mental climate of Europe was beginning at this time; the German historian Albert Mirgeler argues that it involved the evolution of a whole new conceptual distinction between the secular and the sacred.[3]

Although Pope Sylvester II had been an early proponent of reform, the movement had not originated in Rome, but had spread outward from the reformed monasteries of eastern France, principally Cluny (founded in 910). Actually, it was not until after the turn of the millennium, during the abbacy of St Odilo (c.962–1049), that Cluniac monasteries were united under one abbot and that their influence spread widely into Burgundy, Provence and Aquitaine and in the border territory between France and the empire. The Cluniac order's great strength was that it stood outside the feudal system; it was not subject to the local lords and bishops. It was directly responsible to the papacy. In fact, it was Cluny that provided the impetus and the personnel to reform monasteries in Rome itself. Also the reforms that spread outward from Cluny were eventually enthusiastically adopted by the German Emperor, Henry III.

As we saw in the last chapter, the events leading up to Henry's intervention in Roman affairs originated during the papacy of the appalling Benedict IX. Encouraged by a group of Roman clergy and citizens, in late 1046 Henry III arrived in Italy determined to reform the papacy. It was Henry who finally destroyed the power of the barons and families of the *Patrimonium Petri* and set in train conditions for a thorough-going reformation. With the advent of Pope Leo IX (1049–54) the process began in earnest. He was a distant relation of the emperor and had been a reforming bishop in Toul, then just within the western border of the empire, south of Metz. Although appointed pope by Henry III, he insisted on being elected by the Roman church. Himself a man of integrity, the Emperor Henry was deeply conscious of his God-given task to care for the church, and in Leo he was to find an ally. Leo arrived in Rome in the garb of a pilgrim; it was symbolic of a much-needed papal return to spiritual values.

The pope quickly surrounded himself with a team of reformers, including Cardinal Humbert of Silva Candida (died 1061), the Subdeacon (later Archdeacon) Hildebrand (*c.*1020–85), St Peter Damiani (1007–72), as well as the saintly abbots of Cluny, Odilo (*c.*962–1049) and Hugh (1024–1109). The emperor may have been instrumental in commencing the reform, but the process quickly turned against lay interference in church affairs. The reform eventually led to a gargantuan struggle that destroyed the Holy Roman Empire as a political entity, and gave the papacy a hollow, pyrrhic victory that in the end resulted in the Avignon papacy and the Great Western Schism.[4] It was in this era that the papacy adopted the theocratic pretensions that even today it has still not fully jettisoned. The ecclesiastical claims of the modern popes are exactly the same as those of Gregory VII and Innocent III, even if the papacy has retreated from the extreme claims of Boniface VIII. The irony is that, although this period has been closely examined by historians and legal experts, theologians have virtually ignored it; there is hardly any modern ecclesiological reflection on the consequences of the primatial claims made by the popes of this time. There is a kind of theological *Sprung über der Mittelalter* (leap over the Middle Ages). Since this period sees the origin of the assertion of papal monarchy in the strict sense, it cannot be ignored theologically. Today we are faced with the ecclesiological puzzles that derive from the actions of thirteenth-century popes. Gregory IX (1227–41) and Innocent IV (1243–54) were prepared to use every ecclesiastical, spiritual and diplomatic weapon to destroy the Hohenstaufen Emperor, Frederick II (1194–1250), and in the bull *Unam Sanctam* (1302) Boniface VIII (1294–1303) made theological claims that are patently absurd. How seriously are these claims to be taken today? Why have they seemingly been ignored when these popes were certainly claiming to speak authoritatively? Theology has yet to provide an answer to these questions.

What was the reform about?

THIS 250-YEAR PERIOD from the beginning of the eleventh century is generally seen by historians as one of reform and progress. Both the Roman church and the papacy needed rescuing from the abuses of lay control, especially from the control of the feudal families, whose fortified mansions still dotted the urban Roman landscape. Reform was also needed in the wider church, but the evidence is that the zeal of the reformers quickly transmuted into a fierce fanaticism that destroyed the good with the bad. Fundamentally, the reformers set out to break the corrupt stranglehold that the feudal nobility had gained over the church. In a society in which the real source of wealth and power was land, it is understandable that both lords and monarchs treated their geographical domains, and everything and everybody in them, as their personal property. This included the church and churchmen.[5]

We have already seen a vivid example of this: the papacy, and all that went with it, had become the 'property' of the feudal barons of the *Patrimonium Petri*. In this context the spiritual and religious significance of church office was entirely lost. At first the reformers did not include the German monarchs in their sights, but as the conflict developed it transmuted into massive papal confrontation with sacralised theories of imperial power.

The key issue for the eighty years from 1050 was what is now incorrectly called 'lay investiture'. Today we have a clear distinction between the sacred and secular, but it was not so clear to the medievals. For them power and land tenure were inextricably mixed. Thus spiritual and ecclesiastical office, which almost always meant control over portions of land, also brought with it secular power. To control land and property was to have power, and that power had to be fitted somewhere in the feudal hierarchy. So when the bishop or abbot was appointed by the king to office (the majority of episcopal appointments were royal), the candidate was ordained by three bishops; he then knelt before the appointing monarch or lord and was invested by him with a ring and pastoral staff. He thus entered into possession of the feudal estates that went with the office. In all this the medievals found it very difficult to sort out the spiritual and temporal roles.

It is easy to see how this system could be abused: totally unworthy candidates bought bishoprics and monasteries because of the power, lands and wealth attached to them. This was the sin of simony (the buying and selling of church offices), and it was this, and the connected issue of clerical sexuality, that the reformers had primarily in their sights. If reforming churchmen challenged lay dominance, they also had to challenge the sacred power of the monarch, specifically the power of the German emperors. For, as we have seen, the imperial office had inbuilt caesaro-papist pretensions, and the emperor often wielded God-given authority on behalf of both church and state.

There was also a racial undercurrent: the Italians, who saw themselves as the real inheritors of the Roman tradition, resented constant interference by German 'barbarians' in their affairs, including their control of the bishopric of Rome. There was probably also an element of jealousy in this, for the stability and culture of Germany at this time surpassed that of Italy. This should not be pushed too far, for not all of the reformers were Italians. According to Friedrich Heer, the reformers were actually the 'revolutionaries' in this process.[6] He argues that Catholicism is still living with the wedge driven between clergy and laity by this reform movement, and he substantially agrees with Mirgeler that the distinction between secular and sacred in European culture finds its origin in this struggle. Contrary to the views of the historians who see the origins of the concept of papal monarchy back in the theories of Damasus I, Leo I and Gelasius I, it is this period that sees the real origin of the notion of papal monarchy.

The demand for celibacy also became a central focus for the reformers. A key element common to the reformers was their monastic background. Just as celibacy was a characteristic of the monk, so the reformers were determined that it should also be part of the priestly life. It had been customary for centuries for many priests, bishops and even abbots to be married. There was also another group of clergy who had been ordained as celibates, but who had entered into a domestic relationship after ordination. In canonical legislation over a long period in the West there had been calls for celibacy of the clergy, or at least for a limitation on the married clergy's sexual activities. There were three interconnected sources for this demand: the first was the ancient ritual taboo (originating in the Bible and ultimately in pagan custom) about the danger of a priest celebrating Mass after intercourse with his menstruating wife. The menses were seen as infected with demonic magic. The second was the real danger of alienating church property by passing it on from priest-father to priest-son. The third source was connected to the developing theology of Christ's real presence in the eucharist.[7] Just as Christ in his time was born of a virgin, so the eucharistic Christ should be born on the altar of chaste priests. The celibate priest or monk was pure and uncontaminated and was thus completely committed to the service of the church.

But we should not think of this in modern terms. The aim of the reformers was not to deepen the inner life of priests, nor to bring about moral and spiritual renewal. Celibacy was seen as functional and was fundamentally a means of maintaining ritual purity. The essence of priestly 'impurity' consisted in going from handling the body of a woman (possibly menstruating and therefore contaminated) to handling the body of Christ at the altar. The laity needed the sacraments, especially the eucharist, from ritually pure virginal priests who were free of secular ties, including marriage and family. The Lateran Synod of April 1059 decreed that 'no one shall hear the Mass of a priest who, he knows for certain, keeps a concubine or has a woman living with him'.[8] During this period the term 'concubine' commonly replaced the word 'wife' for a priest's partner, and even marital relations between a priest and his wife were described as 'fornication'. For instance, denouncing the bishop of Toul, who had married while he was a layman before ordination, Gregory VII described him as committing 'public fornication'. The Council of Poitiers of 1078 described the children of priests as *ex fornicatione nati*, born from fornication (Canon 8). As a result of the reform, priest's wives lost their legal status; and a number of synods decreed that they could be enslaved or become the property of the bishop. This is also the beginning of the canonical notion that the marriage of a priest was not just illegal, but invalid.

The popes of this period alleged that they argued from 'ancient discipline' to support their reforms. However, the clergy did not see the attempt to impose celibacy as a revival of ancient discipline: they saw it as a dangerous, unwarranted and unprecedented innovation.

Linked to lay control was the besetting scandal of simony: the buying and selling of sacred things. In this period it involved the sale of ecclesiastical offices, such as bishoprics or abbeys. The Council of Chalcedon had forbidden that any charge be made for ordination.[9] But by the eleventh century the simoniacal sale of the sacrament of orders was commonplace, although it was still considered an evil. Simony was one of the charges brought against John XII when he was deposed as pope. In the eleventh-century reform movement simony, like celibacy, also became a symbolic issue because it was a sign of secular ties. The reformers were determined to stamp it out.

Leo IX began his papacy with a series of synods in Rome: his targets were simony, clerical marriage and priestly concubinage. Leo had a powerful personality; his progress from synod to synod and his sermons to assembled clergy left a deep and, on simoniacs, a fearful impression. The papacy had clearly arrived back on the map of Europe, and Leo was determined that it would be a major force in church life. While he strongly supported the claims of the Holy See, his relationship with Henry III never wavered; pope and emperor worked together to reform Christianity.

The last years of Leo's papacy were ruined by his unsuccessful campaign against the Normans in southern Italy, when he himself was captured and imprisoned for almost a year in Benevento. The Normans had first come to the south as anti-Byzantine mercenaries in 1015, but they exploited the instability of the area where Italian and Byzantine inter-acted. In a period of twenty years under the leadership of Robert Guiscard (*c.*1015–85) they seized the remaining Byzantine domains and by 1090 they had also taken Sicily. The Norman kingdom was soon to become a major player in papal geopolitics.

Pope Gregory VII (1073–1085) and reform

THERE WERE NINETEEN years between the death of Leo IX (1054) and election of Hildebrand as Gregory VII. In this period the reform move-ment gathered strength due to the actions of two strong popes, the development of canonical theory, and the fortunate conjunction of new historical circumstances. The key element in these years was a decisive shift in papal policy to exclude the German monarchs from any role in papal, episcopal or clerical appointments or the internal administration of the church.

After the death of Leo, Stephen IX (1057–58) was elected quickly to forestall any interference by the Roman families. Stephen worked hard to limit lay power in church affairs. In this he was supported by both Peter Damiani and Humbert, the erstwhile 'diplomat' to the Eastern church, whose *Adversus Simoniacos* was published about 1058. In it Humbert argued that simony was not just a sinful abuse, but a heresy, and that all consecrations of bishops, and ordinations of priests by such bishops, when the office was obtained by simony, were invalid.[10] In con-trast Peter Damiani, now the cardinal bishop of Ostia, was both more traditional and more tolerant. While he argued against simony, he pre-ferred a policy of co-operation between the secular and spiritual powers and maintained that the emperor had a role in the church.[11]

Pope Stephen IX was succeeded by Nicholas II (1059–61). This pope brought about two far-reaching reforms: he changed the method by which the popes were elected, and he turned for strategic support to the Normans of southern Italy, and thus shifted the geopolitical balance of Western Europe. The popes henceforth could play off the Normans against the Germans. The most radical of Nicholas' ecclesiastical re-

forms was the outlining of a new method of electing popes: Canon 1 of
the Lateran Synod (13 April 1059) stipulated that 'the election of
the Roman pontiff should be in the power of the cardinal bishops . . .
[with] the subsequent consent of the other orders of the clergy and of the
people'.[12] The need for the reform of elections is understandable, given
the previous two hundred years' history. Nicholas did try to maintain
the tradition of wider involvement, for the papal election was not valid
unless there was subsequent consent from the other cardinals and the
Roman clergy and people. But it was the beginning of the disenfran-
chisement of the clergy and laity. Gradually the power of election was
vested in all of the cardinals; 120 years later, at the Third Lateran Council
in 1179, it was decreed that a pope could only be elected by a vote of
two-thirds of the cardinals. Clearly, the popes no longer saw themselves
as merely the bishops of Rome, but as the rulers of the universal
church. The cardinals followed suit. No longer were they the senior
priests of Rome; they were now becoming an elite of the church.[13]

The election by popular acclaim in the church of St Peter *ad vincula*
(in chains) on 22 April 1073 of the Roman Archdeacon Hildebrand did
not occur according to the decree of Nicholas II. He took the style
Gregory VII. He had been part of the reform process from the beginning of his ecclesiastical career. There is something essentially unattractive about the personality of Gregory. Wido of Ferrara, who admittedly
was no admirer of Gregory, commented: 'The Christian people is divided into two with some saying that he is good and others calling him an
impostor and a false monk and an anti-Christian'.[14]

As pope he had three aims: the reform of the Western church, the
Christian reconquest of Spain from the Muslims, and reunion with the
Eastern church. He certainly began the reform of the church, but at considerable cost. In his other two aims he failed dismally. The mainspring
of his reform programme was his conception of the Roman primacy.
This, he argued, was of divine origin. He used the primatial power in
the service of reform, and he expended every effort to root out simony
and clerical marriage. For Gregory the world was the place where good
and evil contended and where he was called by Peter and Paul to confront the unrighteous. Three months after he was elected, he wrote to

the people of Lombardy attacking the simoniacal bishop of Milan and he told them that as pope

> We are so placed that whether we will or no we are bound to pro-
> claim truth and righteousness to all peoples ... according to the
> word of the Lord: 'Cursed be he that keepeth back his sword from
> blood!' that is he that keepeth back the word of preaching from
> reproving the carnally minded.[15]

The text from Jeremiah 48:10 ('Accursed is the one who is slack in doing the work of the Lord; and accursed is the one who keeps back the sword from bloodshed') is cited at least ten times in the correspondence of Gregory, according to Colin Morris.[16] The text became a keynote of the Gregorian papacy.

Basing himself on the work of Humbert, Gregory argued that it was the task of ecclesiastics rather than monarchs to reform the church. The popes now felt strong enough to stand alone and they began to confront imperial theories, rooted in the Gelasian and Carolingian tradition, that as God's anointed both king and pope were jointly responsible for the Body of Christ. Gregory's view distinguished the church, as the spiritual body of Christ, from the state, the natural political community. Both existed within the context of Western society—*Christianitas*—which, in practice, equalled the totality of the social, religious, cultural and political realities that went to make up Christian Europe. The question for Gregory and his immediate successors became: how far is the spiritual and how far is the temporal master in a Christian world? In the truest sense Gregory was the real revolutionary in all this. He sets out a new view of the politico-ecclesiastical economy. By denying the state any right to interfere in church affairs he makes two points: he sharply distinguishes the church from the state, the spiritual from the temporal; he asserts the superiority of the church over the state, even to the extent of claiming the right to depose God's anointed monarch.

Gregory began on the reform path as soon as he was elected. To make sure that the decrees of the Synod of Rome (March 1074) on simony and clerical marriage were put into effect, Gregory sent legates to Germany, France and England to promote reforming synods in those countries and to promulgate the papal decisions. Most of these early efforts at reform were a failure. There were angry scenes in many places; many of the German clergy bluntly declared that they would desert the priesthood rather than their marriages. There was long resistance to the imposition of celibacy, especially in Germany. Uta Ranke-Heinemann has argued that, despite often serious ecclesiastical penalties against both priests and their partners, clerical marriage and concubinage survived well into the sixteenth century in Germany.[17] In practice it probably lasted even longer in Italy. Local synods attempted to enforce the Gregorian discipline: obstinate priests who remained with their wives were often suspended from sacramental practice and lost their benefices. Sometimes they were excommunicated and occasionally declared infamous and heretical. Attempts were made to isolate married priests, and bishops who were slow to enforce the changes were threatened with deposition. The motivation of the reformers was not so much priestly spirituality as control over ritual purity and the lives of clerics. The whole period generally saw a profound depreciation of sexuality, and the monastic ideology of the time reinforced a *contemptus mundi* (contempt of the world) and a devaluation of the body. Nevertheless, a spate of pamphlets and books defending clerical marriage appeared during and after Gregory's papacy.

Attempts through local legislation to prevent simony were equally fruitless. Gregory quickly realised that he would have to take a new direction. So he set out to assert the complete independence of the church from the temporal power and to affirm the authority of Rome over the whole church. At a series of synods the pope prohibited any cleric from receiving a church, abbey or diocese from the hands of any lay person.[18] Excommunication was applied to laymen who invested bishops or abbots. Gregory made no distinction between the spiritual and temporal aspects of church office. The bishop or priest was there to serve the church. The pope claimed that he was returning to the ancient practice of the church, but he omitted any reference to traditional rules, reaching back to the fourth century, requiring the approbation of the emperor or lay lord for ecclesiastical office.

The best statement of Gregory's position is to be found in the *Dictatus Papae* of 1075. The *Dictatus* contains twenty-seven propositions which define the rights and prerogatives of the pope in terms that had hitherto not been used. These propositions, or *tituli*, are the work of Gregory himself. Their exact purpose is not clear: they could have been a table of contents for a canonical collection, or even notes for a sermon that was never given.[19] The *Dictatus* is the clearest statement of the most far-reaching claims ever made by a pope to this point in church history. Commenting on the *Dictatus* from an Orthodox perspective, Aristeides Papadakis emphasises its radical and revolutionary nature and says that the Gregorian reforms were not in any sense traditional. The pope, he says, was guilty of a real ecclesiological mutation. Papadakis says that the reforms created 'a serious breach' both with history and ecclesiastical tradition. He blames the ecclesiological brashness of the pope and his followers on the fact that they were all 'ultramontane' (pro-papal), monastic Germans, totally unaquainted with the Eastern tradition of independence from the pastoral and ecclesiastical supervision of Rome.[20]

Certainly, you can sympathise with Orthodox concerns when you look at Gregory's programme. He says that papal power is divine in origin; because the pope is sanctified by the merits of St Peter, his power is universal and he is subject to judgement by no one (*Dictatus*, 23, 2, 19). His power is absolute and illimitable. The Roman church is set up as the model for the rest of the church: 'The Roman church has never erred, nor ever, by the witness of scripture, shall err to all eternity'.[21] Based on his conception of the primacy, Gregory set out a complete programme of church government. His most extreme claim is his contention that the pope can depose either ruler or emperor (*Dictatus*, 12). From the papal archives Gregory felt he could have justified most of the *Dictatus* from the letters and writings of Leo I, Gelasius I, Gregory the Great and Nicholas I, but none of these popes would have dared to suggest that a pope could depose an emperor.

During his early years Gregory accepted the Gelasian theory of the two powers, sacred and secular, each supreme within its own sphere. But in the *realpolitik* of church government, basing himself on Humbert's *Adversus Simoniacos*, the pope came to assert the absolute primacy of spiritual power.

Anyone then who wishes to compare the priestly and royal dignities in a useful and blameless fashion may say that in the existing church, the priesthood is analogous to the soul and the kingship to the body . . . It follows from this that, just as the soul excels the body and commands it, so too the priestly dignity excels the royal.[22]

Thus the power to bind and loose was now a harsh fact of political existence. But the radical nature of this should not be missed: Gregory was fooling himself if he thought that this was the teaching of Gelasius or Ambrose.

To achieve his programme the realistic Gregory knew that a centralised power-structure was needed. If Rome could not project its authority outward, the whole reform process would grind to a halt. So the chancery was reorganised to deal with incoming issues as quickly as possible. Links between Rome and the local churches were strengthened, legates were dispatched, and the moral reform of papally exempt monasteries was encouraged. Local bishops were summoned to Rome to answer for their actions (the beginning of *ad limina* visits), and the independent power of metropolitans was curbed. The right of the pope to bestow the pallium (the symbol of office) on primates and metropolitans was reasserted.

But all of this was an ecclesiastical side-show compared with the political struggle with the Emperor Henry IV (1050–1106). Given the views of the two protagonists, conflict was inevitable. Henry was the product of a line of kings and emperors who had been responsible for reforming the papacy; they had taken it from the gross debasement of the Theophylact and Crescentii princelings and had laid the foundation of the very reform upon which Gregory himself was building. They had appointed bishops in their own realms and they saw themselves as much responsible for the church as the pope. Henry bluntly told Gregory in a letter refusing to recognise him as pope that Christ had called him to kingship and that he would be judged by God alone.[23]

The detail of the struggle between Henry and Gregory has been outlined in many places.[24] Henry declared Gregory deposed in January

1076; the pope responded by releasing his subjects from their allegiance and excommunicating the emperor. The Saxons rose in revolt, and Henry's other rivals took the opportunity to refuse obedience. The low point for Henry was in January 1077 when he stood for three days in the snow as an excommunicated penitent outside the castle of Gregory's supporter, Matilda of Tuscany, at Canossa (just south of Reggio Emilia on the northern edge of the Apennines).[25] The Emperor's repentance was entirely political, and the pope excommunicated him again on 7 March 1080. In response the bishops of Lombardy (a stronghold of opposition to Gregory) and some of the German bishops declared Gregory deposed and elected a new pope, Clement III, in 1080.[26] In May 1081 Henry occupied Rome, and Gregory's allies began to desert him. Henry returned to Rome in March 1084 and Gregory shut himself up, secure from assault, in the Castel Sant' Angelo. Clement III was enthroned in the Lateran. The Normans came to the rescue of Gregory, but on 25 May 1085 he died in Salerno. Despite Gregory's intention that a reformer be elected, the weak and short-lived Victor III (1085–87) took possession of the Holy See with support from the Normans. After a six-month delay he was succeeded by the cardinal bishop of Ostia, Eudes of Chatillon, a former prior of Cluny and a reformer in the Gregorian tradition. He took the style Urban II (1088–99).

Realising the importance of the cardinals, Urban quickly moved to associate them more closely with himself in the government of the church; they became, in effect, a kind of ecclesiastical senate. While he was conciliatory, he also continued the battle against lay investiture and simony; in the latter part of his papacy he travelled widely attending reforming councils and synods. Right through this period until 1121 there was a series of antipopes in the line begun by Clement III, who died in 1100.[27] These antipopes continued to threaten the influence of the papacy, for they prevented the coherent development of a theory of papal power. At times they even endangered the very existence of the papacy.

Urban also made overtures to the Eastern church. There is a sense in which Humbert of Silva Candida's rude posturing in Constantinople in 1054 was not just personal. It reflected what Papadakis has called 'the rising tide of papalism'.[28] However, negotiations between Constantinople and Rome in 1089 made it clear that reconciliation was not out of the question. The Byzantine empire needed military help on its eastern frontier in Anatolia. The response that Pope Urban had in mind was a crusade to rescue Jerusalem and eventually the Eastern empire from the Seljuk Turks, and then to reunite East and West. It was certainly not what the Emperor Alexius I Comnenus (1081–1118) intended. Urban called the First Crusade (1095–99) at the Council of Clermont. The Crusades were based on the long Christian tradition of pilgrimage to the Holy Places of Christ's life and death. This crusade was successful: it actually liberated Palestine and took Jerusalem on 15 July 1099. The kingdom of Jerusalem was established in 1100, and a series of Latin states (Antioch, Tripoli and Jerusalem) were set up along the Syrian and Palestinian coasts. The problem was that crusades soon became the excuse for settling old scores with, or attacking, the Byzantines. It all led to considerable bitterness in the East.

Urban was succeeded by another Cluniac, Paschal II (1099–1118). A tenacious man, he was determined not to yield on the question of lay investiture. In 1111 the German King Henry V (1106–25) occupied Rome, hoping for a final solution to the investiture problem and coronation as emperor. Paschal proposed the revolutionary suggestion that bishops renounce their lands and become simply pastors of the people! Then there would be no chance for lay interference in church affairs. Henry consented and the arrangement was announced in the middle of the imperial coronation ceremony. Tumult ensued. The solution was repudiated by the cardinals, and in 1112 the pope reneged on the concessions made to Henry V and annulled the coronation! Further efforts at conciliation failed during this papacy, as well as during the papacy of Gelasius II (1118–19). Henry V and his antipope, Gregory VIII (1118–21), were excommunicated.

After on-again, off-again negotiations, the final solution to the investiture problem came with Callistus II (1119–24). It was enshrined in the Concordat of Worms (23 September 1122) and confirmed by the First Lateran Council (March 1123).[29] In the agreement Henry V renounced his right to invest abbots or bishops with their temporalities and guaranteed free canonical elections and consecrations. The first canon of Lateran I condemned simony.[30] The council stipulated that only those elected canonically could be consecrated bishops, and it strengthened the power of the bishop within his own diocese to appoint priests. Lay people were excluded from ecclesiastical affairs. The separation of clergy and laity was complete. Clerical marriage was forbidden. The antipope, Gregory VIII, was deposed, humiliated, and imprisoned for the rest of his life. There was an image of him in the old Lateran palace crushed under the foot of Calistus II.

The major advance that had been made in the years since Gregory VII was the development of the distinction between the granting of the temporal possessions of a diocese or abbey, and the bestowal of consecration and spiritual authority. The development of this distinction was largely due to St Ivo (*c.*1040–1115), bishop of Chartres. The distinction is obvious to us with our clear division between sacred and secular, but it was not so in the eleventh century. Ivo of Chartres was one of the great pioneers of canon law in the Middle Ages. This is significant, for the lawyers were soon to take over the papacy.

Theories of church and state in the twelfth century

THE TWELFTH CENTURY was an extraordinarily dynamic period in European history. There was a renaissance in art, culture, politics, economics and government and a vigorous renewal of religious and ecclesiastical life. This period saw the rapid evolution of political consciousness in England, France and the Norman kingdom of Sicily. It was only the German empire that still languished in the doldrums of instability and exhaustion as a result of the struggle over lay investiture with the papacy. This period also saw the renewal of cities, the regrowth of trade, and the emergence of the republican and commune movements, as the growing independence of urban dwellers caused them to become increasingly truculent toward their lordly feudal rulers. We shall see an example of this in Rome itself.

The city of Rome was also reborn in the twelfth century. There was a great increase in church building and the historian of the city, Richard Krautheimer, mentions three especially—San Clemente, Santa Maria in Trastevere and the Four Crowned Martyrs—which are all products of this age.[31] This was also the period of the rebirth of the idea of Roman antiquity. Those living in the city did not have to search for antiquity, as Krautheimer points out; it was all around them.[32] However, he shows the ambiguity of medieval attitudes to antiquity: for instance, many Romans showed contempt by simply mining classical sites and buildings for construction material for themselves. More cultivated people admired classical monumentality and life-likeness of classical forms, but their lack of real historical perspective meant that their appreciation was superficial. As is true today, it was foreign visitors who most appreciated the classical heritage. But the idea of the world-wide power of ancient Rome was there to be mined by the ideologues of papal power.

This new, more worldly spirit, however, conflicted with the continuing tradition of the more conservative, other-worldly, monastic attitudes of men like St Bernard of Clairvaux (1090–1153). Something of this can be seen in the attacks mounted by Bernard on the scholar Peter Abelard (1079–1142). Bernard was the product of the Cistercian reform of Benedictine monasticism. This was just the most important of several reforms of religious life: in Italy, around the turn of the millennium, the Camaldolese were founded at Campus Maldoli (Camaldoli) in the high Apennines above Arrezo by St Romuld (*c*.950–1027). Their purpose was the standardisation of the hermit life, which previously had been free and uncontrolled. This same pattern of the standardisation of eremitical life was followed by the Carthusians, founded at La Grande Chartreuse by St Bruno (*c*.1032–1101) in 1084. Also in Italy St John Gaulbert (*c*.990–1073) returned to a strict living of the Benedictine rule at Vallombrosa. None of these groups was large, but all are still in existence. Their importance was that they set the pattern for Cistercianism.

The aim of the men who set up their community at Citeaux just south of Dijon in Burgundy was to return to the letter of St Benedict's rule. The prayers and elaborate chanted offices of Cluny were swept away. They restored the primacy of hard manual work and they became industrious, self-supporting communities. Lay brothers (they were called *conversi*) became an integral part of the community. The constitution of the order was laid down in the *Carta Caritatis*, developed under the second abbot, Stephen Harding, and it was approved by Pope

Callistus II (1119–24). In many ways Cistercianism was put on the map of Europe by the arrival of St Bernard who was to become abbot of Clairvaux. One of the truly great men of the Middle Ages, Bernard's personality was forceful, severe and strictly orthodox. It contrasts interestingly with the aestheticism of his contemporary, Abbot Suger (*c*.1081–1151) of St-Denis in Paris. The Cistercian reform spread all over Europe and was an essential element in supporting a reformed papacy.

The twelfth century was also characterised by the emergence of a new notion of society itself. We have already seen the first stage of the church's attempt to extricate itself from the intricacy of its relationship to the German empire. The Gregorian reformers achieved a revolution through the defeat of lay investiture. Overlapping the slow decline of the old model of society is the emergence of a new understanding of the re-lationship between *ecclesia* and *imperium*. The reformers felt that the church had to be totally independent of the state with liberty to pursue its own religious ends, directly subject to God and to no one else. It was never as clear as this in the twelfth century, but these tendencies were very much in evidence and they certainly influenced the legal reformers and canonists who were to be increasingly influential in European so-ciety. Parallel with this is the increasing separation between clergy and laity, with celibacy as the distinguishing clerical mark.

But this does not mean that the medievals distinguished between church and state in our sense. For the concept of the state as a separate entity had by no means developed clearly at this stage. The state still tended to be seen as an arm of the church. The predominant medieval idea was that Europe shared a common ecclesiastico-political ethos and that this was held together by a unique reality: Catholicism. The unity and solidarity of the West, which cut across all national bound-aries, depended on the church, which was the foundation of medieval culture. From this emerged the notion of *Christianitas*—the idea of a common society within which the whole of Europe operated. Since the foundation and integrating element of *Christianitas* was Catholicism, it became natural to see the head of the church as the leader of *Chris-tianitas*. This, of course, could create problems for civil rulers. How-ever, in recognising this papal leadership the medievals did not intend that the pope should have real civil or political jurisdiction over the various nations. His power was meant to be indirect and spiritual. But the discussion certainly was about power—who had it and how it was used.

The great popes of this period were to push the question of papal power to the outer limits. This was to lead firstly to another intermittent struggle with the German empire, and later to conflict with the emerging nation states, especially France. Gregory VII claimed the power to depose kings, but he did not see himself as *Rex Europae* (king of Europe). His successors were less circumspect: several of the popes of the thirteenth century did not hesitate to think of themselves as *Imperatores Occidentis* (the Emperors of the West). The results of this for the church were to be disastrous, and Catholicism is still infected with some of the pretensions of medieval papalism.

The principal effect of the investiture controversy was the enhanced primatial power of Rome. Roman primacy had been asserted and, in theory at least, had been more or less accepted for most of church history. Given the conditions of the first millennium, however, primacy was of limited practical account in the church. But from the time of Leo IX onwards the assertion of the primacy became increasingly important in the practical sphere.[33] Because of the gradual and widespread improvement in communications, papal primacy could be imposed more effectively. Many of the rights of metropolitan and primatial archbishops and local synods passed over to the pope who, since the ninth century, had the right of bestowing the pallium on the various primates. Abbeys and religious orders were increasingly tied to Rome through exemption and privilege and, by the early thirteenth century, it was Rome that approved the constitutions of new orders, such as the Dominicans and Franciscans. Through the reform movement the popes increasingly asserted their authority in the deposition of bishops, the calling of local councils, the solving of local disputes, the sending of papal legates as troubleshooters, and interference in theological debates. Rome's assumption of power increased throughout the twelfth and thirteenth centuries.

Tierney calls this period 'the age of the lawyers', and it was they who developed the underpinning theories.[34] We have already seen the influence of Peter Damiani, Humbert and Ivo. But above all it was the influence of the Camaldolese monk Gratian (?–*c*.1159), who assembled in Bologna the massive *Concordantia canonum discordantium*, or the *Decretum Gratiani*, that became normative. The *Decretum* was an extraordinary and organised collection of canonical and legal texts that had accumulated over the previous millennium. It included decrees and letters of popes, together with decisions of councils and various churchmen. Gratian's *Decretum* quickly became the basic text upon which masters of law commented in the medieval fashion of discussing established texts. For the first time it was possible to achieve the centralisation of administrative unity in the church. While Gratian was supportive of papal centralisation, he still maintained the dualism of Gelasius. The state, he said, was independent of the church in origin, function and competence. He argued that the papal power of deposing the emperor or king was really only a right to excommunicate the ruler for evil behaviour and to free subjects from their obligation of obedience.

Gratian's text inspired an enormous amount of commentary. These (mainly anonymous) commentators were called Decretists, and they split into two groups on the question of the relationship between *sacerdotium* (priesthood) and *imperium* (state power). The moderates were represented by Huguccio of Pisa, later the cardinal of Ferrara, who tried to maintain the dualistic approach of Gratian. He says clearly: 'Both powers, namely the apostolic and the imperial power, were instituted by God; neither depends on the other . . . The emperor holds power in temporal affairs and the pope in spiritual from God alone; and it is thus that authority is separated.'[35] According to Huguccio, popes could depose kings only in co-operation with nobles who could initiate action against a tyrannical ruler.

The opposite group, led by the Englishman Alanus, held that since the pope was the successor of Christ he possessed the *plenitudo potestatis*, full power over spiritual and temporal affairs. It was the pope who bestowed power on the emperor and could take it away again. The only restriction on the pope was that he could not actually use the sword, the *ius effusionis* (the right to spill blood); administration of this belonged to secular rulers. The English humanist John of Salisbury (who, like Ivo, was also bishop of Chartres) argued that the coercive power of the state was derived from the church. Obviously all these theories had practical results. It is to this practical interaction that we must now turn.

The papal struggle with the Hohenstaufens[36]

THE POPES IMMEDIATELY following Gregory VII had a difficult time. This continued until the negotiation of the Concordat of Worms (1122), which ended the long battle over investiture. The First Lateran Council of 1123 was convoked by Callistus II (1119–24) to confirm the Concordat of Worms. However, with the death of Callistus, the old instability returned to the papacy with the interference of the Roman families, this time the Pierleoni and the Frangipani clans. These disputes tended to reflect a deeper, ongoing struggle between older-style Gregorian reformer-cardinals, who still focused on investiture, and younger cardinals, most of them lawyers, who wanted a complete spiritual renewal of the church.[37] The older cardinals were content with the agreement achieved at Worms, but the newer group of lawyer-cardinals wanted to maintain ongoing reform. The result was electoral instability and the emergence of several antipopes.

Before any of this could be resolved, a new church–state crisis confronted the papacy. The German empire had been seriously weakened as a result of the investiture controversy. This was vividly illustrated in the virtual surrender of the lands of Matilda of Tuscany by the Emperor Lothar II (1125–37) to Innocent II (1130–43). Control of this territory had been the subject of constant tension between papacy and empire since the death of Matilda in 1115. She originally left her estates to the papacy in 1077; she renewed this legacy in 1102. However, the territory had never been handed over to the papacy. In 1133 Emperor Lothar accepted the lands back from Innocent as a fief at an annual rent. A series of weak emperors had also allowed their position to be further eroded by the feudal pretensions of the German princes. The empire ran the serious risk of breaking up into its component parts. It was Frederick I Barbarossa (1152–90) who set out to re-establish imperial power and attempted to redefine the relationship of empire and papacy. In this process conflict with Rome was inevitable.

This was clear from the start of Frederick's reign: he announced his election, but did not seek approbation from Pope Eugenius III (1145–53). Eugenius, a Cistercian disciple of St Bernard, had been a vigorous reforming pope but he had great difficulty maintaining himself at Rome because of the power of the Roman republic, which had rejected the temporal power of the pope.[38] A pact between pope and emperor was concluded at Constance in the spring of 1153. The emperor agreed not to make peace with the Roman republic or the Normans, to defend the honour and *regalia* of the pope, and to defend southern Italy against Greek invasion. The pope agreed to honour Frederick and to crown him, to excommunicate anyone who acted against the unity of the empire, and also to defend southern Italy. However, the pope died a couple of months later.

Anastasius IV (1153–54) was elected. Roman-born with great experience in the curia, he was acceptable to the republicans who had dominated Rome since 1143. His conciliatory papacy was all too short. He was succeeded by the only Englishman ever elected: Nicholas Breakspear, Hadrian IV (1154–59). The conflict with the empire was quickly renewed.

The detail of this conflict is not as important as the issues that emerged from it. These first came to the fore at the Diet of Besancon in 1157. In his letter to Frederick, through the papal legate Rolandus Bandinelli, Hadrian bluntly told the emperor to be thankful for his imperial coronation and commented that if the church had been more generously treated by him, *maiora beneficia excellentia tua de manu nostra suscepisset*— Your Excellency would have received greater *beneficia* (benefits) from our hand. The word *beneficia* had two meanings. Did Legate Bandinelli mean it in the feudal sense? In this case the emperor would be a vassal of the pope. Or did it simply refer to a papal 'favour' to the emperor? In the midst of this debate, another of the papal legates undiplomatically commented: *A quo ergo, si a domino Papa non habet imperium?*—From whom then does he [Frederick] have the empire if not from our Lord, the Pope?[39] Naturally this led to a confrontation with the emperor. His argument was that if he was the *Roman* emperor then he ought to control northern Italy, the former territory of Matilda of Tuscany, and even

Rome itself. To settle these issues, Frederick proposed a commission of cardinals and bishops to judge between pope and emperor. Hadrian IV refused, but died in 1159.

Everything depended on the successor to the English pope. The election was very disputed and two popes emerged: the papal party elected the Legate Rolandus Bandinelli as Alexander III (1159–81); the imperial party, Ottavianus of Monticelli as Victor IV (1159–64). This was the beginning of an eighteen-year schism. Alexander was widely recognised as the true pope; support for Victor came largely from the empire. Again the detail of the struggle between emperor and Pope Alexander is not important. Suffice to say that by 1176, due to military defeat, the emperor was forced to make the Peace of Venice with the pope. As a result, they agreed to recognise each other; Frederick admitted the *de facto* independence of the pope in Rome and the *Patrimonium Petri*; much of the rest of the Italian papal territory was restored and Sicily was implicitly recognised as a fief of the papacy; and the imperial antipope, Callistus III (1168-78), was abandoned. He submitted to Alexander two years later. Given his experience of antipopes, Alexander attempted to reform the papal election process.

At the Third Lateran Council (1179) it was decreed that to be elected pope a candidate would require two-thirds of the votes of the cardinal electors.[40] This confirmed the decree of the Lateran Synod of 1059. The purpose was to force the cardinals to compromise and to reach consensus about the candidate in order to preclude the danger of disputed elections. It was meant to prevent damaging splits between a small majority and a large minority. This two-thirds majority requirement remained in force until 22 February 1996.

The immediate successors of Alexander III were, on the whole, not very successful in their struggle with Frederick I. He continued to occupy the lands of Matilda of Tuscany and to regard them as imperial territory. The papacy was virtually surrounded when Frederick arranged a marriage between his son Henry VI and Constanza, daughter of Roger II of Sicily. Empire and papacy were at loggerheads again. Relations between Henry VI (1190–97) and Pope Celestine III (1191–98) reached breaking point, but the sudden death of Henry in Messina from a cold caught while hunting freed the papacy from the dominance of the empire in Germany and both northern and southern Italy. Celestine died two years later.

Innocent III (1198–1216)

ON THE DAY of Celestine's death the cardinals unanimously elected one of the great popes, the Cardinal Deacon Lotario of Segni, who took the style Innocent III. He was an attractive man with a witty sense of humour and a strong feel for the mystical life.[41] He supported St Francis of Assisi; Giotto's famous painting of Innocent's dream of Francis holding up the church gives us a clue to the mystical side of Innocent, an aspect of his personality that is not sufficiently emphasised by most historians. In every way he was an exceptional leader.

Innocent was a man of action rather than of theory. He left no complete *tractatus* on his views on church and state. He had been taught by Huguccio, who held the dualistic view that church and state have independent roles, but that the pope was greater than the emperor because he was the head of the whole of Christian society. Huguccio also argued, however, that the emperor (or king) did not receive his 'sword' from the pope. But by the time Innocent became pope, a truly hierocratic view of the papacy had emerged. This held that secular sovereignty was essentially derived from the church, that the emperor or king was merely the vicar of the pope and the defender of the church. For Innocent, power and the right to rule came directly from God. It did not come from below, from the church, let alone from the people. The pope was the mouthpiece of this divine inspiration.

The result of this hierocratic view was that increasingly the popes saw themselves as the lords and kings of the world, holding the *plenitudo potestatis* and dispensing or withdrawing this power as political contingencies demanded. Certainly Gregory IX (1227–41) and Innocent IV (1243–54) acted in this way in their struggle with Frederick II, and the hierocratic view culminated in the absurdities of Boniface VIII. Canonical theorists after Innocent III pushed the hierocratic position to extreme lengths. The hierocratic view is, of course, out of touch with reality and even in the medieval period it was a sign of the decadence of papal ecclesiology. It is a product of ideology divorced from a theology of the church, and from the facts of both papal and imperial history.

There is debate as to what extent Innocent III was influenced by hierocratic views. The older opinion was that he was a hierocrat who saw himself as the 'lord of the world'. This is questioned now; the reality is that he stands somewhere in between the dualistic and hierocratic.[42] Innocent had a grand vision, paralleling that of the architects and builders of the Gothic cathedrals. He wanted to bring the divine order of the universe to ecclesiastical affairs and the world of politics.[43] To an extent he was successful in this. He thought that the papacy was the source of this divine order in the world of affairs. In his sermon of consecration, drawing on the Petrine text, he said: 'You see then . . . this servant set over the household, truly the vicar of Jesus Christ, successor of Peter, anointed of the Lord . . . set between God and man, lower than God but higher than man, who judges all and is judged by no one'.[44] Here he refers to himself as the 'vicar of Jesus Christ'. It is in the period between Gregory VII and Innocent III that popes shift from referring to themselves as Vicar of Peter to the more all-embracing Vicar of Christ. Innocent says plainly: 'We are the successor of the prince of the apostles, but we are not his vicar nor the vicar of any man or apostle, but the vicar of Jesus Christ himself'.[45] What then, in the context of this approach, was the role of the state? Is it simply a lesser reflection of the papal authority that actually presides over the whole material world? Innocent never really clarified the theory, but in practice he saw himself as presiding over the entire political economy of Europe.

Despite his hierocratic views, Innocent did not at first have it all his own way in Rome. It took him seven years to gain final control of the city from the republic and Roman families. He also re-established the Papal States, so that when he died they straddled Italy. Disappointed in his own imperial candidate, the Emperor Otto IV (1198–1218), Innocent deposed him in 1210 and supported the claims of Frederick II (1211–50). He excommunicated King John (1199–1216) of England and placed the country under an interdict. Effectively, this meant that the sacraments, except anointing for the sick and dying, could not be administered. A number of the medieval popes used the interdict as a weapon of control: Alexander III interdicted Scotland, and Innocent III also interdicted France as a result of the illicit marriage of Philip II Augustus (1179–1223) in 1200. Innocent unsuccessfully tried to intervene in the almost constant feudal war between France and England.

One of Innocent's most disastrous mistakes was the establishment of a Latin patriarchate in Constantinople after the city fell to the forces of the Fourth Crusade (1204).[46] Slaughter and plunder followed the conquest, and the crusaders were correctly seen by the Byzantines as far worse than the Turks. Innocent III had hoped that the Latin patriarchate would lead to reunion, but it actually led to even deeper bitterness between East and West. About 120 years later Barlaam of Calabria told Pope Benedict XII (1334–42): 'It is not so much a difference of dogma that turns the hearts of Greeks against you as the hatred of the Latins which has entered into their spirit, in consequence of the many and great evils which the Greeks have suffered from the Latins at various times, and are still suffering day by day'.[47] The Fourth Crusade was, in fact, the last straw. Although there were continuing attempts to renew contact between the two halves of Christendom, Eastern and Western Christianity were now irretrievably divided.

One of the most attractive aspects of Innocent's papacy was his support for St Francis of Assisi (1181–1226). The pope saw Christ-like poverty as a way of winning back to the church heretical groups who focused on this issue. The notion of a return to the simplicity and poverty of Jesus and the early church was a powerful idea running right through the Middle Ages. Francis brought a lyricism and freedom to the increasingly rigid hierarchical structure of thirteenth-century church and life. The other important order that emerged during Innocent's papacy was the Dominican, founded by St Dominic Guzman (1170–1221). The Dominicans were flexible and well suited to the emerging urban style; they were intellectual and geared to preaching.

One of the early tragedies of the order was that it became involved under Popes Innocent and Gregory IX in the attack on the Albigensians of southern France. Gregory eventually set up the Inquisition (1232) and placed it in the hands of itinerant Dominicans. The Albigensians— or Cathars—were fundamentally dualists who believed that matter was evil, and that they were called to a life of extreme rigorism. They rejected marriage and the sacraments, and in the late twelfth century they had been condemned at a number of local councils. They distinguished between the 'perfect', who lived rigorous, committed lives, and the ordinary 'believers', who expected to undergo the *consolamentum*— baptism in the spirit—at the time of death. The Dominicans had been sent by Innocent III to engage in disputation with the Cathars, but after the murder of his papal legate in 1208, the pope ordered a crusade against them. The Albegensian crusade became both violent and cruel and there was much bloodshed. Part of the reason for this is that the Cathars were seen to be social deviants as much as they were seen as heretics. Throughout the later Middle Ages the distinction between heresy and deviancy was often difficult for contemporaries to sort out for the two were often equated.

Actually it was the Emperor Frederick II who first evolved the idea of an inquisition. It was quickly adopted by Pope Gregory IX, whose papal inquisitors travelled around searching out heretics. From this period onwards the Inquisition became a continuing element of papal policy and control. In 1252 Innocent IV allowed the use of torture as a means of inquiry and a method of proof in inquisitional procedures. The background to this development was the perceived growth of heresy and social deviance among many groups such as the Waldensians and Franciscan spirituals, as well as the Cathars. Edward Peters points out that popes like Innocent III identified heresy with other types of crime.[48] Innocent IV takes this assumption to its logical conclusion in the decretal *Ad Extirpanda*: heretics ought be subjected to the same cross-examination as common criminals and they were thus subject to the real threat of torture. One of the accepted procedures was the withholding from the accused of the names and evidence of the delators (those who had reported them to the inquisition) and witnesses.

It is significant that the Fourth Lateran Council, which Innocent III called for November 1215, devoted much attention to the question of heresy. The council called for a crusade against heretics, and promised that 'Catholics who take the cross and gird themselves for the expulsion of heretics shall enjoy the same indulgence, and be strengthened by the same holy privilege, as is granted to those who go to the aid of the Holy Land'.[49] In the council there was a hardening against the more tolerant individualism of the twelfth century. It detailed temporal punishments for clerical incontinence, condemned clerical drunkenness, and made stipulations about the clergy's dress. The laity are to confess and receive communion each year at Easter time; there are rules about consanguinity and affinity in marriage, an attack on clandestine marriages, and instructions on the social position and dress for Jews.[50] The council called the Fifth Crusade, but Innocent was dead before it got under way.

The struggle with Frederick II (1211–1250)

THE POPE DIED suddenly from fever in Perugia in mid-July 1216. Two days later Honorius III (1216–27) was elected. His papacy was dominated by the conflict with Frederick II and the promotion of the Fifth Crusade.[51] Frederick, like most of the Hohenstaufens, was fascinated with southern Italy and Sicily. He was born near Ancona and ruled the empire and northern and southern Italy from 1211. To try to persuade Frederick to go on crusade, Honorius crowned him Holy Roman Emperor in 1220. Frederick was an intelligent, powerful man, ruthless and amoral, with an ambition to unite Italy under his own control. He saw himself as a new Roman emperor with a divine right to rule, and he felt he owed nothing to the papacy. His views were the antithesis of the hierocratic legalists. He was a sceptic who represented the new lay spirit that was becoming increasingly important. His harem, courtly eunuchs and Saracen mercenaries caused comment all over Europe.

The popes still saw Sicily as a papal fief, and what they feared most was that Frederick would trap the Papal States in a pincer movement by controlling both southern and northern Italy. Innocent III was determined to resist this. Honorius, however, was a gentle, conciliatory man and a far less skilled diplomat. But his successors, Gregory IX (1227–41) and Innocent IV (1243–54), were tough-minded, ruthless popes who were prepared to do whatever was necessary to protect the Papal

States from Frederick's ambitions for a united Italy. They used every canonical and moral weapon in the papal armoury, as well as dubious diplomatic manoeuvring and ruthless pressure on other European leaders to isolate Frederick. The damage that resulted to the prestige of the papacy was considerable, and Innocent IV eventually defeated Frederick by outliving him.

What were the events that shaped Innocent's papacy? Gregory IX, the nephew of Innocent III, twice excommunicated Frederick, but died in 1241 while still at war with the emperor. Following Gregory's death, the cardinal electors, for the first time, were locked in a conclave in squalid conditions, away from outside interference and communication, in order to force them to reach a quick decision. (The word 'conclave' comes from *cum clave* meaning 'with a key'). In practical terms the clergy and the people of Rome were now totally excluded from the election process, and the custom of a conclave was permanently adopted in 1271. However, in 1241 it still took the small group of cardinals two months to elect Celestine IV, who died two weeks later! The difficulty of finding a successor left the papacy vacant for nineteen months until the election of Sinibaldo Fieschi of Genoa. He took the style Innocent IV. He was a canonist whose family had been friendly with the emperor. After tentative negotiations with Frederick, the pope fled to Lyons where he called the thirteenth ecumenical council.

His motives for calling this council were clearly political: the aim was to defeat Frederick. The emperor did not appear, but he was accused of perjury, suspicion of heresy, sacrilege, and repression of the liberty of the church. Despite a strong defence by the jurist Thaddeus of Suessa, the emperor was declared deposed on 17 July 1245. Two things resulted from this. Firstly, in northern Italy there was devastation as a result of the escalation of the struggle between the Guelphs (the pro-papal party) and the Ghibellines (the pro-imperial party). Secondly, Frederick himself responded in a letter to the kings of Christendom. He mounted a stinging attack on the whole clerical and ecclesiastical superstructure with its wealth and power. The emperor called for a return to the primitive church with its poverty and evangelical simplicity. But more importantly he invited the kings to assist the clergy to return to their primitive ideals by helping themselves to clerical and ecclesiastical wealth.[52] It was a temptation that was later to be taken up in one way or another by several kings.

After the death of Frederick, the island of Sicily eventually came into the possession of Charles of Anjou, who was appointed king of Sicily by Urban IV (1261–64) in 1264. The popes still saw Sicily as a papal fief. Charles I died in 1285 after his plans to invade Constantinople were destroyed by the infamous *Sicilian Vespers* (1282), the story of which is inaccurately told in Verdi's famous opera![53] The kingdom was eventually lost to the Aragonese monarchy. However, the whole business was a further drain on papal attention and resources.

The *plenitudo potestatis* (fullness of power) and the primacy

THROUGHOUT THE STRUGGLE with Frederick, and in the period following, canonical theories of papal power continued to develop in an extreme direction. Under Gregory IX decretals were collected from the previous century. These decretals had been influenced, in turn, by earlier canonists. This collection of papal decretals now became the source for further commentary. So the modern habit of popes commenting on their predecessors', and even their own, encyclicals and letters has a long history. The problem is that this methodology has an inbuilt intellectual incestuousness that ultimately leads not to development, but to stultification. This is precisely what happened to medieval canonical thought.

The new school of canonists were called Decretalists, and they swept away the dualism of Huguccio. The greatest of them was Innocent IV. He did, however, leave some room for legitimate political power. His younger Decretalist successor was Cardinal Henri de Suse, known as Hostiensis (died 1271).[54] His line of interpretation follows that of Alanus. He was an English canonist who taught at Bologna in the time of Innocent III who embraced an extreme hierocratic doctrine; he saw the pope as world-king. Hostiensis concedes that there are two authorities on earth, but that the temporal is completely subject to the spiritual. 'Therefore, in the order of greatness, there is only one head, namely the pope. There ought to be only one as our head, one lord of spiritualities and temporalities, because "the earth and the fullness therefore" belong to him who committed all things to Peter.'[55] It was Boniface VIII who later attempted to apply this to the reality of political life.

A term that we have already seen in the context of Innocent III is *plenitudo potestatis*—the fullness of authority and power, both spiritual and temporal. In this period fullness of authority became synonymous in canonical thought with papal primacy. As John A. Watt has pointed out, two historical sources come together to inject meaning into the term *plenitudo potestatis*.[56] The canonists linked the authority granted to Peter in the Petrine text with the notion of imperial or monarchical power that had came into canon law from Roman law, the study of which had been revived at this period. Increasingly, in practice, the popes imitated imperial power.[57] By the time of Innocent III the term *plenitudo potestatis* denoted papal sovereignty.[58] This sovereignty became co-terminus with primacy.

The problem is that this whole development lacks any theological content. It is rooted in the legal tradition and ecclesiastical jurisprudence and in an extraordinarily narrow interpretation of ecclesiology. Primacy is described fundamentally in legal terms. It is split off from the theological definition of the church, and it contains no sense of other ministries. Papo-centrism dominated the Middle Ages, and subsequent papal history, because of an underdeveloped, even primitive, ecclesiology. The power and role of the leader was defined before there was a rounded and evolved notion of the body that was being led. Certainly, this was the result of historical circumstances, but it was also the result of a papal bid for power.

This same tendency is seen in the development of the legal notion that *Papa est iudex ordinarius omnium*—the pope is the ordinary judge of everyone in the church. The term *iudex ordinarius* comes from Roman law. It was argued that if the pope was the *iudex ordinarius* and he held the *plenitudo potestatis*, then there was no limit to his jurisdiction. In this view the pope held 'jurisdictional omnicompetence' over the whole church and hierarchy and thus appeals could be made to him, in the process by-passing and ignoring other local church authority.[59] What today is called 'the principle of subsidiarity' was ignored and as a practical result the competence of the local church was constricted.

But, while the theory of *plenitudo potestatis* has survived in the church, the days of the medieval universal papal monarchy were quickly drawing to a close.

Celestine V (1294), Boniface VIII (1294–1303) and the nation states

IN THE FORTY-YEAR period between Innocent IV (died 1254) and Boniface VIII (elected 1294) there were twelve popes, often with long delays between elections. For instance between Clement IV (1265–68) and Gregory X (1271–76) there was an interregnum of two years and nine months; between Honorius IV (1285–87) and Nicholas IV (1288–92) eleven months; and between Nicholas and Celestine V (1294) two years and three months. There were two periods of six months: between John XXI (1276–77) and Nicholas III (1277–80), and Nicholas and Martin IV (1281–85). These delays were caused by political pressure on the cardinals and deep divisions among them. The Second Council of Lyons tried to bring stability by passing a detailed decree on papal elections.[60] The decree gave the cardinals ten days to come together for the conclave. If they had not elected a pope within three days, a graduated fast was to be imposed on them. This was not immediately successful, for the longest breaks between popes occurred immediately after the council!

These long breaks and the resulting instability eventually led to the incident of St Peter Celestine—Celestine V (1294). He is the only pope who certainly resigned although, as Patrick Granfield points out, there are debates about nine other possible papal resignations.[61] Pope Celestine is instructive on several scores: he shows that saints are not necessarily the best popes and, in the light of the suggestion of modern popes resigning at a predetermined age, he poses the question of what to do with a resigned pope. The whole period also highlights the fact that the church still does not have a mechanism to deal with demonstrably heretical, morally unsuitable or insane popes.

Between the death of Nicholas IV (April 1292) and the election of Celestine V (1294) there was a vacancy of two years and three months. To resolve the impasse the cardinal dean, Latino Malabranca, proposed the name of the saintly 85–year-old hermit, Pietro del Morrone, who, after Benedictine training, had spent most of his life in the high Abruzzi. He had founded a Benedictine congregation under the patronage of the Sicilian monarchy. His spirituality had been influenced by the radical Franciscans, and the cardinals obviously hoped that the saintly pope would save the church. Pietro was elected in July 1294 and took the style Celestine, but he quickly fell under the influence of his royal protector, Charles II, who insisted that he live in Naples. As pope he was incompetent and was easily influenced by both the king and the ambitious Cardinal Benedetto Caetani. Under royal influence he appointed twelve new cardinals, seven of whom were Frenchmen. The groundwork for the Avignon papacy was being laid. By November it was clear even to Celestine himself that resignation was the only way out and, advised by Caetani, he abdicated. A fortnight later, on Christmas Eve in Naples, Caetani himself was elected, taking the style Boniface VIII. He was an ambitious and abrasive man, who quickly decamped to Rome.

While the papacy was caught up in its gargantuan struggle with the German empire, it had seemingly ignored a new development in Europe —the rise of national states. The most important of these were France and England. The days of transcultural, international empires had finished across the world. The Hohenstaufens had fallen, the Byzantine empire was beginning the last stage of its decline, the Muslim world had broken up, the Sung dynasty had collapsed in southern China before the onslaught of Kublai Khan, and the Delhi sultanate had begun to disintegrate. In Europe the papal spiritual empire was also on its last legs.

Boniface had come to the papacy in circumstances that were at least dubious. There was no clear precedent for a resignation, and Boniface's enemies were later to say the election was invalid. After Celestine's resignation he was arrested, escaped back to the mountains, was recaptured and died in confinement in 1296. Boniface quickly got down to work. He seemed to thrive on conflict and his years as pope were characterised by impulsive interference in international affairs, with obvious lack of success. The pope was no longer the 'lord of Europe' and Philip IV the Fair (1285–1314) of France was to be Boniface's nemesis.

Centralised national monarchy was on the rise. This was not to occur without enormous opposition from feudal barons, and urban and communal movements jealously guarded their hard-won liberties against the kings. We should not overestimate the centralisation of these medieval monarchies, but the lineaments of the modern state could be discerned in them. Medieval kings, especially in England and France, struggled to maintain their positions and to fight each other. To achieve this they needed two things: a doctrine to support the legitimacy and independence of their emerging states, and money through taxation to make this a reality. It was St Thomas Aquinas (*c.*1225–74) who provided them with their ideology. Increasingly, they saw the church as a source of finance through taxation.

Following Aristotle and the natural law theory, Aquinas argued that the state was rooted in the social nature of humankind. This is the opposite of what the popes were claiming. Aquinas suggested that civil authority arises from the nature of the state itself.[62] Therefore God intended government and human society; the common good demands that someone must give this process a sense of direction 'because human beings are naturally social animals . . . The social life of the many would not be possible unless someone presided over it to look after the common good.'[63] Aquinas considered that the best form of government was limited monarchy. This clearly stands in contrast to the hierarchical, papal view whereby *potestas* (power) descends from God through Peter to Peter's successor and thus down the hierarchical ladder, just like the great chain of being itself.[64] Aquinas held that church and state should work together, but he is clear that secular power is not derived from the pope nor the church, but from the natural law itself. This helps to explain why on this—and a number of other questions—Aquinas was considered suspect by many of his ecclesiastical contemporaries.

Naturally enough there were theorists on both sides in the dispute between France and the papacy. The most extreme pro-papalist was Aegidius Romanus (Giles of Rome), ironically one of Aquinas' teachers. His *De Summi Pontificis Potestate* provides the foundation for Boniface's bull *Unam Sanctam*. Giles argued from the intrinsic superiority of the spiritual over the material. For Giles, the lordship of the pope was beyond anyone's judgement, and he held that it was implicit in the order of the universe. He even argued that theoretically the pope was the owner of all material goods in the world. Giles' line of argument was that, because souls were spiritual, they were governed by the pope; bodies were subject to souls; material goods existed to serve the needs of the body; *ergo*, all material goods were subject to the pope! At the other end of the spectrum was Pierre Dubois, who held a form of extreme proto-Gallicanism which argued that all church property ought to be handed over to the national and especially to the French monarch.

Philip IV's aims were simple: he wanted to establish a centralised kingdom by bringing feudal barons and the church under monarchical control.[65] As part of his national policy Philip was engaged in war with England over feudal claims in France. This required money. So he taxed the French clergy. However, the Fourth Lateran Council (1215) had decreed that the clergy were not to pay taxes without the consent of the pope. If such taxes were imposed without papal approval, the punishment was anathema and excommunication. However, Lateran IV also decreed that, if the 'bishop together with his clergy foresee a great need or advantage that they consider, without any compulsion, that subsidies should be given by the churches', they may grant church revenues for this.[66] An example might be a crusade, or a 'just war'. The King of France was engaged in a 'just war' against the King of England and vice versa, and they both used this loophole to tax their respective clergy without papal approval.[67]

For the aggressive Boniface, who held the most extreme hierocratic views, this was a direct insult. He responded to the French king in the bull *Clericis Laicos* (25 February 1296).[68] Basically the pope denied the right of laity to tax clergy, and he threatened excommunication and interdict against anyone who imposed or received such payments. In response Philip stopped papal taxes from France, which resulted in dangerously low reserves in the Roman coffers. After some bluster and the concession of the canonisation of Philip's grandfather, Louis IX, the pope was forced to yield in the bull *Etsi de Statu* (1297).

It was at this stage that the king's chief minister, Pierre Flotte, a ruthless lawyer, unafraid of papal censures, began negotiations with the Colonna family. Boniface had deposed two cardinals from this family after they had called for a general council to try him for the murder of Celestine V and to test the legitimacy of his election. But by 1300 the Colonna were in retreat and the pope proclaimed 1300 as the first Holy Year. Hundreds of thousands of pilgrims came to Rome from all over Europe. Boniface's confidence was restored: he was beginning to boast that he was emperor as much as pope.

He again condemned royal interference in church affairs in the bull *Asculta Fili* (December 1301).[69] Here Boniface refers to himself as he 'who holds the place on earth of Him who alone is Lord and Master'. Boniface chided the king and called the French bishops and clergy to Rome for a synod. In April 1302 the first ever Estate General met, and the French nobles and third estate wrote to the cardinals saying they no longer regarded Boniface as true pope. The clergy simply said they could not attend the Roman Synod. The pope insisted, but less than half the French episcopate attended his ineffective synod. This was followed by the bull *Unam Sanctam* (18 November 1302). The bull states the most extreme hierocratic position: the pope argued categorically that the temporal is completely subject to the spiritual. Using the story of Noah when everything was destroyed except what was in the ark and quoting the biblical Song of Songs, Boniface argued that there was no salvation or forgiveness of sins outside the church. (The exegetical apparatus of the bull is allegorical.) In the church, Boniface argued, 'there is one body and one head, not two heads as if it were a monster'.[70] That head is identified with Christ, then with Peter, and then with Peter's successor. Basing himself on the text 'Feed my sheep' (John 21:17), Boniface argued that everyone is subject to the papacy because Christ 'committed to [Peter] all his sheep'. While mentioning the two-sword theory, Boniface held that 'it is necessary that one sword should be under another and that the temporal authority should be subjected to the spiritual'. The pope says that whoever resists the spiritual power 'resists the ordination of God'. Thus the concept of *plenitudo potestatis* in the bull is stated in the extreme form. He concludes the bull with the extraordinary claim: 'Consequently we declare, state, define and pronounce that it is altogether necessary to salvation for every human creature to be subject to the Roman Pontiff'.[71]

Philip's reply was a personal attack on Boniface: the pope was denounced for homosexual misconduct. He was also called a heretic and usurper. A demand was raised for a general council to depose him. He was seized at Anagni on 7 September 1303 by Philip's minister Guillaume de Nogaret and Sciarra Colonna, who demanded that he resign.[72] He refused to accept their demands and was rescued by the citizens of the town. It is said that one of the Colonna thugs slapped him across the face, but he does not seem to have been injured. But he was deeply shaken by the assault on his dignity, and he died in Rome on 12 October. He was succeeded ten days later by Benedict XI (1303–04).

What are we to make of Boniface's papacy and of the extreme papal claims that he enunciated? As pope he was a disaster. His total failure to read what was happening in the contemporary political life of Europe and his extreme clericalism enhanced the secularising tendencies already operative in the French (and later the English) monarchy. But it was his theology that was most outrageous. The extreme teaching of *Unam Sanctam* cannot be justified by any traditional or biblical standard. What therefore is the doctrinal significance and binding force of *Unam Sanctam*? Given that parts of it are clearly time-conditioned, how is it to be reconciled with modern papal teaching authority? Is it, for instance, infallible? Or is it only 'ordinary magisterium' (day-to-day papal teaching that is not definitively binding)? If it is neither of these, what is it?

The Catholic ecumenist George Tavard argues that most late medieval theologians considered that 'the doctrines of *Unam Sanctam* were not received by the church as authoritative'.[73] In medieval times (and still today) reception by the whole body of the faithful was one of the necessary norms for the truth of a doctrine. Some modern theologians, such as Yves Congar and M. D. Chenu, seem to suggest that what is of permanent value in *Unam Sanctam* is that all political action is subject to the ethical demands of the gospel. This generalising tendency hardly does justice to the precise specifics of Boniface VIII. Other theologians hold that only the final sentence is a dogmatic definition. The rest is merely the odd papal claims of the thirteenth century. But, as Tavard correctly asks: how can this last sentence of *Unam Sanctam* be divorced from the body of the text?[74] The whole text has a specific meaning of which the last sentence is merely a pointed summary.

Clearly it is not an 'infallible definition' in the modern meaning of the term; but if it is not infallible, what is its doctrinal status? If, as Pope Pius XII (1939–58) says, Boniface VIII's teaching was a 'medieval conception . . . conditioned by its time', surely the same norm can be applied to the teaching of Pius XII himself?[75]

This is the nub of the problem: when and how does doctrinal teaching, clearly intended by the enunciating pope to be universally binding, become 'conditioned by its time'? What are we to make doctrinally of Boniface's claims, even if they come from the fourteenth century? The simple fact is that this problem has never really been solved.

The excesses of the papacy of Boniface VIII led directly to the move of the popes from Rome to Avignon. And Avignon led straight to the greatest crisis of medieval Christendom: the Great Western Schism.

6

Avignon and the Great western schism

The Avignon papacy (1309–1378)[1]

THERE WAS CHAOS in Rome following the death of Boniface. The Dominican Niccolo Boccasino was quickly elected as Benedict XI (1303–04). During the eight months of his papacy he tried to reach agreement with all the major protagonists of the previous papacy. The French continued to demand that a general council be called to condemn Boniface but, as a staunch ally of the former pope, Benedict tried to defend his memory. Having left the turbulence of Rome, Benedict set up residence in Perugia, but he died almost immediately, 'the victim of acute dysentery', Kelly says, not of poisoning as is often alleged.[2]

After an eleven-month struggle between the pro-Boniface and pro-French factions in the conclave in Perugia, the Frenchman Bertrand de Got was elected with the style Clement V (1305–14). An intelligent but weak man, he was under constant pressure from Philip IV's government. He was also racked with intestinal cancer, which incapacitated him for months at a time. After stints in Lyons and Vienne, he set up residence at Avignon in 1309. The popes were to remain there until 1378. Clement had good reasons for leaving Italy with Guelph–Ghibelline struggles in full swing. There were many precedents for

leaving Rome: between 1100 and 1304 the popes had spent 82 years
in the city and 122 out of it. However, there was far less precedent for
leaving Italy totally.[3]

It is often claimed that the Avignon popes were mere creatures of
the French monarchy. This is not strictly true. While they were subject
to French influence, they did not lose their independence completely
and can be compared favourably with the popes of the Ottonian period.
The city of Avignon was not part of the French kingdom at this time,
but was situated on the western border of the independent papal enclave
of Comtat-Venaissin, which was feudally subject to the Angevin princes
of Naples, who were themselves vassals of the pope.[4] The behaviour
of Philip IV in attempting to limit papal claims can be paralleled in
England, where the four Statutes of Provisors (1351, 1353, 1365, 1389)
attempted to check the power of the pope in making appointments to
vacant benefices. The second statute also prevented cases being withdrawn from the king's courts and appealed to Rome. A further statute of
1393 prevented papal bulls or excommunications being published in
England.

The period in Avignon also tarnished the image of papal universal-
ism, and made it seem French to the rest of Europe. Ullmann makes the
point that Clement's papacy marked the point when the popes abandoned their traditional role as the moral, spiritual and forward-looking
leaders of Europe.[5] They began a kind of 'rearguard' action, and the initiative passed into the hands of the emerging national monarchies.
Perhaps the worst thing that these popes did was to turn the College of
Cardinals into a French club, often through the promotion of relatives.
Clement V, for instance, was notable for nepotism (the appointment of
close relatives, especially 'nephews' to church offices), making six of his
family cardinals.

The money-raising activities of these popes became legendary. The
purpose was to pay for papal building programmes and for the improvement of the city of Avignon. Throughout this period there were also
constant attempts to restore the Papal States. This proved very expensive, and the money for it was raised by the most dubious means. These
fund-raising activities, more than anything else, lost the papacy support

throughout Europe. Despite the attempts to restore the Papal States, there is a sense in which they had lost a sense of the pope's primal role as bishop of Rome, and their continued residence at Avignon is symptomatic of the way they viewed the papacy as an office of administrative power in the church rather than a focus and means of maintaining its unity.

Under the influence of Philip IV, Clement called the Council of Vienne (1311–12). The purpose of the council was political, and although the *acta* of the meeting are extensive, its legislation seems to be in inverse proportion to what was achieved.[6] The Council of Vienne unsuccessfully tried to call a crusade and to reform the church. It condemned the Franciscan Spiritual, Pietro Olivi, as well as the Beguines and Beghards, but both the Spirituals and the devout laity survived. The humiliating process against Pope Boniface VIII was begun under French pressure, but was eventually shelved. However, the council canonised Celestine V as a 'victim' of Pope Boniface, rehabilitated the Colonna cardinals, annulled the former pope's acts against the French monarchy, and lifted the excommunication of Guillaume de Nogeret, the ringleader of the attack on Boniface at Anagni.

The council's one 'achievement' was the destruction of the Order of the Knights Templar, which, of course, was carried out because the French king wanted it. The Templars' problem was that they were wealthy and had incurred the wrath of Philip IV. They were accused of everything from spitting on the cross to homosexuality, from drunkenness to pacts with the infidel to abandon the crusade.[7] These accusations (extracted under torture) have now been discredited. The Templars had played a major role in the crusader states in the Middle East and had accumulated considerable wealth in their 'temples' in London (now the Inner and Middle Temple) and Paris. It was this which attracted Philip IV, and he used both the papacy and the inquisition as ways of getting at their wealth. Sixty-three of the Templars were burned as heretics in 1310 and the order was suppressed in 1312; the grand master, Jacques de Molay, was burnt in Paris in 1314.

After the death of Clement V there was a vacancy of two years and four months before the cardinal bishop of Porto, the Frenchman Jacques

Duese, was elected in Lyons on 7 August 1316, taking the style John XXII (1316–34). The cardinals had been divided along national lines.

John was an elderly, diminutive, but very energetic pope, who increased the centralisation of the church by seizing the power of appointing bishops from many of the cathedral chapters. The ultimate purpose of this was fiscal, rather than pastoral or theological. He did it in order to demand payment to the Avignon curia of annates (the revenue gained during the first year of occupancy of a benefice, which was now to be paid to the papacy). In fact, the Avignon curia virtually invented modern accountancy in its attempts to keep track of and ledger what Mollat calls the 'vast fiscal system' that John XXII created.[8] It was precisely this perception of great wealth that brought to a head the ongoing conflict with the Franciscan Spirituals.

Immediately after the death of St Francis (1226), trouble began in the order over the correct interpretation of Franciscan poverty. Was it meant to be radical, material poverty, as St Francis apparently intended, or should the Franciscans conform to the pattern of life typical of the other mendicant orders? The organiser of the order along conventional lines was St Bonaventure (*c.*1217–74). But the Spirituals held on to Francis' notion of radical poverty. They had much popular sympathy, but they became more and more extreme. A friend of the Spirituals had become pope in the person of Nicholas III (1277–80), and his bull *Exiit qui Seminat* (1279) allowed a breadth of interpretation of the vow of poverty which the Spirituals could exploit. The leader of the second generation of Spirituals was Pietro John Olivi (1248–98); he argued that Nicholas' bull was unchangeable. In a fascinating study Brian Tierney has shown that Olivi originated the doctrine of papal infallibility.[9] Olivi was condemned at the Council of Vienne.

However, in 1322 the Franciscan general chapter taught that Christ and the apostles were radically poor and owned nothing. John XXII declared this to be heresy, and a split occurred in 1325 when a large minority of Spirituals went into schism and accused Pope John of heresy. He responded with an attack on them in a series of bulls which prompted strong protests by both the Franciscan superior-general, Michael of Cesena (*c.*1270–1342), and the fascinating English Franciscan theologian, William of Ockham (c.1285–1347). This led to the excommunication of them both by John. They fled to the court of Ludwig IV, the Bavarian (1314–47). Needless to say, John did not feel himself bound by the decrees of his predecessor Nicholas III, and he did not accept the notion of infallibility, which the pope saw (correctly) as a limit on his own freedom. Here, as Tierney points out, we have the ironic situation of a pope rejecting the teaching on infallibility because he saw it as a limitation imposed by the decrees of his predecessor on his freedom to act.

Late in his life John also condemned a series of propositions taken from the works of Meister Eckhart (c.1260–1327); these were the product of ill-will and bad faith by the Cologne inquisitors. Eckhart had been Dominican provincial in Saxony from 1304 to 1311 and a highly respected teacher and preacher in the order.[10] He is well known in the contemporary world as a speculative and mystical writer whose works are read more widely now, both inside and outside the Catholic church, than ever before.

John excommunicated Ludwig the Bavarian in 1324. Ludwig appealed to a general council and branded the pope as a heretic over his attitude to the Spirituals. He occupied Rome in 1328 and was crowned emperor there by Sciarra Colonna, the Roman noble who had arrested Boniface. An antipope, the Franciscan Nicholas V (1328–30), was elected, but support for him in Rome quickly collapsed when Ludwig returned to Germany in 1329. Late in his life there were serious questions about the orthodoxy of Pope John's personal views on the beatific vision, which were condemned by the University of Paris in 1333. He was something of an amateur theologian and he claimed that the souls of the saved would have to be satisfied with a vision of the humanity of Christ until the final judgement. This arcane and non-traditional opinion was repudiated by his successor.

The rest of the Avignon popes—Benedict XII (1334–42), Clement VI (1342–52) and Innocent VI (1352–62)—were all French and were generally mediocre characters of no great significance. John XXII had set a pattern of nepotism. This pattern continued among all the Avignon popes, and the period also saw the growth of the power of the College of Cardinals. All three popes following John XXII toyed with the idea of returning to Rome. But, afraid of the chaotic situation in Italy, they actually established the papacy even more firmly in Avignon by carrying out an extensive building programme.

It was not just French influence, nepotism and the financial exactions of Avignon that lost the goodwill of the Catholic people for these popes. It was also the growing and pervasive influence of a new way of thinking summed up in the work of three great writers: Dante Alighieri, William of Ockham and Marsiglio of Padua. This new way of thinking, also partially represented by King Philip IV, can be loosely referred to by the ambivalent modern word 'secularisation'. In this specific context it refers to the gradual breakdown of the sacralised idea of European unity characterised by the concept of *Christianitas*. A gradual process of change in social, economic, cultural and political affairs had began. It became increasingly individualistic and this-worldly. The growth of learning among lay people showed that clerical hegemony over education was slowly decreasing, and the study of Roman law supported the idea of powerful kings. Some laity, seeking a deeper form of Christian life, strayed into heresy. But most desired to participate fully in the emerging lay society. There is no clear, hard-and-fast point of change; medieval and proto-modern forces and ideas continued to coexist for several centuries. However, because of the continuing importance of the papacy in European affairs, all three writers had to develop theories on the extent of the influence of the papacy and its interaction with civil government.

Theorists of papal power: Dante, Ockham and Marsiglio

AT FIRST SIGHT Dante Alighieri (1265–1321) does not really belong in this company. Writer of the *Divina Commedia* and one of the greatest poets of human history, Dante, who suffered acutely from the pro- and anti-papal disputes of northern Italy, seems profoundly medieval. But while the allegorical form of the *Divine Comedy* belongs to the Middle Ages, the content—the individual's search for meaning and love through the exploration of ultimate good and evil—is very modern. Dante, an educated layman who had studied Aquinas, was exiled from Florence for his stance against Boniface VIII in 1301. His reflection on the ethics of power, *De Monarchia* (1310?), was condemned as heretical in 1329 and was later placed on the *Index of Forbidden Books*. In it Dante argued that the world needed a kind of international kingship (modelled on the Holy Roman Empire) whose authority was God-given and which stood above national and sectional conflicts to preserve the peace and liberty that humankind needs for human fulfilment. To achieve this the emperor would work with the pope, and the church ought to abandon all worldly possessions and focus its energy on eternal salvation. The influence of the Franciscan Spirituals in this is obvious.

The *Inferno* (Canto XIX) had earlier already placed three papal contemporaries of Dante (Nicholas III, Boniface VIII and Clement V) in hell, plunged head-downward in a hole in flaming rock. These popes were there because they were notorious simoniacs: 'Miserable pimps and hucksters, that have sold the things of God'.[11] These popes had raped the church and Dante did not hesitate to denounce them:

> You deify silver and gold; how are you sundered
>   In any fashion from the idolater,
> Save that he serves one god and you an hundred?
> Ah Constantine what ill were gendered there—
>   No not from thy conversion, but the dower
> The first rich pope received from thee as heir![12]

The reference to Constantine reminds the reader of the *Donation of Constantine* and of the Papal States. These verses convey something of the anti-papal spirit that was increasingly abroad in the fourteenth century. 'Your avarice saddens the world', Dante tells Pope Nicholas III in hell. This was, to an extent, an unjust judgement on a very able pope who had been the champion of the Spirituals.

Dante's slightly younger contemporary was Marsiglio of Padua (1275–1342), doctor of medicine and first medieval theorist of secular power. Together with Jean de Jandun he wrote the *Defensor Pacis* (1324), dedicated to the Emperor Ludwig the Bavarian, who at the time was engaged in a struggle with Pope John XXII. The *Defensor Pacis* is the most radical political work of the Middle Ages. It espouses a thorough-going secular view of the source of power in society, probably because of Marsiglio's antipathy to constant ecclesiastical interference in state affairs. In clear contrast to the hierocratic view, Marsiglio argued that the state is autonomous and supreme, and is the unifying source of all power in society. Although he says that democracy is the best form of government, he allows for an elective monarchy. But Marsiglio is no democrat in our sense; he has no notion of the separation of church and state. In his view the church is merely an instrument of the state.

Marsiglio argues that the church only holds its property in trust; it has no right to taxes or tithes. In return for spiritual services, the clergy receive simple sustenance. Christ instituted the power of order, but not the hierarchy. All priests are equal, and they should be elected to office by the people. The growth of the ecclesiastical hierarchy is social in origin, as is the papacy. Supreme authority in the church belongs to a general council, which should be called by the emperor. Marsiglio's views clearly hand the church over to the control of the state. They prepared the way for the bureaucratic absolutism of the sixteenth-century monarchs.

In many ways William of Ockham (*c.*1285–1347) is a more creative thinker than Marsiglio.[13] Born at Ockham near Woking in Surrey, England, he joined the Franciscans and studied and lectured at Oxford. In 1324 he was summoned to Avignon to answer alleged charges of heresy brought by a former rector of Oxford University. In Avignon he met Michael of Cesena, the Franciscan superior-general, and he became embroiled in the conflict with John XXII over the condemnation of the Spirituals. Ockham called for the removal of John for heresy. As we have seen, he and Michael were excommunicated and both fled to the court of Ludwig IV in Munich where Ockham died in 1347. It was here that he wrote the tracts on papal and imperial power and in defence of the Spirituals.

His importance as a philosopher and theologian is nowadays being increasingly realised. At the core of the revisionist approach that he takes is his epistemology. He denied the reality of universal ideas and emphasised the sheer centrality of individual entities. Ockham argued that there was no need for the multiplication of mediating beings—like universal ideas—for reliable human knowledge. He enunciates

'Ockham's razor': *Entia non sunt multiplicanda sine ratione*—beings should not be multiplied without reason. His individualist epistemology breaks down the synthesis created by Aquinas and the other great medieval thinkers. He believed that this approach, which had enmeshed God, humankind and nature in a vast, interconnected series of links, was a fabrication without support in reality. He believed that the human mind was able to create common categories, but only in a limited sense. Ockham's realism and focus on the individual made him a 'precursor' of contemporary empiricism.

Ockham's politico-ecclesiastical thought was very much the product of his struggle with John XXII. He was deeply opposed to papal absolutism and was influenced by his conviction that John was a heretic. He was also utterly convinced that all power, including papal power, is limited. Otherwise, Ockham says, the Christian life would not be one of freedom but of slavery. In this he also seems proto-modern. The genesis of his political philosophy is his defence of Franciscan poverty in the *Opus Nonaginta Dierum*—The Work of Ninety Days (*c*.1332). But it is in his *Dialogus* (written between 1333 and 1338 and never finished) and the *Breviloquium* (The Short Discourse on Tyrannical Government) that he sets out in detail his views on ecclesiology.

Unlike Marsiglio, who saw the church as a department of the state, Ockham believed in the legal independence of the spiritual realm. His belief that John XXII was a heretic gives us the clue to his approach to the church: it was theological rather than canonical, and in many ways he is the only late medieval thinker to develop a theology of the church. I have already noted the distinct lack of an ecclesiology in the medieval papalist milieu. Ockham, in contrast, provides a clear ecclesiological context for his reflections on power in the church. Theology, he says in the *Dialogus*, is the *scientia superior* (the higher knowledge) and it is the theologian who is able *profundius cognoscere* (to know more deeply).[14] When he discusses the question of heresy, Ockham says that orthodoxy can be discerned through both scripture and tradition, and he understands tradition in the broad sense of something accepted historically by the church at large. The pope cannot add to the sum total of *Catholica veritas* (Catholic truth). At best, he can approve a belief as Catholic and true. Ockham says that the *tota multitudo fidelium* (the whole multitude of the faithful) can err in matters of faith, but he never says that the *tota ecclesia* (the whole church) can be in error. There is a sense in which he is arguing that what today we call 'dissent' is essential to fulfil Christ's promise to be with the church 'all days' to the end of the world (Matthew 28:20). He maintains that when a doctrine is proposed as 'Catholic truth' (in our time it is most likely that the doctrine will be proposed by the pope), it does not attain the status of Catholic truth if it is rejected or resisted publicly by an individual Catholic or group of Catholics. Ockham also distinguishes the Roman church from the whole church. A general council has the authority to judge and correct the Roman church and its bishop. This view was to become a basic principle of later conciliarist ecclesiology.

His final work was the *Tractatus de Imperatorum et Pontificium Potestate* —the Tract concerning Imperial and Pontifical Power (*c*.1347). Here he argues that the pope does not have a *plenitudo potestatis*; rather he has a ministerial pre-eminence, a *principatus ministrativus*. In other words, Ockham correctly shifts the discussion from power to service. Certainly, the popes have limited spiritual power and a carefully confined temporal authority. This limited authority, Ockham says, must always be used cautiously, wisely, and for truly ministerial purposes. It is significant that, despite his personal bitterness about John XXII and Clement VI, Ockham is always the cautious constitutional liberal rather than the anti-papal zealot.[15] His concern was with limiting papal absolutism by introducing checks and balances into the constitution of the church. And his historical context should never be forgotten: he was dealing with forms of papal absolutism that had affected his own religious order profoundly. It was this very papal absolutism that was to be challenged in the fifteenth century by conciliarism. Ockham was certainly the most interesting ecclesiological (and philosophical) thinker of the fifteenth century.

The return from Avignon to Rome

THROUGHOUT THE LATTER period of the Avignon papacy the plague raged throughout Europe.[16] Before the advent of the plague there had been several crop failures, probably due to longer and colder winters and wetter summers. Thus the population was weakened when, in 1348, the Black Death struck for the first time. In the following years more than one-third of the population of Europe died. The other scourge was war. The One Hundred Years War lasted throughout this period, and it was increasingly carried on by mercenaries relying to a considerable extent on a scorched-earth policy. The Black Death and destructive warfare seemed to be God's revenge for the sins of the world and especially for the sins of the papacy. In Germany the Flagellant movement, which began as a kind of mass response to the plague, soon took on an anti-papal tinge. Parallel to this was the development of a mystical and penitential spirituality that centred on the person of Jesus. Although the origins of this can be found in the Franciscan movement, it is best exemplified in Sts Brigid of Sweden and Catherine of Siena. It was also a time of the growth of pious devotions, especially to the passion and death of Jesus. Emphasis on the figure of the dying Jesus made eminent religious sense to people in time of plague.

This unstable background provides a context for the greatest constitutional crisis ever suffered by the Catholic church—the Great Western Schism. This broke out after the popes returned to Rome. Three issues had dominated the policies of the Avignon popes: the achievement of peace in Europe; the recovery of the Holy Land; and the recovery and pacification of the Papal States. The first two policies were total failures. The third became interlocked with the outbreak of the schism.

The facts are straightforward: the fourth Avignon pope, Clement VI (1342–52), maintained a rich court and was a patron of scholarship and the arts.[17] While working to restore order in the Papal States, he remained very French in attitude. Under Clement, respect for the papacy fell, especially in England and Germany. St Catherine of Siena (c.1347–80) thought he was the devil incarnate. His successor Pope Innocent VI (1352–62) was a stern reformer. Because he fully intended to return to Rome, he worked hard to pacify the Papal States. From 1353 his legate in Italy was Cardinal Gil Alvarez de Albornoz (c.1295–1367). Albornoz was an astute politician and an able soldier. The problem in the Papal States was the old tendency toward the reassertion of the power of petty local lords and the breaking up of central and northern Italy into its component parts. In Rome itself the commune movement was resurrected. Cola de Rienzi (*c.*1313–54), tribune of the people, attempted to re-establish the Roman republic in 1347. He was defeated that same year, and in 1352 he fell into the hands of Clement VI in Avignon, who had excommunicated him. Released by Innocent VI, he was used by Albornoz to try to break the power of the baronial rulers of Rome. He was killed in a riot in 1354. Richard Wagner's opera *Rienzi* celebrates his life.

Albornoz continued his warfare and intrigues, and by 1364 he had pacified most of the Papal States. The saintly Pope Urban V (1362–70), encouraged by the Emperor Charles IV (1355–78) and St Brigid of Sweden (1303–73) who was resident in Rome, took the decision to return to Rome in 1367, despite the protests of the French cardinals and monarchy. After a five-and-a-half month journey he entered the city on 16 October. Rome was in a very dilapidated state. So he began a vast rebuilding programme. Urban was visited by the Emperor Charles and the Byzantine Emperor John V Palaeologus (1354–91) who, to obtain Western support against the Turks, became a Latin Catholic.[18] Urban, however, would not consent to the calling of a council of reunion between the Eastern and Western churches and decided to send Latin missionaries to the East. Trouble in both Rome and the Papal States disillusioned Urban and, despite the protests of St Brigid, he returned to Avignon in 1370. He died two months later.

He was succeeded by Gregory XI (1370–78). Determined to return to Rome, he put off the actual departure many times because of lack of funds, the threats of the Visconti rulers of Milan, war between England and France, and revolt in the Papal States. The Papal States were eventually subdued by the legate, Cardinal Robert of Geneva. Strengthened by the encouragement of St Catherine of Siena, who was in Avignon for three months in 1376, Gregory decided to return to Rome.[19] Catherine did not hesitate to speak to Gregory XI in intimate terms, calling him in one letter 'sweetest Babbo mine'! On 13 January 1377 Gregory entered Rome. He was not welcome and soon retired to Anagni. Peace between the Viscontis, the Florentines and the papacy was almost patched up when he died in March 1378. He was the last of the genuine Avignon popes.

The outbreak of the Great Western Schism[20]

THE FIRST CONCLAVE to meet in Rome in seventy-five years was surrounded by both riot and controversy. Everyone in the city demanded a Roman, or at least an Italian, pope. Of the sixteen cardinals who made up the conclave, eleven were French, four Italian, and one Spanish. On Thursday morning, 8 April 1378, amid riots, a non-cardinal who was not present, Bartolomeo Prignano, the Neapolitan-born archbishop of Bari, was elected. He had the advantages of being both Italian and an experienced curial official. That afternoon the populace broke into the conclave; the terrified cardinals, in a foolish ruse to placate the mob, placed the elderly Roman Cardinal Tebaldeschi on the throne. The next day they informed Prignano that he had been elected pope. He accepted, took the style Urban VI (1378–89), presided at Palm Sunday Mass and was crowned on 18 April, Easter Sunday.

He was determined on reform. He decided to start at the top with the cardinals themselves. In his days as an official at Avignon he had been admired for his virtues. But he had a violent temper, and the cardinals quickly realised they were dealing with an unstable, possibly deranged pope. With the onset of summer most of the cardinals, with the exception of the three Italians (Tebaldeschi had died), were at Anagni. With the papal diatribes still fresh in their minds, they decided to do something. The legal advice was that a council was impossible since Urban certainly would not call it. So they issued two declarations: firstly, they claimed that they were not free in the election of Urban; thus he was not pope. He should step down. Secondly, they declared the papacy vacant. They moved to Fondi for greater security, and there on 20 September 1378 they elected a new pope, the erstwhile general who had secured the Papal States, Robert of Geneva. He took the style Clement VII (1378–94). The three Italian cardinals did not vote, but they gave homage to Clement after the election. On 27 September Urban created twenty-seven cardinals and in the following December Clement created six more for his side. He set up his curia at Avignon in June 1379. The schism hardened into two irreconcilable camps: France, Spain, Portugal and Scotland for Clement; the rest of Europe for Urban. While Catherine of Siena, a Dominican nun, thought that Urban was true pope, other saints, such as the Dominican friar St Vincent Ferrer, supported Clement. Catherine did not hesitate to speak her mind to the three Italian cardinals who had not voted for Clement VII, but had given homage to him: 'Ah, foolish men, worthy of a thousand deaths! As blind, you do not see your own wrong, and have fallen into such confusion that you make of your own selves liars and idolaters.'[21]

What are we to make of the election of Urban? There is a fair consensus among modern historians that the mainly French cardinals elected Urban 'under duress'.[22] There is also evidence that their subsequent consent was not given freely. Further doubts are raised by his obvious mental instability, which increased throughout his papacy. According to canon law, the election of a person of unsound mind was illegal. Here it needs to be noted that this was not the mere election of an antipope by a dissatisfied rump in the conclave; it was the whole electoral body saying that they had not been free in Urban's election and that in practice they were beginning to doubt his sanity. The historian Karl August Finke, who has looked closely at the issues, thinks that it is impossible to say whether the election was either absolutely valid or invalid, and the people most intimately involved were invincibly ignorant of which of the two was the valid pope.[23] Therefore, despite the assumptions of some later historians, the fact is that after 1378 there were two doubtful popes.

Yet, at the same time there is a sense the cardinals had staged an ecclesiastical *coup d'état*. To see their revolt against Urban in broader perspective, it is necessary to backtrack a little to Avignon. Here the cardinals had come to see themselves as a corporation and even as a kind of senate around the pope. The notion gained ground that if the cardinals elected the pope, he was bound by their advice and assent in granting privileges. Some thought that his relationship to them was the same as that of a bishop to his cathedral chapter. Most of the French cardinals of Avignon were secular aristocrats whose achievements were modest and whose oligarchic interests and expectations were those of their class. They were the princes of the church and the pope was responsible to them. These attitudes were encouraged under Clement VI. Any attempt to reform the cardinals met with resistance. One of them told Urban VI to his face that if he diminished their honour they would do their best to diminish his.[24] Some canonists argued that the *ecclesia Romana* (the Roman church) was constituted by pope and cardinals and one could not act without the other. The pope's *plenitudo potestatis* was increasingly limited by the need to consult with the cardinals. They also shared in the wealth of the Roman church and this, together with the electoral influence that came from their remaining a small group, made them anxious to limit the number who could be appointed to the college.

With the election of Urban VI they were faced with the problem of a possibly insane pope. They responded by asserting that if they elected an unsuitable pope they had the power to annul that election. What they could not have foreseen was how intractable and extended the schism was to become. It lasted just over thirty-six years, from April 1378 to the beginning of the Council of Constance on 16 November 1414. To try to deal with the impasse that resulted from the schism, theologians and canonists developed the theory of conciliarism.

The canonical background to conciliarism

Conciliarism is the term used to cover the variety of theories put forward to solve the problem of the schism. All of them involved the holding of a general council, and they asserted in some form or other the superiority of a council over the pope.[25] The conciliarist position was different to that of the oligarchic cardinals who simply sought a dominant role for themselves in the government of the church. Generally, the older-style Avignon cardinals did not favour the doctrine of conciliar authority, which was more 'democratic' in tendency. However, both positions were actually derived from the same source: the prevailing corporatist sense that was strong in the Middle Ages and was expressed in the church through the canonical tradition. In the crisis of the schism both these strands eventually resolved themselves into a conciliarist approach as a way of solving the conflicts that arose from having two and eventually three popes.[26]

A key element in the conciliar theory was the concept of an ecclesiastical corporation.[27] This notion is rooted in canonical discussion of the relationship between local bishops and their cathedral chapters. A chapter was made up of the senior priests (canons) of the diocese, and local bishops in the Middle Ages were usually elected by the chapter. However, the ongoing centralising tendencies of the medieval popes, especially the Avignon popes, tended to limit this right. In the thirteenth century chapters increasingly formed into corporations to protect themselves, and by the beginning of the fourteenth century the canons had acquired considerable power, especially during an episcopal vacancy. The notion gained ground that bishops acted as agents of the chapter with a derivative, limited authority. Tierney comments that in the background to this there was a broad Catholic notion that the church was more than a mere hierarchical structure, and that the priests and laity were an integral part of the church's reality.[28]

The next step was the application of the concept of an ecclesial corporation to the universal church. The key person in making this transition was Cardinal Hostiensis. It was he who applied the notion of corporation law to the papacy. He promoted the theory of the intimate relationship between pope and cardinals: as his Latin vividly says, *tanquam sibi inviscerati*—literally, 'as though they [the cardinals] were "intergutted" to him'.[29] In this view the cardinals clearly shared in the *plenitudo potestatis* of the Roman church. But Hostiensis went further. He applied corporation law to the Roman clergy and people. He argued that if the entire group of cardinals was wiped out during a papal vacancy, then the Roman clergy and people could convoke a council to elect a pope and guide the church. So in the broadest sense the whole church could be considered as an ecclesiastical corporation in which all members shared in its authority. These ideas were picked up and developed by the conciliarists.

There are many other theorists whose ideas formed part of the conciliarist background. Among them was Guillaume Durand (died 1330), bishop of Mende, who was certainly compromised by his attachment to Philip IV of France, his opposition to Boniface VIII, and his participation in the trial of the Templars. But at the Council of Vienne he strongly condemned the power of the papal chancery to dominate the church and to overrule even metropolitan archbishops. He was concerned to defend the traditional rights of bishops over and against the pope and curia; he called for a definition of papal primacy. A French Dominican, John of Paris, was another writer from the anti-Boniface VIII camp, but his *De Potestate Regia et Papale* (Concerning Papal and Regal Power) was probably the most balanced study written at the time of the dispute between Philip and Boniface. He held that the church could own property, but that ownership of church goods was vested in the whole Christian community, and that the pope, far from being an overlord, administered the church's property on behalf of the community. John was a follower of Aquinas in that he believed that civil government originated in the social nature of humanity and that regal power ought to be limited by constitutional means. He applied the same norm to the church: the pope is the servant of the community, and if he is deficient in his service he would be liable to rebuke and ultimately dismissal preferably by a council, or, *in extremis*, by the cardinals. The council acts for the whole church and no pope is immune from its judgement.

Earlier thinkers concerned with the schism, such as Conrad of Gelnhausen, opposed the notion of a general council because it could not be held without the authority of the pope and there was no clearly recognisable pope. As Innocent III had pointed out, popes were beyond the judgement of anyone. It was this assumption that had to be transcended, and it was the great Florentine canonist and conciliar theorist Cardinal Francesco Zabarella (1360–1417) who achieved this.[30] He was created a cardinal by John XXIII in 1411. In his collection of proposals for ending the schism, the *Tractatus de Schismate* issued between 1402 and 1408, he held that the whole of the mystical Body of Christ was a corporation and a corporation can exercise jurisdiction even when there is no effective head. Schism, Zabarella argued, creates a quasi-vacancy in the papacy since neither claimant can govern the whole church. In these circumstances the authority of the church could and should be exercised by the *congregatio fidelium* (the whole body of the faithful). This was exercised through a general council. In a schismatic situation a council should be called forthwith—by the popes themselves, or by the cardinals, or by the emperor, or by the civil power. Zabarella held that the convocation was actually secondary, for the council's authority came not from its convocation, but from the whole *congregatio fidelium*. In fact, the extraordinary situation of a schism only reinforced the fact that ultimately the pope only held the *plenitudo potestatis* in a limited and derivative way.[31] In the sixteenth century Zabarella's *De schismate* was placed on the *Index of Forbidden Books* because it asserted the supremacy of a council over the pope. Zabarella brings us to the conciliar period itself.

Eastern church scholars, such as Papadakis, point out that a conciliar solution was only a problem for the Western tradition because, during the Middle Ages, it had become so papo-centric. He shows that the Orthodox were much more accustomed to synodal modes of operation.[32]

The overture to the Council of Constance

THE ROMAN POPE, Urban VI, showed no interest in healing the schism and seemingly descended further into monomania and madness. The Papal States fell into anarchy. His cardinals were confronted with the problem of what to do with a pope who was clearly deranged. Some of them plotted to place him under a guardian, but he forestalled this and in 1384 he imprisoned and brutally tortured six of them. Shortly afterwards five others mysteriously disappeared. He died in Rome in 1389, possibly the victim of poisoning. The alternative pope, Clement VII (1378–94), organised a curia in Avignon and appointed a genuinely international group of cardinals. He hoped that with the death of Urban he would be recognised by the Roman cardinals. But Urban's successor, Boniface IX (1389–1404), showed no willingness to compromise. He gradually regained control of the Papal States and he refused to negotiate with the newly elected Avignon pope, Benedict XIII (1394–1417).

Boniface was totally unscrupulous in his attempts to raise money. He sold church benefices and offices to the highest bidder and exploited the commercial possibility of the sale of indulgences. His successor, Innocent VII (1404–06), was ineffective and continued the policy of refusing to negotiate with Benedict XIII. Innocent's successor, Gregory XII (1406–15), was initially anxious to heal the schism. The Roman cardinals had taken an oath in the conclave that if elected they would abdicate if Benedict XIII of Avignon also did so. In May 1408 nine of Gregory XII's cardinals, convinced that their pope would never resign, abandoned him and made their way to Livorno to enter into negotiations with Benedict XIII. He proved as obdurate as Gregory, and eventually the cardinals of both camps decided to bypass their popes and to call a council at Pisa. It met on 25 March 1409. Eventually there were four patriarchs and twenty-four cardinals from both jurisdictions present, together with 100 bishops, 107 abbots, the generals of the mendicant and other orders, plus canonists, theologians and representatives of universities, cathedral chapters and princes.

The Council of Pisa cited the two rival popes to appear; when they failed to do so it deposed them after a careful legal process and declared them contumacious schismatics, perjurers and obdurate heretics. The council had applied the long-accepted norm that a pope could be deposed if he deviated from the faith. Today historians generally accept that the Council of Pisa was a legitimate council; it was certainly a representative one.[33] If this is correct Pisa had the power to declare that the Holy See was vacant. This position, however, has never been accepted by the modern papacy, which has maintained the legitimacy of the Roman line, and the recent collection of the *Decrees of the Ecumenical Councils* does not include Pisa, but does include Constance.[34]

The Council of Pisa then proceeded to elect Peter of Candia, a Franciscan, as Alexander V (1409–10). As much of Europe rallied to Alexander, his election had probably already fatally weakened the positions of both Gregory and Benedict, but now there were three popes. Tragically, Pope Alexander died in Bologna in 1410. He was succeeded by Baldasare Cossa, a Neapolitan thug and notorious libertine who had studied for a doctorate of law at Bologna and had served the curia of Boniface IX as treasurer. He took the style John XXIII. He was elected because he had been a prime organiser of Pisa, because the cardinals at the council felt that his military experience would assist in the recapture of Rome, and because he already had threatening military forces at his disposal. No doubt generous bribes also helped. Although he was by far the most widely supported of the three papal contenders, his election was a disastrous mistake. By his scandalous life he destroyed the efforts of Pisa to heal the schism.

Between 1411 and 1413 John established himself in Rome, but political events forced him to flee and to appeal to the German King Sigismund (emperor 1433–37), who placed him under enormous pressure to call the Council of Constance. The council began on imperial territory on 5 November 1414 in the local cathedral. August Franzen says that the Council was 'ecumenical from the start'.[35] Tanner also seems to accept its ecumenicity from the beginning. The primary issue facing the council was the healing of the schism, and Tanner says that this could only be achieved by the authority of a council.[36] Working on the assumption that the Roman line was the only valid one, older historians, such as Cuthbert Butler, argue that the council only became 'ecumenical' from 4 July 1415 when the legate of Gregory XII staged a rereading of the bull of convocation.[37] Franzen comments that only Gregory and his supporters took this rereading of the convocation bull seriously.[38] The council also made the same offer to the Avignon pope, who declined. This is important today because some historians and theologians have continued to maintain the figment that this 'convocation' somehow constituted the ecumenicity of Constance. Given that the all-important decree *Haec Sancta Synodus*, declaring the council superior to the pope, had been passed before 4 July, the pro-Roman view tries to maintain that this decree was not part of the council's *acta* and was thus not binding. Franzen shows that the doubtful election of 1378, the three-decade-long schism, and the fact that both Gregory XII and Benedict XIII had already been deposed at Pisa in 1409, made it clear that the council considered that there was no legitimate pope at the time it passed *Haec Sancta*.

The council dismisses popes: Constance (1414–1418)[39]

THE COUNCIL OF Constance was to sit for three years and five months, with forty-five sessions, from 16 November 1414 to 14 April 1418. It adopted the revolutionary approach that it would vote by 'nations'—each one casting a single vote. In this way it was not dominated by the bishops of any one nationality, especially the French or the Italians. Here it clearly followed the pattern set in the medieval universities. The leaders of the conciliar movement at the time of Constance were the

French Cardinal Pierre d'Ailly (1350–1420); John Gerson (1363–1429), chancellor of the University of Paris; and Cardinal Francesco Zabarella. The key role played by King Sigismund, especially in the early stages, is also significant. He was the moving force that got the council under way, he participated in its deliberations, and his presence guaranteed its security. Constance set itself three fundamental aims: to deal with the schism, to reform the church, and to confront the teachings of Wyclif and Huss.

Certainly, there is evidence that the attendance was impressive: according to Ulrich Richental, who was a local citizen and who wrote the contemporary *Chronicle of the Council of Constance*, there were literally thousands of people there.[40] Over the whole period, according to Richental, who was something of a statistician, there were 5 patriarchs, 33 cardinals, 47 archbishops, 145 bishops, 93 suffragan bishops, 132 abbots, 155 priors, 578 doctors (of theology or law) and 5300 simple priests and scholars, plus the king and nobility and literally thousands of camp followers in attendance. These included merchants, shopkeepers, craftsmen, musicians, and over 700 'harlots in brothels . . . who hired their own houses [and those] who lay in stables and wherever they could, beside the private ones whom I could not count'.[41] Apparently the influx of so many clerics and scholars made sure that business was good for all local citizens! Phillip H. Strump gives different figures; he says that 2290 in total attended.[42] Whichever figure is correct, a representative cross-section of the church of late medieval Catholicism was at the council.

The first sessions of the Council of Constance were taken up with the attempt to get John XXIII to resign. He pledged himself to do this in early March 1415, but he then fled from the city accompanied by a considerable group of Italians and Austrians. According to the conciliar sentence that deposed him, John fled from Constance 'secretly and at a suspicious hour of the night, in disguised and indecent dress'. The pope was 'notoriously scandalous to God's church and to this council' because he supported the schism in violation of a promise he had made to the council; he was a simoniac and a man of 'detestable life and morals'.[43] The council was rallied by Zabarella and d'Ailly, with the powerful help of Sigismund. At the third session, on 26 March, Zabarella persuaded the council to declare that it had been constituted in a proper way and that John XXIII's departure had changed nothing. By the fifth session, on 6 April 1415, the fathers were exasperated with John. They were ready to confirm the decree *Haec Sancta*, which had already been prepared by Zabarella. A slightly different version had been passed a week before, on 30 March 1415.[44]

The decree is clear about its purpose: 'the eradication of the present schism' and the 'reform of God's church [in] head and members'.[45] The very directness of the language of *Haec Sancta* conveyed the feeling of the need for direct action in a time of crisis. The first two points of the decree were the most important theologically: firstly, Constance says unambiguously that it is 'legitimately assembled' in the Holy Spirit, that it represents the whole church, and that it has power 'immediately from Christ'. Secondly, as a consequence, 'everyone of whatever state or dignity, even papal, is bound to obey it in those matters which pertain to the faith, the eradication of the said schism and the general reform of the said church in head and members'.[46] *Haec Sancta* also guaranteed the freedom of the council, quashed the decrees and decisions of John XXIII and commanded his curia to remain in Constance.

Meanwhile on 4 July 1415, after 'convoking' the council, Gregory XII authorised his envoy, Carlo Malatesta, to abdicate in his name. Benedict XIII, having refused to abdicate, was tried and deposed on 26 July 1417. The Christian world was now united under a single authority—the Council of Constance. The council went on to declare on 9 October 1417 in the decree *Frequens* that 'the frequent holding of general councils is a pre-eminent means of cultivating the Lord's patrimony'.[47] The time span is clearly nominated:

> The first shall follow in five years immediately after the end of this council, the second in seven years immediately after the end of the next council, and thereafter they are to be held every ten years for ever. They are to be held in places which the supreme pontiff is bound to nominate and assign within a month before the end of each preceding council.[48]

Two key issues emerged in the last period of the council: who were to be the electors of the new pope, and should the reform decrees be passed before or after the election? The council deadlocked on these issues, and there was a danger that it would break up without success. In October it was decided that the electoral college be composed of the twenty-two cardinals then in attendance at the council, plus six delegates from each of the five nations present. Meanwhile the special committee that had been working on reform had five of its decrees passed on 9 October 1417. It decreed that in the case of a future schism a council would assemble within a year to settle the problem. A new profession of faith for the pope was drawn up, which emphasised the teaching of previous ecumenical councils. The practice of translating bishops from diocese to diocese against their will was forbidden. The *ius spolii*, the papal privilege of 'exacting and receiving of procurations . . . and of spoils on deceased prelates and other clerics' was abolished.[49]

The council also condemned fifty-eight articles from the teachings of the Englishman John Wyclif (*c*.1330–84), as well as all of his books. Wyclif, dead thirty years, was condemned as a heretic; the council ordered that his body and bones be exhumed 'to be scattered far from a burial place of the church'.[50] Wyclif's ideas had been taken up by the Czech John Huss, rector of the University of Prague. He came to Constance, under imperial safe conduct, to defend his ideas. Thirty articles from his book *De Ecclesia* were found to be erroneous. He was also condemned as a heretic, degraded, and handed over to the secular authority to be burned. He died at the stake on 6 July 1415.

On 11 November 1417 the new pope was elected: Oddo Colonna, who took the style Martin V (1417–31) He had been involved at Pisa and had been loyal to John XXIII until his flight from Constance. He was to spend most of his papacy retreating from the reforms of Constance and re-establishing the old-style Roman papacy. But conciliarism was far from a spent force.

The Councils of Basel and Ferrara–Florence[51]

WITH THE ELECTION of Martin V, the schism was effectively ended and papacy began to get back to its normal pattern. Once elected, Martin shed any shreds of conciliar thinking, and any attempt that he later made at reform was merely cosmetic. His energy was focused outward, for he faced major financial shortfalls and the Papal States were in chaos. Rome and the area south of it had been occupied by the Neapolitans since 1406. He recovered Rome in 1420 and began a vast rebuilding and recovery programme in the city. Bologna and the Romagna had become independent republics, and central Italy had been freed from Roman authority. Between 1424 and 1429 he gradually recovered much of central Italy and from that he was able to enrich both the church and his Colonna relatives. The whole situation in the Papal States was complicated by inter-city rivalry, and by factions formed around the principal families. In fact, all the popes from Martin V to Julius II (1503–13) had two fixed strategic ideas: to hold the Papal States through political and military action, and to maintain their financial independence. Some of the corruption of the papacy in this period can be traced back to these political, military and financial aims.

Meanwhile the Avignon pope, Benedict XIII, who had refused to recognise the council, had died in 1423 and was succeeded by Clement VIII (1423–29). Clement abdicated in 1429, and this was the effective end of the Avignon line. Despite a distinct lack of enthusiasm for the decree *Frequens*, Martin called a council for Pavia in 1423. It quickly transferred to Siena, but was closed in 1424 due to poor attendance. He called the next one for Basel in 1431, but he was dead before it opened. His successor was Eugene IV (1431–47). Prior to his election, the cardinals had entered into a pact that the new pope would allow the collaboration of the cardinals in the government of the church. While confirming it after election, in practice Eugene was to ignore this agreement.

The ecumenical status of the Council of Basel is debated. Tanner says that there is some doubt about the ecumenicity of the first twenty-five sessions, but he himself seems to accept them by publishing the *acta*.[52] Attendance was small, but it effectively began proceedings in December 1431 with a reaffirmation of *Frequens*. There was widespread expectation that Basel would tackle the issue of church reform. Eugene IV seems to have underestimated this expectation. An invitation to attend had been issued to the Hussites by the council, but as soon as he heard about it Eugene ordered his legate, Cardinal Giuliano Cesarini, to dissolve the assembly. Cesarini refused. On 15 February 1432 the council reaffirmed the superiority of a general council over the pope, and this remained the position of the fathers at Basel.[53]

This led to a stalemate as both sides manoeuvred to gain the ascendancy. By 1433 the pope's position was weak; he had been abandoned by most of his cardinals and was also under pressure from the Emperor Sigismund.[54] At the sixteenth session, on 5 February 1434, Eugene's bull *Dudum Sacrum* of December 1433, withdrawing his bull of dissolution and acknowledging the council's legitimacy, was incorporated into the *acta* of the council, and the papal legates swore *propriis nominibus* (in their own names) to the superiority of a council over the pope. At the eighteenth session, on 26 June 1434, *Haec Sancta* was renewed 'and the attention of all [was] drawn to it'.[55]

However, in the next four years the positions of Eugene and the council were reversed. On the one hand Eugene became more fluid and politically astute in dealing with the council. On the other the conciliar fathers fell victim to their own structure and methodology. Since April 1433 they had worked on the basis of the abolition of all distinctions of dignity and rank, with theologians and priests participating on an equal footing with bishops. The council showed radically democratic tendencies. There were never many bishops at the council and the small number there gradually dwindled. The council increasingly limited papal powers, and in June 1435 it abolished papal taxes and annates. In March 1436 the fathers decided the rules for conclaves; they nominated the number of cardinals who could take part, and put forward a profession of faith for the pope. They also required the pope to consult regularly with the cardinals. As a result the papal envoys had withdrawn in May 1436. In 1437 Basel conceded communion under both kinds to the Bohemian Hussites. The council had also begun negotiations with representatives of the Eastern church concerning a place in which to hold a council of reunion between East and West.

Meanwhile Eugene IV had issued a defence of papal monarchy in his *Libellus Apologeticus*. He suggested that Basel was a revolt of lower clergy against their lords that actually threatened the social order.[56] He maintained that the council was made up of uneducated lower clergy, which

Joachim W. Stieber says was 'quite false'. The pope had four specific complaints against the council. He objected to: (1) the decrease in his power through the notion that the council held the highest ecclesiastical authority over all Christians; (2) the abolition of annates; (3) the imposition of a papal oath of office; and (4) the council's granting of plenary indulgences.

By the late 1430s Eugene had seized the initiative. When summoned to appear in Basel for disobedience, he issued the bull *Doctoris Gentium* (18 December 1437), which gave the council thirty days to wind up its business and be transferred to Ferrara. There had been strong overtures from the Byzantines to bring about reunion, and Greek envoys had been at Basel since 1431. These and the papal minority followed the pope's instruction. Eugene had been trying for years to get the council to Italy, where he and the Roman curia would have more control over it. On 15 January 1338 the Council of Basel suspended the pope, who responded with an excommunication. The council proceeded to elect a new pope—Felix V (1439–49). Both the French king and the Germans supported the Basel remnant, with Charles VII of France passing the Pragmatic Sanction of Bourges (7 July 1438) asserting the supremacy of a council over the pope. This was to be the foundational plank of Gallicanism.[57] The Council of Basel eventually petered out a decade later.

The peripatetic papal Council of Ferrara–Florence–Rome (1438–45) was very poorly attended, although Eugene IV himself was there. The participants were mainly Italian bishops from the Papal States, Venice and Tuscany. Steiber seriously questions the ecumenicity of this council because it could hardly be seen as representative of Latin Christianity. It is questionable if the Greeks who were present were representative of their church either; this is reinforced by the fact that the agreement reached at the council was promptly rejected by the Eastern church when the envoys returned to Constantinople, even though the Ottoman threat to the Byzantine empire had now reached a critical stage.[58]

The council sat in Ferrara for the early part of 1438 and then moved to Florence at the beginning of 1439. The main points for discussion with the Easterners were the use of unleavened bread in the Eucharist, the procession of the Holy Spirit, papal primacy, and purgatory.[59] The imponderable that was not able to be assessed was the deep suspicion of the people of the Eastern empire for Latin Christians, especially after the Crusades, and the lack of any understanding between the people of East and West. By mid-1439 all of the theological issues had been ironed out, including Eastern acceptance of Roman primacy. The bull *Laetentur Coeli* (6 July 1439) set out the decree of reunion. In many ways the bull was as much about attacking conciliarism as reunion with the Greeks, especially in the discussion of papal primacy. After the agreement the council dragged on for another six years in Florence and Rome, and it brought about the reunion between other Orthodox churches in the East and Rome: the Monophysite churches of Armenia in 1349, the Monophysite churches of Ethiopia and Syria in 1441 and 1445, the Chaldeans of present-day Iraq and the Maronites of Lebanon.

The Greek Easterners delayed for twelve years before they proclaimed the decree of union in Hagia Sophia on 12 December 1452 during the final siege of Constantinople. The great city was taken by the Ottoman Turks on 29 May 1453. The union with the West abruptly ended.

Much of the rest of the activity of the Council of Ferrara–Florence–Rome was taken up with attacks on the proceedings and participants of the Council of Basel. Eugene IV had died in 1447, and he was succeeded by a scholar-pope who began the church's relationship with the Renaissance, Nicholas V (1447–55). Through adroit political manoeuvring he brought peace to Rome and the Papal States, got the rump of the council of Basel closed down, reconciled the antipope Felix V, founded the Vatican library, carried on a vast building programme in Rome and hired outstanding artists. Sadly, he left the problem of church reform untouched.

But before we move on to the Renaissance popes we need to note briefly the reassessment of the theological significance of the teachings of the Councils of Constance and Basel that has occurred in recent ecclesiology. In the late 1960s and early 1970s there was a revival of interest in the history of the conciliar movement. This had begun before the Second Vatican Council (1962–65) with the work of the historians of canon law such as Walter Ullmann and Brian Tierney, and Joseph Gill the historian of Ferrara–Florence, who rejects the dogmatic validity of *Haec Sancta*. From 1960 onwards the Belgian scholar Paul de Vooght produced a series of articles and a major book on conciliarism.[60] He holds that the definition of primacy of the First Vatican Council is compatible with *Haec Sancta*. This discussion was continued in Hans Kung's book *Structures of the Church* (1964) and in Francis Oakley's *Council over Pope?* (1969). The latter is the most provocative study to emerge from this revival of interest in conciliarism.[61] Kung and Oakley are the only ones to apply the conciliar debate to contemporary ecclesiology, and they also accept the continuing relevance of the principle of the superiority of a council over the pope. Hubert Jedin, historian of the Council of Trent, sees conciliarism as having a limited validity in an extreme situation. Historical research into conciliarism has continued in the work of Karl August Finke and August Franzen.[62] But this whole discussion has dissipated since the 1970s.[63]

By the time of Nicholas V, the conciliar age was over. From then onwards it was back to business as usual in Rome. The popes continued to act as petty Italian princelings. Although there was considerable cultural achievement during the Renaissance, the late fifteenth and early sixteenth centuries were a time of ecclesiastical disaster for the Catholic church.

It resulted in the crisis of the Reformation.

from the Renaissance to the french Revolution

The Renaissance popes

Nicholas V (1447–55) set a pattern that was to be followed for the rest of the fifteenth century: the popes focused their energy on the recapture and maintenance of the Papal States. The context of this struggle was the incessant internecine strife between the city-states of Italy. They also tried to organise a crusade against the Turks, who were threatening south-eastern Europe and the Mediterranean. However, the pressing need for reform of the church was neglected: corruption, promiscuity, bribery, nepotism, and increasing multiplication of benefices by single office holders came to symbolise the papacy of this period. A number of these popes were genuine humanists and patrons of art, although at the same time in Spain and Germany, with approval from Rome, the inquisition was hunting down, torturing and burning suspected heretics and especially witches, who were all categorised as social deviants.

Nicholas' successor, the minor Spanish nobleman Alfonso de Borgia, took the style Callistus III (1455–58). This pope devoted most of his energy to organising a crusade against the Turks. Like all of the popes of this period he was a nepotist. It was he who brought his nephew, the Spanish adventurer Rodrigo Borgia, into the curia, and made him a cardinal deacon in 1456 and vice-chancellor of the Holy See in 1457. It was through this office that Borgia amassed vast wealth.

His successor, Pius II (1458–64), was the greatest pope of the Renaissance period. He was educated as a humanist and his name, Enea Silvio Piccolomini, was transformed at his election to the style Pius, the reference being to Virgil's 'pius Aeneas'. He turned the villa in which he was born into the model town of Pienza; it still stands as a fascinating tribute to Renaissance town-planning, usually devoid of tourists, just south of Siena. In his early years he had been a strong conciliarist, and had fathered a number of children; he had worked in Germany and had visited other countries, including Scotland, on diplomatic missions. After a serious illness he underwent a conversion and was ordained priest in 1446. As pope he tried to organise a crusade against the Turks and, as an internationalist, was deeply involved in intra-European political affairs. Before his election he had abandoned his concilarist past, and while he remained a keen writer (who wrote his own *Commentarii*, or memoirs), he was increasingly critical of humanism, especially in its more pagan forms.[1] Pius seems to have been influenced by the German reformer and cardinal, Nicholas of Cusa (1401–64), who also began as a supporter of conciliarism, but became strongly pro-papal from about 1437.

Paul II (1464–71)—Pietro Barbo—was a Venetian by birth, and it was he who built Rome's famous Palazzo di Venezia and its accompanying piazza. It was Paul who created the Roman carnival, and he was popular with the Roman populace.[2] He was unsuccessful in organising a crusade against the Turks, but was able to get financial support for the Hungarians and Albanians in their resistance to Turkish expansion. He died suddenly of a stroke, and was succeeded by a Franciscan, Francesco della Rovere, as Sixtus IV (1471–84). Although Sixtus' personal life was exemplary, he ruthlessly advanced his relatives (he came from a poor background), and he involved the papacy so deeply in the internecine affairs of Italy that he effectively secularised it. To finance his wars and his building programme in Rome (which he transformed from a medieval to a Renaissance city) he issued and sold indulgences. Attempts to reconvene the Council of Basel in the last years of his papacy were met with a renewed ban on general councils. His positive achievements were that he attracted the greatest artists to Rome, established the Vatican archives and reformed the Vatican library.

The four successors of Sixtus IV—Innocent VIII (1484–92), Alexander VI (1492–1503), Julius II (1503–13) and Leo X (1513–21)—were all of a type. They were nothing more than utterly worldly politicians, whose personal lives were characterised by promiscuity and scandal. Much of their time was taken up in petty warfare. The possibility of church reform at the highest level came to a standstill under these popes, although much reform had been going on in lay and clerical circles outside Rome. The redeeming feature of these popes—at least from our perspective today—is that they were patrons of the arts and culture, and the treasures of today's Vatican are the result largely of their work.

Innocent VIII was incompetent and corrupt. He legitimated his bastard children and married them off to princely families. He left the Papal States in anarchy. He was succeeded by the Spanish adventurer Rodrigo Borgia, who took the style Alexander VI. He is the most infamous of the popes, at least in popular estimation. He was elected by bribery and corrupt promises. Alexander was nothing more than a debased Renaissance prince, and his personal life was characterised by considerable promiscuity. He was an ineffective politician whose policies were dominated by the interests of his bastard children, of whom the four born to the three-times-married Roman noblewoman, Vanozza Catanei, were the most favoured.[3] Alexander's protracted affair with Catanei began after 1473 and had concluded before 1486. The family biographer, Michael Mallett, says that she was a beautiful woman who brought stability and order into Rodrigo's personal life.[4] Although he was not a great patron of the arts in the sense of Julius II and Leo X, Alexander was responsible for the restoration of the Castel Sant' Angelo and the marvellous Borgia apartment in the Vatican, which can still be seen close to the Sistine Chapel; as Georgina Masson says, it is 'surprisingly small' for a papal dwelling, but its very feeling of intimacy conveys something of the genuine 'feel' of Renaissance life.[5]

Two of Catanei's children by Pope Borgia, the infamous Cesare and the much-maligned Lucrezia, seem to have been Alexander's evil

geniuses. At one stage the pope was apparently determined to expro-
priate the entire Papal States to the Borgia family, and enormous sums
of money were poured into the project of crushing the Roman families
and the other interested parties that would be affected. However,
Charles VIII of France (1483–98) invaded Italy. At the same time a reforming Dominican, Girolamo Savonarola (1452–98), began his prophetic preaching in 1482 in San Marco in Florence. He denounced the
immorality of both the Florentines and the clergy and, supported by the
French, he dominated a kind of theocratic democracy in the city between 1494 and 1495. He attacked Alexander and the curia, and called
for a general council and the deposition of the pope. He was excommunicated in 1497. The Florentines eventually tired of the strictures of
their fanatical friar. He was arrested, tortured and hung in 1498. It has
never been sorted out if he was a genuine saint, or a dangerous dema-
gogue. Alexander himself died in 1503, probably as a result of poison
ironically intended for another cardinal. His son Cesare just survived
the same poison.

Francesco Todeschini, a nephew of Pius II, was elected as Pius III
(1503), but he died after a month. His death was a tragedy for he was a
man of culture and integrity, and there are signs that he would have
attended to the need for reform by calling a general council. He was
quickly succeeded by a Franciscan, Giuliano della Rovere, with the style
Julius II (1503–13).[6] He had bribed his way into the papacy. A ruthless
enemy of Alexander VI, he had spent most of the previous decade in
exile in France. His main aim was to protect the Papal States from
foreign domination. There is a sense in which Julius was romanticised
through his connection with Michelangelo Buonarroti (1475–1564) and
the painting of the Sistine Chapel ceiling, which began in 1508. But he
was actually a completely secularised ruler for whom the outward signs
of religion were merely formalities. The painting of Julius at prayer
by Raphael in the 'Mass of Bolsena' fresco in the Vatican Stanze seems
totally inappropriate for such a worldly pope. More of a soldier than a
priest, his life was largely given over to the re-establishment of the Papal
States. He was completely committed to the expulsion of French and
foreign influence from Italy and prepared to use any political or military

means to achieve this; he was later seen as one of the pioneers of Italian unification.

His success in these Italian wars and the struggle against the French was achieved not only through his own skill, but also through the professional army that he recruited; he no longer relied on mercenaries. He also established the Swiss Guard, which remained a fighting force until 1825, when it became a domestic bodyguard.

Early in his papacy he moved quickly to neutralise the incipient state dominated by Cesare Borgia in the Romagna in the north-east Papal States. Later, in an intricate series of manoeuvres in 1509–10, he succeeded in defeating the Venetians as well as expelling Louis XII (1499–1515) and the French from Italy. Julius did not hesitate to use ecclesiastical censures to achieve this. In response, Louis XII renewed the Pragmatic Sanction of Bourges (see Chapter 6) and demanded that a council be called. This was not unexpected: the French church had largely been under the control of the French monarchy since the passing of the sanction in 1438. But the idea of a council was more threatening to Julius since conciliar ideas were still very much in the air, and the pope had already promised to call a council within two years of his election. He was clearly vulnerable on this point.

After complex negotiations, and supported by a group of rebel cardinals, a French-sponsored council actually opened at Pisa in October 1511. As a counter-manoeuvre against the Pisan council, Julius summoned the Fifth Lateran Council (1512–17).[7] Clearly he was concerned about conciliarism, but he died before the council could achieve anything. Nelson Minnich, the historian of the Fifth Lateran Council, makes the perceptive observation that the papacy will only successfully deal with conciliarism when the issue is transformed from a focus on canon law to theology.[8] It could probably be maintained that this has still not occurred.

Julius was certainly a serious patron of art who encouraged not only Michelangelo, but also Raffaello Sanzio (1483–1520) and Donato d'Agnolo Bramante (1444–1514). It was Bramante whom Julius commissioned to design the new St Peter's. This undertaking was symbolically much more important at the time than the Sistine Chapel project, for it involved the demolition of the 1200-year-old Constantinian basilica. This had been on the edge of collapse since the papacy of Nicholas V. Despite enormous protests, in a 'grand, irrevocable gesture', Julius had it torn down.[9] He told Bramante that he wanted a church that would 'embody the greatness of the present and the future'.[10] The cost of this building, as well as all the other civic improvements in Rome, was paid for by the proclamation of an indulgence. This proclamation was to be a tragic model for Julius' successor.

Julius died ten months after the Fifth Lateran Council opened. He was deeply mourned in Rome. He was succeeded by Giovanni de' Medici, the second son of Lorenzo the Magnificent, who took the style Leo X (1513–21). He had little to recommend him except that he was a Renaissance prince. He was ugly, extravagant, pleasure-loving, cruel and devious. Martin Luther, who had visited Rome in 1510 on the business of his Augustinian order, was understandably scandalised by what he saw there. In view of the outbreak of the Reformation in 1517, Leo was an utterly unworthy pope. But by this stage the papacy was far-gone in its preoccupation with Italian political in-fighting, and seemed to be quite divorced from the reality and needs of the church in the rest of the world.

Although Leo was passively committed to continuing the Fifth Lateran Council at which there were many calls for reform, he gave it no energy or direction. The council had opened under Julius in May 1512 with a speech on the need for reform by the Augustinian superior-general Giles of Viterbo. Much of the energy of the council was initially taken up with attacking the French-sponsored Council of Pisa (1511–12) and the Gallicanism of the Pragmatic Sanction. After the election of Leo X the council focused on peace in Europe and reform of the church. Minnich has analysed a number of speeches on the subject of reform at this council.[11] Typical was that of the curalist Antonio Pucci of the apostolic camera—the fiscal department. He was a biblical scholar and his reform suggestions were practical.[12] Pucci said that the pope assisted by the council had to be the principal agents in the process of *reformatio in capite et membris* (reform in head and members). If this *reformatio* was not carried through by pope and council, God's judgement would be dire.[13] Evils among laity, clergy, bishops and princes were listed. Religious orders come in for a special tongue-lashing. But his criticisms became muted when he reached the higher echelons of the hierarchy; the pope and cardinals got off almost scot-free. Yet he seemed to intuit what would actually happen if nothing was done: 'For unless at this very time of the council . . . we [recover] our reputation which has been almost totally lost . . . there is nothing else left in which we can take refuge and hope'.[14] With a pope of the calibre of Leo X there was neither refuge nor hope.

One of the most interesting proposals at the Fifth Lateran Council was for the establishment of an episcopal college in Rome to represent the interests of the world's bishops. Local bishops felt marginalised by the cardinals and curial officials and were often annoyed by the exemption from their jurisdiction granted to religious orders. These problems about episcopal power have not gone away and were repeated at subsequent councils—Trent, Vatican I and Vatican II. There is a sense in which the position of the bishops in the church has far more theological validity than that of cardinals and the curia. This was realised at the Fifth Lateran Council by several speakers.[15] But like everything at that council, the proposal for an episcopal college came to nothing because of curial vested interests and the sloth of the pope.

The Lutheran crisis (1517)

LEO HAD QUICKLY squandered the money that his predecessor had saved, and he had to borrow heavily from the Roman banker Agostino Ghigi to maintain the papal government. He had to pay for his Italian wars, a projected crusade against the Turks, and the lavish lifestyle that had become endemic in the Roman court. Church offices, including cardinals' hats, were up for sale. But the precipitating cause of the Reformation was the cost of the rebuilding of St Peter's and the subsequent renewal of the plenary indulgence of Julius II to help pay for it.

The actual basis of the curial financial system went back far beyond Julius II and Leo X. As we have seen the business of papal taxes had been reorganised at Avignon by John XXII and Benedict XII. The papal financial bureaucracy evolved a century ahead of similar structures that were developed to support the absolute monarchies of Spain and

England. But for the papacy to develop such a system was a perversion, for it meant that spiritual offices were essentially secularised and put on sale. There was such a close symbiosis of grace and Mammon that simony was a constant threat, if not a reality. If this system began at Avignon, it reached its apogee in the papal court just before the Reformation in order to pay for the Renaissance in Rome.

The particular indulgence against which Martin Luther (1483–1546) revolted had been proclaimed by Pope Leo to pay for St Peter's. He had struck a special deal (about which Luther knew nothing) with the archbishop-elector of Mainz, Albrecht of Brandenburg (1490–1545). Albrecht was a pluralist: he was also archbishop of Magdeburg and apostolic administrator of the diocese of Halberstadt. The idea was that, if Albrecht was to allow the indulgence to be preached in his territories, he would get a percentage of the collection to pay off his loan from the Fugger banking company of Augsburg, which he had taken out in the first place to buy his office from the papacy. He was paying 20 per cent interest to the Fuggers, so the sooner the loan was liquidated, the better! On the face of it, it was hard for Rome to lose (except morally) from this totally simoniacal deal.

A Dominican, Johann Tetzel (1465–1519), a professional indulgence preacher, had been appointed by Archbishop Albrecht in 1516 to preach this jubilee indulgence. There is no doubt that Tetzel used questionable methods in his preaching. A sample shows the corruption inherent in the whole business:

> You should know that all who confess and in penance put alms into the coffer according to the counsel of the confessor, will obtain complete remission of all their sins . . . Why are you standing there? Run for the salvation of your souls . . . Don't you hear the voices of your wailing dead parents and others who say 'Have mercy upon me . . . because we are in severe punishment and pain. From this you could redeem us with a small alms'.[16]

In October 1517 Tetzel was active on the border of Electoral Saxony close to Wittenberg. Many people from Wittenberg had crossed the border in order to obtain the indulgence.

Luther objected to the whole process, and he reacted in the normal scholarly fashion by publishing ninety-five theses on indulgences on 31 October 1517. He had already preached on the topic in October the previous year in Wittenberg, and he was very popular among the towns-people and at the newly founded local university. Luther had reflected long and suffered much personal spiritual pain as, over a number of years, he worked away at developing his theology of grace and justifi-cation. Given his concern for the depth of the human struggle in re-lationship to God and salvation, it is understandable that he was offended by the crude and probably heretical preaching of Tetzel. For through Tetzel the idea gained ground that salvation could be gained by the simple expedient of paying for an indulgence. As the contemporary saying that caricatured Tetzel's 'theology' put it: 'As soon as the coin in the coffer rings, the soul into heaven springs'.[17] There was no need for repentance; all that was required, according to Tetzel, was the simple expedient of paying, and the soul of the friend or relative would be released from purgatory. It was a system that was wide open to abuse.

Luther's theses were intended simply as the basis for an academic discussion; there was no question of turning the whole affair into a revolution against papal authority, nor of upsetting the order of the church. In April 1518 Luther attended a chapter of the Augustinians at Heidelberg, and he defended his theses to great acclaim. But he had offended powerful people and had affected them where it hurt most— in their pockets! In May 1518 he was reported to Rome by the Domi-nicans. They sent a copy of his theses to the curia, plus selections from his devotional works and sermons in Wittenberg. Leo instructed the general of the Augustinians to silence Luther, and in August he was cited to appear in Rome within sixty days.

Luther's great strength was that he was protected by Frederick the Wise, elector of Saxony (1463–1525). In the autumn of 1518, Luther met the very sensible papal nuncio, the Dominican Cardinal Thomas de Vio Cajetan (1469–1534), in Augsburg. Luther was forced by Cajetan to see where his position was leading him. A bull, *Cum Postquam*, on indul-gences, was issued in Rome. The curia were attempting to persuade Frederick to hand Luther over while, at the same time, supporting the

Saxon ruler as candidate for Holy Roman Emperor. Frederick held firm and protected Luther. The church revolt was spreading in Germany. In June 1519 there was a disputation at Leipzig between Luther and the Dominican Johann Eck (1486–1543). At this stage Luther had not gone as far as many medieval theologians such as William of Ockham, but he clearly perceived that the central question in debate was really the power of the pope and the nature of the church, for it was the pope who issued indulgences.

At Leipzig Luther formulated two fundamental principles: papal primacy is not of divine origin; and religious truth is only that which can be proved from scripture. Despite the sensible attempts of the good-willed Cajetan to establish an expert examination of Luther's writings in context, Eck was able to bulldoze through a condemnation in Rome. The papal response was the bull *Exsurge Domine* (15 June 1520), in which Leo X condemned Luther on forty-one counts and declared him a heretic.[18] But it was too late, for Luther already had the support of all of Wittenberg and much of Saxony, and also many of Germany's most influential classes. He publicly burned the bull and was subsequently excommunicated.

The failure of Leo and the Roman curia to respond to the German crisis was due to their political and familial preoccupations, and their lack of real appreciation of what was quickly developing in Germany. When Leo died of malaria in December 1521, he left the church in turmoil and the papacy bankrupt. He had truly lived out his reported comment at the time of his election: 'God has given us the papacy; let us enjoy it'.

Leo was succeeded by a pious, scholarly and well-intentioned Dutchman, Adrian Florensz Dedal, who retained his baptismal name as Hadrian VI (1522–23). Educated at Leuven, he had been a professor and chancellor of the university there, tutor of Charles V, and had worked for the Spanish monarchy in civil administration and church reform. He began his papacy with a determined reform of the curia and the city of Rome. He withdrew all indults (permissions) granted to the secular power to nominate to vacant benefices. He was very unpopular with both the curia and the Roman people because of his demands for reform. The great German historian of the popes, Ludwig von Pastor, says:

> Hadrian now brought himself into complete disfavour with the ecclesiastical bureaucracy—of all bureaucracies the worst . . . According to the Ferranese envoy, no pope ever received so much abuse as Hadrian VI. Prelates and cardinals accustomed to the pomp and luxury of the Leonine period found a continuing stumbling block in the asceticism and simplicity of Hadrian's life.[19]

Unfortunately, Hadrian also misread the situation in Germany and simply demanded that Luther submit to Roman censure. But the pope died before much could be achieved.

He was succeeded after a fifty-day conclave by the weak and indecisive Giulio de' Medici, nephew of Lorenzo the Magnificent, who took the style Clement VII (1523–34). The contemporary commentator Francesco Guicciardini says that the pope was 'rather morose and disagreeable . . . by no means trustworthy and naturally disinclined to do a kindness and very grave and cautious in his actions'.[20] For much of his papacy he was under the influence of the Emperor Charles V (1519–56), although the pope regularly changed sides in the cesspool of European strategic and diplomatic rivalries between the Emperor, Francis I (1515–47) of France and Henry VIII (1509–47) of England. In fact, it was Clement's lack of political skill and principle that led to an imperial invasion of Italy which, in May 1527 culminated in the appalling sack of Rome.[21] The occupation lasted nine months and the city was largely destroyed by the motley, ill-led and largely Protestant imperial army. The population of about 60 000 was reduced by half. The pope spent most of the occupation holed up in the Castel Sant' Angelo.

Like his predecessor Leo, Clement dismissed Luther and the German Reformation as the tiresome and pettifogging arguments of obscure monks. It was a disastrous mistake, for it gave the reformers time to establish themselves in Germany. For the full decade of Clement's papacy, the Emperor Charles V was virtually left alone to deal with the entire Protestant crisis, often betrayed by the policies of Henry VIII and

Francis I. Luther had called for a council, but Clement's fear of this meant that constructive dialogue was never really attempted with the Protestant party.

Just as disastrous was the pope's inaction regarding the marriage of Henry VIII.[22] For most of the first half of Henry's reign England's affairs were largely run by Cardinal Thomas Wolsey (*c.*1474–1530), Lord Chancellor and legate *a latere* of the pope (a personal papal representative who deals with a specific matter or person). It was not that the king surrendered his power; he just let others do the work for him. The ultimate test for Wolsey came with 'the King's great matter', Henry's divorce proceedings. In the early summer of 1527 Henry became infatuated with Anne Boleyn (*c.*1507–36). Although she seemed to be irresistibly attractive to men, she refused to give way to the king's demands until she became his wife. As a result Henry began to claim that he had a serious doubt of conscience regarding his marriage to Catherine of Aragon (1485–1536), the widow of his deceased elder brother Arthur. Henry had married Catherine under a papal dispensation from the law of affinity, given by Pope Julius II; it also mentioned a 'possible' non-consummation. Through Wolsey, Henry sued for divorce from Catherine. But the problem was that Charles V was Catherine's nephew, so for five years Clement VII did virtually nothing except to recall the case to Rome after two years of desultory hearings in England by Cardinal Lorenzo Campeggio and Wolsey. But before the pope eventually found for Catherine, England had gone into schism. Although the pope should not be blamed for the schism, his failure to read the situation correctly and deftly meant that the anti-clerical and anti-papal forces already at work within English society were given a freer rein by King Henry than might have otherwise been the case.[23]

Few mourned Clement when he died in September 1534, and his temporary tomb was smeared with the words *Inclemens Pontifex Minimus* (Inclement and Minimal High Priest).[24] It was an appropriate obituary. He had acted largely as an Italian princeling who had misread the revolution that was already happening in Germany, northern Europe and England.

The Counter-Reformation[25]

THE QUICK ELECTION of Alessandro Farnese, who took the style Paul III (1534–49, was not unexpected. Although he belonged to the reform party in the curia, he was still very much a Renaissance prince. His installation as pope was celebrated with pageants and tournaments, and he revived the Roman carnival. As a cardinal, Farnese had lived a very worldly life, and his beautiful sister Giulia had been one of the mistresses of Pope Alexander VI. He had fathered four children, and two of his grandchildren were created cardinals while still in their teens. He had reformed his ways in 1519 when he was ordained, but he remained totally devoted to the interests of his family. As pope he commissioned Michelangelo to paint the Last Judgement behind the altar in the Sistine Chapel, and he supported art and education. The famous portrait by Titian shows the aged and stooped, but extraordinarily shrewd pope, whose keen, worldly and intelligent eyes look clearly outward toward something in the distance.

Paul was the first pope to realise that the Protestant problem had to be dealt with decisively and that only a council would be able to achieve this. In some ways it was the initial appearance of Protestantism in Italy that confronted the pope with this realisation. As a kind of dry run for reform, he issued in 1536 *A General Edict for the Reform of Ecclesiastical Persons and Places in Rome*.[26] It dealt with issues like clerical dress, care of parishes, regularity of the celebration of Mass by priests (at least once a month), public begging, behaviour at Mass, and the preaching of orthodox doctrine. This edict was the product of a conservative curial committee and there was no mention of reform of the curia itself. But after the appointment of a number of reformers to the College of Cardinals in 1536—men like Pietro Caraffa (1476–1559), Jacopo Sadoleto (1477–1547), Gasparo Contarini (1483–1542), Reginald Pole (1500–58) and Marcello Cervini (1501–55)—the pope was able set up a real reform committee—the *Consilium de Emendenda Ecclesia* (Committee for Church Reform)—made up of these newly appointed cardinals, plus several others.

The report of the *Consilium* was hard-hitting.[27] It singled out the abuse at the core of the problem: the curia's fiscal system, which had led to the splitting of the notion of office in the church from the actual practice of pastoral ministry. The buying and selling of offices bred the idea that ecclesiastical revenues could be divorced from the celebration of the liturgy, the preaching of the word and Christian instruction. This led to a neglect of residence by bishops, religious superiors and parish priests. The *Consilium* did not hesitate to blame the popes for these abuses. The reformers were beginning to suggest that the old system should be swept away completely. In response conservatives made much of the fact that the report of the *Consilium* was leaked to the Lutherans, who used it in their propaganda. Paul III made efforts to reform the Datary and Penitentiary, but the loss in revenue to the Holy See was considerable and in a period of inflation the pope faced considerable monetary problems. These two offices had a stranglehold on papal finances because they granted absolutions from censures and penalties (Penitentiary) and issued and dated papal documents (Datary). It was through these offices that taxes were levied on the bureaucratic paperwork.

Another abuse nominated was that too many bishops held their positions merely for profit and not for pastoral ministry. Cardinals often held several bishoprics—Thomas Wolsey, for instance, was a noted pluralist. Many bishops did not maintain residence in their dioceses: the Italian cardinal Campeggio, for example, was bishop of Salisbury. The constant granting of exemptions by the Datary and the Penitentiary meant that many committed simony and then got absolution from the sin at the same time!

Essentially, what Paul III was doing was introducing what today is called the Counter-Reformation to the papacy. Popular history has been slow to keep pace with leading-edge research: and until the last four decades or so very little had been written in English on the Counter-Reformation, and it is still seen in some popular histories as a belated response to the Reformation. The very term 'Counter-Reformation' (invented some 130 years ago in Germany) emphasises a reactive stance. While the Counter-Reformation interacted with Protestantism, it was, in essence, an independent movement with roots in Spain and Italy going back 150 years prior to the Reformation. This can be seen especially in the area of personal renewal and spirituality. Clearly, the term 'Catholic Reformation' would be more accurate, although it is still not widely used. The fact that there was a desperate need for reform is obvious from the papal history that we have canvassed. Far too many prelates and clergy, including popes, were entirely devoid of any consciousness of the spiritual aspects of their vocation. Concubinage, absenteeism and general loose living were rampant. There had been some effort to re-form the older orders, but this was piecemeal and uncoordinated. Popes and bishops did not give reform the priority it deserved.

The Counter-Reformation took root and grew most strongly in Spain and Italy. In many ways Italy was the place where reform was most needed. From about 1445 onwards reform in Italy centred on the 'oratories'. These were established in Rome, Venice, Bologna, Verona, Genoa and Vicenza. They were composed of lay and clerical members devoted to charitable works. Many of the leading figures of the Counter-Reformation belonged to oratories. One of these oratories was that of St Philip Neri (1515–95).[28] He is primarily responsible for the conversion of Rome itself. He began the religious order the Congregation of the Oratory, and when he died in 1595 the city had changed from the neo-pagan humanism of Leo X and Clement VII to the city of the Counter-Reformation.

In Spain the church had already been reformed, and the Council of Trent had little to add. The country had been united by Ferdinand and Isabella in the late fifteenth century, and they had insisted on church reform as part of their programme to unify Spanish society. They demanded that good bishops be chosen, and noteworthy efforts were made to improve the education of the clergy. The inquisition was used as a repressive instrument to stamp out dissent, so Protestantism never became a real threat in Spain. The great reformer of the Spanish church was Cardinal Francesco Ximenez de Cisneros (1436–1517), archbishop of Toledo. An Observant Franciscan, he lived a life of poverty, austerity and sanctity. He was also a great reformer, statesman and scholar, who founded the University of Alcala, reformed theology and supervised the publication of the Complutensian Polyglot Bible. It was due to his work that the later mystical aspects of the Counter-Reformation flowered in Spain with Sts Teresa and John of the Cross.

The Jesuit order is a key consideration in any discussion of the Counter-Reformation. However, despite the assertions of some historians, the Jesuits can hardly be said to have been founded in response to Protestantism.[29] Ignatius Loyola's origins and inspiration were entirely separate from the work of the reformers.[30] Founded in Paris in 1534, the Society of Jesus was approved by Paul III in 1540 in the bull *Regimini Militantis Ecclesiae*. The key to the success of the Society was the fact that it was contemporary and adjusted to the needs of the times. Members were given a sound formation as novices through the *Spiritual Exercises*, which had been devised by Ignatius as a result of his own spiritual experience. He also insisted on a long and profound spiritual and intellectual formation in order that the members be ready to take up contemporary challenges. Jesuits were not tied down by rigid timetables, the chanting of the divine office or the wearing of a specific habit. They had a freedom and fluidity of movement that meant that they could meet needs as they arose. Jesuits were also seriously committed to the papacy by the taking of a fourth vow to be at the disposal of the pope.

As it worked out in practice, the Society faced two fundamental challenges: evangelisation through the missions in Asia and the Americas, and the challenge of Protestantism. At the time of Ignatius' death in 1556 the Society possessed more than one hundred houses with over a thousand members. There were already eleven provinces, including India and Brazil.

Attempts at reunion and approaches to Protestantism

DURING THE PAPACY of Paul III two distinct approaches emerged within the Roman church as to how to bring about reform and to deal with the Reformation. One approach was to attempt reconciliation with the Protestants; the other was to close ranks and to protect the heartlands of Catholicism in Italy and Spain. The leader of the more open approach was Cardinal Gasparo Contarini (1483–1542), a Venetian layman who had been made a cardinal by Paul III. Contarini recommended meeting the Lutherans and making concessions to them in order to heal the breach. The Englishman Reginald Pole, who served with Contarini on the *Consilium*, shared similar views. Pole, who was descended from Edward IV, and was living in Italy at the time, was critical of Henry's break with Rome. Contarini hoped that a Protestant presence at a general council might achieve reconciliation between the two sides. In fact, both he and Pole had considerable sympathy with the Lutheran view on justification.

Among the Lutherans Philip Melanchthon (1497–1560) represented a similar irenicism, and he was responsible for the moderate and conciliatory Confession of Augsburg (1530), which he hoped would be acceptable to the Catholics. Both Contarini and Melanchthon were present at the last serious attempt to reconcile the Lutherans and the Catholics at the Colloquy at Regensberg in April–May 1541.[31] This was the last of a series of *colloquia religionis* that had been held in Germany under the aegis of Charles V. The first was held at Hagenau in 1540 and the second at Worms in 1541. The final Colloquy in Regensberg reached agreement on most points, including the vexed question of justification. Cardinal Giovanni Morone (1509–80) and Contarini attended Regensberg as papal legates. But the agreement was disowned by Luther, and Contarini himself fell under suspicion of heresy for his views on justification. He died in 1542.

A different approach to the issue of reform was taken by Cardinal Gian Pietro Caraffa (1476–1559). He saw no point in negotiation with the Lutherans. The church should be reformed by a strict application of canon law, internal purification, and the vigorous and repressive use of the inquisition. His approach gained the ascendancy after the failure of the Regensberg Colloquy and the death of Contarini. The repressive approach was strengthened by the fact that Protestantism had already come to Italy. This was signalled by two spectacular conversions in 1542: the famous preacher and vicar-general of the Capuchin order, Bernardino Ochino, fled to the Lutherans in Augsburg. Then the famous Augustinian, Peter Martyr Vermigli, fled to Switzerland and then to England under Edward VI (1547–53). These desertions weakened the influence of the Contarini circle and strengthened the hand of the intransigent Caraffa. Support for the Roman inquisition (which was established in 1542) was further strengthened when in May 1549 Pietro Paolo Vergerio, the bishop of Capo d'Istria, escaped from Italy after the commencement of a trial for apostasy. He had previously been nuncio in Germany.

Concern with Protestantism in northern Italy had led Paul III to establish the Roman inquisition in July 1542. Pastor has emphasised the way in which the Roman inquisition was able to ignore local bishops, with a consequent centralisation of power in Rome. He also notes the 'fiery enthusiasm' of Caraffa in getting the inquisition under way.[32] When Caraffa became Pope Paul IV (1555–59), the inquisition had a free hand: even Cardinal Pole was suspected of heresy, and Cardinal Morone was imprisoned for criticising the persecution of those in Rome thought to be heretics. Heretical books also began to be listed and forbidden: in 1559 the *Index Librorum Prohibitorum* (Index of Forbidden Books) was established.

The Council of Trent (1545–1563)

THE GREATEST ACHIEVEMENT of Paul III was the Council of Trent. Almost as soon as the Lutheran crisis broke out there were cries for a general council to promote reform and to solve the growing religious dissension of Europe. Although Luther claimed that a council could err and that scripture was the sole canon of truth, he still demanded a council in the pamphlet *To the Christian Nobility of the German Nation* (1520).[33] From the Diet of Worms (1521) onwards there was imperial pressure for a 'free, general Christian council in German lands'. (This was the imperial Diet at which Luther defended his teachings before Charles V. It was at Worms that he uttered his famous words *Hie stehe ich. Ich kan nicht anders. Gott helff mir. Amen.*—Here I stand. I cannot do otherwise. God help me. Amen.) The words here are important: 'free' meant a council free of papal domination, for it would be called by emperor and princes, as well as the pope. 'Christian' meant that the council would include the laity (and for the Lutherans, it meant that the

Bible would be sole norm of orthodoxy) as well as clergy and bishops. Also the council would be held within the borders of the empire.

The problem that the Emperor Charles V faced was that for much of this period (1521–29) he was at war with Francis I. In these circumstances Clement VII was able to play for time and he allied himself with France. Clement VII was afraid of conciliarism and put his faith in diplomacy, playing off the French against the empire. The Confession of Augsburg (1530) was a chance for all sides to agree, but the opportunity was lost through the opposition of Luther and the inaction of Clement VII.

Paul III realised that the pressure for a council could not be resisted, but there were periods when he himself stalled for time. On the occasion of Emperor Charles V's visit to Rome in the spring of 1536, Paul gave a firm promise that he would convoke a council. It was called for Mantua in June 1537, only to be put off to 1538. Between 1538 and 1542 the *colloquia religionis* replaced the proposed council. When it was clear that the final colloquy, at Regensberg, had failed, Paul convoked the council for Trent for November 1542. For the next three years there was a history of delay and suspension until on 13 December 1545 the council finally opened.

The historian of the council, Hubert Jedin, says that Trent was symptomatic of the final triumph of the papacy over conciliarism.[34] The change in attitude that had occurred between Basel and Trent was significant. The papacy had survived, and Paul III's convocation demonstrated that it was now confident enough to entrust the reform of the church to a conciliar body. His bull, *Laetare Jerusalem*, set three tasks for Trent: healing of the split between Catholics and Protestants; the reform of the church; and defence of Europe against the Ottoman Turks. The council did not get down to work until January 1546. It worked through three separate sessions: 13 December 1545 to 1 February 1548; 1 May 1551 to 28 April 1552; 18 January 1562 to 3 December 1563.[35] At the first session the papal legates were Cardinals Gian Maria del Monte (the future Julius III), Marcello Cervini (the future Marcellus II) and Reginald Pole (future archbishop of Canterbury). Trent was an independent bishopric in northern Italy in imperial territory, directly below the Brenner

Pass from Innsbruck. Although there were never more than thirty or forty bishops present, there was a serious accommodation problem in the town.

Early progress was slow because of insufficient preparation. However, the council decided early-on to adopt two parallel courses: it would issue dogmatic decrees and ecclesiastical reform decrees side by side.

From the start the Council of Trent confronted the theological issues focused on by the reformers: the relationship of scripture and church tradition, original sin, the sacraments, justification, the role of bishops and the pope, and the nature of the ministry and priesthood. Luther had said that the Bible alone was the sole rule of faith, and he rejected church teachings that were not found there. In response the council fixed the canon of scripture. The Latin Vulgate was declared to be the official Catholic version, and it was decreed that the church alone could 'pass judgement on the true meaning and interpretation of the sacred scriptures'.[36] Commentaries, notes and glosses on scripture were not to be published without 'having been previously examined and approved' by local bishops.[37] But on the difficult question of the definition of tradition, Trent sidestepped the issue because it was felt that theological reflection upon it had not sufficiently matured. It simply stated the existence of tradition without defining it.

Another key issue for the reformers was justification, the process whereby we achieve a right relationship with God. With Luther, the council asserted that God's grace is necessary for the whole process of salvation. However, it also asserted that intrinsic change occurs as a result of the operation of the grace. Luther's teaching that the merits of Christ 'cover' our sinfulness was excluded; the council taught that grace changes us in the inner core of our being. Luther's doctrine of *sola fides* (faith alone) was also explicitly excluded. However, the council asserted that faith was the beginning, the foundation and the root of justification, but that the co-operation of the human will was necessary in the process of justification. The final version of the decree was adopted on 13 January 1547. The text is profoundly rooted in scripture. It was not until four and a half centuries later, in 1999, that Catholics and Lutherans reached agreement on this complex issue.

Connected with justification is the doctrine of original sin. With Luther the council rejected the pelagian idea that original sin and its effects can be removed by the human will and effort. However, Luther's notion that baptism did not intrinsically change the sinful nature of humankind was rejected. The Anabaptist view that 'recently born babies should not be baptised even if they have been born to baptised parents' was also rejected.[38] The council stated that the validity of the sacraments was not simply dependent on the faith of the recipient. The number was fixed at seven. On 3 March 1547 a decree on the sacraments was issued, focusing especially on baptism and confirmation.

The reform decrees of the first session stipulated that bishops must ensure that sound and orthodox theology was taught and that a proper training for the clergy be established.[39] Bishops were allowed an absence of only six months from their dioceses, or financial penalties began to apply. This was aimed especially at pluralists. The same applied to priests and monks living outside their cloisters. Bishops and priests were instructed to preach regularly, but religious priests could only preach outside their own churches with permission from the bishop.[40] Preaching was declared to be 'the chief task of the bishops'.[41]

On 11 March 1547 a decision was made to transfer the council to Bologna within the Papal States. There had been an outbreak of typhus at Trent, but this was merely an excuse; the real reason was to get the council outside the influence of the Emperor Charles V. When the move was made, a number of imperial bishops remained at Trent and the number of bishops at Bologna dwindled. Most were from Italy. They were outnumbered by the theologians. Much of the antagonism between Paul III and Charles V was personal. While no decrees were issued at Bologna, intensive work was done in preparation for later decrees. The council was suspended by the pope on 16 February 1548.

Paul III died on 10 November 1549. He had been one of the truly great popes. A difficult, ten-week conclave followed at which Pole came within one vote of being elected. Eventually the senior legate at Trent, Giovanni Maria del Monte, was elected with the style Julius III (1550–55). Although he was very much a Renaissance prince and his public infatuation with a male youth (whom he named a cardinal) created scandal,

Julius was a believer in reform and in the need for the continuation of the council. He sent Pole to England as papal legate and archbishop of Canterbury when Mary Tudor became queen in 1553. There was a short-lived if somewhat turbulent revival of Catholicism in England, with Pole dying twelve hours after the queen on 17 November 1558.

The new pope recalled the Council of Trent, and it reopened on 1 May 1551. Charles V gave the council cautious support, but it was opposed by Henry II of France (1547–59) and it seemed as though France would make a complete break with the papacy. It was only through the work of Cardinal Guise of Lorraine that this was averted. The council was held up for five months awaiting the arrival of the German bishops. Because much preliminary work had been done at Bologna, on 11 October 1551 the council was able to issue its decree on the Eucharist. This highlighted the real presence of Christ in the Eucharist (against the Protestant emphasis on spiritual presence) and the 'aptness' of the term 'transubstantiation' to describe that presence.[42] On 25 November 1551 a decree on penance and last anointing was issued. The traditional understanding was asserted against the overall rejection of these sacraments by the Protestants. Reform canons were also issued on the relationship of priests and bishops, and regulations concerning procedures in church courts.

Julius III had invited the Protestants to the council and, after protracted negotiations, they were given a safe-conduct and the council at first postponed the definitions on the Eucharist out of deference to them. The Lutherans arrived in January 1552. They made three demands: that all decisions to this point be declared null; that they could sit in the council as equal members; and that the council could decide matters over the head of the pope. There was some consideration of these demands, but it quickly became theoretical when war broke out between Catholics and Protestants in Germany in March 1552. On 28 April 1552 the council decreed its own suspension.

Julius III died in 1555, the year of the Peace of Augsburg, where it was agreed that the local ruler—according to the adage *cuius regio eius religio*—could decide religion for his own region and people. Marcello Cervini—Marcellus II (1555)—was elected.[43] He was the first genuinely committed reformer elected in this whole period. He was a man of scholarship, culture and integrity. But he died of a stroke less than a month later. It was a real tragedy. Pope Marcellus is appropriately commemorated in Giovanni Pierluigi da Palestrina's great polyphonic masterpiece, the *Missa Papae Marcelli*. The Mass probably dates from the early 1560s and was published by Palestrina in 1567.

Marcellus was followed by the fanatical and violent reactionary Gian Pietro Caraffa, who took the style Paul IV (1555–59). He refused to re-convoke the council. He was politically inept, and his anti-Hapsburg sentiments led to conflict with the emperor and with the Spanish king, Philip II (1558–98). As a consequence of this he also fell out with Mary Tudor of England, who had married Philip II; this, of course, was a dis-astrous mistake on her part for it tended to alienate her from the English people. The pope felt that he could push reform through himself, rely-ing largely on the inquisition. He suspended Cardinal Pole as legate to England and even imprisoned Cardinal Giovanni Morone for heresy. One of his few real achievements was the purging of the Datary. When he died there were explosive riots in Rome against his papacy and fam-ily. The headquarters of the inquisition were destroyed.

After a four-month conclave, which was dominated by international problems, the politically astute Giovanni Angelo Medici (no relation to the Florentine Medicis) was elected with the style Pius IV (1559–65). One of the best appointments he made was that of his nephew, the reformer Carlo Borromeo (1538–84), as archbishop of Milan. Under pressure from the French, influenced largely by the growth of Calvinism in France, the pope reconvened the Council of Trent. It was to become a constant of French royal policy to support Protestantism in Germany, while suppressing the Huguenots at home. Calvinism had also spread from Switzerland to Hungary and Poland. The Protestants, including the English, were invited to the council, but refused.[44] The emperor, Ferdinand I (1556–64), as well as the French, hoped that the Protestants might change their attitude if the council was declared a new one, even if held at Trent. The pope left this question open when convoking the council.

When the council met at Trent, it picked up where the last session had left off, only after complex negotiations between the French and the emperor. The first series of reform decrees were issued on 16 July 1562.

The council sidestepped the issue of communion under both kinds (sharing in both the bread and the wine) by handing it back to the pope for decision; the Protestants had already granted the cup to the laity. On 17 September the decrees on the Eucharist were issued. The council taught that the Mass made present sacramentally the one sacrifice of Calvary. At the same time, responding to the corruptions that had crept in during the late Middle Ages, the council issued a set of rules covering the celebration of Mass.

In October and November the council came close to breaking up over the question of the episcopate. The problem arose over the seemingly innocent question of the obligation of episcopal residence. The question was: could the pope release a bishop from the obligation of episcopal residence, or was a bishop obliged by the law of God to reside in his diocese? This led to a tangle of practical and theoretical questions centring on whether the episcopate was of divine right and whether a bishop derived his authority from God or the pope. If a bishop assumed his power and jurisdiction directly from God, what role, if any, did papal primacy play? The Spanish stood for the *ius divinum* of the episcopate, and the council became hopelessly bogged down on the issue.[45] The problem was not solved. It came up again at Vatican I and Vatican II and, in practice, is still not really resolved because the pope can still appoint and dismiss bishops. However, Vatican II made it clear that a bishop is a full member of the college of bishops by virtue of his episcopal ordination, and is a vicar of Christ, not of the pope.

The decree on holy orders was issued in July 1563. The sacramental character of the priesthood was defined, and clerics were obliged to reside in the place of their ministry. The conciliar call for seminary training for all clergy in every diocese was also issued in this period. Questions about the choice of bishops, diocesan government, episcopal visitation, dispensations, indulgences and the reform of religious orders were all considered. Marriage was defined as a sacrament. The decree *Tametsi*, which attempted to stamp out clandestine marriages, declared that for a marriage to be valid it had to be celebrated before a priest and two witnesses. Thus the power of the church over marriage was strengthened. In late 1563 the Legate Morone rushed the council to a conclusion when international tensions began to close in again. Its final session was on 3 December 1563 and its decrees were confirmed by Pope Pius IV on 26 January 1564.

A *Catechism of the Council of Trent* was issued in 1566 (Carlo Borromeo was largely responsible for it), a reformed *Breviary* in 1568 and a new *Missal* in 1570. A revised *Index of Forbidden Books* was issued in 1596.

Theologically, it had been a careful council, leaving contentious theological issues open. It had certainly attempted to restate the traditional orthodox positions on the issues raised by the Reformation. But it trod warily so that legitimate debates were not peremptorily closed. But it was a radical council in matters of reform of the church. A number of historians, such as G. R. Elton, have argued that an 'incisive break' was made by Trent and that a new reality was created; this was Roman Catholicism which, Elton argued, differed essentially from the old Latin church of the Middle Ages.[46] There is a sense in which he is right: Trent did signify a mutation in the history of the church. Something new, which can be identified with modern Roman Catholicism, did emerge. The disciplinary reforms, far more than the doctrinal decisions, led to the Roman Catholic 'thing' of which Elton speaks. The reform of the curia, increasing centralisation in Rome, the establishment of the seminary system, contributed much to what is explicitly 'Roman' in Catholicism. But this Romanism was never unchallenged. Gallicanism in France, Febronianism in Germany and to a lesser extent Jansenism in France, all challenged papal authority and Roman centralisation. Complete papal control of the church did not really emerge until after the First Vatican Council (1869–70).

But there is a sense in which Elton is profoundly wrong. For the Catholic reformers saw themselves as the inheritors of the faith of the Middle Ages. There is a clear continuity of doctrinal teaching between the medieval and the Counter-Reformation periods, especially on questions such as justification and the sacramental system. The Catholics of the Counter-Reformation did not try to undercut the whole history of the church by returning to some imagined pure New Testament faith, but they recognised the ongoing nature of the church's tradition and tried to be true to that tradition.[47]

The spiritual and cultural core of reformed Catholicism lay in the rich but austere religious climate of Counter-Reformation Spain.[48] While the Jesuits were the active, ministerial expression of the Catholic renewal, it was the Carmelites, Sts Teresa of Avila (1515–82) and John of the Cross (1542–91), and the great artists inspired by Carmelite mysticism, El Greco (c.1541–1614) and Tomas Luis de Victoria (c.1548–1611), who created the transcendent, interior landscape and imagery of what was to form the core of Catholic spirituality and art. Their mysticism expresses a controlled yet passionate intensity, a movement outward and upward as they reach beyond themselves. They largely transcended the cramping orthodoxy and austerity of sixteenth-century Spanish Catholicism 'to create a paradoxical freedom and space, in which we can perceive the permeable borders of earth and heaven, between the transcendent and natural world', between nature and grace.[49]

The post-Tridentine papacy and the theory of papal monarchy

TRENT PROVIDED CATHOLICISM with the sheet anchor of clear doctrine, and its practical reforms provided the possibility of turning away from the corruption of the past. The inquisition had saved Italy from Protestantism, but at the terrible cost of intellectual repression. Jesuit influence became pervasive throughout Italy as the fathers toured the various states and drew influential people to reformed Catholicism. They also influenced Carlo Borromeo, who set up Milan as a model diocese for the rest of Italy.[50] A series of reforming popes began with Pius V (1566–72). He was a Dominican with experience as an inquisitor. His reforms were considerable, but he relied heavily on the inquisition (he personally attended its meetings), and reform was achieved only at the cost of sacrificing virtually all liberty of thought. Like Paul IV he was harsh to the Jews and expelled them from the Papal States. It was Pius V who set up the Congregation of the Index as separate from the inquisition. His involvement in international affairs was disastrous. He even clashed with Philip II of Spain. He excommunicated and 'deposed' Elizabeth I (1558–1603) of England in 1570, a foolish move that placed

English Catholics in an impossible position. His one political success was the defeat of the Turks by the Holy League of Spain and Venice at the naval battle of Lepanto. But the Turks quickly recovered from this.

His successor, the canonist Gregory XIII (1572–85), after whom the Gregorian calendar is named, was a more moderate and practical reformer. He made sure that only good candidates were appointed bishops, and he used the system of nuncios to try to ensure that reform was carried out at the local level. He also set up the college system in Rome to train indigenous clergy for their own countries. The Jesuits were given the Roman College (now the Gregorian University) and the important German College. The English College in Rome was also established which, along with the English seminary established by Cardinal William Allen in Douai, trained clergy for the English mission. The pope also approved St Teresa of Avila's reform of the Discalced Carmelites and the foundation of the Oratory of Philip Neri. He was not particularly successful either in the government of the Papal States, which degenerated into anarchy, or in international affairs. But both Gregory and his successor encouraged missions in Asia, the Philippines, and Central and Latin America. This was the high point of colonial expansion of Spain and Portugal.

Gregory's successor, Sixtus V (1585–90), was an inflexible Franciscan, the son of a poor farm worker. It is reported that Elizabeth I said that he was the only man in Europe fit to be her husband! He ruthlessly restored order to the Papal States and refilled the papal coffers by prudent administration and new taxes. He also massively rebuilt Rome, and his name can be found everywhere on buildings and monuments around the contemporary city. He improved the layout of the city, restored its water supply, built new bridges across the Tiber, completed the dome on St Peter's and enhanced the Vatican library. However, the pope's treatment of ancient buildings (including the Lateran palace, which he pulled down) horrified many Romans. It was Sixtus who moved the great Egyptian obelisk to the centre of the piazza of St Peter's.[51]

But his lasting achievement was the reorganisation of the Roman curia. The structure that Sixtus established lasted until the further reorganisations in 1908 under Pius X (1903–19) and in 1967 under Paul VI

(1963–78).[52] By setting up a renewed curia Sixtus finally broke the power of the College of Cardinals who, from his reform until the nineteenth century, were largely administrative heads of the Roman departments, bureaucrats in the Papal States, theologians, or assistants to the pope. The large majority of them lived in Rome or central Italy. Sixtus limited the number of cardinals to seventy. The reorganisation of the curia was based on congregations, or committees of cardinals with permanent administrative support. They resembled departments in a modern bureaucracy. Fourteen congregations were set up, with nine devoted to church affairs and six to the secular affairs of the Papal States. The congregations devoted to church affairs remained pretty much the same until the reform by Paul VI after the second Vatican Council. The nine congregations for church affairs were:

(1) The Congregation of the Inquisition. Under Pius X this was to become the Supreme Sacred Congregation of the Holy Office. It is now the Congregation for the Doctrine of the Faith.[52a]
(2) The Consistorial Congregation, which dealt with bishops.
(3) The Congregation for the Oriental Churches.
(4) The Congregation of the Sacraments.
(5) The Congregation of the Council of Trent, which dealt with the discipline of the clergy and laity.
(6) The Congregation of Religious.
(7) The Congregation of Rites, which dealt with liturgy and canonisation of saints.
(8) The Congregation of Seminaries and Universities.
(9) The Sacred Ceremonial Congregation, which dealt with papal ceremonies.

The important Congregation of Propaganda Fide began as a commission of cardinals to supervise foreign missions in 1599, and was organised as a congregation by Gregory XV in June 1622. A missionary training seminary, the *Collegium Urbanum*, was attached to Propaganda, as it came to be called, in 1627. As well as foreign missions, non-Catholic European countries were also brought under the aegis of Propaganda.

In Sixtus' reform there were also three tribunals—the Penitentiary, the Rota and the Apostolic Signatura—and four offices—the Apostolic Chancery, the Datary, the Apostolic Chamber and the Secretariat of State—which acted as the papal foreign ministry. The pope also decreed that bishops must make regular *ad limina* visits to Rome (they were required to come every five years) and submit annual reports. Sixtus was generally hated in Rome, and when he died of malaria in 1590, the mob tore down his statue.

With the death of Sixtus V the city became more relaxed. Three popes followed in quick succession. The promising Urban VII (1590) died after only twelve days as a result of malaria. Gregory XIV (1590–91) lasted ten months, and Innocent IX lasted through November–December of 1591. From now until 1800 all of the popes were the product of upper-class birth or at least a wealthy or elite family, a legal education and secure patronage as they worked their way up through the Roman curia. Once they reached the rank of cardinal they were able to draw on connections that had been built up over many years in order to become *papabile* (a potential candidate for the papacy).

Within a month of the death of Innocent IX, a Florentine, Ippolito Aldobrandini, was elected with the style Clement VIII (1592–1605). The cardinals could not have made a better choice. Clement was a peaceful and devout man who had risen through the curia, and he continued and consolidated the reform movement along the lines already established. He tried to bring reconciliation to the warring Catholic powers. He reluctantly received Henry of Navarre back into the Catholic faith, accepted the Edict of Nantes granting freedom to the French Huguenots, and recognised Henry as king of France (1589–1610). The pope also helped to negotiate the Peace of Vervins (1598) between France and Spain. In this way he broke the all-pervasive Spanish influence in Rome. During Clement's papacy several million Ukrainian Orthodox recognised Rome while retaining their own liturgy. However, the pope's reconciliation did not extend to the Dominican friar Giordano Bruno (1548–1600), a supporter of Copernicus, who was tried by the inquisition and burned in Rome in 1600 for the heresy of 'pantheism'. Clement VIII was a friend of St Philip Neri, and he made the Jesuit Robert Bellarmine a cardinal. Both of them tried to moderate the pope's stubbornness, with little success.

Clement VIII died in 1605 and was succeeded by the short-lived Leo XI (April 1605). Camillo Borghese was elected in May 1605 and he took the style Paul V (1605–21). He asserted papal authority, even in the civil sphere, in an almost medieval fashion. But what was appropriate for Innocent III made no sense in the increasingly secularist atmosphere of post-Reformation Europe. It was during the papacy of Paul V that a new theological view of the pope's role emerged into the full light of day. This view was articulated most clearly by St Robert Bellarmine.

Papal primacy was denied by all of the reformers. The pope was seen as the anti-Christ by Protestant apologists. For Protestants supreme authority lay in the word of God and church order was based on the community. In the Calvinist tradition much of this power was exercised by elders. Trent and papal apologists were forced to respond to the Protestant interpretation of church government. The council, as we have seen, sidestepped the issue of the relationship of bishops and pope. But this failure laid the way open for an explanation of papal power without a corresponding explication of episcopal authority. An ecclesiological disjunction between the pope and the bishops emerged at the expense of the bishops. As a result Catholicism has had a significantly unbalanced church structure since the early seventeenth century with a very strong bias in the papal direction.

One of the key theologians in this process was the Jesuit St Robert Bellarmine (1542–1621), born in Montepulciano in Tuscany.[53] It is his articulation of the role of the papacy that has become the accepted teaching today. In the sixteenth century monarchical absolutism emerged with Ferdinand and Isabella, Henry VIII, Elizabeth I, Francis I and Philip II. These monarchs were supported by increasingly efficient bureaucratic structures. In the wake of monarchical absolutism, in the early seventeenth century the theory of the 'divine right of kings' was articulated. The notion was that kings were responsible to God alone, that their will was the source of law, and that subjects owed obedience to every morally lawful command.[54] It is significant that this notion of divine right was current at the very time when Bellarmine articulated his theory of papal monarchy. Bellarmine was a controversial theologian and under papal obedience he developed his Roman lectures into the massive three-volume *Controversies against the Heretics of our Times*, two million words of argumentation typical of the post-Reformation period, published between 1586 and 1593.[55]

He articulated a theory of absolute papal monarchy. Christ is the supreme head of the church. The pope is his vicar, his ministerial head on earth. The pope has absolute power to rule the church. He succeeds to his rights and prerogatives *iure divino* (by divine right) and not merely *iure ecclesiastico* (by ecclesiastical right). There is nothing particularly original in this. Bellarmine held that general councils can err and the pope must give his confirmation to a council's decrees for them to be genuine. He taught that the pope cannot be judged, deposed, or punished by a general council. If he becomes a heretic he simply ceases to be pope and then can be judged and deposed by the church. The pope is the supreme judge in deciding controversies on faith and morals, and what he formerly teaches is, by that very fact, infallible. The only limit to papal power that Bellarmine allows is in the area of direct interference in the concerns of secular authorities. 'Temporal rulers . . . held their authority from God, though in his view it was mediated to them through the consent of the peoples they ruled.'[56] This view led to the first volume of his *Controversies* being placed on the *Index of Forbidden Books* for a brief time by Sixtus V!

Not all Bellarmine's work was directed against Protestants. Some of his best controversial works are directed against the Servite friar Paolo Sarpi, the theological adviser to the doge and the republic of Venice. The high-handed Paul V had excommunicated the doge and council and placed the republic under an interdict in May 1606 in a dispute over papal jurisdiction in Venice. The tough-minded doge, Leonardo Donato, was unwilling to let Paul get away with the interdict. Under pressure, the Venetian clergy ignored the interdict. Enter Fra Paolo Sarpi (1552–1623), the Venetian-born Servite friar: he was employed by the republic as an official theological apologist. A friend of Galileo and a scientist of distinction, he was also a linguist and mathematician. His connections with leading Protestants caused suspicions in the inquisition. His views became increasingly anti-papal and he was strongly opposed to the Jesuits. Sarpi seems to have been an intelligent, broadly educated man who revolted against the intellectual constraints of the Counter-Reformation. His theological position was basically conciliarist (he republished Gerson), and his fundamental loyalty seems to have been to Venice, his birthplace.

In Rome Bellarmine received a papal command to respond to the books and pamphlets emanating from Venice. Sarpi and others had claimed that secular rulers (including the pope, who was the prince of the Papal States) derive their power directly from God. Bellarmine simply denied the divine right of kings (and doges), for their authority, he argued, is derived from heredity or election. (He is not consistent here, for he had argued in the *Controversies* that temporal rulers held their authority from God even if mediated through the consent of the ruled.) Not so the pope: his power comes directly from God. Kings and princes can lose their crowns, can alienate or resign their power. The pope is different: 'No one can diminish or take away the power of the Supreme Pontiff, not the college of cardinals, nor a general council, nor the Pope himself, because papal authority comes immediately from God, and is not subject to the control of any created will'.[57] This teaching of Bellarmine has essentially been the accepted dogmatic position on papal primacy since this dispute in the early seventeenth century. This papo-centric Counter-Reformation attitude has been characterised as a 'fortress mentality' that has carried through right until our own day.[58] But there were other forces at work that offered a counter-balance to the Bellarmine view of the papacy.

Gallicanism and Febronianism

GALLICANISM HAS A bad name as a result of its subservience to the French monarchy. It is true that this was a key political element. But Gallicanism was also a theological approach to the church's constitution flowing from a specific ecclesiology. This emphasised episcopalism and the need for a strong conciliar tradition, as well as the idea of reception—the notion that acceptance of a teaching by the Catholic community is an essential element in verifying the truth of that teaching. The origins of Gallicanism lie in the dispute between Philip IV and Boniface VIII (see Chapter 6). Gerson and d'Ailly gave the theory a strong conciliarist emphasis during the Great Western Schism. In July 1438 the French church, under monarchical pressure, acted to limit papal authority in France through the Pragmatic Sanction of Bourges. In this the French monarchy asserted its right to administer church property independent of Rome and to nominate candidates to vacant benefices. In 1516 a concordat between Leo X and Francis I replaced the Pragmatic Sanction; this concordat, which remained in force until the French Revolution (1789), gave the king the right to nominate to all major church offices. In the sixteenth and seventeenth centuries a series of French theologians evolved politico-theological theories that limited the authority of the papacy in France over both the church and the bishops. The reforms of Trent were never officially accepted in France, although it was in France that many of the practical reforms of the council were first carried out: an illustration is the establishment of seminaries by St Vincent de Paul (1580–1660) and Jean-Jacques Olier (1608–57).

The core of Gallicanism was expressed in the *Four Articles* of 1682. The *Four Articles* were drawn up by Bishop Jacques Bénigne Bossuet (1627–1704) of Meaux in the dispute between Louis XIV (1643–1715) and Innocent XI (1676–89) over the appointment of bishops and the control of the revenues of vacant French dioceses. The *Four Articles* express the essence of Gallicanism. The first rejects the right of a pope to depose a king, or to interfere either directly or indirectly in civil affairs. The second asserts the full validity of the decrees of the Council of Constance on the superiority of a general council over the pope. The third declares that the actions of the pope are to be regulated by the canons of the church, and in France by the laws and customs of the Gallican church. The fourth is the theological article: it states that in questions of the faith, the pope has the major power of discernment, and his decisions apply to all. But his judgement is not irreformable (infallible) unless the consent and acceptance of the church is given.

The *Four Articles* were condemned by Alexander VIII (1689–91) in 1690. Though they were withdrawn by king and clergy in 1693, Gallicanism was taught right through until the French Revolution in the theology faculties. It certainly remained the accepted stance of French Catholicism until the emergence of nineteenth-century ultramontanism (see Chapter 8). It even spread to the Irish clergy through some of the early French *émigré* lecturers at Maynooth in the revolutionary period. At the First Vatican Council there were still bishops who held Gallican views.

But Gallicanism was more than the bare views articulated in the *Four Articles*. Typical of popular theology textbooks in eighteenth-century France was Dom Jamin's *Pensées Théologiques relatives aux Erreurs du Temps* (1768). He makes it clear that the Roman church is the centre of ecclesial unity and that, while Christ is the supreme head, 'the Roman Pontiff is the ministerial head'. The pope's power was limited by the canons.[59] The importance of episcopalism was also emphasised:

> The bishops are bishops by divine right; they hold their power immediately from Jesus Christ, and not from the sovereign pontiff whose equals they are, except in the primacy, which was established by Christ only to show forth unity . . . They judge with him in matters of faith and discipline, but their jurisdiction is limited by their diocese: whereas that of the Pope has no limits.[60]

The theory of reception of teaching is also a major element in Gallicanism, but Jamin limits it to the episcopate: '[The pope] can make new laws and propose them to the church; but they have not the force of general laws except by the acceptance of his colleagues in the episcopate'.

Febronianism is, to an extent, a kind of German Gallicanism. It was developed by Bishop Johan Nicholas Von Hontheim (1701–90), auxiliary bishop of Trier, writing under the pseudonym Justinius Febronius. Commissioned by the archbishop-electors of Trier, Mainz and Salzburg, Von Hontheim undertook a major historical investigation of the development of papal power. His book *De Statu Ecclesiae* criticised the medieval development of the papacy and advocated keeping as much power as possible at the local level in the hands of the bishops and the civil power. The book was placed on the *Index of Forbidden Books* in 1764. A similar development occurred in Austria, when Joseph II (1765–90) developed what is called Josephism, also a form of political Gallicanism. W. A. Mozart's archbishop, Hieronymus Von Colloredo, was influenced by this movement.[61] Joseph II reformed the church in the Hapsburg territories by closing decrepit and useless monasteries, encouraging education and a simple, straightforward, almost Protestant-like piety among the people. The key issue was that he as an enlightened despot controlled the church in his territories. Fundamentally, both these movements had 'Gallican' tendencies and their supporters wanted to reform the church independent of the papacy: both were strongly opposed to the influence of the Jesuits. Febronianism and Josephism had much in common with Jansenism, although this was, in itself, an independent movement.

The popes of the seventeenth and eighteenth centuries

THE POPES OF this period were, generally speaking, a mediocre group and, as the Enlightenment period progressed, Rome became increasingly irrelevant in European affairs. The seventeenth century had begun well. Gregory XV (1621–23) had reformed the papal election process in another effort to exclude international political influence, he had seen the reimposition of Catholicism on Bohemia and had canonised the great figures of the Counter-Reformation: Teresa of Avila (1515–82), Ignatius Loyola (1491–1556), Philip Neri (1515–95) and Francis Xavier (1506–52). The mention of Xavier reminds us of the foreign missions, and, as we saw, it was Gregory who established the Congregation of Propaganda Fide in 1622 (now the Congregation for the Evangelisation of Peoples) to encourage and guide Catholic efforts in the new worlds of the Americas and Asia. The early work of the congregation was outstanding, although as time went on it became less adventurous.

The first half of the seventeenth century saw the great Baroque creations of Gian Lorenzo Bernini (1598–1680) all over Rome. Urban VIII (1623–44), 'the Barbarini pope whose bees buzz all over Rome', was responsible for the completion of St Peter's and for the extraordinary Bernini carvings of the pregnant niece of the pope on the pedestals of the *baldacchino* over the high altar in St Peter's.[62] It was also Urban VIII who finally forced his friend Galileo Galilei (1564–1642) to abjure the Copernican system and who placed the great scientist under house arrest.

The outstanding pope of the seventeenth century was Innocent XI (1676–89). A holy and frugal man influenced by Jansenism, he restored the papal finances and spent much of his time engaged in a long struggle with Louis XIV over Gallicanism. He also opposed Jesuit influence, although they retained some power in the inquisition. It was Innocent who pulled together an alliance against the Turks, who had again invaded Eastern Europe. The alliance saved Vienna and helped to reconquer Hungary. In the early eighteenth century the popes Clement XI (1700–21), Clement XII (1730–40) and Benedict XIV (1740–58) gave strong support to missionary work, although these three popes saw the question of the Chinese rites come to a head. The Jesuit Matteo Ricci (1552–1610) had arrived in China in 1582, and he had reached Peking by 1601. By their policy of favouring traditional Chinese ceremonies (which they held were basically civil in nature) and the use of indigenous religious terminology, the Jesuits were able to build up a sizeable Christian community among the upper, scholarly classes.[63] The Franciscans and Dominicans came to China in the seventeenth century and they favoured a more proselytising approach among the poor. The Paris Foreign Missionary Society, influenced by the Jansenists, was virulently anti-Jesuit. These orders denounced the Jesuits in Rome, and the 'rites' controversy came to a head in the early eighteenth century, especially under Clement XI. His condemnation of the Jesuit approach was repeated by Clement XII and Benedict XIV. These were very stupid decisions. In China it was perceived as an attack on the imperial dynasty, and it eventually gave grounds for the K'ang Hsi emperor (1662–1723) and his successors to persecute Christians.

The eighteenth-century popes were not impressive.[64] Benedict XIV was very much the enlightened despot. He was conciliatory in his international dealings and had wide scholarly interests and ecumenical tastes. But he was not able to halt the slow decline of the papacy.[65] This was revealed above all in the suppression of the Jesuits by Clement XIV (1769–74) in 1773. Opposition to the Jesuits began among the other religious orders, especially the Dominicans, in the disputes about grace and freedom. This was continued in the Jansenist attack on so-called Jesuit 'moral laxity'. The other orders kept up the pressure through the

Chinese rites controversy. But by the mid-eighteenth century the core of the opposition to the Society had moved into the corrupt Bourbon courts of France, Naples and Spain. The Jesuits were far too independent and influential for the anti-clericalism of the enlightened despots. However, it was from Portugal in 1759 that the Jesuits were first expelled by the Marquis de Pombal (1699–1782). Pombal was an Enlightenment sceptic who was determined to make the church an instrument of the state. The Jesuits stood in the way of this. In 1767 they were deported from Spain and its empire and from Naples and Sicily.

Despite enormous pressure from the Bourbon courts, Clement XIII (1758–69) refused to dissolve the order. It was a different story under his successor, the Franciscan, Clement XIV. He was unable to prevent the partition of Poland in 1772, and failed significantly in international affairs. After a series of delaying manoeuvres that achieved nothing, he published the brief *Dominus ac Redemptor Noster* (1773) decreeing the complete dissolution of the Society of Jesus. The Jesuits were the victims of the failure of papal policy. The destruction of the Society was seen as a victory for 'enlightenment', but it was merely a concession to the threat of schism that the Bourbons held over Rome. Within three decades these same corrupt Bourbons were to be swept away by the enlightened secularists of the French Revolution. They were no loss to anyone. Clement XIV died a year later in deep depression.

The elimination of 23 000 Jesuits was an enormous loss both to the church and to culture in Europe. The Society survived in Germany, Prussia and Russia due to the support of local monarchs who appreciated its educational work. In the United States, as well as England, small groups of Jesuits continued working, so that the tradition was there when the Society was restored in 1814.

Meanwhile the inadequate Pius VI (1775–99) was elected. He faced the challenge of the French Revolution. The first direct conflict with the revolutionary government came over the Civil Constitution of the Clergy (12 July 1790).[66] The ordinance was meant to affect only the civil aspects of the church. It reflects legalist and clerical Gallicanism and is slanted toward 'presbyterianism'. Parish priests would be elected by the parish; bishops were to be elected by *citoyens actifs* (active citizens); and dioceses were to conform to the borders of the new *départements* (civil administrative units). The newly elected bishops were to receive their *institutio canonica* from the metropolitan. The pope would be notified. The church was made a part of the state. Freedom of opinion and religious toleration were guaranteed in the *Declaration of the Rights of Man*. After an oath of fidelity to the Civil Constitution was imposed, the bishops refused their approval and, despite their Gallican leanings, they appealed to the pope. Pius VI stalled for time to see what the attitude of Louis XVI (1754–93) would be; and the king was waiting for the pope! The oath split the clergy. Only seven of the bishops took it; the others refused it and left France. Charles Maurice Tallyrand (1754–1838), the bishop of Autun, assisted by Jean Baptiste Gobel (1724–94), who was to become constitutional archbishop of Paris, set out to consecrate a new episcopate.[67] A majority of the priests took the oath, but many with reservations. The non-jurors, who refused to swear the oath, were expelled from their appointments.

Eventually the pope condemned the Civil Constitution in March 1791. The king was unwilling to break with the papacy, and from this point onward he turned away from the revolution. The new government soon tired of trying to settle the religious issue. But the clerical oath had become identified with patriotism. Non-jurors were identified with *émigrés* and enemies abroad. The new Legislative Assembly decreed that they were to be considered under suspicion of revolt against the law, and in the 1792 September Massacres, 225 priests were executed. On 20 September 1792 the National Convention assumed power. The monarchy was abolished, and in January 1793 King Louis XVI was executed. The Terror became an instrument of state policy under Maximilian Robespierre. The National Convention pushed for total de-Christianisation. By this time the priests and bishops who had supported the Civil Constitution were in an invidious position. They were in schism in a state that was becoming increasingly anti-Christian. A new, pagan calendar was established. The Constitutional church fell apart and a new revolutionary cult was introduced—the cult of Reason. On 8 June 1794 the Feast of the Supreme Being was celebrated in Nôtre Dame.

With the fall of Robespierre and the Termidorian Reaction of mid-1794, the Terror receded. But the principles of the French Revolution had spread to Italy. The newly emerging French general, Napoleon Bonaparte, took Milan in 1796 and then invaded the Papal States and imposed the Peace of Tolentino on Pius VI in February 1797. In February 1798 the Roman Republic was set up and the pope deposed. War broke out again in Italy and, after a brief stint in Florence, Pius VI was taken over the Alps to France.

When Pius died a prisoner in Valence in July 1799, many presumed that the papacy had at last come to an end. But he had left secret instructions for the election of a successor. Ten months later in Venice, Luigi Barnaba Chiaramonte, a Benedictine, was elected with the style Pius VII (1800–23).[68]

The modern age of papal history had begun.

8 The Nineteenth-century papacy

Pius VII (1800–1823) and Napoleon[1]

THE SAVANTS OF the French Enlightenment had assumed that, when he died as a revolutionary prisoner in the summer of 1799, Pius VI would be the last pope. But the year also saw French power in retreat: the Revolutionary General Bonaparte (1769–1821) was trapped in Egypt, and the Austrians controlled northern Italy and the Legations. (The Legations were the north-eastern portion of the Papal States just south of the Po valley, which were administered by papal legates.) The cardinals were scattered across Italy, several of them in financial distress. Nevertheless, there was only a two-month delay before a conclave met in Venice under Austrian protection and influence.

The key issue facing this conclave was the actual survival of the Papal States.[2] The Austrians were determined to expand their empire by holding onto northern Italy, and the Neapolitan kingdom had occupied Rome and the Marches. The Josephist tradition was still strong in Austria, and through the election of a pliant pope, the Hapsburgs hoped to gain control of the papacy. The conclave lasted three and a half months, deadlocked over the election of a pro-Austrian candidate. Eventually, as we saw in Chapter 7, the Benedictine monk Luigi Barnaba

Chiaramonte was elected and took the style Pius VII. He was an excellent choice. The impasse had been broken due to the efforts of the secretary of the conclave, Monsignor Ercole Consalvi (1757–1824).[1a] The new pope immediately appointed him cardinal secretary of state. He was to become the greatest of papal diplomats, and together and separately pope and secretary were to spend the next fifteen years opposing the yet-to-be-proclaimed emperor, Napoleon Bonaparte. Pope Pius quickly removed himself from Austrian influence and returned to Rome, arriving in July 1800.

On the journey to Rome he heard about Napoleon's victory over the Austrians at Marengo (14 June 1800). French power in Italy was now restored. Two years later a peace treaty with Great Britain was signed. The First Consul, Napoleon, was now supreme and he moved quickly to restore relations with the church. Neither Pius nor Consalvi was a reactionary, and the pope had already proclaimed that democracy was compatible with the church. So he was happy to work with the French state. Napoleon himself was hardly a 'good' Catholic: in Egypt he had defended Islam, in France he was a Gallican, and in Italy he often posed as pro-papal. At heart he believed that religion was part of life and he was determined to make it an agent of the law.

Protracted and difficult negotiations were carried on in Paris, first by Monsignor (later Cardinal) Giuseppe Spina and then by Consalvi. On the French side the chief negotiator was the abbé (later cardinal) Bernier, with the French foreign minister, ex-bishop Talleyrand, and a tantrum-throwing Napoleon regularly interfering. An eventual concordat was signed on 15 July 1801, but it was not published until March 1802 with Napoleon's *Organic Articles* attached. The terms of the actual concordat were weighted in favour of France, but there was no suggestion of theological Gallicanism, even if the government behaved in a Gallican way by retaining the right to nominate bishops. Consalvi had wanted Catholicism to be made the state religion, but the most he could obtain was recognition of it as the religion of 'the majority of Frenchmen' and a guarantee of freedom for the church, although this freedom was to be severely limited by police powers contained in the *Organic Articles*. The appointment of parish priests required government approval. Bishops and priests were to be paid by the state. The question of episcopal appointments caused real problems for Rome.[3] Napoleon wanted to eliminate the old episcopate (many of them were still living abroad, especially in England, as *émigrés*). In the brief *Tam Multa* the pope requested all bishops in office to resign within ten days. Most who were resident in France did so. The opposition came from the *émigrés*. Forty-eight bishops resigned and thirty-seven refused. A smaller episcopate was appointed and diocesan boundaries conformed to those of the new *départements*. The high resignation rate was significant: it was a symptom of the end of episcopal Gallicanism.

The *Organic Articles*, which were never agreed to by Consalvi, channelled ecclesiastical communications with Rome through the government, gave control of seminary formation to the First Consul, and applied undefined police regulations to the church, especially to worship. Napoleon simply saw the church as a department of state. The same fate befell the concordat negotiated with the first consul over the Northern Italian Republic. This included the Legations, and there was a feeling among curial conservatives that 'democratic' rulers like Napoleon were satanic and could not be trusted. This was reinforced by Napoleon's civil code which allowed divorce. The danger perceived by conservative cardinals was that the civil code would be applied in the Papal States.

In 1804 Napoleon was immensely popular in France, and so his nomination as emperor by the senate 'by the grace of God and the Will of the people' was supported by a massive vote in France.[4] But Napoleon saw himself differently: he was no democrat, but one of God's elect who was joining the anointed, crowned heads of Europe. The Corsican upstart was the 'new Charlemagne'. That is why he wanted a papal coronation, but it was to be in Nôtre Dame de Paris, not in Rome. The pope would come to him. But there were reservations in Rome, especially with the insultingly brief invitation. It was eventually agreed that 2 December 1804 was to be the date of the coronation. After an exhausting journey across the Alps in a heavy Berlin coach, the pope reached Paris. Jacques Louis David's famous painting of the coronation scene shows Napoleon, having crowned himself, crowning Empress Josephine, with Pius VII looking on slightly bemused, but blessing the event. The pope was popular with the crowd, and he enjoyed his time in Paris. But no concessions were forthcoming from Napoleon. On the slow journey homeward the pope delighted the people he met; here was a pope they could relate to, not like the princes of the eighteenth century. A modern, populist papacy was in the process of being conceived.

Relationships between papacy and empire quickly degenerated.[5] There was tension over the divorce legislation in the civil code and the transference of marriage into the civil sphere. There was further trouble over Pius' refusal to support Napoleon's projected invasion of Britain. In private he called the pope a 'lunatic'. In summer 1806 the Holy Roman Empire was wound up; Napoleon was now supreme. He demanded the abolition of the Papal States. The pope was under enormous pressure, and in June 1806, to placate Napoleon, Consalvi resigned as secretary of state.

The threat of excommunication made Napoleon hesitate, and it was 1808 before he occupied Rome and the remnants of the Papal States. The pope remained ruler of the city and its surrounds. On 17 May 1809 Napoleon declared Rome a 'free imperial city' and abolished the papal government entirely. Pius responded by excommunicating the emperor. In July 1809 the pope was arrested on the initiative of the Rome police chief, General Radet, and was sent secretly to France. It became a bureaucratic nightmare: Napoleon had not approved the arrest and described it as 'a piece of utter folly'. The pope was taken first to Grenoble and then, on the emperor's orders, back to Savona via Avignon.[6] The entire papal government, including the archives, was moved to France,[7] Rome was integrated into the French empire, and Napoleon expected that the pope would establish himself at either Paris or Avignon. The inquisition was closed and the civil code (with its marriage regulations and divorce) applied in the Papal States and Rome. In retaliation, the pope refused to co-operate by canonically instituting bishops appointed by Napoleon. For three years (1809–11), pope and emperor remained at loggerheads. Just after the invasion of Russia began in June 1812, Pius VII was moved on Napoleon's order to Fontainebleau, near Paris. It was a dreadful journey for Pius, who was suffering from a urinary tract infection.

However, by the beginning of 1813, after the Russian disaster, things were changing rapidly. The pope was seen as a 'martyr' even in Protestant England, the younger French clergy were becoming anti-Gallican;

and the emperor was no longer seen as militarily invincible. But just at this moment of possible triumph, the isolated pope gave way to pressure and on 25 January 1813 agreed to a compromising set of 'heads of pro-posals', which Napoleon then published dishonestly as a concordat. But with the return of his old advisers, including Consalvi, the pope repudi-ated the so-called 'Concordat of Fontainebleau'.

It was a short-lived triumph for Napoleon, who had been defeated in October 1813 at the Battle of the Nations near Leipzig. The pope was freed and returned to Rome. He re-entered the city in triumph on 24 March 1814. Napoleon abdicated two weeks later. The pope left Rome briefly during the '100 Days', and returned finally on 7 June 1815.

The Congress of Vienna, the Papal States and the church

CONSALVI WAS ANXIOUS to participate in the peace negotiations with France. The meeting was initially held in Paris; the papal nuncio, Mon-signor Annibale della Gegna, arrived too late to influence events. Con-salvi furiously castigated the man who was later to become Leo XII.

The final defeat of Napoleon at Waterloo in early 1815 brought the kings back to power. But it was a very different Europe over which they now ruled. The principles articulated in the French Revolution and spread by the French armies had created a new consciousness that was to change the course of European history. The final peace settlement was worked out at the Congress of Vienna, which began in March 1815. Consalvi attended, sharing Pius VII's conviction that the restoration of the temporal power in the Papal States was essential in the light of the disasters of the Napoleonic period. But Consalvi did not have an easy time at Vienna. Both the Austrians, who had ambitions in northern Italy, and the French strongly opposed the restoration of the Papal States. The Bourbons and the Hapsburgs were still inherently Gallican and Josephist, and they were against the temporal power of the pope. The sticking point was the Legations which, as Klemens von Metternich (1773–1859), the Austrian chancellor, reminded Consalvi, had been signed away by Pius VI in the Treaty of Tolentino in 1797. It was only Pius VII's enhanced prestige in Europe, and Consalvi's friendship with British foreign secretary Castlereagh, that persuaded the powers to restore the papal dominions. Consalvi had visited London in 1814 and had been received at court. The statesmen of 1815 claimed that they wanted to return to conditions prior to 1789. At Vienna they enunciated the principle of legitimacy: the continuing legitimate rights of kings were to be respected. But their application was not consistent. The Holy Roman Empire was not restored, and it was primarily the legitimate rights of the monarchs of Russia, Austria, Prussia, France and Britain that were respected.

Consalvi's aim at Vienna had been to ensure the neutrality of the papacy by restoring the Papal States, yet at the same time to maintain the legitimist status quo by stamping out liberalism, democracy and freedom of the press. These aims proved to be irreconcilable. E.E.Y. Hales has rightly commented that Consalvi's remarkable achievement at Vienna would later prove to be utterly disastrous.[8] The secretary insisted on keeping the Legations, largely because they were the only economically viable part of the Papal States. But during the Napoleonic regime they had been united with Lombardy, their natural economic, geographic and political setting. Under the French occupation laymen had shared in government, and they did not wish to return to the inefficiency and corruption of the clerical regime.

While Consalvi recognised the need for some reforms in the Papal States, especially in the Legations, he was opposed by the obscurantist *Zelanti* cardinals led by Bartolomeo Pacca, who had shared Pius' exile in France.[9] But the problem was that from the perspective of the educated laity, many of the reforms introduced by the French were a vast improvement on the tradition-bound papal legal and administrative systems. The Papal States became a halter around the pontifical neck and linked the popes psychologically and politically to legitimist ideology. The central issue was the conflation of the spiritual with the temporal. The true interests of the church were sacrificed by the popes of the nineteenth century to the maintenance of a temporal order that was already moribund.[10] This extended to the identification of the fate of the Papal States with that of the universal church. The popes projected their problems with democracy and free speech in the Papal States onto the whole church and condemned these movements everywhere.

An odd contradiction emerged in the life of the church. For much of the century many Catholics rejected the prevailing liberal philosophy of democracy and freedom of expression. In one sense this was a return to the status quo that had existed before the French Revolution—the union of throne and altar. But in another sense it was a new claim: no longer was the church to be subservient to the state, as in the old Gallican and Febronian theories. Rather, it was the duty of the state to protect ecclesiastical rights and exclude any challenge to the doctrinal dominance of the church. The argument ran: if the Roman church was the true church, then the state had an obligation to suppress untruth, especially when it took the forms that threatened Catholicism.

However, in practice, an increasing number of nineteenth-century Catholics rejected the papal doctrine of the right relationship of church and state. In developing liberal-democratic societies like the United States and the Canadian and Australian colonies, Catholics based their claim to freedom of religion, and in British colonies to direct government support, on the liberal principle of equality. The same kind of attitude developed among Catholics in countries like Belgium, Ireland, Britain, Prussia and the German- and Russian-occupied parts of Poland. After the publication of the encyclical of Gregory XVI, *Mirari Vos* (1832), Catholics in the New World and in much of Europe found themselves in the odd situation of claiming a right from their governments that had been outlawed by the pope and that their co-religionists were unwilling to grant in predominantly Catholic countries.

During the nineteenth century the Catholic church became a geographically universal church. In 1800, with the exception of Latin America, the church was almost wholly confined to Europe. By 1900 Catholicism was established on all the continents. The world Catholic population in 1815 was about 118 million, of whom 100 million were in Europe and 15 million in Latin America. By the beginning of the twentieth century the number of Catholics had increased to 382 million, of whom only 194 million were in Europe.[11] This, of course, must be seen within the context of the vast increase in population during this century.

With the growth of European imperialism in Asia, the Pacific and Africa, the foreign missions grew. The Congregation of Propaganda Fide returned to full operation in 1815 and missionary activity was encouraged. Just within the British empire, the achievement of the congregation by 1840 was considerable. Church structures were organised for Upper and Lower Canada, Malta, the Cape of Good Hope and Mauritius, New South Wales, and much of the Pacific. At the same time the relationship between Britain and Ireland was dealt with by the congregation.

This period also saw the restoration of the Jesuit order (1814) and the foundation of a considerable number of new missionary and teaching orders, among the first of which were the Society of the Sacred Heart by St Madeleine Sophie Barat (1800), and the Oblates of Mary Immaculate by St Eugene de Mazenod (1816). The great missionary expansion of the nineteenth and twentieth centuries had begun.

Romanticism and ultramontanism

IDEOLOGICAL FORCES WERE also at work that were to shape the theology and ideology of the papacy over the next 175 years. The roots of 1789 were in the Enlightenment, but the French Revolution was really a bridge period. Overlapping it, a new and dynamic movement swept across Europe—romanticism. The emphasis in the movement was on feeling and nature.[12] Romanticism was initially a reaction against intellectualism and the symmetry of classicism and the industrialisation of Europe. This is quintessentially expressed in the lines from the hymn 'Jerusalem' by William Blake (1757–1827) that speak of the call to 'build Jerusalem in England's green and pleasant land' in stark contrast to the 'dark satanic mills'.

Romanticism also found expression in a religious revival. In a sense ultramontanism is a manifestations of romanticism within Catholicism. The term 'ultramontanism' is derived from *ultra montes*, beyond the mountains, in this case the European Alps. The ultramontanist looks over the Alps from Western and Northern Europe to papal Rome for inspiration. Ultramontanism originates in France and taps into the anti-revolutionary and reactive aspects of romanticism. Its origins lie in the philosophy of traditionalism.[13] The key writers of this movement were Louis de Bonald (1754–1840), Joseph de Maistre (1754–1821), and

Hugues Felicité Robert de Lamennais (1782–1854). De Bonald and de Maistre were nobles who spent many years in exile; their attitude to revolution was profoundly sour. The traditionalist movement gives expression to the longing for peace, stability and security that was common among the emerging middle class in the early nineteenth century. It was a reaction against the French Revolution. Traditionalists argued that it was by adherence to a perennial tradition that truth and stability were maintained in society. Revolutions were wrong because they interfered with the transmission of this truth. Family and state were both God-given, and there was an indissoluble union between church and monarchy.

De Maistre was more a political theorist than a theologian. He wanted to destroy the 'twin evils' of revolution and nationalism. His most important work was *Du Pape* (1819), where he says that the Revolution '*est satanique dans son essence*' (is satanic in its essence). He did not merely want to restore the status quo before 1789 for he was opposed to Gallicanism, which he equated with 'Anglicanism'. The key to his political philosophy is the idea of sovereignty. Subjects are bound to obey the sovereign government for it must be assumed to be right; it is, in a practical sense, 'infallible'. He held that religious truths are also social truths and they exist for the common good. For this reason the practical 'infallibility' of government becomes the absolute 'infallibility' of faith. He saw the infallible papacy as the symbol of spiritual authority, and monarchy as the symbol of temporal authority. For De Maistre the Catholic church was the one safeguard of political stability. These untheological and patently absurd views had considerable influence on the development of French, and later European, ultramontanism. Although the roots of ultramontanism lie further back, the real origins of the movement lie in this conflation of papalism with traditionalism in the early nineteenth century. Two other interesting elements of ultramontanism are that, firstly, it largely identified the ecclesial with the political and that, secondly, in origin it was primarily a lay movement. The lay tradition was to be continued by the journalist Louis Veuillot, who in the 1850s and 1860s became the leader of French ultramontanism.

Linked to these ideas is the book by Count Francois René Chateaubriand (1768–1848), *Génie du christianisme*, published in 1802. Chateaubriand attempted to negate the Enlightenment's rationalist attack on Christianity by transferring the debate about religion from the realm of reason to that of feeling. He argues that Christianity is true because it is beautiful. A similar current is present in the Protestant thinker Friedrich Schleiermacher (1768–1834), who defines religion as 'a sense and taste for the infinite'.

It was Lamennais who brought the ambiguities latent in ultramontanism into focus. Unlike the other traditionalists, Lamennais was a priest, ordained in 1816. His life was characterised by illness and a morbid disposition, and his intellectual development by changes of opinion. He began as a traditionalist, and in the first volume (of four) of his *Essai sur l'indifférence en matière de religion* (1817) he condemned the right of private judgement and called for the restoration of Catholicism as the religion of the French state. He saw ecclesiastical authority as essential for right order in society. But unlike the other traditionalists, he gradually became sceptical of royalist regimes and moved in the direction of an ultramontanist democratic theocracy presided over by the pope. These ideas were expressed in *Les Progrès de la révolution et de la guerre contre l'église* (1828). Here he called for the church to free itself from the restored Bourbon monarchy and to abandon its privileges. Leo XII invited him to Rome and was ready to make him a cardinal; Lamennais refused. A group of young intellectuals (Charles de Montelambert, Henri Lacordaire and Prosper Guéranger) gradually formed around him, and they founded the newspaper *L'Avenir*. Its motto was 'God and liberty'. The French bishops, especially those with Gallican leanings, were particularly annoyed and put pressure on Rome to silence the troublesome abbé. It was Gregory XVI who did precisely that.

The popes before Pius IX[14]

THE TRADITIONALIST MOVEMENT provided a context for the restored papacy. When Pius VII returned to Rome in 1815, he not only faced the task of restoring the Papal States; he also faced a church in chaos as a result of the long interruption of the papal government. To return order to church–state relationships, concordats were negotiated with Prussia (1821) and Russia (1818), and the 1801 concordat with France was renewed (without the *Organic Articles*). In 1822 the papacy recognised the independence of the Latin American republics. When he died in 1823, Pius VII had restored the reputation of the papacy and had turned Rome again into an international and artistic capital.

After his death the tentatively moderate regime in the Papal States was abolished. A difficult conclave followed, at which the erstwhile nuncio in Paris, della Gegna, was elected with *Zelanti* support (these were generally reactionary cardinals who wanted a 'non-political' pope), and took the style Leo XII (1823–29). The 'liberal' Consalvi lost the secretariat of state; he was briefly pro-prefect and then prefect of Propaganda and died in 1824. With Leo XII the nineteenth-century papacy, properly speaking, begins. He saw himself as a religious rather than a political pope. He set a pattern that was to be followed by his successors: his encyclical letter *Ubi Primum* (1824) denounced contemporary errors, the rising influence of liberalism and the de-Christianisation of society. The Papal States reverted to an economically stultified police state. During the brief and slightly more open regime of Pius VIII (1829–30), Catholic Emancipation was passed in the United Kingdom (13 April 1829), and the United States bishops held their first provincial synod. He was succeeded by a Camaldolese monk and former prefect of propaganda, Bartolomeo Alberto Cappellari, who was elected with the style Gregory XVI (1831–46).

Under Leo XII the situation in the Papal States got increasingly worse. The Sanfedisti, or Army of the Holy Faith, a kind of papal guerrilla movement that had begun in 1799, was reactivated, and it worked to stem the growth of the anti-clerical secret societies, generally called the *Carbonari*. The struggle between the two led to civil unrest, especially in the Ravenna area. Despite executions and oppressive measures by the cardinal legates, the papal government was unable to suppress revolt. This came to a head in Bologna in February 1829 at the time of the election of Pius VIII. The same thing happened when the legates were absent again for the conclave of 1830–31. Most of these revolts were led by laymen of aristocratic birth. Anti-clericalism centred in the upper classes and among the bourgeoisie, especially in the Legations. In Rome and the *Patrimonium Petri* the papal government was still reasonably popular. The key point of opposition was hostility to priestly control. Increasingly the presence of the Austrians north of the Po in Lombardy became a key element in internal affairs in the Papal States, and the government of Gregory XVI invited Vienna to use its forces to suppress the second revolt. The Austrian occupation of northern Italy was itself colonial in nature and was deeply resented by Italians throughout the century.

Gregory XVI was austere and resolutely anti-modern. Kelly notes he even banned railways in the Papal States, calling them *chemins d'enfer* (ways of hell)![15] He was opposed to Italian nationalism and as pope did not hesitate to use the Austrians for protection. To safeguard their interests in Italy, the French also intervened, and both powers maintained a military presence in the Papal States until 1838. Throughout Gregory's papacy there were revolts and civil strife. The papal army was made up largely of expensive foreign mercenaries who were a drain on the papal exchequer. Increasingly the Papal States were seen as 'the sick man' of Europe.

The pope was as intransigent theologically as he was politically. In 1799 he had published *The Triumph of the Holy See and the Church against the Attacks of the Innovators*. In this he advocated papal infallibility and the maintenance of the Papal States. As prefect of Propaganda in 1830, he had condemned the liberal revolts that broke out in Catholic Belgium against the Protestant Dutch monarchy, and in Catholic Poland against the Orthodox tsar. Previously the Catholic Irish had been told by the Propaganda Fide Congregation in 1814 that they should not be concerned if the Protestant king of England had veto power over episcopal appointments in Ireland. Pope Gregory was utterly opposed to liberalism because he saw God, not the people, as the source of all sovereignty. His experience of democratic ideas in his own state soured him against all forms of human freedom, in both theory and practice. He was convinced that liberalism was rooted in indifference, and his opposition to all forms of it came to a head in his condemnation of Lamennais.

Calling themselves 'pilgrims of liberty', Lamennais and his friends Montelambert and Lacordaire had gone to Rome in November 1831 to obtain the approval of Gregory XVI for their movement. There was something naive about their expectations; it is hard to believe they were unaware of the ecclesiastical machinations going on around them. While Lamennais was still in Rome, the pope condemned the Polish revolt; Lamennais' own condemnation soon followed. In March 1832 in Munich he received the encyclical letter *Mirari Vos*, which was directed against him. In it the pope explicitly condemned all forms of Catholic liberalism and especially

> the evil smelling spring of indifferentism . . . [from which flows] the erroneous and absurd opinion—or rather, derangement—that freedom of conscience must be asserted for everybody. This most pestilential error opens the door to the complete and immoderate liberty of opinions, which works such widespread harm in both church and state.[16]

Hales correctly comments that Gregory condemned Lamennais because liberal principles could not be applied in the Papal States.[17] The full tragedy of Lamennais was played out when he died in 1854 unreconciled with the church.

While Gregory encouraged reactionary regimes in Europe, in the new world the church was growing apace. In the United States, Canada and Australia Catholicism began to prosper in free, liberal societies. Gregory encouraged the missionary movement, whose impetus really began during his papacy. He established new dioceses and vicariates, approved a large number of new missionary orders of both men and women, helped in the reorganisation of others, condemned the slave trade, and even encouraged the training of indigenous clergy and local hierarchies in mission territories. In Rome he also encouraged archaeological research. Yet despite these positive notes, this papacy showed no comprehension of the forces at work in the nineteenth century. Sadly, Gregory strongly reinforced the pattern of the alienation of the church from modern culture.

The papacy of Pius IX (1846–1878)[18]

GREGORY DIED IN 1846. Giovanni Maria Mastai-Ferretti, the bishop of Imola, was elected, taking the style Pius IX. He had the reputation of being a liberal. He had been critical of the papal government and had shown sympathy with Italian national aspirations. Citizens of the Papal States were delighted when he planned for railways and street lighting and declared an amnesty for prisoners. He allowed some freedom of the press and of assembly, and set up a consulta (consultative assembly) in October 1847. It looked as though he would fulfil at least some of Lamennais' dreams and unite Italy. But the reality was, of course, that Pope Pius was being swept along by his popularity; feeling rather than intelligence always dominated his practical judgement and, as Metternich correctly observed, it was impossible for the pope to share his absolute rule with a democratic assembly. As Pius quickly learned, the spiritual and the temporal were so intimately intermixed in the Papal States that it was impossible to sort them out.

The year 1848 was one of revolutions throughout Europe.[19] But most of these were quickly overthrown or subverted. In Paris in February, King Louis Philippe gave up without a fight; he was replaced by Bonaparte's nephew Louis Napoleon, who by the end of 1848 was president of the republic and by 1852 had been proclaimed emperor as Napoleon III (1852–70). In Frankfurt there was a series of revolts and in Berlin there were widespread riots. These were quickly suppressed. In the Austrian empire there was a revolt in Hungary and unrest elsewhere, which led to the fall of Chancellor Metternich. But eventually imperial rule was reimposed. In both Naples and Lombardy revolts broke out. But Austria soon regained control in northern Italy.

Rome also was affected by revolutionary pressures. The democratic assembly in Rome became increasingly liberal. The pope's premier, Count Pellegrino Rossi, was assassinated, and on 24 November 1848 Pius IX fled to Gaeta in Neapolitan territory. A revolutionary republic was established in Rome by the anti-clericals Giuseppe Mazzini and Giuseppe Garibaldi. They invoked a 'new religious synthesis of God and the People'. World attention was focused upon them. It was the newly established French republic, under the influence of the former secret society member Louis Napoleon, that came to the rescue of the pope. The city was retaken in July 1849, and the pope returned in the spring of 1850. At Gaeta the pope had appointed a lay cardinal (he was eventually ordained to the deaconate), Giacomo Antonelli (1806–76), as secretary of state. It was he who had obtained French help for the recapture of Rome.[20] His financial dealings were suspect, and at the time of his death curial finances were in disorder.

Pius IX should not be seen as a simple reactionary, dominated by Antonelli and the Jesuits. He was more a man of feeling than of thought, and he correctly intuited the increasingly conservative mood of the European bourgeoisie. He also recognised the shift within nineteenth-century Catholicism toward a more feeling-based religiosity that focused on Marian piety; apparitions, centring on the pilgrimage shrines of La Salette (1846) and Lourdes (1858); and devotion to the Sacred Heart, the Blessed Sacrament, and other aspects of the humanity of Jesus.[21] The pope had proposed the definition of the Immaculate Conception before the 1848 revolution. He sought the opinion of the bishops through the encyclical *Ubi Primum* (February 1849), although there was no formal process of episcopal consultation. The actual definition occurred on 8 December 1854. It began a century of intense devotion to the Blessed Virgin within Catholicism. These more tactile devotions became spiritually linked to the promotion of ultramontanism, so that the two went together. Saint-making was also a characteristic of this papacy. Although the Society of Jesus had only been re-established some three decades previously, the order's influence grew in this papacy, and a Jesuit, Carlo Maria Curci, founded the autonomous but semi-official papal newspaper *La Civilta Cattolica* in 1850.

The role of Antonelli was also significant. He acted until 1870 as a kind of papal 'prime minister', and it was under him that the post-1848 Papal States were restored. But this arrangement was only to survive for another decade. With the collapse of the Roman republic, leadership in the movement for Italian unification passed to Turin and the Piedmontese monarchy. A new and popular feeling of *italianita* (Italianness) was spreading. The prime minister of Piedmont, Count Camillo Cavour (1810–61), was the ruthless pragmatist who turned *italianita* into the reality of Italy. Much of the papal opposition to Turin's sponsorship of the Risorgimento (the Italian-unification movement) was based on its secular legislation and anti-clericalism. Cavour was determined to control northern Italy and integrate the Legations into Piedmont, and he was strongly opposed to any form of confederation of Italian states under papal leadership.

As a result of the defeat of the Austrians at Solfarino and Margenta in 1859, Lombardy, Tuscany, Parma, Moderna, the Legations and Umbria become part of a united Italy under the Piedmontese monarchy. To protect the Papal States Pius had commissioned the Belgian Monsignor Frederic de Mérode as minister for war to raise a volunteer army; this move was opposed by Antonelli, who realised that it would annoy Napoleon III. The Neapolitan kingdom collapsed in 1860 before the irregular forces of Garibaldi, and was also absorbed into the Italian kingdom. To stop him marching on Rome, which would have brought France into the conflict, Piedmont seized the Marches and Umbria, and defeated Mérode's volunteers. By year's end all that was left to the pope was the *Patrimonium Petri*. This was protected until 1870 by a French force, assisted by volunteer papal Zouaves.

After the downfall of Napoleon III following the Franco-Prussian War, the French garrison was withdrawn and, after token resistance by papal forces, Italian troops occupied Rome on 20 September 1870. The pope was offered the Law of Guarantees in 1871 by the Italian government, which gave him possession of the Vatican and other Roman buildings and granted him important immunities. He refused this offer and retired to the Vatican. The Roman question was not settled until 1928.

Pius IX and the church

THE GRADUAL LOSS of the Papal States in many ways set the scene for the latter part of Pius' papacy. The pope perceived this as an assault on the church and as a direct result of modern errors and attitudes. Throughout the nineteenth century there had been repeated condemnations of modern thought. The loss of everything except the *Patrimonium Petri*, and the anti-Catholic measures of the Piedmontese government, persuaded the pope to issue the *Syllabus of Errors* and the encyclical *Quanta Cura* on 8 December 1864. The other immediate occasion was the Catholic

Congress at Malines in 1863. Inspired by French and Belgian liberal
Catholics, over three thousand people gathered at the Malines Congress
and called for 'a free church in a free state'. The *Syllabus of Errors* was
drawn up by the Barnabite priest (later cardinal) Luigi Bilio. Antonelli
was opposed to issuing it for political reasons. It was a confusing document and did not bear Pius' signature, but it represented the pope's
view and was symptomatic of his alienation from the modern world. Its
essence was expressed in the last error condemned: that 'The Roman
Pontiff can and ought to reconcile himself with progress, with liberalism,
and with modern civilisation'. The *Syllabus of Errors* was a grab-bag of
propositions condemned in encyclicals and speeches of the pope, and it
covered topics such as rationalism, pantheism, indifferentism, socialism,
secret societies, Bible societies, the rights of the church and the pope's
civil power.[22] Its sources often referred to quite specific situations, but
listing them altogether gave the impression of an entirely negative
response by Rome to the contemporary world. In fact, it was an attack
on liberal Catholics and liberalism everywhere but, as Antonelli had
argued, it was an error of judgement in view of the opposition, misunderstanding and difficulties that it caused for Catholics in democratic
countries.[23]

Another aspect of the Pius IX papacy was that Rome again became
a pilgrimage centre. Transportation made travel easier and pilgrims
flocked to the city. The influence of the new ultramontanism enhanced
the influence of the papacy in the church. Roman centralisation grew,
not only bureaucratically, but also through the religious orders moving
their headquarters to Rome, the establishment of many new orders of
pontifical right, and the building of national seminaries in Rome where
elite diocesan students were trained for the priesthood and imbibed
the *Romanita* (the Roman spirit). Many of them subsequently became
bishops.[24] The Congregation of Propaganda Fide continued its leadership
in missionary work under its long-lasting prefect, Cardinal Alessandro
Barnabo. The nineteenth and early twentieth centuries saw the greatest
missionary expansion in the history of Catholicism and Christianity.
Propaganda Fide encouraged this, and hundreds of new dioceses and
vicariates were set up in the British, French and German colonies, and
in Asia and Africa, as well as the United States, Canada and even Europe

itself. Pius IX re-established the English hierarchy in 1850 and the Dutch hierarchy in 1853. Concordats were negotiated with Russia, Spain, Austria and the Latin American republics.

The First Vatican Council (1869–1870)[25]

THE MOST IMPORTANT EVENT of the papacy of Pius IX was the First Vatican Council. There was widespread questioning in the nineteenth century of basic Christian beliefs. Because of this there was mounting pressure in the church for the reassertion of the fundamental dogmatic basis of Christianity. The idea of a council was first suggested in 1849 as a way of achieving this; certainly the pope began to talk to some of the cardinals about it from December 1864 onwards. Pius was also influenced by the growing influence of neo-ultramontanism. The term 'neo-ultramontanism' was coined by Wilfred Ward to characterise the more extreme nineteenth-century movement in contrast to 'traditional' ultramontanism represented by Bellarmine.[26] On 26 June 1867 Pius IX announced his intention of holding a council, and he set 8 December 1869 for the opening. In a ham-fisted but well-intentioned move, all Orthodox bishops were invited to return to Roman unity so that they could attend the council. Anglicans and Protestants were also invited to submit.

In the lead-up to the council it was the neo-ultramontanes who were best organised. They focused on one aim: the most extreme possible definition of infallibility, passed by acclamation without debate. The leaders of this movement were Henry Edward Manning, archbishop of Westminster, Ignaz von Senestrey, bishop of Regensberg, Victor Deschamps, archbishop of Malines and Conrad Martin, bishop of Paterborn; but there were many other supporters from France and Italy and to a much lesser extent from non-Hapsburg Germany. Neo-ultramontanism developed among those who saw the pope as the last stronghold of authority and stability. A strong apocalyptic note, derived from De Maistre and traditionalism, sounded in this movement. Theologically, the neo-ultramontanes wanted to make everything that the pope said infallible. They held a very different view to the moderate ultramontanes of the Bellarmine variety.

Neo-ultramontanes happily used the popular press; and their views lent themselves to the journalistic 'theology' typified by Louis Veuillot's newspaper *L'Univers*. This paper was held in high regard by Pius IX. Veuillot had a stranglehold on the mindset of most of the French clergy.[27] Unlike the treatment of Lamennais by Gregory XVI, Veuillot was encouraged by Pius IX, even to the extent of supporting him against the French bishops.[28] Cuthbert Butler speaks of Veuillot's 'entirely untheological extravagances'. Typical is this extraordinary statement referring to the pope: 'We all know certainly one thing, that is that no man knows anything except the Man with whom God is forever, the Man who carries the thought of God. We must unswervingly follow his inspired directions.'[29] Such heresies were never contradicted by Pius IX nor by anyone in the curia.

In England most bishops were cautious ultramontanists, but a form of extreme neo-ultramontanism was promoted by Archbishop Henry Edward Manning of Westminster and the layman William George Ward, through both *The Tablet* and the *Dublin Review*.[30] Both were converts, and Manning had a curious ability to identify his own ideas with those of God. W. G. Ward was Manning's theologian, and Butler describes him as 'prone to adopt positions of extreme intransigence'.[31] Ward's position was simply that the pope's every doctrinal statement was infallibly directed by God. In Italy the neo-ultramontanist position was held by *La Civilta Cattolica*, especially after the sacking of its founder, the Jesuit Curci.

The position of the Roman curia was, interestingly, more complex. There was some opposition from within it to the definition. Secretary of State Antonelli, for instance, was an inopportunist on political grounds. Hasler claims that a considerable number of senior curialists and other important bishops were opposed to the definition of infallibility, and that there was understandable fear in the curia of the results of a council, including the possibility of schism.[32] Hasler's figures are probably inflated, but there certainly was quiet opposition among a minority in the curia and papal household. The majority of the bishops followed Bellarmine and belonged to the moderate ultramontane school, even if they had not articulated that view as their own. Many saw the great danger in simply defining the doctrine by acclamation without discussion, as was promoted by the neo-ultramontanes. Even the Roman universities generally held a moderate ultramontane view. They accepted infallibility but they wanted it carefully limited. This view ultimately prevailed, at least on infallibility.

A sizeable minority of bishops at the First Vatican Council opposed the definition. There were two groups: those who had theological reservations about infallibility, and those who considered the timing of the definition inopportune. The first group was small. There were a few French Gallicans like Bishop Henri Maret, dean of theology at the Sorbonne, Augustin Verot, bishop of Savannah, Georgia, USA, and Felix de las Casas, bishop of Constantine and Hippo in Algeria.[33] Several others had their own theological objections. The most significant was the learned historian bishop Karl Josef Hefele of Rottenberg. Between 1855 and 1875 he published a seven-volume history of the councils.[34] Hefele did important work as a consulter in Rome before the council, and Butler thinks that he was one of the few who seriously questioned the doctrine of papal infallibility.[35] It is significant that this questioning came from the best historian at the council.

The German priest Johann Ignaz Von Döllinger (1799–1890), professor of history at Munich, had considerable external influence on the council. He began as an ultramontane, but gradually moved to opposing infallibility. The call in *La Civilta Cattolica* for infallibility by acclamation, and the extremism of people like Manning and Veuillot, worried Döllinger. He wrote a series of articles, published in book form as *The Pope and the Council* under the pseudonym Janus, attacking the whole institution of the papacy from the Middle Ages onwards with its political pretensions, curial centralisation and ultramontanism. He feared that a form of neo-ultramontanism would be defined. His book caused tremendous discussion in Germany.

Most of the rest of the minority bishops believed in a moderate infallibility, but considered it was inopportune to define it at that particular time. Certainly, they were opposed to the neo-ultramontanes and were supported by liberal Catholics everywhere. Many of these bishops were in touch with the broader non-Catholic world, and they did not want to create further alienation between the church and culture. They also believed that it was dangerous for the papacy to be divorced from the context of the church and the magisterium (teaching authority) of the bishops. These issues troubled, among many others, prelates like Cardinals Freidrich von Schwarzenberg of Prague, Josef Othmar Rauscher of Vienna, Filippo Maria Guidi of Bologna, all of the Hungarian bishops, Archbishop Peter Richard Kenrick of St Louis (who, like many of the US bishops, was concerned about the obstacle that infallibility would create for Protestants), Bishop Felix Dupanloup of Orleans, Bishop David Moriarty of Kerry, and the famous pan-Slavic and Croatian nationalist Bishop Josef Georg Strossmayer of Bosnia, Slovenia and Sirmium (Djakovo in modern Eastern Slovenia).[36]

Vatican I was the largest council ever held: Butler says that by the end of December 1869 there were 800 fathers present.[37] This number seems inflated; the average attendance was between 600 and 700. Both Butler and Hales say that there were about 200 bishops from Italy representing about 30 million Catholics.[38] Germany and central Europe, in contrast, were represented by about 60 bishops and a Catholic population of 70 million. Döllinger questioned the ecumenicity of the council because of the preponderance of bishops from Italy and Spain; there is no doubt that Germany and the Hapsburg territories were under-represented. The minority opposed to infallibility amounted to about 140.[39]

The council began on 8 December 1869. The preponderance of the neo-ultramontanes was shown early at the second general congregation, of 14 December 1869. A totally pro-infallibilist deputation De Fide (on theology and dogma) was elected. Not a single member of the minority was on it, except Archbishop Johannes Simor of Esztergom, Hungary, who was on the pro-infallibilist list by mistake! The task of the deputation De Fide was to revise the theological schemas according to the comments of the bishops; the final wording of texts was decided by the deputation. Manning was primarily responsible for the political manoeuvres that led to this. The English Bishop William Ullathorne commented that 'All the cautious people, as opposed to the *Zelantes*, feel that the Archbishop's [Manning's] rooms are the centre of a determined intrigue, and that if they get their committee it is because they are organised, restlessly active, and have the strongest backing'.[40] Butler admits that this biased election was 'a serious blot on [the council's] doings', but he excuses the pope, saying it was against his wishes.[41] If that is the case, why did Pius IX not do something about it? Hasler accuses the pro-infallibilists of manipulation.[42] Certainly, it hindered the council's freedom and destroyed the possibility of reaching moral unanimity. In the first months of 1870 there were widespread complaints about procedure: there was no time limit on speeches, many of which were rhetorical exercises in florid Latin, and because of conditions in the aula (the council was held in the area behind the high altar of St Peter's Basilica) many of the speeches could not be heard. There was no clear agenda and many felt there was no real discussion, just set-piece speeches.

Vatican I produced only two documents: the dogmatic constitution on the Catholic faith (*Dei Filius*) and the dogmatic constitution on the church (*Pastor Aeternus*).[43] *Dei Filius* originally came to the council on 10 December 1869 as a schema on Catholic doctrine against the errors of the day. It was severely criticised by the bishops; Rauscher of Vienna said it was 'too long and elaborate, too abstract and obscure, and that it did not meet the needs of the times'.[44] The pope and the curia were surprised by the vehemence of the rejection, and on 10 January it was sent back to the deputation to be rewritten. It was returned on 18 March. One hundred and seven bishops spoke, and the constitution was finally passed on 24 April 1870.

It is not a particularly impressive document. It condemns pantheism and materialism and asserts God's creativity. God can be known by the light of natural reason but faith, inspired by the Holy Spirit, leads to a knowledge of God's revelation. Faith is a free act that finds its fullest expression in membership of the Catholic church which, itself, is a witness to faith. However, the third chapter contains a statement that has had vast repercussions for the contemporary church. It introduces the term 'ordinary and universal magisterium'. This is now juxtaposed with the term 'infallible magisterium', so that the pope can exercise both an ordinary and an extraordinary magisterium. The statement in *Dei Filius* is almost hidden away:

Wherefore, by divine and catholic faith all those things are to be believed which are contained in the word of God as found in scripture and tradition, and which are proposed by the church as matters to be believed as divinely revealed, whether by her solemn judgement or in her ordinary and universal magisterium.[45]

The history of the term 'ordinary magisterium' is interesting.[46] It first appeared in a papal document in the letter *Tuas Libenter* to Archbishop Gregor von Scherr of Munich in December 1863. Von Scherr had allowed Döllinger to organise a conference of Catholic scholars in Munich, and he was rebuked by Pius IX for this. The term 'ordinary magisterium' had been coined by the Jesuit theologian Josef Kleutgen (1811–83), one of the redactors of *Dei Filius*. Through him the term passed into the conciliar decree.

The final chapter of *Dei Filius* asserts that there can be no disagreement between faith and reason. It says that any appearance of contradiction is 'specious', for it is the result of the fact that the human reason is mistaken or has embraced unsound views.[47] The church alone determines 'the truth of enlightened faith . . . Hence all faithful Christians are forbidden to defend as the legitimate conclusions of science those opinions that are known to be contrary to the doctrine of faith, particularly if they have been condemned by the church'.[48] Thus the source of all truth is faith as defined by the magisterium.

The council discussed reforms of ecclesiastical discipline, which were debated between 10 January and 18 March. These 'disciplinary schemata were subjected to the same fire of criticism as the dogmatic schema'.[49] In the light of Vatican II some of these discussions were prescient. The first reform schema was *De Episcopis*. It was attacked by Cardinals Schwarzenberg of Prague and Melchers of Cologne and Archbishop Darboy of Paris as far too theoretical and lacking any real sense of the bishops' status and position in the church. Both Melchers and Schwarzenberg spoke of over-centralisation in Rome and of the need to reform the curia. Eastern patriarchs and bishops were also concerned, especially with the strong centralising tendencies of the Congregation of Propaganda Fide and its prefect Barnabo. The patriarch of the Chaldeans, Joseph Audu, was 'scolded' by the pope for defending Easterners against the Latin regime and Western canon law. The revised schema *De Episcopis* was never returned to the floor of the council.

The debate on the schema on papal primacy and infallibility began on 13 May 1870. Two versions of the schema that eventually became *Pastor Aeternus* had already been circulated and written comments submitted. On 27 April the deputation De Fide began recasting the schema in the light of these written comments. The theologians of the deputation produced a report strongly favouring ultramontanism. They argued that infallibility was part of original revelation and that therefore historical problems were apparent rather than real.

The debate on the schema as a whole began on 15 May. This was the decisive debate. It lasted until foreclosure on 6 June; sixty-five bishops spoke, thirty-nine in favour, twenty-six against. The major objections were that infallibility was not part of the apostolic tradition but, as Verot said, 'was an opinion introduced by piety and zeal'.[50] Cardinal Schwarzenberg and Bishop William Clifford of Clifton, England, argued that both primacy and infallibility could not be considered apart from a theology of the church. The Eastern rite bishops stressed that the doctrine would place an insurmountable obstacle to reunion with the Orthodox. In a clear reference to Veuillot, Archbishop Darboy of Paris said that the bishops were being forced against their better judgement to define infallibility by demagogues outside the council. He stressed that he opposed a definition that emphasised a personal and separate papal infallibility, cut off from the context of the church. A number of bishops pointed out that the doctrine would alienate Protestants and prevent conversions because the doctrine would be intolerable to people of goodwill.

Two of the most telling speeches were delivered by Bishops Hefele and Maret. Hefele argued that the orthodoxy of Leo the Great's *Tome*, which was an *ex cathedra* (infallible) statement, was actually judged to be orthodox by the bishops at Chalcedon. True to his historical training, he also argued that the pro-infallibilists could not posit the doctrine as revealed and then argue that historical facts to the contrary could be dismissed. He forcefully referred to the condemnation of Honorius I (625–38) by the Third Council of Constantinople. Maret was reproved by the president, Cardinal Bilio, when he argued that if the council declared the pope to be infallible, the council was, *ipso facto*, superior to the pope. This, said Bilio, was intolerable. The council was merely confirming rights the pope already had.

The best arguments for the definition were put by Archbishop Deschamps of Malines. He stressed that infallibility was not personal and absolute, but that it belonged to the papal office and could only be exercised under strict conditions. This was to be borne out in the actual definition. When Manning spoke, he said that as the only convert in the council he was sure that infallibility, far from being an obstacle to conversion, was

> a powerful attraction for those outside the church. The religious Protestant mind in England desired an escape from the confusion and chaos of the innumerable sects, and the lack of any tribunal able to teach with authority . . . the definition will more than anything else promote conversions and the return of [England] to the faith.[51]

Manning said that infallibility was already a Catholic doctrine and 'all are already obliged to hold it'.[52]

Following this general debate, the council turned to the specific question of the primacy; this discussion lasted from 6 June to 13 July. Butler admits that papal primacy is more of an ecumenical problem than infallibility.[53] The basic reason for this was pointed out by many bishops at the council: the ecclesiology of the council was defective and incomplete. 'Here . . . is a summary of Catholic doctrine on the church in which there is no account taken of the hierarchy, episcopate, ministry, ecumenical councils: simply church and pope.'[54] '*Stupefacti sumus*' (We are astonished), said one bishop. A recast schema on the church, including an emphasis on the role of bishops, was prepared, but the council was prorogued before it saw the light of day.

The first two chapters (on Peter and the continuation of the Petrine primacy in the popes) caused little discussion. It was the third chapter on the definition and extent of the primacy that caused most controversy. The fact of the primacy was accepted by the vast majority. But the problem was that there was no context for it. In fact, there is a sense in which primacy was not carefully considered at Vatican I. The bishops were under enormous pressure, not just from the pope, the curia and demagogues like Veuillot, but also from pressure to deal with the agenda quickly. This came from internal forces in the council, but also from the outside. These debates about papal power were occurring as the strategic pressure of Italian unification was growing on the remnants of the Papal States. The Franco-Prussian War broke out on 18 July 1870, the day the council ended. Within two months of being declared infallible, Pius IX lost Rome to a united Italy.

The primacy question quickly focused on two issues: the meaning of the 'ordinary and immediate' jurisdiction of the pope, and the role of the episcopate in the church. The word 'ordinary' here is used in the canonical sense meaning 'not delegated'. In other words it means that the power of the office comes with the office itself; one has the power if one has the office. The word 'immediate' means that the pope can act directly in any part of the church; he does not have to go through another person or body. This sense of absolute power was reinforced when, in what Butler describes as a serious mistake by the deputation De Fide, a clause strengthening papal power even more was suddenly introduced into the canon at the end of the chapter on primacy without debate.[55] The purpose of the canon was to sum up the chapter. The clause inserted is in italics:

> If anyone says that the Roman pontiff has merely an office of super-
> vision and guidance, and not the full and supreme power of jurisdic-
> tion over the whole church, and this is not only in matters of faith and
> morals, but also those which concern the discipline and government
> of the church dispersed throughout the whole world; *or that he only
> has the principal part, but not the absolute fullness, of this supreme power*; or
> that this power of his is not ordinary and immediate both over all and
> each of the churches and over all and each of the pastors and faithful:
> let him be anathema.[56]

In this purely legal definition, power in the church is completely centralised in the pope.

The debate on the schema on infallibility began on 15 June and ended on 4 July. Key minority speeches came from Cardinals Rauscher and Filippo Maria Guidi of Bologna. Rauscher emphasised the formula of St Antoninus (1389–1459), a Dominican theologian at the Council of Florence, and later archbishop of Florence. 'The successor of St Peter using the counsel and seeking the help of the universal church, cannot err.'[57] Rauscher also emphasised that infallibility cannot be divorced from the indefectibility of the church. Guidi was also a Dominican. He argued that the pope was not personally and in and of himself infallible, but only within the context of the church's belief and only to the extent that the pope's teaching reflected that of bishops and theologians. It was another attempt to keep infallibility within the context of the church. Both Butler and Hasler report that Guidi was upbraided by Pius IX for his speech.

Against this emphasis on episcopal consultation, Cardinal Paul Cullen of Dublin stressed the specific authority conferred on Peter by Christ. But the minority was still committed to arguing for placing papal authority within the context of the church. Archbishop Thomas Connolly of Halifax, Canada, put the question bluntly: is the pope infallible by himself, or does he require the counsel and assistance of the church? Hasler asserts that Pius IX used Barnabo of the Propaganda Fide Congregation to threaten missionary bishops like Connolly to get them to switch to the pro-infallibilist side.[58] After eleven mid-summer days of exhausting speeches without time limits, the problem had clearly focused on whether papal infallibility was personal, separate and absolute. The presidents decided to foreclose the debate. The schema and amendments went back to the deputation De Fide. The request of the minority that infallibility be contained within the context of the church was reasonable. They feared that the separate, personal and absolute notion would divorce the pope from the church. But the deputation De Fide would not hear them; they were determined to exclude the Gallican position, which emphasised that the pope was infallible only if the bishops and the church subsequently accepted his teaching.

A week later, on 11 July, the deputation De Fide reported back through Bishop Vincent Gasser of Brixen in the Austrian Tyrol. His exposition on the schema is important for an understanding of the eventual definition. He made it clear that the deputation De Fide held that infallibility was personal and that it was independent of the consent of the church. Two days later there was a trial vote. Out of 601 bishops voting, 451 voted *placet* (yes), 88 voted *non placet* (no), and 62 voted *placet iuxta modum* (yes with reservation). It was now clear that infallibility would be passed, and minority bishops began leaving Rome rather than publicly vote against *Pastor Aeternus*. Only two stayed on to vote *non placet* on 18 July: Edward Fitzgerald of Little Rock, Arkansas, and Luigi Riccio of Cajazzio in southern Italy.

What had been approved? The key text of *Pastor Aeternus* is the actual definition:

> We teach and define as divinely revealed dogma that when the Roman pontiff speaks ex cathedra, that is, when, in the exercise of his office as shepherd and teacher of all Christians, in virtue of his supreme apostolic authority, he defines a doctrine concerning faith or morals to be held by the whole church, he possesses, by the divine assistance promised him in blessed Peter, that infallibility which the divine Redeemer willed his church to enjoy in defining doctrine concerning faith or morals. *Therefore such definitions of the Roman pontiff are of themselves, and not by the consent of the church, irreformable.*[59]

The last sentence (in italics) of the definition was included at the last minute to exclude the possibility of any form of Gallican interpretation. Although the intention here may well have been innocent, the preoccupation with anti-Gallicanism meant that the impression was reinforced that the pope ruled the church doctrinally without the need to consult the bishops.

However, because there had been so much debate, the actual definition is moderate, and infallibility has only been exercised once: in the definition of the Assumption of Mary by Pius XII in 1950. In the process the pope consulted all of the world's bishops before the definition. The real problem for the future church was not infallibility, but primacy and ordinary magisterium. They have had much more effect in subsequent church history.

The definition of papal infallibility led directly to the Old Catholic schism. Small groups in Germany, Austria and the Netherlands rejected the doctrine. No bishop joined them. They united with the Church of Utrecht and eventually formed a loose confederation with the Anglicans. Vatican I also led to a strengthening of anti-clericalism which found its most potent expression in the German Kulturkampf. The failure of the council to respond to the real needs of the times marginalised the church from the major intellectual currents for the next ninety years.

When he died on 7 February 1878, Pius IX had created the modern papacy.[60] The structure of church government that was to last until the present time was now in place, and in many ways the intellectual attitudes that were to characterise official Catholicism right up to the papacy of John Paul II were now established. It had been a significant papacy in every sense of the word.

Leo XIII (1878–1903)

GIOACCHINO PECCI WAS elected quickly. He was aged sixty-eight at the time and was seen as a short-lived, 'caretaker' pope. He was a gifted Latinist and deeply dedicated to the theology of St Thomas Aquinas. He had experience as an administrator in the Papal States; he had had a difficult stint as nuncio in Brussels (1843–46), and was recalled and appointed bishop of Perugia. He was made a cardinal in 1853. He had visited Paris, London, Cologne and other European cities. He was well aware of contemporary culture. In fact, there is a sense in which one can note a sharp contrast between the Pecci and the Mastai papacies. If Pius IX approached the government of church in a largely instinctual, emotional way, Leo XIII was the intellectual. If Pius viewed the modern world as the enemy, then Leo saw it more neutrally as the context in which ministry was carried out. If Pius was a plump man of the people, Leo was thin, aloof, and stood on his dignity. Even a short walk in the Vatican gardens turned into a ceremonial procession. This contrast should not be taken too far, but there was a genuine difference between the approaches of the two popes. Having said that, there is also a strong sense of continuity between the two. Leo XIII was deeply conservative;

he continued the centralising tendencies inherited from the Mastai papacy and was as preoccupied as his predecessor with the recovery of the Papal States.

Leo XIII used the encyclical letter as his major means of communication with the church and bishops. His first encyclical was *Inscrutabili Dei* (1878), which set the pattern for his papacy: he had a strong sense of his great predecessors and the role of the papacy in history and its connection with culture. He was convinced that the theology of St Thomas Aquinas would help Catholicism deal with cultural currents in the modern world. The encyclical *Aeterni Patris* (1879), recommending the use of Thomistic theology, caused a sensation as there were still many opposed to the movement. Thomism was to remain normative in Catholic universities and seminaries until the Second Vatican Council (Vatican II). Leo also insisted in his later letter on historical studies in 1883 that scholars ought to return to the original sources and not depend on subsequent interpretations. He allowed certain scholars access to the Vatican secret archives.

Leo was also aware of the development of critical methods in biblical research, especially among Protestants, and the encyclical *Providentissimus Deus* (1893) encouraged scripture studies and even criticism, although he saw dangers in 'higher criticism'. In 1902 he set up the Pontifical Biblical Commission. He had a strong ecumenical sense. His special interest in England was expressed in the letter *Ad Anglos* (1895), which, however, did not mention the Church of England. That same year he set up a commission to investigate the validity of Anglican orders. Ignoring the commission's conclusions, the bull *Apostolicae Curae* (1896) declared 'ordinations carried out according to the Anglican rite have been and are absolutely null and utterly void'.[61]

The social question was also a major focus of Leo's papacy. The context in which he wrote was European industrialisation, the increase in population and consequent migration to North America, and the capitalist exploitation of workers. The socialists and communists had proposed a radical revolutionary solution to the problem, but moderate Catholic reformers encouraged the development of a social conscience, workers' rights, education and basic economic justice. Among them

were Frederic Ozanam (1813–53), the founder of the St Vincent de
Paul Society, and the bishop of Mainz, Wilhelm von Kettler (1811–77).
The violence of the Paris Commune (1871) forcefully reminded Europeans of the centrality of the social question. Leo XIII attempted to
respond to this. He rejected the socialist and communist solution in
Quod Apostolici Muneris (1878). In defining the nature of the relationship
between church and state in *Immortale Dei* (1885), he maintained that
civil authority came from God and not from the people; he argued that
the ideal state was arranged according to Gospel principles. He admits
that the church is indifferent to the form that the government takes and
that Catholics ought to take part in the public affairs of all forms of
government, although he made an exception for Italy, where Catholics
were still forbidden to participate in the Italian state which, in turn,
enhanced its secularising tendencies.

Leo's central teaching on social issues is found in *Rerum Novarum*
(1891), which provided the foundation of the development of Catholic
social doctrine in the twentieth century.[62] It is a carefully balanced document that is essentially conservative. He admits that it is difficult to
define the relative rights and mutual duties of rich and poor, capital and
labour. The pope blames capitalism for the condition of the working
class, but he warns against a socialist and revolutionary solution. The
right to own property is a natural right. But this natural right must be
balanced by the fact that God has given the earth to all. Leo says that
inequalities are inevitable and the class war wrong. True human worth
does not lie in wealth or poverty but, like Christ, in nobility of life, generosity of spirit and moral qualities. The church has a key role to play in
social questions by influencing people's consciences so that they will act
according to duty. He is supportive of trade unions.

Although Leo was deeply concerned with the recovery of the Papal
States, he and his secretary of state from 1887, Cardinal Mariano Rampolla, were diplomatically adroit. They negotiated a concordat with the
German Chancellor Bismarck who had used the Kulturkampf since
1871 as a weapon against Catholics; Bismarck feared they would subvert
the newly unified Germany under Prussia. But Bismarck's attack had
actually strengthened the determination of Catholics, and gradually

through 1886 and 1887 most of the anti-clerical laws in Germany were reversed. In contrast, Leo and Rampolla failed in their attempt to rally French Catholicism to the Third Republic, but at least Rome showed a willingness to try to negotiate in a situation in which the viciousness of both sides was extraordinary.[63] Charles Péguy's comment *Tout commence en mystique et tout finit en politique* (Everything [in France] begins with mystical belief, but ends in politics) may be a Frenchman taking his country too seriously, but it does point up the problem that pragmatists found themselves caught in a quasi-philosophical cross-fire that polarised opinion and made a negotiated settlement impossible. Defeat in the war of 1870–71 left France divided and bitter. A Bourbon restoration seemed a foregone conclusion, and the church was solidly behind this. But the monarchists were divided, and from 1875 with the proclamation of a republican constitution, the anti-monarchists gained strength. The republicans never had a large majority, however, and until 1914 almost half of France (including many in the army) were alienated from the republican government.

After the election of 1881 the debate shifted to the control of education. The anti-clerical minister Jules Ferry set out to break ecclesiastical control of schools. This led to a confrontation with the church. Republican moderates and Leo and Rampolla attempted a compromise, but extremists on both sides refused to make concessions. Throughout the late 1880s and early 1890s the pope and a minority of Catholics attempted to get the French church to come to terms with the Republic —the so-called *Ralliement*—but this eventually failed. Ferry had said that his aim was 'to organise humanity without God and without kings'.[64] In contrast, the socially aware aristocrat Albert de Mun commented: 'The Church and the Revolution are irreconcilable; either the Church must kill the Revolution, or the Revolution will kill the Church'.[65] The tragedy of the period is that people acted on these stark oppositions.

The enormous expansion of the church outside Europe continued in this papacy with the establishment of 248 dioceses.[66] Emigration from Europe to the United States, Canada and Australia led to the growth of the church in these areas. In the New World, the church had prospered within the context of democratic and liberal regimes, and to an extent Leo XIII recognised this. However, the unfortunate condemnation of 'Americanism' in 1899 showed that Rome still had little understanding of the church's relationship with the democratic regimes that characterised the English-speaking world. Also it is clear that by this stage even the pope's attitudes were hardening toward the modern world.

But there is no doubt that Leo XIII was a great pope. When he died on 20 July 1903 he had restored the international prestige of the papacy.

Pius X (1903–1914) and modernism

IF LEO XIII's PAPACY had been a cautious attempt to come to terms with the modern world, then Pius X's was a repudiation of it. There is a real sense in which this papacy belongs to the nineteenth century rather than to the twentieth. Giuseppe Sarto, patriarch of Venice, was elected after a difficult conclave in which the real issue was the election of Rampolla, who was expected to continue the political policies of Leo XIII. The archbishop of Cracow, Cardinal Puzyna, introduced a veto on behalf of the Austrian emperor against Rampolla, but it probably came too late; Rampolla's candidacy was already lost. Finally, Sarto was elected as a compromise candidate because he would be a 'religious' rather than a 'political' pope. Roger Aubert calls Pius X 'a conservative reform pope' whose instincts were to mistrust anything progressive.[67]

Pope Sarto devoted himself to the renewal of the inner, pastoral life of the church. He reorganised the curia, began the codification of canon law, reformed seminaries and catechetical instruction, changed the emphasis in church music, and encouraged frequent communion. In external relations the pope and his secretary of state, Cardinal Rafael Merry del Val (1865–1930), followed a rigid line, decisively turning away from the diplomatic approach of Leo XIII. This policy led to the separation of church and state in France, and also had serious repercussions in Spain and Portugal.

The divisions of French society in the last decades of the nineteenth century found their clearest expression in the Dreyfus affair. The bitterness aroused by extreme Catholic attitudes led to a revival of anti-clericalism. The Combes government (1903–05) enforced the law against religious orders (many religious were exiled to the United Kingdom), but it did not have the numbers to force a separation of church and state. Partially due to Pius X's unwillingness to compromise, partially to French anti-clericalism, and partially to the ability of Aristide Briand to steer it through the legislative process, the Law of Separation (of church and state) was finally promulgated in December 1905. As a result French Catholics were alienated from the Republic and vice versa. The pope remained resolutely anti-democratic: he condemned the French lay Catholic movement, Le Sillon, in 1910 because of its independence of the hierarchy, as well as Romolo Murri's Azione Popolare, a Catholic Action movement that was the forerunner of Christian Democracy in Italy.

In internal affairs the pope was also determined on change. Prior to Pius X there had been partial attempts to reform the curia, but in 1907 he carried out a major reordering of the congregations that was to last until after Vatican II. However, the changes were cosmetic; there was no change of attitude by curial officials. The 1917 Code of Canon Law (*c*.246) entrusted the task of determining theological truth to the Supreme Sacred Congregation of the Holy Office. As a result it controlled the church during the first half of the twentieth century. It delayed Catholicism's participation in ecumenism for decades; it excluded millions from the sacraments in Spain, Mexico and later Italy for voting communist; and it created an obstacle course of prohibition and condemnation for those theologians who were to be the foundational thinkers of the Second Vatican Council. It went far beyond the traditional task of discerning orthodoxy from heresy, and its procedures were above control or appeal. It suppressed licit and discussable areas of thought and conduct. The most influential man of this papacy was the Spanish Capuchin Cardinal Joseph Calasanz Vives y Tuto (1854–1913), prefect of the Congregation of Religious. A prolific textbook writer, with no comprehension of contemporary culture, he was anti-liberal. He had come to the Vatican in 1884 and had been made a cardinal in 1899. His early life was marked by several exiles. He was a compulsive worker, which resulted in nervous breakdowns and sadly in eventual madness.

The other significant aspect of Pius' reordering of the Vatican was the reform of canon law. This work began in secrecy in 1904 under the guidance of Pietro Gasparri, who became a cardinal and secretary of state in 1914. Parts of the code were issued at various times, such as the decree *Ne Temere* (2 August 1907), which required all Catholics to marry before an authorised Catholic priest and two witnesses, and declared invalid any marriage contracted outside the church by a Catholic. The code was finally published in 1917, and it inflated the juridical aspects and centralisation of the Latin church. In it the solemn and ordinary teaching authority were equated (*c.*1323) and heresy and error were conflated (*c.*1324). Thus basic and traditional distinctions were abandoned in a purely canonical context without reference to theology.

More positive aspects of this papacy were the encouragement of regular reception of communion, the reform of church music, and the strengthening of catechetical instruction. Largely as a result of Jansenism, but with roots going back to the Middle Ages, the practice of frequent reception of communion had almost disappeared among Catholics. Pius X set out to change this, and a new attitude to the Eucharist has emerged since his papacy. He also reacted against the operatic elements that could be found in church music, especially in Italy, and he strengthened the revival of plainchant and classical polyphony.

Although these positive aspects must be remembered, Pius X's anti-intellectualism was to result in the Catholic church turning inward for the next six decades, largely divorcing itself from the cultural currents of modernity and setting up a sense of separation between the church and the world. This can be seen above all in the modernist crisis.[68] This came to a head in the 17 July 1907 decree of the Holy Office, *Lamentabili*, which condemned sixty-five propositions taken largely from the works of the leading modernist Alfred Loisy (1857–1940); however, the first propositions condemned concerned the authority of the magisterium and the Roman congregations. This was followed on 8 September 1907 by Pius' encyclical *Pascendi Dominici Gregis*, which attacked the covert enemies of the church as 'modernists'.[69] Fundamentally, the modernist crisis centred on a split between those who wanted the church to deal with and express itself in terms of the emerging modern cultural forms of the twentieth century, and those who rejected this reconciliation completely. The leading modernist Loisy described it as a 'tendency' rather than a specific movement. The modernists were Catholic philosophers, theologians, biblical scholars and historians who adopted contemporary cultural ideas and literary methodology and applied them to Catholic thought. Although there was a certain naivety among these scholars about the contemporary world, they were committed to the use of the newly developed tools of historical criticism, especially in the areas of biblical studies and church history. Modernist tendencies were also found in the fields of the philosophy of religion and apologetics.

The papal reaction was very negative. *Pascendi* accuses the modernists of intellectual dishonesty: 'None is more skilful, none more astute than they, in the employment of a thousand noxious devices'.[70] The encyclical says that the core of modernism is what Pius calls the principles of immanence and symbolism and what today would be called the relativity of language. He gives various meanings to the term 'immanence', but finally associates it with pantheism and the destruction of the objectivity of the 'supernatural order'. He says that the modernists state that faith is merely a heightened religious consciousness that evolves from nature itself; Loisy and the Irish-born English Jesuit George Tyrrell (1861–1909) are the only modernists who might come close to saying something like this, although it could also refer to the idea of the philosopher Maurice Blondel of the correspondence between the Christian message and the deepest needs of humankind. As the anti-modernist oath, which was imposed on all ordinands and any priest or bishop taking up any important pastoral office, and which remained in force until 1966, says:

> I hold in all certitude and I sincerely profess that faith is not a blind religious feeling arising from the secret depths of the 'subconscious', under pressure from the heart and the impulses of the morally informed will, but that it is a true assent of the intellect to truth

extrinsically acquired ex auditu [i.e. from a source extrinsic to the hearer], an assent by which we unhesitatingly believe all that has been said, attested and revealed by a personal God, our Creator and our Lord.[71]

The pope argues that from this relativisation the conclusion can be drawn that the dogmatic formulations of faith are not statements about reality but mere symbols, the meaning of which can change radically over time.

At the core of the different approaches between the modernists and Pius X is the question of experience and historicity. For the pope, faith is seen in a normative, static sense demanding an intellectual assent; and the mysteries of faith are seen as almost objective realities that can be clearly and permanently expressed within the neo-scholastic theological tradition. The development of doctrine occurs within that context. For the modernists, faith is fundamentally experiential and it develops in an organic and continuous way in, through and sometimes despite the vagaries of personal and cultural history. In many ways this debate has continued throughout twentieth-century church history and has never been fully resolved.

The result of the condemnation was a clamp-down on all forms of Catholic scholarship that did not conform rigidly to the papal line. David G. Schultenover's study *A View from Rome* is a provocative interpretation of the actions of Pius X and the Vatican in terms of the 'Mediterranean mentality'.[72] Schultenover argues that Latin clerics like Pius X and others had no real possibility of understanding what was happening in the rest of the Western world because they were culturally bound by their projection of their own personal, familial and social structures onto the whole church. Gabriel Daly comments that in the long term the ecclesiastical reaction to modernism is more important than the movement itself. He calls this a 'species of ecclesiastical patriotism enforced by an oath'.[73] The integralist fanaticism of the shadowy group around the Vatican Monsignor Umberto Benigni, and the organisation called the *Sodalitium Pianum* (the Sodality of Pius V) has been exposed by the historian Emile Poulat.[74] From within the secretariat of state, Benigni secretly attacked those whom he considered 'modernists' or even 'semi-modernists'. Many serious scholars—such as the biblical expert Father M.-J. Lagrange, OP, the historians Louis Duchesne and Pierre Battifol, the philosopher Lucien Laberthonniere—were silenced or had their scholarly activities curtailed. The Jesuit Tyrrell was expelled from the order and excommunicated, and was finally refused ecclesiastical burial. Loisy also was excommunicated. In a cautious judgement Aubert says that, given the merciless treatment of many scholars and the fear of scholarship among the clergy that the antimodernist reaction engendered, the papal reaction to modernism 'must be assessed negatively'.[75] This judgement can be extended to much of the papacy of Pius X. He may have been a saint in the conventional sense of being a pious and good person, but the Sarto papacy set a pattern of repression of scholarship and the rejection of a genuine encounter between modern culture and Catholicism that really lasted until the Second Vatican Council.

Pius X died on 20 August 1914, right on the eve of World War I.

9 Benedict XV to 1958

Benedict XV, the church and the war

IN EARLY AUGUST 1914 the world went to war. In four years the old order was swept away and the twentieth century really began. As the British Foreign Secretary Sir Edward Grey remarked: 'The lamps are going out all over Europe; we shall not see them lit again in our lifetime'. But this war was not confined to Europe; modern weaponry and European colonialism meant that most of the world was involved. Total war was a new concept. It involved the conscription of the entire citizenry of highly organised modern states, a practice first introduced by Napoleon. Both Pius IX and Leo XIII had condemned conscription. The war resulted in the loss of millions of men who were led by largely incompetent generals, trained for the wars of the nineteenth century. David Thomson correctly compares World War I to a kind of 'Frankenstein monster', the activities and consequences of which could not be predicted or controlled.[1] It left Europe utterly exhausted, with tens of millions killed, and caused massive physical destruction.

During the war the Vatican was sidelined as Catholics on both sides, consumed by nationalism, fought each other to the death. But while the war changed the world, in many ways the Vatican attempted for the next fifty years to continue along the path set by the popes of the nineteenth century. The church stood over and against the world because it saw itself as a *societas vera et perfecta* (a true and perfect society) with its own laws, governance and ways of operating. These stood in stark contrast to secular, civil society. Certainly, after the loss of the Papal States, there was a movement away from opposition to democracy and liberalism, but in a sense papal power, as Giuseppe Alberigo points out, had modulated across from concern with the civil sphere and particular forms of government to concern with control of Catholic life and particularly of the sphere of theology and doctrine.[2]

During the first five decades of the twentieth century there was an ever growing bureaucratic centralisation of the church and a progressive attempt, especially by the Holy Office, to control doctrine, morality and religious practice as a way of regulating the entire life of Catholics. Other sources for discerning truth in the church were completely marginalised or neglected. Alberigo perceptively compares this authoritarian attitude to the ideological states that emerged in Europe after World War I.[3] Yet, despite the untrammelled power of the Holy Office, this same period saw the emergence in the church of a renewal in patristics, theology, church history, and later biblical studies, which was to provide the foundation of the Second Vatican Council.

Giacomo della Chiesa, the archbishop of Bologna, elected pope on 3 September 1914, faced a unique situation. He took the style Benedict XV (1914–22). With John XXIII, he is one of the great popes of the twentieth century. His papacy, overshadowed by World War I, has been consistently underestimated by historians.[4] An experienced diplomat and a protégé of Rampolla, he worked throughout the war to try to get both sides to state their aims so that an armistice and eventual peace could be negotiated. His peace initiative of 1917 was ignored by the belligerents. Because he maintained strict neutrality, he was accused by all sides of favouring the other. The French were convinced that the pope was supportive of the Central Powers. With the Allied governments controlled by anti-Catholics like Clemenceau, Lloyd George and Woodrow Wilson, and even faraway Australia by William Morris Hughes, the papacy really had little chance of participating in the peace conference at Versailles. This was sealed by the determination of Italy through the secret Treaty of London (April 1915) to exclude the papacy from any participation in the peace negotiations.

The settlement imposed on Germany and the Central Powers, largely dictated by Clemenceau, was vindictive, and the pope protested about the intolerable treatment of the defeated countries, particularly Austria. At Versailles in 1919 the seeds were sown that would eventually result in Nazism and World War II.

Although nationalism had made Catholics on all sides willing belligerents, attitudes toward the church began to change after the war. In France and Italy anti-clericalism slowly disappeared; priests and seminarians had been in the trenches. In France 25 000 priests, seminarians and male religious served in the military; 4608 were killed.[5] Nuns had been there to nurse the wounded. Catholics were less and less accused of a double allegiance—to their country and to the Vatican. As a result of this change of attitude Benedict, and his secretary of state Cardinal Pietro Gasparri (1852–1934), were able to lay the foundations for a settlement between the state of Italy and the Holy See. The pope cautiously supported the League of Nations and was also able to restore relations with France and Portugal. The religious orders were allowed to return to France after the war, and the Jesuits to Germany.

Benedict sent his successor, Monsignor Achille Ratti, to the newly established states of Poland and Lithuania as apostolic visitor and later as nuncio. Ratti remained in Warsaw in August 1920 during the Soviet invasion, and felt that the Bolsheviks were the greatest threat to European civilisation. This was to become an important thread in the next two papacies. Pope Benedict also appointed Archbishop Eugenio Pacelli (later Pius XII) as nuncio to Bavaria in May 1917. In Munich he witnessed the 1919 Bolshevik uprising and formed the same view of communism as Ratti. Between 1920 and 1929 Pacelli was nuncio to Germany, eventually moving the nunciature to Berlin.

In the internal life of the church Pope Benedict curbed the cruder excesses of anti-modernist integralism. His first encyclical, *Ad Beatissimi* (1914), which set out a programme for his papacy, not only called for

peace on earth, but tried to bring some reconciliation between traditionalist and progressive Catholics. But he did not change the prevailing
atmosphere in Rome of deep suspicion of any view that deviated from
the neo-scholasticism embraced by the Holy Office. Gabriel Daly has
shown that a rigid neo-scholasticism was the dominant characteristic of
papal theology between the two Vatican councils.[6] Benedict proclaimed
the new Code of Canon Law in 1917; as we saw in Chapter 8, work on
this had begun under Pius X, and it was brought to completion under
the guidance of Gasparri. The pope also encouraged the study of the
Orthodox churches and their theology and established the Pontifical
Oriental Institute in Rome.

He was also deeply interested in missionary work and insisted that
missionaries focus on the task of evangelisation and not just be agents
of their own national brands of European cultural imperialism. He also
called for the training and ordination of indigenous clergy in missionary
countries, which laid the long-term foundations for the enculturation of
the church in the Third World. This is symptomatic of an openness to
the wider world that Benedict XV inherited from his mentor, Cardinal
Rampola. He dissolved the sharp dichotomy between church and piety
on the one hand and the real world of politics and events on the other
created by Pius X.

Benedict died tragically early at the age of sixty-seven in January
1922 and was succeeded by the archbishop of Milan, Achille Ratti, who
took the style Pius XI (1922–39).[7] Interestingly, there had been serious
concern among German-speaking cardinals and diplomats that Ratti was
pro-Polish and anti-German. The historian of the popes, Ludwig von
Pastor, now Austrian ambassador to the Holy See, was also concerned.[8]
Ratti was able to reassure the German cardinals in the conclave. A
scholar himself, as pope he maintained the reversal of anti-modernist
integralism, but only within the cautious limits set by the Holy Office.
In fact, it was in the four decades after 1920 that the Holy Office exercised its most potent control through bureaucratic procedures that were
above all appeal. This fitted in with the attitude of the new pope: he was
something of a martinet and he ran the Vatican in an almost despotic
fashion. One diplomat commented that after his election everyone kept

repeating '*obbedire*, obey'.[9] The attitudes of both pope and curia chimed in well with the approach of the newly arrived dictators. The first of these was Benito Mussolini (1883–1945).

Reconciliation with the Fascists and the corporatist state

MUSSOLINI HAD BEGUN his career as a socialist and anti-clerical atheist; in 1909, while living in Trent, he published the scurrilous novel *Claudia Particella, Mistress of the Cardinal*, in which he referred to priests as 'tuberculosis microbes'. Even as late as 1919 he called for the separation of church and state, and Benedict XV protested about Mussolini's 'blasphemies'.[10] He broke with the socialists during the war, and in 1915 the word 'fascist' was first used. In the chaos that followed the war, the fascists gradually gained power by organising themselves as a political party. By October 1922 Mussolini was prime minister. He consolidated his authority, and by January 1925 he had complete power. As dictator, the erstwhile anti-clerical now had to deal with the church, and the papacy had to deal with him.

Since the occupation of Rome in 1870, the popes had retired to the Vatican and assumed the role of persecuted prisoners who had been unjustly deprived of their state. There was some truth to this stance because, while the Italian government had offered the popes the so-called Law of Guarantees, which was wisely rejected, between 1870 and 1922 the Quirinal behaved badly toward the Vatican. As a result there was widespread sympathy for the difficult position of the papacy in anti-clerical Italy. To protect its seizure of the Papal States the Italian government was determined never to allow the papacy to be recognised as a sovereign power with a claim on any territory in Italy; successive Italian governments kept up the pretence that the pope was merely a private Italian citizen who was allowed to occupy some historical buildings in central Rome which really belonged to the state of Italy. This is why the secret Treaty of London (1915) made it a precondition of Italian entry into the war that the papacy be excluded from any subsequent peace conference. Italy could not risk allowing the pope to have international standing.

In response to Italy's occupation the popes had forbidden Catholics under pain of excommunication to play any part in Italian politics after 1870, the so-called *Non Expedit*. This was slowly dropped in the first decades of the twentieth century. As a result in early 1919 the Sicilian priest Don Luigi Sturzo (1871–1959) organised the Partito Popolare Italiano (PPI). Benedict XV assisted the party indirectly by finally lifting the *Non Expedit*. The PPI was immediately successful, and by the end of 1919 it had become a dominant force in Italian politics. Only the Socialists were larger. But with the advent of Pius XI in February 1922 the situation changed. Pius' vision of Catholic Action, which differed considerably from that of Sturzo, subjected the lay apostolate to priests and these, in turn, to the close scrutiny of the hierarchy. Sturzo believed in the autonomy of lay action, and he very quickly fell out of papal favour. In October 1922 Mussolini formed a government, and he needed the support of the church. In a series of favourable moves toward the church, he attempted to ingratiate himself with the Vatican, but the cynical realist Gasparri was cautious. However, by January 1923 secret negotiations between the secretary of state and Mussolini were under way and, as a sweetener to the fascists, there were Vatican suggestions that the papacy would sacrifice the PPI. The pope and Gasparri, already deeply suspicious of the apparent confusion of democratic politics, had tentatively thrown in their lot with Mussolini, who appeared to be offering a permanent settlement of the Roman question.

The view of Pius XI was that priests (like Sturzo) ought not participate in politics unless the 'Altar of Family' were threatened. As a result he separated Catholic Action from the PPI and advised Sturzo to leave Italy. The priest resigned from the party in July 1923 and went first to London and then, in 1940, to the United States. The driving force behind the elimination of Sturzo and the PPI was Monsignor (later Cardinal) Giuseppe Pizzardo, then Substitute in the secretariat of state. Given subsequent history, the decision to abandon the PPI was probably mistaken. It certainly showed that the Vatican still felt that democratic processes were both secular and confusing. It was a continuation of nineteenth-century papal attitudes.

It is generally held that the great diplomatic achievement of the Ratti papacy was the Lateran Treaty and Concordat of 1929.[11] Throughout

the 1920s feelers had been put out by the Fascist government for a reconciliation with the Holy See. But Gasparri and Pius XI attempted to
drive a hard bargain and did not give in easily. Direct secret negotiations
began in 1927, but a settlement was not reached until 11 February
1929. The treaties made Mussolini popular among Catholics, despite
the fact that he had conceded very little. Basically, the Holy See recognised the kingdom of Italy with Rome as its capital. A real sticking point
had been a claim by the Vatican for a corridor to the sea. Mussolini resisted this, hoping to control Vatican contacts with the outside world by
isolating its territory in Rome. In the treaty a Vatican City of just over
40 hectares was established as an independent sovereign state with the
pope as a foreign ruler in the middle of Rome. A large compensation
was paid to the Vatican by Italy for the final surrender of claims to the
Papal States. About 60 per cent of this was invested in Italian consolidated stock, thus establishing a pattern of tying Vatican investments to
the Italian monetary and corporate sector.

The concordat was negotiated to govern the relationships of these
two overlapping states. Catholicism was recognised as the official religion of Italy, and Catholic canonical legislation on marriage became
the norm for Italian law. Catholic Action was recognised; church schools
were given support and religious education was allowed in all state
schools. Informally, but influentially, the church now gave its support
for Catholics to vote for the Fascists in the March 1929 election. They
won in a landslide. This was not the end of trouble between church and
state. Most of the tension between the Vatican and the Fascists through
the 1930s centred on the question of education, the power to influence
and conscript youth and the role of Catholic Action.

However, the agreement reached between the Fascists and Pius XI
had a deeper significance. For Pius XI encouraged the growth of the
corporatist state which, to some extent, was realised in Mussolini's
Italy.[12] Papal social theory has never shown much sympathy for capitalism, nor for democratic liberalism. Of course, it made sense in the
1920s and 1930s for Pope Ratti to be suspicious of democracy, for in
Europe in this period democratic regimes were often struggling to survive. Also there was a strong European Catholic tradition of suspicion of

constitutional liberalism and the notion of an individualistic, capitalist democracy. Rather than strictly democratic policies, Pius called for the development of centrally organised states with what he called 'intermediary associations' that would give individuals a collective voice. The model for this was seen in the structured interrelationships of the Middle Ages, especially in the guilds. The societal context of these intermediary associations, however, was strictly hierarchical. The corporatist view was expressed in the encyclicals *Quadragesimo Anno* (1930), commemorating the fortieth anniversary of *Rerum Novarum*, and *Divini Redemptoris* (1937), on communism. In fact, *Quadragesimo Anno* is a critique of Fascist corporatism, for the pope calls for free intermediary structures in society in contrast to the dictatorial regime in Italy. But the pope is also highly critical of the liberal theories of what he calls the 'so-called Manchester school', which concentrated enormous power in the hands of a few capitalists. Although the papal approach offers a useful critique of individualistic capitalism, it was the anti-democratic and authoritarian elements in the pope's philosophy that were emphasised in the 1930s. In practice Pius XI stressed a kind of benign paternalism, but this was hardly the way the corporatist state actually worked under Mussolini, let alone under the Nazis in Germany.

Pope Pius is equally critical of the extreme solutions offered by communism as practised by the Soviets and other left-leaning regimes. Unfortunately he does not distinguish communism as practised by the Soviets from the kind of democratic socialism that could be found in the English-speaking world. This created confusion and alienation from the church among many left-leaning Catholics. It was also used to justify attacks by the Catholic right on co-operation between Catholic parties and socialist parties. One of the worst examples of this is Vatican pressure in the depths of the Depression on the Zentrumspartei (the Catholic Centre Party) in Germany to abandon a tacit understanding with the social democrats in favour of coalition with the Nazis.

Corporatist notions also gave support to a number of European rulers, such as the Austrian chancellors Monsignor Ignaz Seipel (1930–32) and Engelbert Dollfuss (1932–34). The priest Seipel was allowed to carry on a long political career on the grounds that Austria was under threat from the socialists.[13] The murder of Dollfuss in 1934 by the Nazis showed that it was the extreme right that was the real challenge to the stability of the state, not the socialists. The clericalist Austrian regime managed to defeat the Nazi *putsch*, and Kurt Von Schuschnigg ruled the country for another three years. Perhaps the fullest expression of the clericalist-corporatist state is to be found in Portugal under Antonio Oliveira Salazar (effectively dictator from 1932 to 1969). In Portugal economic growth was sacrificed for societal stability and Catholic corporatist values. General Francesco Franco in Spain set up a similar state to Portugal, but it was one in which fascist and military elements were predominant.

However, in France the pope took a different line with the neofascist movement, Action française. Founded in 1898, it quickly became associated with a brilliant but atheistic writer and journalist, Charles Maurras (1868–1952). He was utterly opposed to democracy and liberalism as practised in the Third Republic, and he promoted a traditionalist crusade, for the monarchy and authority. Even though he was a pagan and a positivist, he saw the church as a support for his crusade, and he promoted the notion of the union of throne and altar. For him the church was a useful vehicle for political and social stability. In his earlier years he viciously attacked social Catholicism and any move to compromise with democratic forces. After the failure of the Ralliement he gained strong support among French bishops, priests and conservative Catholics. Pius X called him a great defender of the church. His movement grew during World War I, when it was seen as highly patriotic. But in the 1920s he moved in an increasingly fascist and anti-Semitic direction when, at the same time, many French Catholics were moving toward a more moderate stance. The pope was strongly supportive of reconciliation between Germany and France. This was opposed by Maurras, and Action française began to turn on the church. Among Catholics pressure began to build for a papal condemnation of the movement, and this occurred in March 1929. The movement survived the condemnation, and its political influence continued, especially under the Vichy regime during World War II. Many influential right-wing Catholics continued to subscribe to its ideas, including the Jesuit cardinal Louis Billot (1846–1931) who agreed to renounce his red hat because of his association with the movement. Maurras was tried in 1945 and spent six years in prison. The movement died with him.

The papacy and the Nazis

THE MOST EXTREME manifestation of the fascist corporatist state was Nazi Germany. At first the Vatican was inclined to see Adolf Hitler and the Nazis as counterweights against communism, which since the Wall Street financial collapse of 1929 and the economic depression of the early 1930s was becoming increasingly influential across the world. This was especially true in Germany, which had suffered a virtual economic collapse. The Nazi emphasis on 'common-interest before self-interest' also squared with the corporatist views in the ascendant in Rome. Also, in 1930 Gasparri retired, and the new secretary of state, Eugenio Pacelli, was the former nuncio to Germany.

In many ways the Vatican itself had been responsible for the weakening of the German Catholic Centre Party, which had achieved so much for the church in the 1920s. Papal discouragement of Catholic parties and priestly participation in politics, together with distrust of democratic processes, left the Centre Party vulnerable precisely at the time when it needed all its strength to counteract Hitler. Hitler's aim was to use the church in his ascent to power and then deal with it when his power was established. The Vatican, like so many others, was taken in by the future Führer's appearance of moderation. In order to eliminate the Centre Party, which opposed granting him dictatorial powers to deal with the economic crisis, he bypassed it by suggesting a concordat with the Vatican.[14] This would have the bonus of giving him the international respectability of having been approved by the church. Already the Vatican had negotiated concordats successfully with several German *Länder* (states).[15]

The negotiation of the Reich concordat was extraordinarily quick by Vatican standards. It is difficult to work out the reason for this. The best interpretation that can be placed on it is that Rome feared that Hitler would close Catholic schools and abolish the church's youth movements. Given that the struggle for the youth had become a central issue in Italy, this is plausible. Just as the PPI had been sacrificed a decade previously to placate the Fascists, so the Centre Party was now sacrificed without compunction to keep the Nazis on side. The terms of the concordat guaranteed Catholic schools and the right to run Catholic cultural and educational organisations, so long as they were confined to cultural and educational activities and played no part in politics. Priests were similarly limited. Owen Chadwick argues that, however reluctant, the German bishops 'were convinced that they must protect their youth groups, processions, even sermons, from the onslaughts . . . [of] thugs and brownshirts, and that the only way to achieve this was by establishing a clear legal situation for the Catholic church within the Reich, accepting the probability that this state run by gangsters would not be likely to honour all the provisions they signed'.[16]

But in reality hardly any of the provisions were honoured. For the Vatican and the German church the Nazi concordat was a serious mistake. The agreement was widely criticised at the time, and was a deadletter from the time of its signing. Part of the problem was that the Vatican had been outsmarted by Hitler at its own game. In many ways Pius XI was more tough minded than his secretary of state. It is in this negotiation with Germany that we begin to get clues to the personality of Pacelli and to the attitudes he later evinced as pope during World War II. It was not so much that he was pro-German, although he had sympathy with Germany because he had seen the results of the Versailles *diktat* on ordinary Germans in Munich in 1918–19. It was more that he was essentially a diplomat who believed that everything could be solved by compromise and negotiation. His view was that even if the optimum situation could not be obtained, at least a concordat might prevent worse evils. In the case of the Führer this was a total misreading of the situation.

The Nazi attacks on Catholicism increased, so that by 1937 the pope was ready to denounce the regime publicly. As early as 1936 the German ambassador to the Holy See, Diego Von Bergen, was telling the German Foreign Office that the pope confronted him and was furious with Germany, although he claimed that Pacelli was displeased with the pope.[17] In Rome the line that Nazi Germany was a shield against the

Soviet Union was by now wearing very thin. The pope decided on an encyclical against the regime in early 1937, and it was probably largely written in one night in Rome by Cardinal Michael Von Faulhaber (1869–1952), archbishop of Munich, with assistance from a couple of other German cardinals, especially Cardinal Adolf Bertram (1859–1945), archbishop of Breslau. Entitled *Mit Brennender Sorge* (With Burning Anxiety), it was smuggled into Germany and secretly distributed and read from all the pulpits of the country on Palm Sunday, 1937. It was a scathing attack on Nazi race theories and neo-paganism, and it denounced the regime for its attacks on the church and Catholics. It is probably the most direct and outspoken of all papal encyclicals. It was not able to halt the persecution of the church; in fact, it increased the attacks. But the situation of Catholics never remotely reached the dreadful intensity of the persecution of the Jews.

The Vatican and communism

IF THERE WAS a hesitancy at first to attack the Nazis, it was because they were seen as a bulwark against the Bolsheviks. The Vatican shared the fear, widespread in Europe at the time, of Soviet expansionism abroad and communist takeover at home. Also communism was a godless philosophy that persecuted churches, denied the right of private property, and wished to overthrow the social order completely. Interestingly, Pius XI saw liberalism and communism as interconnected. Both individualism and collectivism were condemned in *Divini Redemptoris*.

Before Pius XI, the Vatican had a tradition of opposition to socialism and communism.[18] Leo XIII in the encyclical *Quod Apostolici Muneris* (28 December 1878) denounced the results of 'socialism, communism and nihilism': these were that marriage and private property were attacked and, worst of all, 'impious hands' had been raised against crowned heads by attempted assassinations. In *Rerum Novarum* Leo had again defended the right to private property as a natural right, and he condemned the socialist solution to the social question. But he did admit that 'rapacious usury' and capitalist concentration of wealth in the hands of a few created a kind of slavery of the teeming masses. Little or nothing was said by Pius X regarding socialism, and Benedict XV was too caught up with the war to develop anything of significance.

But the then Monsignor Ratti had experienced the Bolshevik armies at first hand in Warsaw in August 1920. He was the only diplomat who did not leave the capital. His experience in Poland also made him aware of the complex ecclesiastical problems arising in the borderlands between Ukraine, Russia and the newly formed Polish state. In fact, the war of 1919–21 between Russia and Poland was fought over these border regions, with the eventual Peace of Riga (March 1921) extending Poland somewhat eastward into part of Ukraine.[19] Interconnected with Polish–Russian antagonism was the desire of the Latin-rite Poles to absorb Eastern-rite Catholics in Ukraine and Western Russia.

In 1921 famine broke out in the Soviet Union; the Holy See, after complex negotiations, sent a relief mission.[20] In the Vatican hope was held out for the conversion of Russia which, of course, meant the Orthodox. This was not realised, but priests did enter the Soviet Union and provided modest relief. Overlapping this relief mission, complex secret negotiations were carried on by Pacelli through the German government with the Soviets; a French Jesuit bishop was sent secretly in 1926 to the Soviet Union, and after several trips he consecrated and left behind four bishops and a number of apostolic administrators.[21] Eastern-rite Catholics were subjected to a Latin-rite bishop in Moscow. The dialogue through Pacelli continued, but by late 1928 this also had collapsed. By the end of 1927 Stalin had secured complete power, and Trotsky and Zinoviev had been expelled from the party.

Just before the Fifteenth Party Congress (1927) Stalin called for the complete liquidation of the clergy.[22] In April 1929 the Permanent Commission for Questions of Religion was established and anti-religious legislation and propaganda were stepped up. In response the pope called for a crusade of prayer for the persecuted Russian Catholics. The Soviets used the Lateran Treaty with the Fascists as an excuse to break off all negotiations with the Vatican. Pius XI's eastern policy, as Hansjakob Stehle shows, became tangled in the nationalistic ambitions of the Poles in their eastern borderland.[23]

But socialist persecution of the church was not confined to the Soviet Union. In both Mexico and Spain socialist governments attacked the church and killed priests and nuns. Mexican syndicalist-communist governments had persecuted the church, and especially the clergy, since the early 1900s. This came to a head under President Plutarco Elias Calles, who ruled Mexico for a decade after 1924 and who founded the PRI, the Institutional Revolutionary Party, which governed the country until 2000. Under Calles the persecution, especially of priests, was intense. The most famous example is the now beatified Father Miguel Pro, who was shot by firing squad in 1927. Things improved after 1934, although obstacles to church work continued for another twenty years. At times the Calles persecution was appallingly violent and at one stage the number of clergy in the country dropped to around two hundred.

In Spain, anti-clericalism broke out from 1931 onwards: the Jesuits were expelled, Catholic schools were taken over and divorce was per-mitted. Between 1934 and 1936 there was a right-wing backlash led by José Maria Gil Robles. But in the elections of early 1936 an extreme anarchist-syndicalist Popular Front government was elected, and in July Generalissimo Francesco Franco, with logistical help from Mussolini, invaded the mainland from Spanish Morocco. The Spanish Civil War began. It was fought with dreadful brutality on both sides, and more than half a million people were killed. This civil war was a defining moment for some of the best European minds, and it divided Western intellectuals as nothing else had done since the French Revolution. Liberals often moved further to the left, while many Catholics came to see communism as the true enemy of the church. In many ways it was the Spanish Civil War that motivated the encyclical *Divini Redemptoris* of March 1937 condemning communism. This encyclical became norma-tive for Catholic attitudes to communism for the next two decades. Part of the problem was that, with the exception of the Nazis, Pius XI was not equally scathing on the fascists. He had a narrow, conservative vision and he tended to see the left as the sole source of all evil.

Pius XI and the church

IN THE INTERNAL affairs of the church, this same narrowness obtained. In contrast to Benedict XV, who allowed Catholics a fair degree of pol-itical autonomy as is shown by his attitude to Sturzo, Pius XI promoted

Catholic Action and the lay apostolate, but always in terms of laity assisting the church because of a shortage of clergy, and because priests could not enter some areas because of their clerical dignity. Lay Catholic action was always to be under the control of priests, who in turn obeyed their bishops, who themselves reported to Rome. Although it gave many laity a sense of their Christian dignity and encouraged their participation in the apostolate, it was always subsumed into the hierarchical and priestly ministry. In fact, the first break with Mussolini came over the issue of Italian Catholic Action and Mussolini's determination to control Italian youth.

It was also during this papacy that the Jocists or Young Christian Workers was established by a Belgian priest, Joseph Cardijn. They stood in contrast to clericalised Catholic Action. It was this movement that established the methodology of *see, judge, act*: see reality, judge it in the light of the Bible and discussion in the Young Christian Workers group, and then act in the real world to change things. This movement was to have wide influence in the church leading up to the Second Vatican Council, and its remote influence has continued through liberation theology.

Following the lead of Benedict XV, Pius XI was very supportive of overseas missions. He encouraged the professional study of missiology (theological study of evangelisation) and also promoted the ordination of indigenous clergy, which moved the emphasis in missionary work away from a colonial notion of the church to one that was local. In this both Pius and his predecessor were remarkably farsighted. In 1922 the pope appointed an apostolic delegate to China, and there was a strong emphasis on the need to break the stranglehold that France and the colonial powers had gained over missionary work in the country. A remarkable Belgian priest, Vincent Lebbe, deeply influenced the development of indigenous clergy and a local hierarchy in China.[24]

Pius was also concerned with the influence of secularisation on Christian institutions such as the family. The encyclical *Casti Connubii* (December 1930) attacked the modern vision of marriage and reproduction and the increasingly free availability of divorce. It was significant that the encyclical's strong condemnation of contraception came just after the Lambeth Conference of the Anglican church had given cautious approval to very limited use of contraception. The pope, however, speaks bluntly about the evil of contraception which he sees as a sin against nature that is 'shameful and intrinsically vicious'.[25] The primary writer of the encyclical, the Jesuit moralist Arthur Vermeersch, was deeply concerned with what he thought was a population decrease in his native Belgium, which he maintained resulted from a too easy access to contraception.

A new, and in many places extreme, political and social world had emerged in the two decades of the Ratti papacy. Although Pius XI had shown real courage and some creativity in confronting these problems, his papacy also manifested elements of his autocratic and Rome-bound vision. This is reflected in many of those who surrounded him, especially men such as the Substitute Monsignor Giuseppe Pizzardo. Certainly, the pope also showed an open side, especially to new scientific ideas and to intellectual developments outside the church. It was he who brought in Marconi to set up the Vatican Radio. He was also interested in scholarly issues. In the latter part of his papacy he took a firm stand against Nazi anti-Semitism. His now famous comment 'Spiritually, we are all Semites' was uttered in the context of a Mass for pilgrims in Rome in September 1938. He commented that 'Abraham is our patriarch and forefather', and he went on to say:

> Anti-Semitism . . . is a movement with which we Christians can have nothing to do. No, no I say to you it is impossible for a Christian to take part in anti-Semitism. It is inadmissible. Through Christ and in Christ we are the spiritual progeny of Abraham. Spiritually, we are all Semites.[26]

In 1938 this was a comment that showed insight, courage and leadership and can here serve as the pope's epitaph.

Pius XII, the war and the Jews[27]

Pius XI was almost immediately succeeded by his secretary of state, Eugenio Pacelli, who took the style Pius XII (1939–58). His experience as a diplomat, especially in Germany, and his travels in Britain, France, Argentina, Hungary and the United States gave him contact with a wider world than any previous pope. In many ways his complex papacy has been subsequently subsumed by the claims that he was 'soft' on the Nazi Holocaust. Pacelli was elected on 2 March 1939, six months before the outbreak of the war. The threat of war was his immediate problem and he worked hard to avert the coming conflagration. It came with the German invasion of Poland. Throughout the war he constantly called for peace, and he kept the papacy strictly neutral; he used the term 'impartial'. The papacy also set up an extensive relief operation and a tracing service for missing persons and prisoners.

However, it was the pope's attitude to the Jewish Holocaust that is still widely questioned.[28] This became a widely popularised issue after the opening in February 1963 of the play *The Representative* (or *The Deputy*) by Rolf Hochhuth, which has now been performed all over the world. The play accuses Pope Pacelli of total indifference to the Holocaust. The play is based on the figure of Colonel Kurt Gerstein, a chemist who became an SS officer in order to try to confirm what was happening in the concentration camps. In mid-1942 he visited Belsen and witnessed mass extermination in operation.[29] Gerstein claims he tried to give a report on what he had seen to the Berlin nuncio, Archbishop Cesare Orsenigo, but was turned away from the nunciature. He then tried to get the report to the Vatican through Bishop Konrad Von Preysing of Berlin, an avowed anti-Nazi. There seems to be little doubt that his report did get to Rome. It would have simply confirmed what was already obvious to the church, with contacts all over the Nazi-occupied continent, that a mass extermination of the Jewish people was under way. With the release of much of the documentation, the portrayal of Pius XII in Hochhuth's play can now be dismissed as a complete caricature. But the nagging question remains: given that he knew what was happening, could the pope have done more? Was he 'soft' on Germany?

To answer this question the extreme situation in which Pius XII found himself has to be recalled. While pogroms and genocides had been attempted before, never had such logistical sophistication and technological efficiency been applied. It is generally held that the Wannsee

Conference of ministerial bureaucrats (20 January 1942) made the decision to carry out the *Endlosung*, the 'final solution', to the Jewish question. But the issue goes back much further. The Nazis had always been anti-Semitic. But this does not mean that they initially intended to eliminate the Jews by killing them. Various solutions were considered, including the 1940 idea of transporting them all to Madagascar. It seems reasonable to argue that the idea of killing all European Jews slowly crystallised in Hitler's mind in the first years of the war.[30] Thus the Wannsee Conference was the bureaucratic meeting that activated a previously taken decision. Whatever the origins of the notion, the reality is that the activation of the final solution came at the beginning of 1942. Dreadful things had happened prior to that date, and the concentration camps were already fully operative. But from 1942 the focus shifted to the extermination camps, such as Birkenau, which began in 1941. It was a kilometre from Auschwitz. The emphasis put on the elimination of Jews is shown by the fact that for the next three years much-needed resources for the war were poured into the final solution. Local police and the European railway system were drawn into the process; a large number of ordinary people played a part.[31]

This whole developing context must be remembered in assessing the pope's reaction to the Holocaust. Certainly, by the end of 1942, when the systematic killing of all Jews was well under way, the pope must have known what was happening. He apparently intended to denounce it in his Christmas message. But only a generic condemnation was issued.[32] It is this generalising tendency that has led to criticism of Pius XII. Some have argued that it is the role of the pope to speak generically and for local bishops to apply the teaching. That is hard to sustain in the light of very specific papal condemnations, both before and after the war. The whole question of Pius XII and the Holocaust has again been refocused by John Cornwell's book *Hitler's Pope*, which says unequivocally that Pacelli was anti-Semitic.

My own view is that Pius XII probably shared in the anti-Semitism typical of right-wing Catholics in the inter-war period. However, this does not completely explain his inaction. Carlo Falconi's *The Silence of Pius XII*, which shows little sympathy for the Roman curia and is highly critical of the pope, probably comes closest to a reasonable explanation of

Pacelli's behaviour.[33] Falconi has no doubt about either the pope's knowledge of what was happening, nor of his courage to act if that was necessary. In fact, he argues that there is good evidence that the pope would
have been willing to die himself if that would have helped. So why did he
not speak? Falconi divides the reasons into two groups: external and
internal. Firstly, external: he was deeply worried about Soviet communism, especially once the tide of the war in the east turned against the
Germans. He felt that if he contributed to the weakening of the Nazi
regime he might leave the way open to Stalinist tyranny right across
Europe. Even more important was the fear he felt for the church's survival. What would be the result of a grand gesture for the church? One
has to say that this attitude is sectarian, given that so many innocent
people were dying. But perhaps in the situation it was understandable.
Further, he was pessimistic about what good a grand statement might
achieve. It could lead to even worse excesses. Although Pius XII was
later to become the master of the big gesture, his diplomatic training
and whole ecclesiastical attitude made him deeply suspicious of grand-
standing. One can be critical of this but it was, and probably still is, part
of the Roman ecclesiastical mindset. Pius was nothing if not Roman.
Falconi also shows that Pius XI had been silent in the face of the worst
Nazi attacks on the Jews and other minorities before the war.

Falconi suggests that, psychologically and spiritually, Pius XII was
placed in an appalling moral dilemma, which was heightened by his personal religious faith. Although he never doubts the pope's sincerity or
deeply held faith, he suggests that his religious attitude derived from a
dogmatic and juridical view of religion, rather than from a mystical,
spiritual and prophetic one. Falconi blames the cardinal electors of 1939,
who felt that the church needed a diplomat to deal with the Nazis and
the international situation. He makes the interesting argument that,
because the Nazis scorned diplomacy, a diplomat was the last type of
person the church needed. Falconi seems to suggest that what was
needed was someone who was prepared to risk everything in terms of
the structured church establishment in order to make a stand against the
evil that the Nazi regime represented. In other words, Catholicism
needed a papal prophet. What Falconi does not take into account is that

church history shows that papal prophets are few and far between! But none of this should distract us from something that Falconi also admits: it is easy to judge the pope *post factum*. He was caught up in a complex, fast-moving and dreadful situation, and any statement from him could have the most horrendous effects. It was a terrible moral dilemma and it seems to have crippled him.

This image of moral paralysis is reinforced by Cornwell. In an enlightening chapter he discusses Pacelli's spirituality.[34] His constant spiritual reading was the late-medieval classic *The Imitation of Christ*. This emphasised the interior life and encouraged a piety that stood in opposition to the profane. It engendered a split between personal holiness and the ethics demanded of a churchman in the world. It further crippled the possibility of the pope taking a prophetic stand against the Nazis. It created a 'fatal moral dislocation' in the pope's personality.

Pius XII and theology

FOCUS ON THE insoluble problem of the pope's attitudes to the Holocaust can distract from the important theological developments that occurred during the Pacelli papacy. The modernist crisis had in many ways condemned the church to intellectual and cultural stultification, and had promoted a narrow and unimaginative neo-scholastic integralism. The stultifying dominance of the Holy Office remained supreme throughout this period. But in an institution as large and creative as the Catholic church it is impossible to destroy intellectual life entirely. As early as 1924 a German theologian, Karl Adam (1876–1966), had published *The Spirit of Catholicism*, a popular work that argued that *Pascendi* and the anti-modernist oath did not forbid the historical method, but presupposed it.[35] Slowly, through the 1930s and 1940s, the work of thinkers began a change that was to come to fruition in the Second Vatican Council and the modern church. The roots of this go back to a renewal in historical and patristic studies, especially in the area of the liturgy.

Worship was one of those areas favoured by Pius X, and so the historico-liturgical studies that began in the late nineteenth century continued right through the first half of the twentieth. Inspired by Abbot Prosper Guéranger (1805–75) of Solesmes, the liturgical movement began with a monastic phase, originally in France, and then later in the century in Germany and Belgium. The historical work of English scholars was an often unrecognised part of the pioneering work: the convert layman Edmund Bishop (1846–1917), who did much of his work as a Catholic at Downside Abbey, the Australian-born Downside monk Richard Hugh Connolly (1873–1948), and the Anglican Benedictine Gregory Dix (1901–52), all contributed much to studies of the early liturgy. Perhaps the most important Continental scholar was a Benedictine, Lambert Beauduin (1873–1960), of the Abbey of Mont-César in Belgium, who shifted the focus of liturgical research from history to theology, and finally to pastoral and parochial life.

The revival of liturgy went hand in hand with the revival of ecclesiology. German theologians since the beginning of the nineteenth century had emphasised the more mystical, less institutional aspects of the church. The fount of this was the patristic ecclesiology of Johan Adam Möhler (1796–1838).[36] For Möhler, whose theology is profoundly ecumenical, the church was much more than its structure; it was a living reality, a symbol of Christ's presence in the world. These ideas were adopted and developed especially by Odo Casel (1886–1948), the Maria Laach Benedictine monk. He emphasised the *mysterium* embedded in the liturgy and saw worship as the process whereby believers enter into the very life structure and living reality of Christ.[37] These ideas were popularised by Romano Guardini (1885–1968), who saw the liturgy as the primary way in which one experienced the church.[38] The Austrian priest Pius Parsch (1884–1954) was concerned to popularise the liturgical movement, and his book *The Church's Year of Grace* was a practical guide for priests and people to the liturgical year. In the 1940s pressure grew for the use of the vernacular in the liturgy and for a serious reform of the whole worship of the church; this centred firstly on the need to restructure completely the Easter Triduum (Holy Thursday, Good Friday, Easter Saturday). This led to a conservative reaction, especially in Germany, and even during World War II many pressured Rome for the suppression of the liturgical movement.

Although the liturgical movement began in Europe, it was the American Benedictines who spread the ideas in the English-speaking world. The centre of this was St John's Abbey at Collegeville, Minnesota. Liturgical ideas were popularised in the periodical *Orate Fratres* (the name was later changed to *Worship*), founded by the monk Virgil Michel (1888–1938); he also founded the Liturgical Press. Not only did Michel succeed in translating European ideas into the Anglo-American world, he also succeeded in relating liturgy to the practical life of Catholics, so that their relationship with Christ was closely related to their responsibility for the world in which they lived. In other words, worship was linked to justice.

It was in the middle of the war that Pius XII first intervened in the controversies over the theological and liturgical movements. In the encyclical *Mystici Corporis* (29 June 1943) he confirmed the ecclesiological developments that found their genesis in Möhler. In the twentieth century the emphasis on the mystical, inner core of the church had found contemporary expression in the work of the Belgian Jesuit Emile Mersch (1890–1940) who, like Möhler, had returned to patristic images of the church. Also, influenced by the renewal in biblical studies, Mersch used the New Testament emphasis on the body of Christ as a primary ecclesiological image. Sadly, he was killed in an air-raid; his great work *The Theology of the Mystical Body* restores this biblical notion to the centre of ecclesiology.[39] Although *Mystici Corporis* emphasises the juridical aspects of the church, it also focuses on the presence of Christ in the church, and it tries to show how the two are united. While the pope identified the mystical body entirely with the Catholic church, the encyclical also highlighted the role of the laity, although it still manifested something of the hierarchical clericalism of the time.

The pope directly addressed the liturgical movement in the post-war encyclical *Mediator Dei* (20 November 1947). Generally speaking, he approves and supports the liturgical movement; in fact, the encyclical is very positive in tone and is probably the finest of Pius XII. It is divided into four parts: the first sets out a theology and history of the liturgy and stresses the church's authority. Interestingly, he does not exclude the use of the vernacular. The emphasis in the second part is on eucharistic worship and in the third on the liturgical year and the office. The final part deals with practical issues that range from devotional practices to altar-boys. The first result of the movement was the re- newed liturgy of the Easter Triduum of 1953. Work had begun on this secretly in 1948. Pius XII introduced several other liturgical reforms and laid secure foundations for the important changes in the liturgy that were to come with the Second Vatican Council.

The other even more significant doctrinal encyclical of the 1940s was *Divino Afflante Spiritu* (30 September 1943), which permitted the use of modern historical and critical methods in scriptural study. It was the beginning of the contemporary Catholic interest in the Bible. Given that this was a prime theological target in the modernist controversy, the encyclical must have come as a surprise to many in the church. It was issued on the fiftieth anniversary of Leo XIII's *Providentissimus Deus,* which, although conservative, also cautiously opened the way to use of critical methods and tools. Pius XII opened up the whole field by approving, at least implicitly, the use of form criticism and the develop- ment of modern biblical theology. Again, the foundation was laid for the Second Vatican Council, and this encyclical was perhaps the greatest achievement of the Pacelli papacy.

The year 1950 had been proclaimed a Holy Year by the pope, and about three million pilgrims came to Rome to receive the plenary indulgence. Of these about two and a quarter million were Italians and over half a million were Europeans. Papal audiences became very im- portant, and it was in these audiences that the tall, ascetic-looking pope literally pontificated on a vast range of topics. In many ways this was the first manifestation of papal mass tourism in the modern sense, even though something of this had begun under Pius IX. It was also the begin- ning of media focus on the papacy as the centrepiece of the Catholic church. This media focus has followed a direct line from Pius XII to John Paul II. As part of the Holy Year event the pope canonised two young Italians, Maria Goretti and Dominic Savio, both of whom were proposed as models of sexual purity for youth.

This same year saw the infallible proclamation of the doctrine of the Assumption of Mary into heaven on the Feast of All Saints (1 November

1950). There was no doubt that this doctrine had firm roots in tradition, going back to the early church. The pope wanted to be seen con-
sulting the world bishops about this doctrine, but this was done by mail
rather than in a general council, which was the normal place for such
consultations and declarations. There had been some discussion of a
possible council during the papacy of Pius XI, and a concrete proposal
had been put forward in 1939 by Archbishop Celso Constantini, who
had returned from the nunciature in China to become secretary of
Propaganda from 1935 to 1953.[40] The idea of a council was taken up
again in 1948–49, and the task of studying possibilities was placed in the
hands of the assessor of the Holy Office, the then archbishop Alfredo
Ottaviani, and an extremely conservative Belgian Jesuit, Pierre Charles.
It is possible that the theological material studied by this Holy Office
committee constituted the basis of the condemnations included in the
encyclical *Humani Generis* of 1950.[41] The proposed council was soon
placed in the too-hard basket, and the proclamation of the Assumption
was preceded by episcopal consultation by mail.

The war years seem to have been theologically the most open of
Pacelli's papacy, but there was a strong Roman reaction against new
theological developments from just before 1950. The encyclical *Humani
Generis* (12 August 1950) was basically directed against the theologians
of the so-called French *nouvelle théologie* (new theology), which included the Jesuits Henri de Lubac (1896–1991) and Jean Daniélou
(1905–74), along with Yves Congar (1904–95) and Marie-Dominique
Chenu (1895–1990), both from the Dominican house of studies, Le
Saulchoir.[42] The *nouvelle théologie* had emerged as Jesuit and Dominican
scholars searched for a culturally relevant theology in the late 1930s and
especially during the war, when many of them served in various armies.
These war experiences confronted them with human, ethical and theological questions that were simply inconceivable to Roman theologians.
Based on the more dynamic philosophy of Maurice Blondel (1861–
1949), Joseph Maréchal (1878–1944) and Emanuel Mounier (1905–
50), the aim of the thinkers of the *nouvelle théologie* was to move beyond
the neo-scholasticism that dominated ecclesiastical study by returning to
the biblical, patristic and medieval sources. They were also interested

in re-engaging pastoral experience and the role of the laity with theology. They were explicitly ecumenical in intent and recognised that theology and doctrine divorced from historical context made no sense in the modern intellectual culture.

De Lubac, who together with Congar was probably the key theological figure in the *nouvelle théologie*, had been one of the principal Catholic writers in the spiritual resistance to French Fascism and Action française, and in June 1942, during the Nazi occupation, he wrote bravely against anti-Semitism and was for a period under Gestapo surveillance.[43] With Jean Daniélou, de Lubac began the series *Sources chrétiennes* in 1942 to provide the church with critical editions of patristic authors. Fundamental to his theology is the notion that there is a deep desire or passion for God planted in everyone, and that there is no division between nature and the supernatural; both are intimately intermingled. This is a view also held by his fellow Jesuit, the Austrian Karl Rahner (1904–84). De Lubac's seminal book *The Mystery of the Supernatural*, which returned to the views of Sts Augustine and Thomas Aquinas on the relationship of nature and grace, was placed on the *Index of Forbidden Books* in 1952. The other key figure in the movement was Yves Congar. During the war he spent five years as a prisoner of war in Colditz Camp. He was a Catholic pioneer in the ecumenical movement who always maintained close contacts with parish life.

Lurking behind the whole *nouvelle théologie* movement is the figure of the Jesuit palaeontologist and thinker Pierre Teilhard de Chardin (1881–1955), who had not been permitted to publish any of his ideas publicly at that stage and was under Roman suspicion.[44] Even in the early 1920s his work was suspect, and in the late 1940s he was still denied permission to publish *The Phenomenon of Man*.[45] His contribution to modern theology is enormous, if somewhat undifferentiated. Basically he argues that matter matters because it is imbued with purposive, spiritual energy that moves ever higher toward greater complexity and reaches its apogee in Christ. His great strength is that he addressed what is arguably the most important theological issue facing us today: the reintegration of the material and the spiritual and the jettisoning of dualism. A close friend of de Lubac, who always remained faithful to him in life and after his death, Teilhard held that the ultimate end of the evolutionary process is mystical.

The tragedy of *Humani Generis* is that this encyclical paralysed the intellectual development of the church for another decade and negated much of the good that had been achieved earlier in the Pacelli papacy. It was the apex of the influence of the Holy Office's repressive approach to theology. The encyclical reflected the views of two of the Holy Office's consulters, the Jesuit Charles Boyer and, more importantly, the Dominican Reginald Garrigou-Lagrange (1877–1964), for many years professor at the Angelicum in Rome. Garrigou-Lagrange, a supporter of Action française, anti-Semitism and the Vichy regime, was a rigid neo-Thomist whose theology lacked any historico-critical perspective. He even considered the thought of his fellow neo-Thomist, Jaques Maritain (1882–1973), to be highly dangerous! The new theology was caricatured in the encyclical as attacking the foundation of Christian culture. Theologians were told that the papal magisterium was the proximate and universal norm of truth, that a decision by the pope in controversial questions was final and binding, and that the task of theology was to show how the doctrine of the magisterium was found in the sources. The encyclical condemns those who accept the theory of evolution, as well as monistic or pantheistic speculations. These were said to give comfort to communists! The condemnation of 'polygenism', which suggests that the human race is not descended from a single pair, is clearly directed at Teilhard. There is also a generalised condemnation of the philosophy of existentialism. The encyclical would not have been so tragic if it had not resulted in both de Lubac and Congar and several others being silenced and losing their teaching positions, and the French Dominican and Jesuit provincials losing their jobs.

By 1950, the Roman curia was in a state of *immobilismo*—complete stultification. Patronage was rife; with no retiring age, cardinals hung on to office until death. In fact, even the Jesuit preacher and founder of the Better World Movement, Riccardo Lombardi, who was close to the Vatican, spoke of the need for reform.[46] Despite the fact that Pius had expanded the size of the College of Cardinals both numerically and nationally, his authoritarian and solitary style increasingly diminished their role. This was reinforced by his speech making, which was often couched in incomprehensible rhetoric. There was hardly a topic he did not cover.[47] He seemed to live for work. He had no apparent interest in other people, in the outer world, or even in relaxation. The pope was often perceived by people as almost 'quasi-divine'. However, during the illnesses of his declining years, power slipped into the hands of curialists.

Pius XII's death in October 1958 marked a turning-point. He was succeeded by John XXIII (1958–63). An extraordinary renewal was at hand.

10 The council and conciliar popes

John XXIII (1958–1963) and preparations for a council[1]

ANGELO GIUSEPPE RONCALLI, patriarch of Venice, was elected pope after a three-day conclave. He took the style John, and the numeration XXIII indicated that Baldassare Cossa, elected in the Pisan line in 1410 as John XXIII, and dismissed by the Council of Constance in 1415, was considered an antipope by Rome.[2] In the Roman view the last legitimate John had died in 1334.

Roncalli had been born in a village near Bergamo, Italy, in 1881, had lived his early years as a priest during the modernist crisis, and had served as a medical orderly and chaplain in World War I. Appointed to Bulgaria by Pius XI in April 1925 as apostolic visitor without diplomatic status, his task was to explore possibilities for reunion with the Bulgarian Orthodox. This turned out to be a chimera, but it was an excellent introduction to the complexities of Orthodoxy. Just prior to going to Bulgaria he met the Benedictine Dom Lambert Beauduin (1873–1960), the pioneer liturgist who was also an expert on the Eastern churches. Their significant friendship was to last until Beauduin's death when Roncalli was pope. In November 1934 Roncalli was appointed apostolic delegate to Greece and Turkey, an even more difficult and sensitive post than Bulgaria. He was in Turkey throughout the war. Because the country was neutral, it quickly became a centre of both espionage and contact between the belligerents. As papal representative, even though without strict diplomatic status, he became a pivotal person through whom much diplomatic traffic passed.[3] He was even marginally involved in the overtures of the anti-Hitler plotters to the Allies.

At the end of 1944 he was appointed papal nuncio to France; he was to remain there until 1953. In Paris he found himself confronting several problems. Firstly, the provisional government of Charles de Gaulle demanded the sacking of the bishops who had collaborated with the Vichy regime. Pius XII had refused an episcopal purge, and Roncalli negotiated the issue successfully with the French government; as a result only three collaborator-bishops resigned. Secondly, it was during Roncalli's time in Paris that the worker priest movement developed. During and after the war the conviction had grown that France was a *pays de mission* (mission country), and to try to reach the working classes, Cardinal Emmanuel Suhard had in 1946 permitted several priests to work in factories. Peter Hebblethwaite says that Roncalli was very influenced by Suhard's pastoral ideas.[4] Many of Suhard's priests took part in trade union activities, and inevitably became involved with the French Communist Party. This led to trouble with Rome. There had always been suspicions in the Holy Office and in Rome about the worker priests' ministry, but Roncalli had to some extent protected them, and the theologians of the *nouvelle théologie* (see Chapter 10). He was now under Roman suspicion himself, and the ideas generated by both these movements must have influenced him. There were about ninety worker priests when recruitment was suspended. In June 1953, after the departure of Roncalli, the movement was suppressed by Roncalli's successor as nuncio, Paolo Marella, later a cardinal, on orders from the Vatican.[5]

Clearly, Rome had not been entirely happy with Nuncio Roncalli. Pius XII complained that he was often 'away' when most needed, and his humane, warm and open style would not have been popular in the curia. Meriol Trevor describes him as personal and light in touch, but he was shrewd and worked hard to avoid involvement in purely internal French matters.[6] He met and was popular with a wide range of people and was never narrowly ecclesiastical. He left Paris in January 1953 and was appointed a cardinal and patriarch of Venice.

In Venice he found his true *métier* in full-time pastoral work. Roncalli was a paradoxical mixture of the pietistic attitudes of his generation of Italian clerics, combined with an openness that allowed him to live and let live. While his spirituality was traditional and simple, it always remained humane and gentle, as his spiritual diary, *Journal of a Soul*, demonstrates.[7] Despite his long years in the diplomatic service, he was never a career curialist. He was also a competent historian and antiquarian.

The long illness that led up to the death of Pius XII had left the curia in disarray, but still under the control of a self-serving group of career curialists. Roncalli emerged as one of the possible candidates before the conclave, but it took eleven ballots to elect him. He was clearly perceived as transitional. However, his humanity, affability and humour were in sharp contrast to the austere and remote Pius, and he quickly became very popular with the media. People sensed in him a warmth, gentleness and genuine spirituality. Right from the start the themes that were to typify his papacy quickly emerged: unity in the church, unity with other Christians, and peace in the world based on true justice and charity.

Pope John's papacy was an open one from the start. This can be seen in his encyclicals. The description of non-Catholic Christians as 'separated brethren' first appeared in *Ad Cathedram Petri* (29 June 1959). His great encyclicals *Mater et Magistra* (15 May 1961) and *Pacem in Terris* (11 April 1963) looked toward a world of peace built on justice, human rights and international social equity. *Pacem in Terris* is the quintessential expression of the utopia of a reconciled world to which the pope looked forward. In the immediate wake of the Cuban missile crisis of 1962, it was he who began the openness to the USSR and initiated the policy that was to become in the next papacy the famous *Ostpolitik*.[8] The first products of his openness to the communist world resulted in the release of the Ukrainian Archbishop (later Cardinal) Josyf Slipyj (1892–1984), metropolitan and archbishop of Lvov, who had spent eighteen years in Soviet jails since 1945. Also the pope received Nikita Khrushchev's daughter Rada and son-in-law Alexi Adjubei, editor of *Izvestia*, in the Vatican.[9]

It is now clear that right from the beginning of his papacy John intended to call a general council.[10] There is some evidence that Cardinals Ernesto Ruffini and Alfredo Ottaviani may well have encouraged the idea, but the real inspiration clearly lay primarily with the pope.[11] He announced his intention on 25 January 1959 to a surprised and un-enthusiastic group of cardinals in the chapter house of St Paul's Outside the Walls. Right from the beginning the pope intended that the council be pastoral, open and ecumenical in the broadest sense, and in October 1959 general invitations were sent to 'separated Christian churches'. Most significantly, the pope intended the council to be a transition: from the defensiveness of Trent and Vatican I into a new phase that drew much more broadly on the Catholic tradition and was open to the world and ready to learn from it.[12] This was what Pope John called *Aggiornamento*, or at other times, a 'new Pentecost'.

Control of the conciliar preparations was placed in the hands of the newly appointed secretary of state, Cardinal Domenico Tardini (1888–1961), who was much more at home in the papacy of Pius XII. The aim of Tardini and the curia was an in-house council approving, but not debating, previously prepared documents.[13] Most of the curialists were similar to each other: Italian career bureaucrats, of limited theological knowledge. Some were good canon lawyers and most had been educated within the narrow confines of the Roman seminary system.[14] In the curia the prevailing view was that John had made a bad mistake in calling the council. A preparatory commission was set up, and between January 1959 and October 1962 there gradually occurred what Etienne Fouilloux has called the 'slow emergence from inertia'.[15] Part of the reason for this inertia was that the conciliar tradition had been to an extent lost due to papal centralisation since Trent.

The pope decided that, instead of a questionnaire that constrained the world's bishops, there would be a letter of invitation to send in ideas and suggestions about topics to be discussed at the forthcoming council. It went out under Tardini's name in June 1959 and covered such issues as doctrine, clerical and Christian life, and the issues confronting the church. All answers were to be given in Latin.[16] Fouilloux has analysed the *vota* or suggestions that came in; there were 1998 responses out of the 2594 invited to write, a 77 per cent response rate, which is excellent.[17] He notes that the *vota* manifested the diversity of Catholicism rather than its unity. Although there were some innovative views, most were 'timid' and 'cautious' and many were 'narrow-minded'. It was this caution and timidity that the curialists banked upon in imposing their own notion of the council.[18] Many curial cardinals showed disinterest, and some open contempt, for the idea of a council.

But there were other powerful forces at work in the church. In order to facilitate ecumenism, John set up the Secretariat for Christian Unity in March 1960, directed by the German Jesuit and biblical scholar Cardinal Augustin Bea, who had been the main author of *Divino Afflante Spiritu* and the confessor of Pius XII. Some of the bishops began to demand that preparation for the council turn outward to the world and its needs. The French bishops asked that the council confront the problems of the developing world, an idea echoed by Cardinals Josef Frings of Cologne and Bernard Alfrink of Utrecht, who also spoke of the need for decentralisation in the church. Archbishop Lorenz Jaeger of Paderborn, in north-western Germany, wanted a broad ecumenical approach, and he called for a council that would be democratic, collegial and open. He urged lay participation. Cardinal Giovanni Battista Montini of Milan said that the church must adapt to the needs of the age.

In the period prior to the council a parallel preparation was carried on by theologians. It was Hans Küng, then a young outspoken Swiss-born theologian, who succeeded in actually spelling out an alternative agenda from that of the curia. In *The Council and Reunion* and in a series of lectures around the world, he outlined a whole conciliar programme that was truly prophetic.[19] He pointed out that the announcement of the council had led to a real change of atmosphere in the church. His book strongly emphasised the need for renewal and reform of the Catholic church as a preliminary to reunion with the separated churches. In this sense the council would be truly ecumenical. The phrase *ecclesia semper reformanda* (a church always in need of reform) re-entered the ecclesiastical vocabulary. As part of an ecumenical attitude, he emphasised the

use of the Bible in theology and worship and the development of a vernacular liturgy. Ecumenism was not to be only among Christians but
extended to dialogue with other cultures and religions. There should be
an emphasis on the universal priesthood of all believers. Finally, there
was a need for a reform of the Roman curia and abolition of the *Index of
Forbidden Books*.

As we saw in the preceding chapter, the theological foundations of
the council had been laid, at times at great personal cost, by scholars
during the previous thirty years. Yves Congar had focused on historical
ecclesiology and ecumenical theology. It was Karl Rahner who was to
emerge as the most important Catholic theologian of the century. His
theology developed out of a synthesis of Thomist, existentialist and tran-
scendentalist philosophies, especially the thought of Martin Heidegger.
Rahner's most influential work began to be published in 1954 in the
series of essays *Schriften zur Theologie* (Theological Investigations). The
synthesis of his thought is to be found in *Foundations of Christian Faith*
(German edition, 1964; English translation, 1978). Other important
theologians in the lead-up to Vatican II were M.-D. Chenu, Jean Daniélou
and Henri de Lubac. The American Jesuit John Courtney Murray
(1904–67) sketched out a *modus vivendi* for the church in a liberal,
secular, democratic society. Most of these thinkers had been silenced by
Ottaviani's Holy Office. There was a growing group of Catholic scholars
working in biblical studies; often they were deeply in debt to the
pioneering work of their Protestant colleagues.

The Second Vatican Council (1962–1965)[20]

THE COUNCIL OPENED ON 11 October 1962. The pope's opening
address sketched a vision of vast optimism. He insisted that the church
must look outward to contemporary existence. He disagreed with the
'prophets of doom who announce ever more unhappy events'. The
council was not about condemnation: 'Today . . . the Bride of Christ
prefers using the medicine of mercy rather than severity'.[21] Zizola
shows that the theological schemas prepared by the curia did not cor-
respond to the attitude that the pope had emphasised in his opening
address.[22] So the way was left open for the reformist majority, but in

order to seize the initiative they needed leadership. This soon emerged, and many timid and negative bishops underwent something of a 'conversion' at the council.

It was the largest and most diverse council in history: there were 2443 voting participants in the first session, the vast majority of whom were bishops.[23] The numerical superiority of the Italians, who had dominated Trent and Vatican I, was gone. Present throughout the sessions were about fifty Orthodox and Protestant observers, despite the attempts of many in Rome who opposed their presence. They exercised a profound psychological influence on the deliberations. Their attendance constantly reminded the bishops that Catholicism did not exhaust Christianity, and that the imperative of Christian unity must be kept before the council.

The First Session of Vatican II lasted from 13 October to 8 December 1962.[24] Each morning the bishops gathered in St Peter's—tiered stands had been erected on both sides along the length of the nave—for Mass and then debate in Latin. Afternoons and evenings were increasingly taken up with meetings, conferences and lectures as participants and theologians attempted to sort out the issues for themselves. On the very first day the curia tried to stampede the council into accepting its list of members of conciliar commissions. Led by Cardinals Achille Liénart (Lille) and Josef Frings (Cologne), the bishops put off these elections for three days, and as a result the elected commissions got a much broader spread of representation.[25]

In very general terms the council divided into a progressive majority and a small, consistent minority who opposed everything for which Vatican II stood. But the actual constellations were more complex: Cardinal Ottaviani, for instance, was strongly opposed to nuclear deterrence, whereas many United States bishops who supported religious liberty, which Ottaviani strongly opposed, supported their government on the morality of nuclear weapons. There were always different constellations of bishops who opposed various reforms and these shifted consistently.

The first session debated schemas on the liturgy, revelation, communications media, church unity and the nature of the church. The schemas previously prepared by the curial theologians, under the guidance of Ottaviani and the Dutch Jesuit Sebastian Tromp, were summarily rejected by the large majority. These were on revelation, ecclesiology and church unity. This came to a head in the debate about the schema on revelation which, having been prepared by the Ottaviani–Tromp commission, was a restatement of the old 'two sources' notion: the Bible was one source of God's revelation, and church tradition another. But in the years prior to the council the idea gained ground that there was no distinction between scripture and tradition, and that tradition is the church's ongoing interpretation of scripture in the demands of everyday life.[26] This meant that scripture was not a second and independent source of revelation; it was simply the flip-side of tradition. This view was much more acceptable to Protestants.

This more open attitude was constantly repeated by the other leaders of the majority—Cardinals Paul Léger (Montreal), Franz Koenig (Vienna), Bernard Alfrink (Utrecht), Leon-Joseph Suenens (Brussels) and Maximos IV Saigh, Melkite patriarch of Antioch (Damascus, Syria). Bishop Emile De Smedt of Bruges (Belgium), the finest speaker of the council and one of its best theologians, summed up the majority view of the three schemas prepared by the Holy Office when he said that they smacked of Romanism and were characterised by triumphalism, clericalism and juridicism. De Smedt also emphasised the importance of ecumenism.

Because the pre-conciliar liturgy commission had been fairly widely representative, debate on the schema on worship reversed the roles of progressives and conservatives. The progressives supported much that was in the schema and the conservatives wanted it radically changed. The debate centred on the issues of the use of local languages in the Mass and sacraments (the so-called 'vernacular'), communion under both kinds, the concelebration of Mass (several priests celebrating Mass together), and the power of local conferences of bishops to decide on liturgical changes for their own cultures, with general reference to Rome. While there was strong opposition to liturgical reform from some Italians, interestingly it was some of the English-speaking bishops who provided the stoutest opposition to the use of the vernacular, to concelebration, and to communion under both kinds. No decisions were taken at the first session and, like all other topics, the schema went back to the commission for rewriting.

Little was achieved in a superficial discussion about the mass media. There was some recognition of its potential, but generally the attitude of the bishops showed little comprehension of the importance of communications. The discussion was also shelved for the next session.

The first session concluded on 8 December with very little in terms of concrete results. But the bishops had begun to think for themselves. It was clear that this would not be a council that merely approved prepared texts. It had gained its own momentum. A co-ordinating commission was set up with wider representation, and the schemas had gone back to much broader commissions for rewriting. The curia had been put firmly in its place.

Pope John XXIII died on 3 June 1963, possibly the most important pope of the whole post-Reformation period. He had succeeded in initiating a revolution in the church; he had brought the post-Reformation church and papacy to an end, and had made the the ecclesial world more open to the secular. His humanity, humility and unostentatious sanctity had touched people, and many were genuinely sad when he died. But the future of the council, if it was to continue, lay in the hands of his successor. The conclave of 1963 was to be one of the most important for many centuries.

The election of Paul VI (1963–1978)[27]

Giovanni Battista Montini, the archbishop of Milan, was elected on the sixth ballot of a two-day conclave that was numerically the largest in history.[28] He took the style Paul VI. It was the first conclave for centuries in which non-Italians numerically predominated. This was another of John's achievements: a more internationalised College of Cardinals now represented the broader Catholic church. In the conclave the anticonciliar cardinals, led by Giuseppe Siri of Genoa, had first tried to exclude both Giacomo Lercaro of Bologna (who was considered too liberal) and Montini. Lercaro was closer to Pope John, and eventually his twenty or so votes shifted to Montini. A number of the conservatives also shifted to the cardinal of Milan; perhaps they intuited something of Pius XII in him. He was elected on the sixth ballot.

He had been born near Brescia in northern Italy in 1897. His father was a newspaper editor who was later a member of the Italian parliament who was strongly opposed to fascism. From 1922 to 1954, with the exception of a brief stint in the Warsaw nunciature, Montini worked in the secretariat of state, eventually becoming assistant to Pacelli. When Pacelli became Pius XII, he worked closely with him. Always a moderate, he was anti-fascist, pro-democratic and widely read in French Catholic social thought and philosophy, especially in the work of the convert lay philosopher Jacques Maritain (1882–1973). Maritain was a Thomist philosopher who had great influence on Catholic social thought in the 1940s and 1950s, shifting it in a genuinely democratic direction. Maritain taught at the Institut Catholique in Paris and the Institute of Medieval Studies in Toronto, as well as Princeton and Columbia Universities. From 1945 to 1948 he was French ambassador to the Vatican.

Montini had been deeply involved in the Catholic student movement and after 1945 supported moderate elements in the Italian Christian Democratic Party. Here we see something of Maritain's influence upon him. His nine years in Milan gave him considerable pastoral experience, and in 1958 he was made a cardinal by John XXIII. Pope John also involved him in preparations for the council, and he was an active member of the Central Preparatory Commission. In 1960 he visited Brazil and the United States, and in 1962 he took an extended trip to Zimbabwe (then Southern Rhodesia), Upper Volta, Nigeria and Ghana.[29]

Paul VI faced an immediate and daunting task: how to continue the council along the lines clearly favoured by the majority and yet, at the same time, win over persistent minority, especially curial opposition? Although he had gained the two-thirds majority requirement in the conclave, more than twenty cardinals had not voted for him. The evidence is that most were curialists, and Pope Paul's concern was that they would be alienated from the council as long as they feared that unorthodox views predominated within it.[30] In some ways this problem is the key to the pope's attitude to the council, and to much of the rest of his papacy: it was a constant compromise between keeping the reactionaries in the curia and elsewhere on side, while attempting to grapple with modernity and the realities of contemporary ministry.

Vatican II—continued

POPE PAUL QUICKLY ANNOUNCED that the council would continue. At the beginning of the second session (29 September to 4 December 1963) he set out four major tasks for the succeeding sessions.[31] First, he called for a doctrinal presentation on the nature of the church; second, he wanted an inner spiritual renewal of the church; third, he pledged the church to work for Christian unity and asked forgiveness for the papacy's part in causing disunity; fourth, he broadened the notion of ecumenism to include a dialogue with the wider world.

The council debate opened with a consideration on the revised schema on the church. It contained chapters on the people of God, the hierarchy, and the role of Mary in the church. A fierce debate broke out over the chapter on the hierarchy and specifically on the question of episcopal collegiality, the notion that the bishops together with the pope govern the church and are ultimately responsible for its ministry. A minority saw this as an encroachment on papal primacy and denied that it was based in either scripture or tradition. At this period the restoration of the permanent deaconate was also debated. Many speakers saw this as a threat to the celibacy of priests: who would choose to be celibate if they could be full-time deacons and marry? Most support for the deaconate came from missionary countries that were already suffering from shortages of priests. Discussion on this schema dragged on, and it became clear that the council was in crisis and floundering. The only ones to profit from this were those who wanted the council to fail. To break the deadlock, a straw vote was taken; it became clear that both collegiality and the permanent deaconate would gain the necessary two-thirds vote. The schema on the pastoral office of bishops was introduced. It reflected the pre-conciliar juridicism and was rejected and sent back to the commission for a complete rewriting.

In November the schema on ecumenism was introduced. It was more widely accepted, but debate immediately focused on Chapter 4, which dealt with the relationship of the Catholic church to the Jewish people, and Chapter 5 on religious liberty. Introducing the schema, Cardinal Bea spoke of the terrible consequences of anti-Semitism and of the difficult question of the status of the state of Israel.[32] This became a crisis issue for Arabic Christians who, as the Coptic patriarch of Alexandria Stephanos I Sidarouss said, would be in a difficult situation when they returned home to minority status in Muslim countries fiercely opposed to Israel.

It was De Smedt who focused the religious liberty question.[33] Everyone who followed their own conscience in religious matters, he argued, had a right to authentic religious freedom. Nothing can take the place of a free judgement of an individual conscience. It had been John Courtney Murray who had developed the theory of the compatibility of Catholicism with a free, secular society, and the strongest push for religious liberty came from the United States bishops. This created no problem for bishops from democratic countries. But there was strong opposition from many Italian, Spanish and Latin American bishops where Catholicism was the majority religion. The two problem chapters on the Jews and religious liberty were eventually pushed into a temporary limbo in the second session.

Meanwhile some work had been brought to a conclusion. The *Constitution on the Sacred Liturgy* and the *Decree on Social Communications* were adopted on 4 December 1963.[34] The liturgy constitution laid the foundation for the most radical overhaul of Christian worship in church history, and has had the greatest impact on ordinary Catholics in parishes. But the ill-considered *Decree on Social Communications* has subsequently been forgotten. Now there was a sense that something had at last been achieved. However, Paul VI's role in the second session seemed ambivalent. Throughout his papacy he often seemed to vacillate. At Vatican II he seemed unwilling to support the majority, to make a stand. But he had to guarantee the freedom of all, and humiliation and confrontation are not the way of the Vatican, especially in dealing with its own.

The pope concluded the session by announcing a pilgrimage to Jerusalem and a meeting with the ecumenical patriarch of Orthodoxy, Athenagoras. This took place in January 1964. This action strengthened the ecumenical thrust of the council, and as one of the first major papal journeys, it had a world-wide impact. Much work went on between the sessions. The Council for the Implementation of the Liturgical Constitution was set up in 1964 with Cardinal Lercaro as president and Father Annibale Bugnini (1912–82) as secretary.[35] But there were enormous problems in combining the work of this committee with existing bodies, the Congregation of Rites and the conciliar commission on liturgy.

Another problem was the escalating cost of the council. Many felt that the third session would have to be the last. In the month before the third session opened Paul VI published his first encyclical, *Ecclesiam Suam*. The keynotes of his papacy were sounded in the letter: profound awareness of the world, dialogue with it, and a willingness to work to renew it. But the council was heading for trouble. There is a sense in which it was trying to achieve too much, especially within the context of the conflicting forces at work within it.

The third session, from 14 September to 21 November 1964, saw both the climax and major crisis of the council.[36] The session began with the presentation of nine rewritten schemas: on the ministry and life of priests, the missions, lay apostolate, religious life, Christian education, the church in the modern world, the sacrament of marriage, the Eastern churches, and the church. Eventually several of these were combined, eliminated or integrated. The text on the laity was still inadequate and held that the ministry of laity was delegated by the clergy and ignored lay sharing in the priesthood of Christ. Likewise the text on the ministerial priesthood emphasised piety, avoided the question of celibacy, and gave the impression that priests were second-class citizens after bishops. These schemas were sent back for rewriting.

The important schema on *The Church in the Modern World* was introduced on 20 October. Pope Paul was one of the prime movers of this, and he was determined to see it through the council. It eventually evolved into the most significant document of the council: its aim was to shift the focus of the church outward to the world. The discussion on this schema ranged across a whole spectrum of modern issues, including a ban on nuclear weapons, social justice, sexuality, population and contraception.

However, dissatisfaction with the administration of the council had been simmering throughout the third session, especially with the secretary-general, Archbishop Pericle Felici, who, it was felt, was manipulating the council on behalf of the conservative minority.[37] Feelings reached a crisis point on 14 November, when the revised schema *On the Church* was given to the bishops. The third chapter on collegiality was the storm centre. Felici informed the council that a 'superior authority' (whom everyone presumed to be Paul VI) had imposed a *nota explicativa praevia* (a preceding explicative note) to the chapter to preclude any encroachment on the primacy by the notion of collegiality.[38] Confusion reigned: was the *nota* part of the text? 'No,' said Felici. What was its purpose then? Felici said the bishops had to understand the text and to vote in terms of the *nota*. Why had the pope imposed the *nota* on the council as a precondition for voting? He wanted moral unanimity when the text was voted on, and he knew that the minority would never agree unless the *nota* were imposed. The pressure on the pope from the minority conservatives from the beginning of the session had been considerable.[39] However, many bishops were furious with this action, which was considered arbitrary and unnecessary. The *nota* probably did not alter the sense of the text, but the question remained: did the pope have a right to determine the interpretation of the text in advance? A somewhat gloomy council eventually adopted the texts of the *Dogmatic Constitution on the Church*, the *Decree on the Eastern Catholic Churches* and the *Decree on Ecumenism* on 21 November 1964.[40] The now separate declarations on religious liberty and the Jews were put off until the next session.

When the session closed many of the bishops were depressed, as were the observers from the other churches. It was clear that there would have to be a fourth session and that enormous work would have to be done in between. But the minority were happy. There was a core group of 200 to 300 who formed the Coetus Patrum Internationalis (the International Group of Fathers) who opposed religious liberty, collegiality, ecumenism, the deaconate and openness to the Jews.[41]

Soon afterward the pope flew to Bombay for the International Eucharistic Congress. While the immediate focus was Catholic, the long-term papal aim was to reach out to the other great faiths. Pope Paul was also invited to address the General Assembly of the United

Nations in New York, and he did so in October 1965 during the fourth session. He was the first pope in office to visit the United States. Meanwhile between the sessions work had continued on all the outstanding documents. Prior to the opening of the fourth session, Paul VI announced that he would reform the Roman curia and that canon law would be revised. The questions of mixed marriages and birth control continued to be openly discussed.

The fourth and final session lasted from 14 September to 8 December 1965.[42] This session was largely fought out in the committees framing the schemas, rather than in St Peter's. It also saw the beginning of the debate about the role of women in the church. The pope opened the session with the announcement that he would follow the council's advice and establish a World Synod of Bishops through which he could consult the bishops and collaborate with them.[43] It was a concession, but the synod's rules determined that the pope called it at his discretion, presided over it, determined its agenda, and decided how its results would be communicated.

The council was now under pressure; this had to be the last session, if only for financial reasons. The *Declaration on Religious Liberty* was the first item on the agenda. The debate was protracted, and the reactionary Coetus opposed it in every possible way. The core of the *Declaration* was that no human power could command conscience. Modern society was recognised as essentially pluralistic. It did not pass until the second-last day of the council. The *Decree on the Pastoral Office of Bishops in the Church* and the *Decree on the Sensitive Renewal of Religious Life* eventually passed without further debate.[44] Few people took post-conciliar renewal more seriously than did religious orders, but the decree itself was not an impressive document. Debate continued on the schemas on the *Church in the Modern World*, priestly life, and the missions. Simmering under the surface of the discussion of priestly life was the celibacy issue. Paul VI became quite emotional over this and forbade all discussion of it in the council as inopportune. This was the first issue withdrawn from the council by the pope.

The revised schema on *Relations with Non-Christian Religions* (an expansion of the schema on the Jews) came before the council again in mid-October. The issue was as divisive as ever. Bishops from Arab countries were still convinced that a declaration on the Jews would imply recognition of the state of Israel. Despite the fact that the schema was directed to Hindus, Buddhists, Moslems and the other religions, it was the section on the Jews that received the most attention. There was a note of anti-Semitism in the opposition, especially among the Coetus. Two hundred and fifty bishops opposed it to the end. The rewritten *Dogmatic Constitution on Divine Revelation* was also opposed to the end by a small minority.[45] It had been rewritten by a group of theologians, including Karl Rahner, Yves Congar and Josef Ratzinger. It highlighted the intimate connection between the Bible and tradition and the fact that revelation is essentially God's self-communication. It says that although the foundational revelation occurred in the time of Christ, the process of revelatory salvation is a continuing one. The *Decree on Priestly Formation*, the *Declaration on Christian Education*, the *Decree on the Apostolate of the Laity* and the *Decree on the Missionary Activity of the Church* were all passed by mid-November.[46] These decreees are unimpressive documents. The *Decree on the Ministry and Life of Priests* has subsequently been shown to be particularly problematic.[47] The French Dominican Christian Duquoc has argued that the fundamental problem of the contemporary priesthood is to be found in this decree. He claims that it places the priest in an irreconcilable bind between the demands of a contemporary ministry and an outdated theology of priesthood.[48] He argues that this tension shows itself in all of the contemporary problems related to the priesthood.

The last big issue the council surmounted was the *Pastoral Constitution on the Church in the World of Today*. Despite enormous work on the text by ten sub-committees, there were still many problems to be resolved when it was submitted to the council. There was a long discussion on marriage and sexuality, but the question of birth control was unhappily skirted at the pope's request. It seemed a contradiction of episcopal collegiality. If there was any issue the bishops ought to have been consulted on, it was this. This was the second issue withdrawn from the council by the pope. Over 450 bishops said the schema was too soft on atheism and communism. The question of nuclear war and deterrence was fully debated. This was the time of the escalation of the Vietnam War, and the question of conscientious objection also arose. World population was also mentioned, and a group attempted to use the pope's name to introduce a condemnation of contraception into the schema. It was finally approved on 7 December 1965.[49] That same day the pope and the Orthodox Patriarch Athenagoras agreed to 'consign to oblivion' the mutual excommunications that had poisoned the relationship between Catholics and Orthodox since 1054. On 8 December 1965 the council concluded.

It had been a mixed blessing. Although the Second Vatican Council had unleashed an ecclesial revolution, there is a sense in which it failed. Perhaps the fundamental problem was that the council tried to do too much. It was meant by Pope John to be 'pastoral' and not preoccupied with condemnation. But in hindsight it might have been better had it focused on major theological statements and allowed the church in the post-conciliar period to work out the pastoral implications of the basic shift in theological emphasis that it achieved. Fundamentally, the theological documents of the council are essentially transitional rather than finally prescriptive. Because of the need to obtain moral unanimity and the agreement of as many of the minority as was possible, the council's statements are also compromises that allow different theological models to coexist. Karl Rahner has perceptively commented that a general council is as much the beginning of a new discussion as the conclusion of an old one. In other words, Vatican II signals a decisive shift of emphasis in an ongoing discussion.

New emphases have to be incarnated in structures in order to be fully realised. The problem is that the practical structures for the realisation of the new vision articulated at the council have never been decisively put in place. Enormous energy was expended in the renewal of the church and its institutions in the years immediately following the council, but now, thirty-five years after Vatican II, many in the church feel that much of that energy seems to have been wasted. However, because we are still in the process it is difficult to come to a final assessment of this.

Paul VI and the implementation of the council

THE WORK OF Vatican II did not finish on 8 December 1965. It continued through a ten-year period of practical reforms across the life of the church: worship, ecumenical relations, episcopal conferences, the rejigging of the curia, the updating of religious orders and the priesthood, the rewriting of canon law. It also occurred through a new spirit of openness that spread throughout the church. But the compromises that had been made at Vatican II and the failure to reform the Roman curia thoroughly provided opportunities for those who wished to maintain the old values and power structures.

The period immediately after 1965 saw a whole series of post-conciliar documents applying and expanding the reforms of Vatican II.[50] For instance, between 1963 and 1981 forty separate documents were issued on the reform of worship, which set out the practical applications of the *Constitution on the Sacred Liturgy*. There were sixteen documents on ecumenism and ecumenical activities, fifteen on the reform of religious life, six on the priesthood, and six from the Synod of Bishops. Of these, the most important were clearly those on worship, ecumenism and religious life. Ecumenism was a priority for Paul VI; his meetings with Archbishop Michael Ramsey of Canterbury (24 March 1966) and the Ecumenical Patriarch Athenagoras in Jerusalem (6 January 1964), Istanbul (25 July 1967) and Rome (26 October 1967) were highlights of his papacy.

One of the least noticed but important post-conciliar documents was the apostolic letter of Paul VI, *Matrimonia Mixta* (7 January 1970).[51] It dealt with the complex issue of marriages between non-Catholics and Catholics, but it also impinged on ecumenical relationships, especially in countries where there was a significant number of Anglican, Orthodox or Protestant Christians as well as Catholics. The pope tried to engage the bishops of the world in the preparation of the letter but received little response. Collegiality is a two-way street. Probably because of the lack of input, the letter is not as radical as it could have been.

In terms of church structure, one of the key post-conciliar documents is the apostolic constitution *Regimini Ecclesiae Universae* of 15 August 1967. In this Paul VI attempted to reform the Roman curia. The key elements in the constitution are that all curial appointments are limited to a five-year term; all Vatican staffers must resign at the age of seventy-five; all appointments are cancelled at the death of the pope. As a result Paul VI to an extent broke the ongoing power and tenure of the cardinals who were prefects of the congregations. There are no longer any 'supreme' dicasteries (the term that congregations use to describe themselves)—and under John Paul II's adaptations there are no 'sacred' ones either.[52] Now all curial departments are juridically equal. Some nomenclature was changed: Propaganda became Evangelisation of Peoples, and the Holy Office became the Congregation for the Doctrine of the Faith. The Secretariat of State (or Papal Secretariat) has now emerged as the core of the Vatican. All business flows through this body; it has become a kind of curia within the curia. In Paul VI's reform the Council for the Public Affairs of the Church administered church relationships with civil governments and the papal diplomatic service. In a further streamlining under John Paul II, the Secretariat of State has been divided into two sections: the first deals with general church affairs, and the second with relations with states. In this sense the secretary of state has now truly become a kind of papal prime minister, rather than just a foreign minister. The curia has been largely internationalised and the old Italian career structure has been considerably modified.[53]

But the curial leopard has not really changed its spots: the old methods of power, manipulation, delay and control still remain. Although Paul VI faced fierce protest over his changes to the curia, it has to be said that at most he rejigged the old structure rather than radically changed it. It was this failure to tackle the structural problem at a fundamental level that has led to the revival in the contemporary Vatican of some of the worst aspects of the pre-conciliar curia. This is illustrated by the renamed Congregation for the Doctrine of the Faith (CDF). Its name has been changed (although its address has remained the Palazzo del Sant'Uffizio), and its processes have been modified by the decree *Integrae Servandae* (7 December 1965). Pope Paul attempted to shift the focus of the congregation from the condemnation of error to the encouragement of orthodox doctrine and to the discussion of disputed questions. The 'fraternal' correction of errors was envisaged as a last resort. If this had been followed through, things might have really changed in the congregation. But the major problem was that the change of emphasis was entrusted to those who had most resisted it. A scholar from the Catholic University in Leuven, Monsignor Charles Moeller, was brought in as CDF secretary, but he soon returned to Belgium. He commented that it was 'like asking the Mafia to reform the Mafia'.[54] In 1968 a Yugoslav, Cardinal Franjo Seper, was appointed prefect. The International Theological Commission was set up in 1967 to work alongside the CDF.

In 1969 the French Cardinal Jean Villot was appointed secretary of state, succeeding the aged Cardinal Amleto Cicognani. But during the papacy of Paul VI the key men in the Secretariat of State were the Substitutes, Archbishops (later Cardinals) Giovanni Benelli and Agostino Casaroli. The industrious and dynamic Benelli dealt with ordinary affairs and Casaroli with foreign affairs, including the controversial *Ostpolitik*, the Vatican's attempt to negotiate with the communist regimes of Eastern Europe. Giancarlo Zizola has pointed out that the Papal Secretariat, which was meant to be a co-ordinating body of the curia has, in fact, become a duplicate curia that surrounds and cossets the pope.[55] This has been reinforced by the changes of John Paul II, who has strengthened the position of the Secretariat of State even more.

A whole series of new secretariats and other bodies were set up in the curia between 1960 and 1967, such as the Secretariat for Christian Unity (1960), the Secretariat for Non-Believers (1965) and the Pontifical Council for Justice and Peace (1967). The increase in the number of curial officials is significant, although by modern bureaucratic standards the numbers are still very small: Thomas Reese says that in the mid-1990s there were about 1740 people.[56] It was this increase that largely contributed to the Vatican's financial deficits right up until the mid-1990s. Guiseppe Alberigo comments that it was in the late 1960s that the restructuring of the curia was really abandoned and that, in fact, the new curial offices paradoxically brought even more aspects of the church under Vatican control.[57] The reforms of 1967 actually enhanced papal power. This is not to say that the curia did not change; it did. The sense of curial officials as baroque noblemen disappeared, a genuine internationalisation occurred, and there was a certain streamlining of administration. Especially in the 'new' curia some able and broad-minded people were appointed, including some women, but not many of these open and pastoral people are left now. At heart, things did not change: the same self-enclosed, ministerially inexperienced and narrow attitudes characterise those who work in the contemporary curia.

Two encyclicals: *Populorum Progressio* (1967) and *Humanae Vitae* (1968)

THERE IS A SENSE in which Paul VI was profoundly concerned with the world and his encyclical *Populorum Progressio* is one of the most radical of all papal documents. It is truly international in approach. It deals fundamentally with the north–south divide and the gap between the rich and the poor. This, the Pope says, will only be resolved by the full human development of all people. Genuine humanism will be achieved by integral development, which will come about through social justice and equity in international relations. He even recognises that there is a population problem (para. 37). The problem with the encyclical is the ambivalence of the meaning of the word 'development', which so often occurs at the expense of the environment. However, the Pope does seriously question theories of rationalist economics and the dominance of market forces. The inspiration of the encyclical had been the papal visit to India, French Catholic social thought and the influence of Barbara Ward, who had spoken to the council. Closely tied to his broad vision of the world was the conviction that the church was called to proclaim the Gospel. This was expressed best in his apostolic exhortation *Evangelii Nuntiandi* (8 December 1975).[58] Many regard this as one of the finest theological products of the Montini papacy. This extraordinarily open document linked evangelisation to justice to the poor, and salvation to liberation.

With an ongoing commitment to Third World Catholicism, the pope went to Colombia, visiting Bogota and beginning the Latin American Bishops' Conference in Medellin in August 1968. It was at Medellin that the Latin American bishops first expressed the idea of salvation in terms of the theology of liberation. They were inspired by *Populorum Progressio*. In July of 1969 the pope travelled to Kampala, Uganda, where he stressed the importance of the church being part of the local culture. He told the African churches that the Catholic tradition could be expressed in ways that were suited to the culture of Africa.[59] The pope's longest trip was to the Far East and Australia in November 1970. He also visited Fatima, Portugal, and the World Council of Churches and the International

Labor Organisation in Geneva. He had begun the policy of papal trips, and much of it was motivated by the desire to spread the message of social justice.

Tragically, it is not Paul VI's social radicalism that is remembered but his moral conservatism. So often his papacy is defined by the encyclical *Humanae Vitae*. The history of the encyclical is well known.[60] The pill, which made artificial contraception readily available, only came into widespread use in the 1960s. Prior to that Pius XI had condemned all forms of artificial contraception in *Casti Connubii* (1932). The introduction of oral contraceptives seemed to shift the moral focus of discussion, and some Catholic moralists argued that the use of the pill was permissible. They based this on the principle *Lex dubium non obligat* —a doubtful law does not oblige. Many Catholic couples, for whom the issue was more than theoretical, began to use the pill. Pope Paul turned to the Birth Control Commission, set up by John XXIII to advise him. The only non-professional people on the commission were the Americans Pat and Patty Crowley, a married couple from Chicago and the founders of Christian Family Movement, who provided the most telling evidence against the so-called rhythm method. In 1966 a final majority report recommended change in papal teaching on contraception. A minority on the Commission wanted the traditional teaching maintained. The report remained secret until it was leaked to the *US National Catholic Reporter*, who handed it on to *The Tablet* in London.[61]

Ottaviani and conservative moralists, of whom one of the most important was the American Jesuit John C. Ford (1902–89), put Paul VI under intense pressure to maintain the old line. Ford argued that the real issue was authority rather than contraception: he said that any change would gravely weaken papal teaching authority for it would seem to indicate that the church had been wrong for centuries, and specifically that Pius XI was incorrect. This had already been confronted by the commission; the teaching on contrception was not of apostolic origin and was never part of the infallible magisterium. But the Birth Control Commission was quietly and decisively set aside.

The Pope appointed another secret commission, headed by Ottaviani.[62] The issues that concerned this secret committee were the consistency of the magisterium's teaching and the fear of government-organised family planning as well as general hedonism.[63] These are the real reasons for *Humanae Vitae*. But the argument in the encyclical is based on the natural law. Conception was a natural result of intercourse, and the processes of nature could not be artificially vitiated. Every conjugal act must be open to the transmission of life.

The encyclical argued that all bishops, priests and Catholic faithful must give internal assent and commit their consciences to the papal teaching. The pope admitted that many would not agree with him in his interpretation of the natural law, but he wanted them to obey nevertheless. This was interpreted by many as hypocrisy. The results of this encyclical for the church community have been considerable. Many Catholics left the church. Others, bereft of sensible pastoral advice, limped along for years denying themselves communion. Most priests were as confused as laypeople, but their pastoral sense guided them toward a tolerant and helpful attitude. It led to many good priests and even to one American bishop leaving the ministry. The encyclical was the beginning of a drop in Mass attendance, especially in the fertile age group. Perhaps it also had the result of bringing many Catholics to moral maturity in one step. They assumed personal responsibility for their own moral behaviour. No longer could they ask the church to decide their morals. They learned to use and develop their own consciences. The encyclical was not, as Cardinal Suenens pointed out in 1969, a collegial action. The pope had called a synod that year to discuss collegiality, but as Suenens said, Paul VI had ignored collegiality in the contraception decision.[64] Suenens was quickly supported by Karl Rahner, Hans Küng, Bishop Christopher Butler and other theologians. Nothing was resolved at the synod on collegiality. There can be no doubt of the pope's good intentions, but he seemed to become increasingly fearful of supposed threats to papal primacy.

Ostpolitik—and financial scandals[65]

OSTPOLITIK IS THE TERM used to describe the complex policy initiated by John XXIII and continued by Paul VI to try to get some religious freedom for the approximately 60 million Catholics living under the communist governments of Eastern Europe. Pope John realised that a purely anti-communist stance was insufficient and he tried to develop a different approach. Both he and Pope Paul VI hoped that through dialogue with communists the constant threat to world peace would be lessened. Although not always successful, the approach was ahead of its time and showed the independence of Vatican 'foreign policy' from the conventional approach of the Western alliance. The man who ran the *Ostpolitik* for both popes was Archbishop Agostino Casaroli (1914–98), later to be cardinal secretary of state. He was supported by the diplomats Archbishops Achille Silvestrini and Luigi Poggi, with Cardinal Koenig of Vienna playing an important intermediary role.[66] There was a parallel reconciliation going on with the Russian Orthodox church, largely cultivated by Cardinal Jan Willebrands of the Christian Unity Secretariat. This led to strong opposition by Cardinal Josyf Slipyj, the head of the Ukrainian Catholic church, after his release from Stalinst prisons. The Ukrainian Catholics had been forcefully incorporated into the Russian church in 1946 by Stalin. The whole problem was complicated by the fact that a married clergy was traditional in the Ukrainian church, but in countries like Canada, Australia and the United States they were forbidden to marry. So, in the early 1970s, Slipyj threatened dire consequences. It was suggested that the Ukrainian church might abandon union with Rome.

In contrast, the Polish hierarchy, led by the primate, Cardinal Stefan Wyszynski, did not object outright to the *Ostpolitik* but felt that the negotiations were too diplomatically oriented to be useful.[67] There is some truth to this judgement, although concessions were won in Yugoslavia, Hungary and to a limited extent Czechoslavakia. Another strong opponent of the *Ostpolitik* was Cardinal Joseph Minszenty, who fled to the United States legation in Budapest after the failure of the Hungarian revolution in 1956. Eventually, he was forced by the Vatican to resign as archbishop of Esztergom in 1974, and he died in Vienna the next year.

The latter years of Paul VI's papacy and the early years of that of John Paul II were marked by a series of financial scandals. In a series of foolish moves, Paul VI and his financial advisers allowed themselves to become involved with some of the most notorious con-men of the century. Although the general lines of this scandal are clear, the exact interconnections between the Vatican and the shadow-side of international finance are hard to clarify. Certainly by the late 1960s it was clear that the Vatican had financial problems. The Chicago-born Archbishop Paul Marcinkus was the rising star at the Instituto per le Opere de Religione (IOR)—the Institute of Religious Works—set up by Pius XII in 1942 as an investment arm of the Vatican. It acts as a merchant bank and was thus involved in the world of international finance. As an ordinary bank most of its deposits come from religious orders, private individuals and other church-related agencies. It is popularly, if inaccurately, known as the Vatican Bank. Historically, it is significant that the church has condemned usury since the Council of Arles (314). However, by the mid-twentieth century the Vatican itself was running a bank that speculated in the short-term money market.

Marcinkus thought that Vatican investments should be moved out of the Italian stocks favoured by his predecessor, Cardinal Alberto Di Jorio, and placed in various international companies that were felt to be safe. At the time there were accusations that the Vatican was trying to sidestep Italian currency laws and taxes on its portfolio. The IOR was also being clearly used by some Italians as a channel to the tax havens of Switzerland and the Caribbean to avoid Italy's financial regulators. In a secret meeting in 1969 Marcinkus introduced Paul VI to a Sicilian banker, Michele Sindona. This was a foolish move, for Sindona's Mafia and criminal connections were well known. He was also a member of the notorious right-wing pseudo-Masonic lodge, Propaganda Due (P-2), founded by the Fascist, Licio Gelli. Sindona used his Vatican connections to facilitate criminal financial deals, and it is also clear that Marcinkus did nothing to stop him. By 1974 two banks run by Sindona had crashed, and he was wanted in both Italy and United States. The Vatican tried to distance itself from him. But it had already lost a massive amount of money through the Sindona connection. Estimates range between $US30 million (the official figure) and $US200 million. Sindona died suspiciously of poison in an Italian prison in 1986.

Through a connection with Paul VI's private secretary, Don Pasquale Macchi, the Vatican then brought in as an adviser the Milanese banker Roberto Calvi, president of the prestigious Catholic-run Banco Ambrosiano. The IOR quickly became a large stockholder in the Ambrosiano.

Calvi was a highly talented thief. Like Sindona, he used his Vatican connections to facilitate a whole range of illegal dealings. In July 1981 Calvi was convicted of the illegal export of Italian currency. Further investigations by Italian banking authorities uncovered massive fraud by Calvi. He was found hanged under Blackfriars Bridge in London in June 1982. Through Calvi the Vatican had become involved in the theft of $US1.6 billion from the Banco Ambrosiano. In late 1982 John Paul II appointed a committee of cardinals to investigate the whole sorry affair. Marcinkus was eventually charged by the Italian authorities, but he was protected by Vatican diplomatic immunity and eventually retired to the United States. While denying all responsibility in the Ambrosiano affair, the Vatican made reparation by paying $US250 million to the Ambrosiano's creditors. The source of this money has never been explained. Many writers have subsequently charged the Vatican with criminal misbehaviour. The very best that can be said is that its financial administration was irresponsible. It vividly demonstrates the foolishness of allowing priests to participate in the world of international finance. Vatican finances are now under the control of the Prefecture for the Economic Affairs of the Holy See, and to some extent the financial problems have been solved. The Vatican is slowly becoming more open about its costs and expenditure.[68]

The last years of Paul VI's papacy were overshadowed not only by financial scandals, but also by the growing right-wing Lefebvrist schism, the departure of many priests and religious from the active ministry, and a spreading disillusionment among Catholics across the world about the application of conciliar renewal. Many hoped that the pope would retire at the age of seventy-five and that a synod of world bishops would elect his successor. He seems to have toyed with the idea for a while, but eventually only further internationalised the College of Cardinals and decreed that cardinals aged over eighty be excluded from future conclaves. He suffered from ill-health for the last couple of years of his life. The power and influence of the Substitute secretary of state, Archbishop Giovanni Benelli, throughout this last period of his life was considerable. Benelli had implemented the details of the pope's reform of the curia and had virtually run the secretariat of state for the last years of the Montini papacy. He was made cardinal and archhishop of Florence just over a year before the pope died.

Paul VI died on 6 August 1978. He left an ambivalent legacy. He had saved the church from schism and he had tried to implement Vatican II. But for many Catholics he had never gone far enough and had not decisively dealt with curial and reactionary attempts to subvert the council's vision. Also his reputation never recovered from the disaster of *Humanae Vitae*. Yet even in 1978 time had not run out, and there was still a chance to realise the vision that was inherent in Vatican II.

In a month of optimism between 26 August and 28 September 1978, it seemed as though that radical vision might be realised.

The year of three popes[69]

THE CONCLAVE THAT mct on 25 August had a record 111 cardinals and was the first to meet under Paul VI's reforms. Cardinals aged over eighty were excluded, although their influence on the pre-conclave discussions was considerable. There were only twenty-seven Italians who were eligible as electors. The cardinals met daily to prepare for the election. In public discussions before the conclave it became clear that what Western Catholics wanted was, in the words of a group that included Hans Küng, Yves Congar and Edward Schillebeeckx, 'a man of holiness, a man of hope, a man of joy . . . who can smile. A pope not for all Catholics but for all peoples. A man totally free from the slightest taint of financial organisational wheeling and dealing.' On 26 August 1978, twenty days after the death of Paul VI, the 65-year-old Albino Luciani, the patriarch of Venice, was elected on the third ballot. It was an extraordinarily quick conclave. He promised to be a new style of pope. He was from a working-class background, and all of his priestly and episcopal experience had been in pastoral work and seminary teaching. He had never had anything to do with the curia, although he had been active in the Italian Bishops' Conference. He chose the unusual style of John Paul. It is impossible to say where he would have stood on theological matters, despite assertions that he was assassinated because he was going to disown *Humanae Vitae*, as well as clean up the Vatican Bank and the curia.

He died late in the evening of 28 September while reading in bed. There was no autopsy and rumours of murder by poisoning found concrete form in the book *In God's Name* by David Yallop.[70] Yallop maintained that John Paul I was murdered by a group that included Cardinal Jean Villot (the secretary of state), Cardinal John Patrick Cody of Chicago, Archbishop Marcinkus, and Sindona and Calvi.[71] This tendentious account was refuted by John Cornwell.[72] Cornwell maintained that Luciani died because no one took care of his health and made sure he took medication for his heart condition.

And so Rome prepared for another conclave. This time it was clear that the pastoral candidate would also have to have good health and be younger. The conclave was much longer and clearly more divided. At first the candidates were Benelli and the reactionary Siri of Genoa. It was only when it became clear that neither could get the needed two-thirds plus one that the cardinals began to look outside Italy.

Cardinal Franz Koenig of Vienna put forward the name of Karol Wojtyla of Cracow. He had travelled widely, spoke fluent Italian, and came from a communist country. At fifty-eight years of age, he seemed to have much to recommend him. After eight ballots, he had obtained a large majority. He took the style John Paul II. The election of a Polish pope brought great excitement to the church. Ordinary Catholics felt that as a non-Italian he would take a different approach to his predecessors. Among the well-informed there was a feeling of bemusement.

Everyone was quickly disabused as to the way the new Polish papacy would go.

11 pope john paul II

The formation of Karol Wojtyla

POPE JOHN PAUL II came to the papacy with a unique background.[1] Not only was he shaped by this, but he was also an academic with a body of philosophical writing to his credit that was, until his election, only available in Polish, a language not generally known by most Western theologians. What non-Polish Catholics were soon to discover was that his views were both well developed and very different to those of his European and Anglo-American theological counterparts. His specialisation has always been philosophical anthropology and ethics. He generally belongs to the continental personalist school of thought, but his personalism overlays a deeply ingrained neo-Scholasticism.

Geography is also profoundly important for John Paul. Karol Jozef Wojtyla was born in the small market town of Wadowice on the Skawa River some 40 kilometres south-west of Cracow. It had been part of the Austro-Hungarian province of Galicia until the reunification of Poland in 1918. His home town is 25 kilometres south of Oswiecim (the German Auschwitz) and 100 kilometres south of the national shrine of Our Lady of Czestochowa at Jasna Gora. Both places are significant: his devotion to the Blessed Virgin is both deep and obvious. He is also profoundly influenced by the Holocaust. Perhaps two and a half million people, mainly Jews, were murdered at Auschwitz and the extermination camp at Birkenau, and in the slave-labour camps that surrounded Cracow, such as the one in the suburb of Plaszow (it was here that the famous Oskar Schindler's factory was situated), and this has clearly had a deep effect on the development of Wojtyla.[2] He has spoken of Auschwitz as 'the Golgotha of the modern world'.

His most formative years were spent under the German occupation. It was a vicious and brutal period which lasted until the arrival of Soviet troops in January 1945. He had entered the Jagiellonian University in 1938 as a student of Polish language and literature. During the war years he had been influenced a lay mystic Jan Tyranowski, who introduced him to the study of the great sixteenth-century Spanish spiritual writer, St John of the Cross. They had met at the local parish, where Tyranowski ran a theological discussion group. In late 1941 Wojtyla joined the underground seminary in the residence of Archbishop (later Cardinal) Adam Sapieha of Cracow. The young Wojtyla never seems to have looked back in his commitment to the priesthood. With the defeat of the Germans and the reopening of the university in 1945, he returned and took final examinations in theology in August 1946. He was ordained priest by Cardinal Sapieha on 1 November 1946.

Sapieha sent him to Rome in 1946 to do a two-year doctorate at the Angelicum University. His mentor there was the French Dominican, Reginald Garrigou-Lagrange (1877–1964), whose theology was rooted in the anti-idealist, neo-scholastic tradition of the nineteenth century (see Chapter 9). Garrigou-Lagrange had been close to Action française in the 1930s, and during World War II he had supported the Vichy regime. He was also a vigorous opponent of the *nouvelle théologie*; in fact, it was he who gave the movement its name. At the same time he argued that all Christians are called to radical holiness, in contrast to the prevailing view that only members of religious orders and clergy were committed to seek 'perfection'. This view was shared by Wojtyla. In Rome he was able to continue his interest in Spanish mysticism, and under Garrigou-Lagrange's direction he completed a thesis entitled *Doctrina de Fide apud S. Joannem de Cruce* (The Doctrine of Faith According to St John of the Cross).[3] In the thesis Wojtyla argued that, while the mind rose above conceptual theology in its ascent to mystical contemplation, it never abandoned the substance of revelation, which it came to perceive from the perspective of a more profound wisdom. In other words, no matter how advanced the mystic, he or she never left behind the objective truth of revelation and the reality of the church that expressed divine truth.

The degree was awarded on 19 June 1948. While in Rome he lived at the Belgian College and came to know the work of the Jocists—the Young Christian Workers—founded by the priest Joseph Cardijn in 1925 (see Chapter 9). He also looked closely at the work of the French worker priests, and probably shared Cardijn's criticism of the movement that it was an example of priests interfering in the work proper to the laity. After completing his Roman degree, Wojtyla returned to Poland. He had a brief curacy in a small rural parish and was then moved from 1949 to 1951 to a much larger urban parish in Cracow. Some of his poems were published.

He returned to the Jagiellonian University in 1951 and began a study of the German philosopher Max Scheler (1874–1928).[4] The title of his second thesis was *An Assessment of the Possibilities of Building a System of Christian Ethics on the Basis of the Principles of Max Scheler* (1953). Scheler was a phenomenologist, a social philosopher and a convert to Catholicism. He left the church at the time of the break-up of his second marriage. He was a strong German nationalist during World War I, and he loathed British and American culture. Deeply influenced by Edmund Husserl (1859–1938), Scheler's thought centred on the existence of moral values, and he held that ethics and philosophical anthropology lay at the core of philosophy, rather than metaphysics. For him values are objective essences that are intuitively accessible to the person through feelings and experiences. Thus, although his writing has something of the dense impenetrability that is characteristic of all phenomenologists for the English-speaking reader, he emphasised a philosophy that was socially committed. Scheler was not a Thomist; he was much more Augustinian in attitude. In this, and in his social commitment, he influenced Wojtyla's thought in another direction from the scholasticism of Garrigou-Lagrange.

Wojtyla as Polish bishop

IN OCTOBER 1953 Wojtyla began lecturing in philosophical ethics at the local seminary and in 1954 at the Catholic University of Lublin, the only independent university in the old Soviet bloc. In 1956 he became professor of ethics at Lublin. Throughout this period, in order to maintain pastoral contact, especially with tertiary-educated young people in Cracow, he commuted the 200 kilometres between the two cities each week. *Love and Responsibility*, published in Polish in 1960, was the product of both his lectures on ethics and his discussion and guidance as a chaplain to young people. Although his approach is extraordinarily frank, especially in the area of sexuality, the purpose always seems to be to justify neo-scholastic doctrine within the context of the personalist norm. It worth noting that, as Michael Walsh points out, many of his philosophical *adversarii* (opponents) at this time are from the West and include in particular English—and, to a slightly lesser extent, American —philosophers.[5] The thinkers he quotes as opponents are predictable: Jeremy Bentham, John Stuart Mill, Thomas Malthus, Sigmund Freud, and the like.

On 4 July 1958, at the very young age of thirty-eight, Wojtyla was made auxiliary bishop of Cracow. His play *The Jewellers Shop*—again, a kind of priest's-eye view of marriage—was published in 1960. Appointed apostolic administrator of Cracow in 1962, he became archbishop in 1964 when he was forty-four. He thus attended the whole of the Second Vatican Council, where he was generally identified with the progressive majority. He was created cardinal by Paul VI in May 1967. As archbishop he held a diocesan synod, and was mildly reformist. But he was also close to the people and very popular. In questions of church–state relations in Poland, Wojtyla always took a secondary place to Cardinal Stefan Wysznski, the primate, who was the clearly recognised leader of the bishops in various struggles with the communist government.

But the cardinal from Cracow was increasingly active in Rome through membership of several curial congregations. He also did a considerable amount of travelling, visiting the United States on a couple of occasions as well as Canada, Australia, New Zealand, the Philippines and Papua New Guinea. He usually stayed with Polish communities in each of these countries, which meant that his experience of the wider church was very limited. But he did have many visitors in Cracow from all over the world, and there is no doubt that many of his views on the wider church were formed before he was elected pope. In 1976 he gave the Lenten retreat to Paul VI and the Roman curia. This was later published as *A Sign of Contradiction*.[6]

Wojtyla as pope

THERE IS A WIDESPREAD perception that the great political success of this papacy has been the role of Wojtyla in the fall of the old Soviet Union and the freeing of the satellite states of Eastern Europe. Recent authors, such as Jonathan Kwitney, and Marco Politi and Carl Bernstein, attribute the fall of the Soviet empire almost totally to him—with help from Ronald Reagan and the CIA.[7] However, there are limitations to this view. Certainly, there was concern within the Kremlin when Wojtyla was elected. It is true that the Soviet Union collapsed from within under the weight of gross inefficiency, maladministration, corruption and economic stagnation; it is also true that the election of a pope from within the Soviet bloc assisted the movement toward disintegration. John Paul, of course, had enormous influence in Poland, especially through his support of Solidarity. Several papal visits to his homeland placed the Jaruzalski regime under enormous pressure. If this were the only important aspect of John Paul's papacy, his role in the eventual collapse of the Soviet bloc would make this papacy an important one. But there is much more to his papacy than this.

There is a real sense in which John Paul II himself is a 'sign of contradiction'. He is the first non-Western European pope for over a thousand years and the first non-Italian since the death of Hadrian VI in 1522. He is also the youngest pope since Pius IX (1846). This meant that he came to the papacy with a store of goodwill and excitement among many people who hoped for a new papal approach to many issues in the church. Much of this goodwill has now been dissipated, especially in the West.

But the contrast with his Italian predecessors is deeper that this. He has never been a 'normal' clerical priest. His training for the priesthood was not carried out in a conventional seminary, but in hiding in the archbishop's palace during the darkest days of the Nazi occupation. His entire ecclesiastical career has been lived out in the unique situation of the ultimately successful struggle of the Polish church against an avowedly communist and atheistic state. The achievement of this required a tight sense of Catholic identity, and a determination to wrest control of culture and the structures of society from the atheists. After his election Wojtyla attempted to realise on the world stage his vision of the meaning of life and of the role of the church. He has launched a 'new evangelisation' that aims at permeating culture and society with Christ's 'saving power'.

He has also projected himself as a populist-catechist, a man at home with ordinary people. His training as an actor has not been wasted: he has the ability to use the mass media and to communicate with enormous crowds. He has subtly shifted the papacy away from the notion of the pope as an aloof, almost 'quasi-divine' figure to an accessible man-of-the-people image. His relationship with the media is an ambivalent one: although he has generated far more column inches and more time on radio and television than all the other popes put together, he does not trust journalists nor their product, which he sees as shallow, intrusive and manipulative. As a catechist-preacher he sees the media primarily as a tool of evangelisation. For him it is a propagandistic agent of the proclamation of the 'good news'. He seemingly has no real comprehension of the critical and informative role of the media, especially in a Western democratic society. Yet, paradoxically, few modern leaders have been so well presented in the media; in many ways this is because of shrewd placement and promotion. A key figure in this has been Dr Joaquin Navarro-Valls, head of the Press Office of the Holy See and a member of Opus Dei.

Perhaps the most obvious sign of this accessible image is the fact that this pope has travelled more than any pope in history.[8] Travel and communication have created a sense of an omnipresent papacy. 'Previous popes have claimed a universal jurisdiction and pastorate; John Paul II has made it a reality.'⁹ By the end of 2000 he had travelled well over a million miles in ninety-one pastoral trips, visiting more than 126 countries.¹⁰ Some of these trips have been very brief; others, such as the 1986 journey to Bangladesh, Singapore, Fiji, New Zealand, Australia and the Seychelles—six countries in twelve days—have almost epic status. His trips to Africa and Latin America—regions vitally important for Catholicism—have taken in almost every country on the two continents. There is no doubt that his linguistic skills are considerable and that his ability to relate to enormous crowds is remarkable. Just as remarkable is his ability to become the central focus of a visual image; he is the first pope to have exploited television to the full. He has argued that the purpose of these pastoral trips is to strengthen the faith of the local church and to be a symbol of the unity of the universal church.

However, the fact is that the results are ephemeral. As the Jesuit Bartolomeo Sorge, the former editor of the *La Civiltà Cattolica*, has suggested, the trips resemble summer rain: they refresh, but are without lasting effects. By the 1990s the effect of the constant travel started to dissipate, although the visits to Cuba (January 1998) and Mexico (January 1999) were real successes. Although the pope can still command attention in the media, it is more likely to be critical, especially in Western countries. This was vividly illustrated in the trip to Germany in June 1996, where the reaction to him was very negative. Yet the pope is still attractive to certain types of younger people: huge crowds greeted him in August 1997 in Paris.

The pope's teaching

IF THE POPE SEES himself as a catechist and pastor on overseas trips, this is only one aspect of his view of himself as a teacher in the church. In the course of his papacy he has issued a series of encyclicals and other writings that range across issues dear to his heart, including ethics and morals, the millennium, labour and the social question, Christ and the redemption, the Blessed Virgin Mary, sexuality and contraception, the family, the priesthood, womanhood, and Slavic Christianity and culture; they constitute a body of theological work in their own right.¹¹ These are not new issues for Pope John Paul; he has been thinking about them for most of his life. Several encyclicals in this corpus particularly stand out as expressing the main theological themes of his papacy: among them are *Redemptor Hominis* (4 March 1979), *Sollicitudo Rei Socialis* (30 December 1987), *Veritatis Splendor* (5 October 1993), *Tertio Millennio Adveniente* (10 November 1994), *Fides et Ratio* (14 September 1998), and *Ut Unum Sint* (25 May 1995).

In many ways *Redemptor Hominis* is the thematic encyclical for the Wojtyla papacy, for it highlights the centrality of Christ's redemption, the effects of that redemption on contemporary humankind and the church's responsibility to maintain the truth. Significantly, the first paragraph of the encyclical refers to the millennium, which John Paul sees as 'a new advent, a season of expectation'.[12] While the redemption of Christ gives humankind its essential dignity, the pope argues that contemporary technology alienates us from ourselves and from the natural world around us. He says that 'The ascendancy of technology demand[s] a proportional development of morals and ethics'.[13] The church, he argues, has a special responsibility to bring humankind back to essential truths, and the papal magisterium is entrusted with the task of enforcing that task (para. 19). All of these themes have become central to this papacy.

Sollicitudo Rei Socialis develops the thought of Paul VI's great encyclical *Populorum Progressio* (1967). John Paul outlines what he means by authentic human development and decries 'blind submission to pure consumerism'.[14] This encyclical, as well as *Centisimus Annus* (May 1991), on the one hundredth anniversary of *Rerum Novarum*, gives forceful expression to John Paul's quite radical critique of capitalism and his contempt for the vacuous consumerism that he sees dominating the West.

Prior to the publication of *Veritatis Splendor* (6 August 1993), there had been much speculation about whether the forthcoming encyclical would invoke infallibility to enforce the teaching of *Humanae Vitae* against contraception. In fact this did not happen; it was apparently strongly opposed by Cardinal Josef Ratzinger, although the pope made it clear in *Veritatis Splendor*, which deals with fundamental moral questions, that circumstances could never change the nature of an intrinsically evil act, such as contraception. He attacked the moral relativism that he claimed is characteristic particularly of Western democratic societies. He further argued that the church's moral teaching is in crisis because of dissent within the church itself. The problem, the pope claimed, was a real misunderstanding on the part of some Catholic moralists concerning freedom of conscience. For John Paul freedom of conscience fundamentally means the freedom to act according to the moral truth as revealed, especially by the papal magisterium. It does not primarily refer to personal freedom to interpret circumstances or intentions in order to act according to one's own moral decision. Michael Walsh has compared *Veritatis Splendor* to Pius XII's *Humani Generis* (1950), where various groups of theologians were criticised with descriptions of their theological opinions which were 'travesties' of their actual views.[15]

The theme of the third millennium is one to which John Paul has returned in several encyclicals. He has set out a vast programme of preparation for Catholics for the millennium Jubilee and has devoted an encyclical to this theme: *Tertio Millennio Adveniente* (November 1994). He sees the Jubilee as part of the Christian duty to sanctify time. The encyclical *Fides et Ratio* (14 September 1998), on faith and reason, characterises post-modern society as having lost the desire for ultimate truth, which cannot be found by reason alone. He says that the modern cultural and techno-scientific enterprise must be impregnated by faith and the existence of absolute truths and universal moral imperatives.

Perhaps the most remarkable and atypical encyclical of the latter part of the Wojtyla papacy is *Ut Unum Sint* (May 1995) on the papal commitment to ecumenism. In it he says that his essential ministry is to act as *servus servorum Dei* (the servant of the servants of God); this 'designation is the best possible safeguard against the risk of separating power (and in particular the primacy) from ministry'.[16] He asks forgiveness for the responsibility of the papacy in divisions among the churches. He commits the Catholic church to continuing dialogue and even concedes the need of finding a way of exercising the primacy which, while not renouncing what is essential, is nevertheless open to the new situation of the churches. He frankly admits that the exercise of papal primacy 'constitutes a difficulty for most other Christians'. This is certainly true in the case of the reformed communions, and their response to the encyclical was negative. The Orthodox have been equally critical: the Ecumenical Patriarch of Constantinople, Bartholomeos I, who had spent three days with the pope in the Vatican in June 1995, criticised the encyclical and the Catholic church for claiming a world primacy of jurisdiction and an infallibility that is both personal and independent of the whole church. Given the centralisation of church governance that we have seen from the time of Vatican I and Pius IX up to and including the papacy of John Paul II, this criticism seems perfectly justified.

However, the pope's invitation to reflect on the nature of the primacy has been taken up by a number of Catholics, including the German theologian Hermann J. Pottmeyer and also Archbishop John Quinn in a lecture at Campion Hall, Oxford, in June 1996, and in his subsequent book *The Reform of the Papacy*.[17] Pottmeyer argues that *Ut Unum Sint* signals a willingness on the part of the papacy to shift its emphasis from a hierarchical to what he calls a 'communio' ecclesiology. By this he means that the universal church is a fellowship or communion of local churches held together by the Spirit of God, and manifesting itself in the college of bishops in union with the bishop of Rome. Collegiality is practical expression of this. But the practical problems that Pottmeyer (a member of the CDF's International Theological Commission) does not address are taken up by Archbishop Quinn in his Oxford lecture and book. Quinn describes *Ut Unum Sint* as 'revolutionary' precisely because it shows that the First Vatican Council definition of the primacy 'was not the last word'. Among a whole range of practical issues, such as the place of 'loyal dissent' in the church, the process of appointment of bishops, the reform of the college of cardinals, and the need for a practical expression of collegiality, Quinn says that the key issues remain over-centralisation and the need for serious reform of the Roman curia. He sees the church's response to *Ut Unum Sint* as a moment of grace that we cannot afford to let pass.

Ut Unum Sint reminds us that John Paul has produced a unique corpus of papal writings, for his official pronouncements have a more personal and direct feel; they are far less pretentious and, at least to English readers, they are not written in the convoluted 'Vaticanese' favoured by his predecessors. They clearly bear the Wojtyla stamp and it is obvious that it is he, rather than some anonymous expert, who is the primary redactor. This does not mean that others have not had a hand in the composition, but they are men very much of the Wojtyla intellectual stamp.

Another product of John Paul's determination to lead the church in a specific theological direction is *The Catechism of the Catholic Church*.[18] In some ways this is modelled on the *Catechism of the Council of Trent* of 1566. The notion of a post-Vatican II, worldwide catechism was first publicly proposed by Cardinal Bernard Law of Boston at the Extraordinary Synod of Bishops in November–December 1985, held to celebrate the twentieth anniversary of the end of Vatican II.[19] The idea was taken up by the pope (he had probably prompted Law to suggest it), and he proposed a compendium of Catholic doctrine that would become the norm for the church. It is not a catechism in the sense of mere questions and answers, but is a continuous text divided into numbered paragraphs. Although it was prepared through a consultation process with the world bishops, it bears the strong stamp of the pope. It was prepared in French, and the first edition was published in that language in November 1992. The English translation became embroiled in controversy over the use of inclusive language and did not appear until 1994. It has been assessed by most experts as a very uneven document. Parts of it, such as the section on the liturgy, are useful and close to the spirit of Vatican II. But other parts have been roundly criticised: the material on creation and the fall is very restrictive and closed and takes no account of modern scriptural, historical and theological studies. There is little on world religions (except Judaism) and even less on ecumenism. The approach of the text to sexual morality is extremely restrictive. There is no doubt that it reflects the pope's own theological agenda. Whether the church needs such a catechism remains an open question, and some Catholics doubt that it is possible to construct a text that is broad enough to embrace the multifaceted nature of Catholicism in every country and culture.

The pope, the curia and saint-making

ONE OF THE FIRST problems that John Paul faced after election was the
Vatican's ongoing financial scandal, as well as the Holy See's crippling
annual operating deficit (in 1991 it was about $US87.5 million).[20] The
pope had asked a Commission of Cardinals to investigate, and this led
to the appointment of Cardinal Edmund Szoka, former archbishop of
Detroit (1981–90), as president of the new Prefecture for the Economic
Affairs of the Holy See.[21] It had been reorganised in 1988 and it now
acts as an internal auditor for the Vatican.[22] The prefecture is supervised
by a Council of Cardinals. In the late 1990s the Vatican came out of the
red with a small surplus. As well as the considerably improved administration initiated by Szoka, part of the reason for this surplus may be that
the pope's book *Crossing the Threshold of Hope*—published in 1994 in
Italian and in English by Random House of New York—together with
The Catechism of the Catholic Church, brought considerable advances and
royalties to the Vatican. Also the Office of the Administration of the
Patrimony of the Holy See, which deals with both the investments and
the practical administration of the Vatican, has vastly improved its oper-
ations. Because of a change in the Italian taxation system the diocese of
Rome is no longer a charge on the Vatican's exchequer, thus saving a
$US5 million deficit.

Pope John Paul has pretty much left the curia in the shape he inherited from Paul VI. However, he has strengthened the role of the
Secretariat of State, and there have been complaints from within the
Vatican that the rest of the curia, with the exception of the Congregation for the Doctrine of the Faith (CDF), have been marginalised.
Certainly Cardinal Josef Ratzinger has emerged as a very influential
figure in the Wojtyla papacy. The famous *Ratzinger Report* of 1985 gives a
clue to his thinking and to that of Pope John Paul.[23] The *Report* signals
the need for a restoration of an 'integral' Catholicism and a recentralis-
ation of the church. There is a real sense in which both pope and cardinal reject the claim of individual religious freedom that finds its roots in
the Reformation, and the rational and intellectual spirit of the Enlightenment. There is a profound suspicion in this papacy of genuine democracy in the sense of individual freedom of expression, as practised in the

Western European and Anglo-American world. When John Paul speaks about 'religious freedom' he really means the freedom to practise Catholicism, or the liberty to embrace it. There is something deeply paternalistic about it all. In the 1990s the pope has become less critical of Western permissiveness and consumerism, presumably because the countries of the old Soviet bloc, including Poland, have embraced capitalism and all its attendant evils and ugliness with great enthusiasm.[24]

Pope John Paul has also established several new Pontifical Councils: for the Family in 1981; for Culture in 1982; for Pastoral Care, for Health Care Workers and for Interreligious Dialogue in 1988. The work of the Pontifical Council for the Family closely follows John Paul's own agenda: it promotes responsible parenthood and reproduction according to the teaching of the popes, it participated in the United Nations World Conference on Population—largely because of its concern with abortion, rather than any real commitment to doing anything about overpopulation—and it works worldwide to defend human life and oppose abortion legislation. Its first president was the Canadian Cardinal Edward Gagnon, and it is now presided over by the Colombian Cardinal Alfonso Lopez Trujillo, a strong opponent of liberation theology. The Pontifical Council for Culture was further reorganised in 1993 when it was merged with the Pontifical Council for Dialogue with Non-Believers. Its president is the former rector of the Institut Catholique in Paris, the scholarly Cardinal Paul Poupard. The function of the council is to promote dialogue with those who are not religious believers and to participate in discussion about culture in the contemporary world. The Pontifical Council for Interreligious Dialogue was set up for discussion between Christian and those from non-Christian religious traditions. In 1988 he also set up the Commission for the Cultural Heritage of the Church and, significantly, the Labour Office of the Holy See to deal with the industrial problems of the laity who work for the Vatican.

This image of a centralised church as the dominant moral and spiritual force in the world seems to be structurally confirmed by the growth of Vatican diplomacy in this papacy: in 1978 there were 89 nuncios and 21 apostolic delegates; in 1998 there were 167 nuncios, 18 apostolic delegates and 24 papal diplomats attached to international organisations.[25] The aim of this and of the constant papal travel is to reach past governments, and even bishops, directly to the mass of the people. It seems ironically like a modern attempt to re-establish a kind of papal monarchy that alone possesses permanent moral and spiritual values. This is meant to stand in stark contrast to the constantly shifting relativities of the post-modern, democratic world.

Pope John Paul has also taken a far more conciliatory approach to the Lefebvrist schism than Paul VI. He established the Pontifical Commission Ecclesia Dei in 1988 to assist the return to full communion with the church of priests and religious associated with the schism led by Archbishop Marcel Lefebvre.

Canonisations and beatifications have played a prominent role in this papacy.[26] The process is dealt with by the Congregation for the Causes of Saints, which studies the lives of those proposed as saints according to revised norms drawn up in 1983 in the apostolic constitution *Divinus Perfectionis Magister*. Now the process can begin with nomination by a bishop from any diocese in the world. Only one miracle is now required in place of the three formerly required. The miracle is usually a medical cure that cannot be explained by science. The processes have been streamlined so that a broader cross-section of people can be included in the canonisation process. Up until September 1998 John Paul had carried out a record sixty-two canonisations, involving 326 people being declared saints, most of them martyrs.[27] The number of beatifications has also been extraordinary: 872.[28] Although there are still many saints and blesseds from the traditional sources (the Catholic countries of Europe, including many priests, as well as founders and members of religious orders, especially from Latin counties), there has been a significant shift of emphasis. This includes focusing on the sanctity that can be found among Third World Catholics and missionaries, and specifically among the laity. There have been several large groups of Asian martyrs, including 103 Koreans, 16 Japanese, 117 Vietnamese, as well as a group of Thai nuns. There are also groups of martyrs from Armenia and Mexico as well as individual saints and blesseds from the United States, the United Kingdom, Papua New Guinea and Australia.

Prominent martyrs from the Nazi period include St Maximilian Kolbe, a Polish priest killed at Auschwitz; Blessed Titus Brandsma, a

Dutch Carmelite priest who protected Dutch Jews; and St Edith Stein, a convert from Judaism who became a Carmelite nun and was also executed at Auschwitz. Three controversial groups include eighty-five martyrs from the post-Reformation period in England, Scotland and Wales (this was interpreted by some as anti-ecumenical), several groups of Spanish religious and priests killed during the Civil War, and a large group of teaching brothers killed during the French Revolution. Surprise beatifications include the Franciscans Fra Angelico, the great medieval painter, and the medieval Oxford theologian John Duns Scotus.

Concern has been expressed about the streamlining of the process of saint-making. The role of the devil's advocate has been abolished and much of the historical work is not as good as it should be. The task of the devil's advocate was to discover reasons why a person's cause should not proceed. It made sure that the candidate for sainthood was looked at very critically and objections were answered by the promoter of the cause. Serious concerns about some who have been beatified have been swept aside, and the sheer number of saints and beatified, while it may satisfy the pious aspirations of small groups, seems to serve no useful purpose for the wider church. Also the influence of church politics is never far away. For instance, the failure to proceed with the cause of Archbishop Oscar Romero, archbishop of San Salvador (El Savador), asassinated by right-wing vigilantes while celebrating Mass in his cathedral, is clearly political. Romero is seen as a hero of liberation theology, even though he was theologically very conservative. Liberation theology is deeply out of favour in the Wojtyla papacy. In an odd juxtaposition the beatification of Pope John XXIII has been deliberately linked with that of Pius IX, a hero of the modern reactionary right. Increasingly the titles 'saint' and 'blessed' are being devalued.

Theology, women, and ecumenism in the Wojtyla papacy

ALTHOUGH THE MODERN POPES have always kept a tight rein on theology, under John Paul II the task of theology has been defined in even narrower terms: fundamentally, Rome has come to see the theologian as an apologist who, in strict subordination to pope and the bishops, clarifies and defends official papal and church teaching. Thus the task of theology is not to explicate the faith in terms of the culture, but simply to explain the teaching of the magisterium. From the beginning of this papacy prominent theologians have been targeted because of their writings. The Congregation for the Doctrine of the Faith—presided over from 1967 by the Yugoslav Cardinal Franjo Seper, and, since 1981, by the former archbishop of Munich, Cardinal Josef Ratzinger—is the key curial body in dealing with theologians. Although appointed to 'reform' the CDF along the lines proposed by Paul VI, Seper quickly became more Roman than the Romans, and after the appointment of the Dominican archbishop Jerome Hamer, the CDF returned to its old ways of anonymous denunciation, trials and condemnations. The German moralist and Redemptorist priest Bernard Häring has described the painful process that theologians undergo in dealing with the CDF in his book *My Witness for the Church*.[29] The usually mild-mannered Häring is critical of the competence of the theological experts used by the CDF, and quotes Cardinal Michele Pellegrino of Turin saying that these people show a 'complete proportionality between ignorance and arrogance'.[30]

The second year of the John Paul papacy in 1979 saw the beginning of the censuring of theologians. Early that year an investigation was opened into the French Dominican Jacques Pohier.[31] The case is not well-known in the English-speaking world and was over-shadowed by the more famous Schillebeeckx case. In April 1978 the CDF asserted that Pohier's book *Quand je dis Dieu* (When I Say God), published the previous year, contained 'clear and certain' errors of faith concerning Christology and scripture. Pohier co-operated with the CDF procedure and was open to discussion of his views, but within twelve months of the first accusation he was suspended from the priesthood. Subsequently he was virtually forced out of the order and the priesthood. Then, in the middle of 1979, the book *Human Sexuality*, a study commissioned by the Catholic Theological Society of America, was condemned.[32] Later in the year a Brazilian liberation theologian, the Franciscan Leonardo Boff, was 'silenced' for twelve months. At the same time Hans Küng's *missio canonica* to teach theology was withdrawn by Rome. Küng, according to the CDF, could no longer be called a 'Catholic theologian'. The precipitating issue was his approach to the theology of infallibility, but the CDF investigation had gone back to the period before Vatican II. Under the terms of the 1933 concordat between Nazi Germany and the Vatican, pressure was brought to bear on the local bishop, Georg Moser of Rottenburg-Stuttgart, to persuade the education minister of Baden-Wurttemberg to remove Küng from the Catholic faculty of the state-run Tubingen University. He was pushed out of the Catholic faculty, but the university created a special chair in ecumenical theology for him. The Dutch Dominican Edward Schillebeeckx had also been under investigation by the CDF for a number of years during Paul VI's papacy. The Schillebeeckx case originally centred on the Dutch theologian's views on Christology in his book *Jesus: An Experiment in Christology*.[33] One of the key issues in the book was the question of Jesus' resurrection. But from 1980 onwards the issue was the orthodoxy of his views in the series of historical and theological essays that comprised his book *Ministry*.[34] After protracted negotiations, Ratzinger issued a letter of rebuke of Schillebeeckx in 1985.

Throughout the 1980s a series of theologians came under the scrutiny of the CDF. The moralist Charles Curran lost his post at the Catholic University of America in 1987 after an eight-year process, which ended with a civil court case, in which Curran defended the right of theologians to dissent from non-infallible papal teachings. Leonardo Boff, after several visits to the CDF, especially over his book *Church, Charism and Power*, and long debates about the nature of Latin American theology, eventually left the priesthood. Bernard Häring, a German, compared the treatment he personally received from the CDF to that meted out to him by the Nazis. The Swiss theologian, Waldbert Buhl-mann was equally critical of CDF processes.

The case of the Sri Lankan theologian and Oblate priest Father Tissa Balasuriya has led the CDF to try to reform its own procedures. It was alleged that Balasuriya's book *Mary and Human Liberation* contained 'errors', probably the most egregious of which was that the book supported the ordination of women. Balasuriya was suddenly excommunicated on 2 January 1997 and his book declared heretical after he refused to swear to a personal profession of faith explicitly drawn up for him by the CDF. Balasuriya's excommunication was widely covered in the media, and he received strong support from Catholics and theologians from around the globe. The CDF was widely criticised. On 15 January 1998 the excommunication was lifted after Balasuriya agreed to sign Paul VI's *Credo of the People of God*, a procedure he had suggested himself before the excommunication.

As a clear result of the widespread criticism that has continued since 1979, brought to a head by the Balasuriya excommunication, the CDF issued on 29 June 1997 a new set of *Regulations for Doctrinal Examination*. These outline procedures for the examination of 'writings or opinions which appear contrary to correct faith and dangerous'. Although there are new safeguards in the *Regulations*, they still do not meet even minimal standards for human rights procedures. The respected canonist Ladislas Orsy says that the regulations 'have their roots in past ages which did not have the same vision of the dignity of the human person and the same respect for honest conscience that is demanded the world over today'.[35] This is ironic in view of the fact that the pope does not hesitate to call for respect for worldwide human rights outside the church.

Another theological issue that has come to head in the 1990s is the question of the ministry and ordination of women in the Catholic church. From well before his election, Pope John Paul had very definite views on the role of women. This is not for one moment to suggest that he is a misogynist in the old clerical sense, as has been maintained by some. In fact, three strong women have deeply influenced his personal and philosophical development: early in his life it was Halina Kwiatkowska, who went on to become a fine theatre performer; from the mid-1950s onwards Dr Wanda Poltawska, a Cracow psychiatrist, has influnced his thought and writings on sexuality; and from 1974 the philosopher Dr Anna-Teresa Tymieniecka has acted as a collaborator and editor of his book, *The Acting Person*.[36] Perhaps it was the influence of these women that led the pope to proceed with the canonisation of St Edith Stein, the Jewish-born phenomenologist who had studied at Frieburg under Edmund Husserl and Martin Heidegger. A convert to Catholicism in 1922, she entered the enclosed Carmelite order and was eventually executed at Auschwitz in 1942. Despite strong Jewish opposition, she was canonised in October 1998. She was exactly the type of woman who would appeal to Pope John Paul. There is no doubt that he sees women as the equal of men, but, although women can aspire to intellectual and professional equality, they are biologically bound by their maternal role. He sees woman as 'mystery', because new life comes out of her. The mystery of womanhood finds its culmination in Mary, the mother of Jesus, because out of her comes the source of all life. Because nature itself determines the role of women, talk about 'rights' to abortion, contraception and ordination are meaningless.

Wojtyla's views on sexuality, which seem to have been influenced considerably by Poltawska, were first developed in his book *Love and Responsibility* (Polish edition 1960, English trans. 1981).[37] Basing himself on what he calls the 'personalistic norm', he argues that sexual intercourse finds its sole human expression within the context of marriage. All other sexual activity is a kind of 'consuming', an eating-up and destruction of another, because there is no life-long commitment. It is to act according to a 'utilitarian' norm rather than a 'personalist' one. The personalist norm excludes all forms of artificial contraception, for conception is the natural result of intercourse, even if it does not always happen. To introduce anything artificial (such as the pill) to impede that possible result is to distort the natural purpose of the act, and thus to act in a morally reprehensible manner. As he says: 'Nature cannot be conquered by violating its laws'.[38]

Within this kind of anthropological context it is inevitable that John Paul II would oppose the ordination of women. His apostolic letter *Ordinatio Sacerdotalis* (22 May 1994) completely excludes the possibility of women ever being ordained priests in the Catholic church. In fact, the CDF was later to claim that this teaching 'has been set forth infallibly by the ordinary and universal magisterium' (28 October 1995). Although the exclusion of the ordination of women was welcomed by the Orthodox, it did cause considerable concern among Anglicans and those Protestant churches that already ordain women.

In fact, the ecumenical record of the Wojtyla papacy is mixed. The emphasis has been on dialogue with Eastern Christians, although relations with the Orthodox have been severely strained over Catholic incursions into post-communist Russia and the appointment of a hierarchy there for Latin Catholics; as well, there are tensions between

Orthodox and Catholic Ukrainians over the return of Catholic churches
seized by Stalin and given to the Russian Orthodox in Ukraine. While
relationships between Protestants, Anglicans and Roman Catholics have
continued to grow at a local and national levels, there has been extreme
caution toward the Western Christian churches by the Vatican during
this papacy. One of the more hopeful ecumenical signs is the 1995
encyclical *Ut Unum Sint*. Another good sign has been the 1999 agreement between Lutherans and Catholics on the question of justification.
The Anglican–Roman Catholic International Commission has continued
to produce splendid documents, of which *The Gift of Authority* (1999)
in many ways responds to John Paul's call in *Ut Unum Sint* for help in
coming to grips with the problems of authority in the church. But it fails
to confront the hard realities of the John Paul papacy in which authority
is often confused with arbitrary power.

Pope Wojtyla has taken other noticeable initiatives in interreligious
dialogue. Symbolic of this was the Day of Prayer for Peace in Assisi
in October 1986, when he met with the leaders of the great world
religions. He has also been willing to reach out to the Islamic world, as
in a speech in Tunisia in April 1996 where he says that God wants us to
know each other more deeply.

Perhaps the greatest strength of this papacy and the issue for which
it will be remembered most positively is the attitude of the pope towards
the Jews. Although no real apology has been offered to them for the
silence of so many church-people and the role of Pius XII in the face of
the Holocaust, there is no doubt that Pope John Paul was deeply serious
when he described Auschwitz as 'the Golgotha of the modern world'.
Never again can there be even the remotest theological or religious justification for any form of anti-Semitism: John Paul II has made it utterly
irreconcilable with Catholicism.

New religious movements and old religious orders

THERE IS A real sense in which the Wojtyla papacy has been in two
minds. On the one hand the pope has insisted on doctrinal orthodoxy;
on the other hand he has encouraged a range of fundamentally anti-

intellectual new religious movements (or 'new ecclesial movements', as Archbishop Paul Cordès of the Pontifical Council 'Cor Unum' calls them), as well as new religious orders. Most of these are 'enthusiastic' groups in the proper meaning of the word 'enthusiasm'—driven by a kind of religious frenzy or intensity of religious feeling, leading to extravagant and often immature public manifestations of belief. In some ways you see the influence of these groups most vividly in Rome itself, where increasing numbers of them are either studying in Roman seminaries and universities, or are moving into various roles in the Vatican curia. They range from the clean-cut, right-wing clergy of Opus Dei or the Legionaries of Christ, to the wild enthusiasm of the charismatics, and the guitar-strumming of the Neo-Catechuminate. In this papacy the new religious movements have come into their own.[39] Because of clear papal favour they have extraordinarily wide and increasing influence in the church and in the Vatican. John Paul sees them as the proponents of the so-called 'new evangelisation', which he clearly wants to become the key focus of the church's work in the new millennium. A half million members of these movements assembled in Rome in May 1998.

Although these movements have strong support from some the hierarchy, many bishops are suspicious of their activities, their lack of a strong intellectual tradition and culture, and their unashamed elitism. Increasingly, they have taken on the characteristics of sub-cultures, and in practice they seem to see themselves as separate from 'ordinary' clergy and laity. More and more priests associated with these movements are being promoted to the hierarchy, especially in Latin America. In fact, the clergy of these movements are developing as a kind of parallel hierarchy. In some places it is almost as though there were two levels of church: the elites from the movements, and the 'ordinary' Catholics.

Opus Dei, the oldest of the new religious movements, was founded in 1928 in Spain by Monsignor José Maria Escriva de Balaguer who, despite controversial circumstances, was beatified in 1992 by the pope.[40] According to Escriva the purpose of the Opus is to spread throughout society an awareness of the universal call to holiness and to the apostolate within the specific context of each person's ordinary life. Escriva's collection of aphorisms, *El Camino* (The Way), has been through several

editions since it was first published in the 1930s. It has been hailed by
some as a spiritual classic, although to others it seems conventional and
pedestrian. At first the Opus saw itself as a lay institute, but in November 1982 it was transmuted by John Paul II into a personal prelature
with the title of the Prelature of the Holy Cross and Opus Dei.[41] (A
'personal prelature' is an unusual canonical structure, personal rather
than territorial in character, which is established for a specific purpose.)
This organisation has been strongly supported and patronised by Pope
John Paul. A significant number of its priests have been made bishops,
including the current successor of Archbishop Romero of San Salvador,
the Spanish-born Fernando Sanez Lacalle, and the archbishop of Lima,
Cardinal Juan Luis Cipriani. The Opus has close links with the former
Fujimori regime in Peru.

According to the 2000 *Annuario Pontificio*, 1734 priests, 344 major
seminarians and 81,954 laypeople are committed members of Opus
Dei.[42] The Opus, with headquarters in Rome, operates virtually as an
extraterritorial organisation not subject to local bishops but responsible
only to its prelate, currently Bishop Javier Echevarría Rodriguez. It is
often criticised for its secrecy, its recruitment methods, and its attempts
to penetrate powerful governing and business elites.[43] It had influence in
the Franco regime in Spain and the Pinochet regime in Chile.

The Focolare (literally hearth or fireplace), or Work of Mary movement, was founded by Chiara Lubich in 1943 in Trent in northern Italy
and was approved by Rome in 1962. The idea of Focolare is to change
the world through the radical observance of gospel ideals. There are a
number of different branches within a larger movement: celibate groups
of men and women; married people and priests who identify with the
aims of Focolare; and a young people's movement. Although it is not
literally a secular institute, Focolare has about 4000 vowed members
and about two million people affiliated worldwide.[44] Although there
are problems with movement, especially the adulation offered to the
founder, it is probably somewhat less sectarian in tendency than the
other groups mentioned.

Another Italian movement that is very similar to Opus Dei is Com-
munione e Liberazione (Communion and Liberation) founded by the

Milanese priest Luigi Giussani. It formed out of the student unrest of the late 1960s in Italy and sees itself as a renewal movement, which in 1993 claimed 90 000 members in Italy and 10 000 elsewhere.[45] It is still largely an Italian movement with close connections to local politics and business. Theologically, it is probably the closest of the new movements to the present pope. Its formal membership is divided into two groups: committed lay celibates (about 800 in 1993) and members of the fraternity who make a life-long commitment to the movement. It is often in conflict with the Italian hierarchy, and Cardinal Carlo Maria Martini of Milan is a strong critic of it.

The Neo-Catechumenal Way (or Neo-Catechuminate—they are popularly known as the 'Neo-Cats') is the most widespread of these new religious movements within Catholicism. Founded in the slums of Madrid in 1964 by Kiko Arguello and Carmen Hernandez, it has set out to 're-catechise' Catholics. It believes that Catholics baptised in infancy are still really pagans at heart; they need to be formed in fellowship and sharing, personal commitment, simplicity of life, and a determination to take the Christian message to others. It is trying to replicate the early Christian process of the catechuminate. Catholics lacking adequate formation in faith are seen as 'quasi-catechumens'. In order to reconvert them it forms separate communities within the context of established parishes, and the process of the new or neo-catechuminate can take up to twenty years. In the late 1990s there were probably about 300 000 members in 600 dioceses with 10 000 small communities in 3000 parishes.

The other new movement is actually a religious order of priests in the proper sense: the Legion or Legionaries of Christ, which was founded by Marcial Maciel in Mexico City in 1941. There are now 350 priests and more than 2300 members active in seventeen countries. Most of their work is educational.

All of these movements have sectarian tendencies, and all of them have received support from John Paul II. They are hierarchical in structure, closed and secretive about their inner life, anti-intellectual and integralist in theology with a strong commitment to the leadership principle. The founder is seen as the sole prophetic source within the movement. Significantly, all of them are Latin in origin. They are often judged to be divisive in the way that they operate within the mainstream church. They have seemingly been favoured by the pope largely because they share something of his millennial enthusiasm.

Although the new religious movements have been favoured in the John Paul papacy, the traditional religious orders have been kept on a tight leash. It is clear that in some ways the pope is not particularly happy with the relative freedom that religious, particularly clerical, orders enjoy in the church. He seems to have almost tested his strength against the most powerful of them, the Society of Jesus. In August 1981 Father Pedro Arrupe (1907–91), the far-sighted superior-general of the Jesuits, had a stroke; instead of the usual procedure of the Vicar-General, the American Father Vincent O'Keefe, taking over the Society, the pope imposed his own delegate, Paolo Dezza, almost blind and seventy-nine years old. However, Dezza proved to be an extremely astute operator, and in September 1983 the Dutchman Peter-Hans Kolvenbach was freely elected by the General Chapter of the Society. It is hard to decipher what the pope hoped to achieve by the appointment of Dezza; possibly it was just a signal that he was in charge.

Several other orders have been placed under the papal spotlight, including the Franciscan friars and the Carmelite nuns. The most recent case has been that of the priests of the Society of St Paul, an Italian order that has specialised in media, particularly publishing. Since early 1996 the order, and especially the Father-General, have been under curial pressure because of complaints about views expressed in the Paulists' highly successful Italian publications *Famiglia Cristiana* and *Jesus*. Again the exemption of religious orders has seemingly been the issue that has led to papal displeasure.

As the first years of the new millennium pass there is no doubt that we are in the twilight of the Wojtyla papacy. What will come after it remains to be seen. In my conclusion I would like to speculate just a little about what that might be.

conclusion[1]

AND SO WE COME to the end of this vast survey of papal history and the development of the papal office. It is appropriate that it is published at the beginning of a new millennium. There is a sense in which the papacy, like European culture itself, has come to a crossroads. In what direction does the future lie? Can we say what the issues for the church and the next popes will be? The Catholic church confronts a moment of choice.

Let us begin by looking at what has happened to the papacy in the last 150 years.

Firstly, never before has the papacy been so powerful. Its theological claims are now supported by the global reach of the mass media. For instance, John Paul II's ability to use his office and his personality to communicate his vision of the church has given him a peculiar ability to impose his agenda on the church. By his constant travel he has in effect turned himself into a kind of 'world bishop'. Modern communications have created an entirely new situation in church history: a seemingly omnipresent papacy. Previous popes, such as Innocent III, had claimed a universal jurisdiction and pastorate, but they did not have the facilities to realise it. John Paul II has made this a reality. He has taken the notion of primacy as defined at the First Vatican Council to its logical conclusion. In its entire history the Catholic church has never been more centralised. The pope has given a new lease of life to the papal monarchy.

Secondly, this is reflected especially in the internal government of the church. This papacy has brought the renewal of Catholicism that followed the Second Vatican Council to a halt. It has not been a restoration of the pre-1960 church; rather it has been the reassertion of the papacy as the sole source of all authority and truth in Catholicism. What we have now is not so much a triangle with the papacy at its apogee, as a kind of papal octopus with tentacles reaching to every part of the church. This is not solely the creation of John Paul; it has been in the process of development for several centuries now.

Thirdly, increasingly the papacy, supported and encouraged by the new religious movements, is putting forward the notion that Christianity is the sole panacea for all the contemporary world's ills. In this view the church alone brings salvation and identity to a world lost in relativities and uncertain identity. Thus the church has an immense, public role to play in the world as the saviour of 'genuine' civilisation and culture. It is a paradoxical return to Boniface VIII's notion of all creatures being saved in and through the papacy. It is a form of unsubtle, almost fundamentalist, Catholic triumphalism. Having lost the Papal States, the papacy is now trying to seize a symbolic sovereignty by going straight to the mass of people. In his very first address Pope Wojtyla called for 'the boundaries of states, economic and political systems, the vast fields of culture, civilization and development' to be opened to Christ's saving power. As Giancarlo Zizola points out, this notion of 'Christian reconquest' dominated the papacies of Pius X, Pius XI and Pius XII.[2] That same message was being hammered out by the pope in 1999 in India when he offended many Hindus, and the nationalist Hindu government, by calling for a renewed effort in missionary evangelisation.

Fourthly, the modern papacy has never really embraced ecumenism, whether it is directed to other Christians, or to the great world religions. To do that would be to recognise the essential relativity of its own power and authority. This is something the curia will never let the papacy do. In the years since the First Vatican Council we have seen not only 'creeping infallibility' whereby each and every papal statement is granted an almost delphic status, but also a 'galloping primacy' whereby the curial power of jurisdiction over each and every part of the church is becoming more and more intrusive. The papacy is the greatest obstacle to genuine ecumenism.

So what choices face the church at the beginning of new millennium?

Firstly, it has to recognise that the weight of the papal office is now too much for one person to bear.[3] Structural change and reform are inevitable: the longer they are delayed, the more difficult and painful it will be for the church. The Roman curia will not reform itself; its inertia will have to be confronted. This incubus needs to be swept away and replaced by a smaller papal secretariat. Increasingly change will have to come from below, from the bishops and the laity. Decision-making power will have to be devolved, and local bishops and national conferences of bishops are the traditional and theologically correct places for that devolution. Subsidiarity is the realistic expression of devolution. The role of the papacy in the church needs to be de-emphasised and the focus of ecclesiology should be shifted to the local church, to the universal church as a communion of local communions.

Secondly, the church desperately needs to recover its original synodal structure. Serious consideration needs to be given to the abolition of the College of Cardinals, which, after all, only seized the role of papal electors in the eleventh century. The World Synod of Bishops must be revived and given the authority to govern the church in a collegial way with the pope. These reforms can only come about through an ecumenical council.

Thirdly, the silly pretensions inherent in the notion of the church as the primal source of salvation for the world must be jettisoned. There needs to be a return to the more subtle, intelligent, and traditional notion of the church as a leaven in the midst of society favoured by Vatican II and Paul VI. This will mean that the papacy will have to learn to live with democratic pluralism and respect for individual conscience. If this is not faced, the church runs the risk of losing intelligent and educated people who have rejected Catholic fundamentalism and have learned to live with fidelity to their faith in a pluralistic world.

Fourthly, in developed countries the profound crisis of meaning and spirituality challenges the church to rethink its whole approach to ministry and evangelisation. In a post-modern, scientific, and technological world the church must begin to listen before it rushes in with answers. Unless the questions are heard, the church risks becoming irrelevant and reducing itself to a sect. This may be the way some of the reactionary new religious movements want to go, but it is not in accord with the Catholic tradition, which has always engaged with culture.

Fifthly, the church cannot avoid the question of women and their place in the world and in the ministry. Education and liberation are not only basic rights of women; they are the key to the control of fertility which, in turn, has implications for the control of world over-population.

Finally, I will conclude in the same spirit as I began—with a sense of hope for the future. The papacy is the greatest and longest-lasting institution in the history of the West, and possibly the world. It has survived for so long precisely because it is paradoxically so adaptable. Its greatest strength is its long history and the durability of its tradition.

Despite all appearances to the contrary, it will change. It has never been a static institution. It is precisely this which will help it survive on into the third millennium of Christian history. The promise of Jesus to Peter will live on in his successors in the Petrine office.

NOtes

Preface

[1] Christopher Dawson (1889–1970), who converted to Catholicism in 1914, was author of several significant books on the interaction of Catholicism and Western culture. *The Making of Europe*, London: Sheed and Ward, 1932, is his most influential book.

[2] Philip Hughes, *A Popular History of the Catholic Church*, London: Burns & Oates, 1939.

1 From the New Testament to Constantine the Great

[1] John P. Meier, *Matthew*, Wilmington, Del: Michael Glazier, 1980, p. 335.

[2] Meier, *Matthew*, pp. xi–xii. See also Raymond E. Brown and John P. Meier, *Antioch and Rome: New Testament Cradles of Catholic Christianity*, New York: Paulist Press, 1983, pp. 12–72.

[3] Meier, in Brown and Meier, *Antioch and Rome*, p. 70.

[4] See Meier, *Matthew*, pp. 263–6.

[5] Raymond E. Brown, *The Churches the Apostles Left Behind*, New York: Paulist Press, 1984, p. 75; see also pp. 75–83.

[6] Raymond E. Brown, Karl P. Donfried, John Reumann (eds), *Peter in the New Testament: A Collaborative Assessment by Protestant and Roman Catholic Scholars*, London: Geoffrey Chapman, 1973, pp. 85–92.

[7] Veselin Kesich, 'Peter's Primacy in the New Testament and the Early Tradition', in John Meyendorff (ed.), *The Primacy of Peter: Essays in Ecclesiology and the Early Church*, Crestwood, NY: St Vladimir's Seminary Press, 1992, p. 46. See pp. 44–57.

[8] See Meier, *Matthew*, pp. 178–86.

[9] Meier, *Matthew*, p. 180.

[10] Meier, *Matthew*, p. 181.

[11] See the ecumenical discussion of the use of the word 'church' here in Brown, Donfried and Reumann, *Peter*, pp. 91–2.

[12] Meier, *Matthew*, p. 182.

[13] Kesich, 'Peter's Primacy', pp. 51–3.

[14] Oscar Cullmann, *Peter: Disciple Apostle Martyr*, Philadelphia: Westminster Press, and London: SCM Press, English trans. 1953. Originally published in German in 1952.

[15] Cullmann, *Peter*, p. 227.

[16] J. M. R. Tillard, *The Bishop of Rome*, Wilmington, Del: Michael Glazier, English trans., 1983, pp. 92–101.

[17] A collective term used for the Pauline letters I Timothy, II Timothy and Titus.

[18] Unless otherwise indicated, dates given for the emperors and popes are for the period of their reign.

[19] Brown and Meier, *Antioch and Rome*, p. 98.

[20] Quoted in J. Stevenson, *A New Eusebius: Documents illustrative of the history of the Church to A.D. 337*, London: SPCK, 1957, p. 1.

[21] See the discussion of the Roman Christian community in John Murray, *The Epistle to the Romans: The English Text with Introduction, Exposition and Notes*, Grand Rapids, Mich.: Wm. B. Eerdmans, one-volume edition, 1968, pp. xvii–xxii.

[22] Frederick J. Cwiekowski, *The Beginnings of the Church*, Dublin: Gill and Macmillan, 1988, pp. 114–15.

[23] Quoted in Stevenson, *A New Eusebius*, pp. 2–3.

[24] W. H. C. Frend, *The Early Church: From the Beginnings to 461*, London: SCM Press, third impression, 1986, pp. 30–4.

[25] Clement of Rome, *First Letter to the Corinthians*, trans. by J. B. Lightfoot (ed. by J. R. Hamer), *The Apostolic Fathers*, Grand Rapids, Mich.: Baker Book House, 1974, p. 15. Originally published by Macmillan (London) in 1891.

[26] Cwiekowski, *The Beginnings*, p. 132.

[27] For the details of this see Jocelyn Toynbee and John Ward Perkins, *The Shrine of St Peter and the Vatican Excavations*, New York: Pantheon Books, 1957, and also Umberto M. Fasola, *Traces on Stone: Peter and Paul in Rome*, Rome: Vision Editrice, 1980.

[28] For a useful diagram showing where the Circus was in relationship to both the Constantinian and present-day basilica, see Fasola, *Traces*, pp. 104–5.

[29] See Stevenson, *A New Eusebius*, p. 3.

[30] Eusebius, *History of the Church from Christ to Constantine*, trans. G. A. Williamson, London: Penguin Books, revised edition 1989, p. 63.

[31] J. E., Walsh, *The Bones of Saint Peter*, Garden City, NY: Doubleday, 1982.

[32] For a good summary and assessment of the evidence, see Daniel Wm O'Connor, *Peter in Rome: The Literary, Liturgical and Archaeological Evidence*, New York: Columbia University Press, 1969, especially p. 209.

[33] This material should be read in light of my treatment of these issues in *Papal Power*, pp. 139–44.

[34] The *Liber Pontificalis (LP)* has been translated by Raymond Davis as *The Book of Pontiffs*, Liverpool: Liverpool University Press, 1989. A second volume, *The Lives of the Eighth-Century Popes*, also translated by Raymond Davis, was published by Liverpool University Press in 1992. *The Annuario* is published yearly by the Vatican Press.

[35] Eusebius, IV, xxii, 1–3, Williamson trans., pp. 129–130.

[36] J. N. D. Kelly, *The Oxford Dictionary of Popes*, Oxford: Oxford University Press, 1986, pp. 6–8.

[37] For a description of the site, see Louis Nolan, *The Basilica of San Clemente in Rome*, Rome: Vatican Polyglot Press, 1934, pp. 158–70. For more contemporary information, see Amanda Claridge, *Rome: An Oxford Archeological Guide*, Oxford: Oxford University Press, pp. 284–88.

[38] Claridge, *Rome*, p. 288.

[39] Karen Jo Torjesen has developed these arguments in her interesting book *When Women Were Priests*, San Francisco: HarperSanFrancisco, 1993.

[40] Kelly, *Dictionary*, p. 8.

[41] I Clement, 1 and 57, Lightfoot trans., pp. 13, 37.

[42] Kelly, *Dictionary*, p. 8.

[43] I Clement, 40, Lightfoot trans., p. 30.

[44] I Clement, 42, Lightfoot trans., p. 31.

[45] For translations of the *Letters*, see Lightfoot, pp. 63–88.

[46] For a translation of the *Letter to the Romans*, see Lightfoot, pp. 75–9.

[47] Ignatius, *Romans*, Introduction, see Lightfoot trans., pp.75–6.

[48] For an Orthodox view of this notion, see Nicholas Afanassief, 'The Church Which Presides in Love', in Meyendorff, *The Primacy*, pp. 126–8.

[49] Ignatius, *Romans* 3, Lightfoot trans., p. 76.

[50] This is the interpretation of George La Piana in 'The Roman Church at the End of the Second Century', in *Harvard Theological Review* 18 (1925), pp. 201–77.

[51] Denis Minns, *Irenaeus*, London: Geoffrey Chapman, 1994, p. 121–22.

[52] Ernst Käsemann, *New Testament Questions of Today*, London: SCM Press, 1969, p. 237.

[53] See Kenan B. Osborne, *Priesthood: A History of the Ordained Ministry in the Roman Catholic Church*, New York: Paulist Press, 1988, especially pp. 89–129, 130–60.

[54] See Marta Sordi, *The Christians and the Roman Empire*, London: Croom Helm, 1983, pp. 25–132.

[55] An antipope is one who is elected pope in opposition to another held to be canonically chosen. Hippolytus is listed as such in Kelly, *Dictionary*, pp. 14–15. But nowadays, as Kelly points out correctly, this has 'been increasingly called into question' by scholars.

[56] It was the Australian-born patristic scholar and monk Richard Hugh Connolly who established the Hipppolytan authorship of the *Apostolic Tradition* in his *The So-Called Egyptian Church Order and Derived Documents* (Cambridge Texts and Studies, viii, 4, 1916). For an up-to-date translation of the *Apostolic Tradition*, see R. C. D. Jasper, and G. J. Cuming, *Prayers of the Eucharist: Early and Reformed*, New York: Oxford University Press, 1980.

[57] See Sordi, *The Christians*, pp. 100–7.

[58] For an example text, see Stevenson, *A New Eusebius*, pp. 228–9.

[59] Cyprian, Letter XX, quoted in Stevenson, *A New Eusebius*, p. 235.

[60] Cyprian, *De lapsis*, 5, 6, quoted in Stevenson, *A New Eusebius*, pp. 229–30.

[61] Cyprian, *The Unity of the Catholic Church*, trans. Maurice Bévenot in the *Ancient Christian Writers* series, Westminster, Md: Newman Press, 1957, vol. XXV, pp. 43–67.

[62] See Bévenot trans., p. 40.

[63] Cyprian's Letter to the Ephesians, 43, 5, quoted in Robert B. Eno, *The Rise of the Papacy*, Wilmington, Del: Michael Glazier, 1990, p. 57.

[64] Kelly, *Dictionary*, p. 21.

[65] Sordi deals with the Diocletian persecution in *The Christians*, pp. 122–32.

[66] Eusebius describes the persecution in chap. 8 of *The History of the Church*. See also Sordi, *The Christians*, pp. 122–32.

[67] Kelly, *Dictionary*, pp. 24–5. See Davis' translation of the *Liber Pontificalis*, p. 13.

2 The Consolidation of the Papacy

[1] Georgina Masson, *The Companion Guide to Rome*, London: Collins, 1972, p. 309.

[2] The present-day title of the basilica, San Giovanni in Laterano, dates from a rebuilding of the church after an earthquake in the late ninth century. It was completed in 904 by Sergius III (904–11).

[3] Richard Krautheimer, *Rome: Profile of a City, 312–1308*, Princeton: Princeton University Press, 1980, p. 31; see also pp. 2–31.

[4] For the spread of Christianity at the beginning of the fourth century see Tom Cornell and John Matthews, *Atlas of the Roman World*, Oxford: Phaidon, 1982, pp. 177–9.

[5] For Constantine and Constantinople, see John Julius Norwich, *Byzantium: The Early Centuries*, London: Viking, 1991, pp. 62–79.

[6] See Sordi, *The Christians*, p. 133–44, for a discussion of this issue.

[7] Norman P. Tanner (ed), *Decrees of the Ecumenical Councils*, London: Sheed and Ward and Georgetown University Press, 1990, vol. I, p. 2.

[8] In the fourth century a 'council' and a 'synod' were not clearly differentiated. Both were gatherings of bishops. Slowly the word 'council' came to be reserved for ecumenical gatherings of the whole episcopate, and 'synod' for more local gatherings of bishops.

[9] For a detailed study of the Donatists, see W. H. C. Frend, *The Donatist Church: A Movement of Protest in North Africa*, Oxford: the Clarendon Press, 1952. For selective documentation, see Stevenson, *A New Eusebius*, pp. 313–23, 326–30.

[10] Quoted in Stevenson, *A New Eusebius*, p. 319.

[11] See Pierre Batiffol, *Cathedra Petri: Etudes d'Histoire ancienne de l'Eglise*, Paris: Editions du Cerf, 1938, p. 51. The Latin literally means 'holds the major dioceses'.

[12] Constantine quoted in Stevenson, *A New Eusebius*, pp. 326–7.

[13] Nicaea is now Iznik, in north-west Turkey, not far from the south-eastern shore of the Sea of Marmara.

[14] For a clear summary of Arius' teaching, see J. N. D. Kelly's *Early Christian Doctrines*, London: Adam and Charles Black, fourth edition, 1968, pp. 226–31.

[15] Socrates, *Ecclesiastical History*, I,5, quoted in Stevenson, *A New Eusebius*, p. 340.

[16] He should not be confused with Eusebius (*c*.260–*c*.340), bishop of Caesarea (on the coast of Palestine), the writer of the *Ecclesiastical History*.

[17] See Kelly, *Doctrines*, pp. 231–7.

[18] Henry Chadwick, *The Early Church*, Harmondsworth: Penguin Books, 1967, p. 237; see also pp. 237–46.

[19] Davis, *Pontiffs*, p. 27. See also Kelly, *Dictionary*, p. 30. The *Liber Pontificalis* text actually outlines the task of the *primicerius notariorum*—the senior clerk or secretary of the Roman church.

[20] Batiffol, *Cathedra Petri*, pp. 41–2.

[21] Canon 6 in Tanner, *Decrees*, vol. I, pp. 8–9.

[22] In *Papal Power* (p. 164), I largely followed the account given in Kelly, *Dictionary*, pp. 32–3, of the struggle between Damasus and Ursinus. I acknowledge that my account there was one-sided and needed to credit more fully those sources that favoured Damasus. However, this does not mean that I have changed my interpretation of this pope's theological views, nor my criticism of him.

[23] Davis, *Pontiffs*, p. 29

[24] Davis, *Pontiffs*, p. 1. This attribution to Damasus is false. The first redaction of the *Liber Pontificalis* dates from after 530.

[25] For the survival of Roman paganism, see Joseph Vogt, *The Decline of Rome: The Metamorphosis of Ancient Civilisation*, London: George Weidenfeld and Nicholson, English trans., 1967, pp. 144–55.

[26] For the civil and military background, see Vogt, *Decline*, pp. 87–176. For a military explanation of decline during the fourth century, see Arther Ferrill, *The Fall of the Roman Empire: The Military Explanation*, London: Thames and Hudson, 1988, especially pp. 51–85.

[27] Tanner, *Decrees*, vol. 1, pp. 25–30.

[28] Tanner, *Decrees*, vol. 1, p. 32.

[29] Walter Ullmann, *A Short History of the Papacy in the Middle Ages*, London: Methuen, 1972, p. 14.

[30] Jean Steinmann, *Saint Jerome*, London: Geoffrey Chapman, 1959. See pp. 111–55 for his period in Rome.

[31] Jerome, *Letter* 15, 2, quoted in Eno, *Rise*, p. 85.

[32] Steinmann, *Jerome*, pp. 134–42.

[33] Ullmann, *A Short History*, pp. 12–13.

[34] Steinmann, *Jerome*, pp. 151–55.

[35] Jerome, *Letter* 45, 6, quoted in Steinmann, *Jerome*, p. 155.

[36] Vogt, *Decline*, pp. 155–76.

[37] A recent study of Ambrose is Neil B. McLynn's *Ambrose of Milan: Church and Court in a Christian Capital*, Berkeley: University of California Press, 1994.

[38] Ambrose, *Letter* 21, 4. Translation from S. L. Greenslade, *Early Latin Theology*, London: SCM, 1956, p. 204.

[39] Ambrose, *Sermon Against Auxentius*, PL, vol. 16, col. 1018. My own translation. The PL refers to the collection of Latin patrology by Jacques Paul Migne, *Patrologiae cursus completus: Series Latina*, Paris Garnier, 1844-91.

[40] Ambrose to Theodosius, *Letter* 11, 4, PL, vol. 16, col. 946.

[41] See Kelly, *Doctrines*, pp. 417–18.

[42] Trevor Gervase Jalland, *The Church and the Papacy: A Historical Study*, London: SPCK, 1944, pp. 268–70. For Siricius' *Letters*, see PL, vol. 13, col. 1131–96.

[43] Siricius, *Letter* 1, quoted in Jalland, *Church*, p. 269.

[44] Jalland, *Church*, p. 271. Tillard, *Bishop of Rome*, pp. 97–8, also refers to this identification.

[45] Ferrill, *Fall*, pp. 102–16.

[46] Augustine, *Concerning the City of God: Against the Pagans* (Book III, chap. 30), trans. Henry Bettenson, Harmondsworth: Penguin, 1972, p. 131.

[47] Ferrill, *Fall*, pp. 56–67.

[48] Jerome, *Letter* 77, 8, PL, vol. 22, col. 695–6.

[49] For a military assessment of Theodosius, see Ferrill, *Fall*, pp. 68–85.

[50] See Ferrill, *Fall*, pp. 83–116. For the barbarian tribes, see Hans-Joachim Diesner, *The Great Migration: The Movement of Peoples Across Europe, AD 300–700*, London: Orbis Publishing, 1982.

[51] Peter Brown, *The World of Late Antiquity: From Marcus Aurelius to Muhammad*, London: Thames and Hudson, 1971, p. 122.

[52] Kelly, *Dictionary*, p. 36.

[53] Innocent, *Letter* 37, 1. For his extant letters, see PL, vol. 20, cols 68–80.

[54] Innocent I, *Letter* 29, quoted in Jalland, *Church*, p. 282.

[55] Innocent I, *Letter* 30, 2, PL, vol. 20, col. 590.

[56] Augustine, *Sermon*, 131, PL, vol. 38, col. 734. Jalland, *Church*, (p. 283) shows that the Latin saying contains no more than three words that are authentically Augustine's.

[57] A more benign interpretation of Zosimus' interactions with the North African bishops is given by Jalland, *Church*, pp. 285–91.

[58] See Aloys Grillmeier, *Christ in Christian Tradition: From the Apostolic Age to Chalcedon (451)*, London: A. R. Mowbray, English trans., 1965, pp. 329ff; Kelly, *Doctrines*, pp. 223–343; R. V. Sellers, *The Council of Chalcedon: A Historical and Doctrinal Survey*, London: SPCK, 1961.

[59] Louis Duchesne, *The Early History of the Church*, London: John Murray, English trans., 1924, vol. 3, p. 226.

[60] Duchesne, *Early History*, vol. 3, p. 234.

[61] For the dispute leading up to Chalcedon (451), see Sellers, *Chalcedon, passim*; Grillmeier, *Christ*, pp. 453–95; and Duchesne, *Early History*, vol. 3, pp. 220–71.

[62] For a copy, see Colman Barry, *Readings in Church History*, New York: Newman Press, 1960, vol. I, pp. 97–102.

[63] Davis, *Pontiffs*, p. 37. Kelly, *Dictionary*, p. 43, says he was born in Rome of Tuscan parents.

[64] Diesner, *Great Migration*, pp. 71–84.

[65] Leo the Great, *Third Sermon on the Anniversary of his Consecration*, PL, vol. 54, col. 146. My own translation. Leo's writings can be found in PL, vols 54–6.

[66] This notion is discussed in Tillard, *The Bishop of Rome*, pp. 92–101.

[67] Duchesne, *Early History*, vol. 3, p. 297.

[68] Sellers, *Chalcedon*, pp. 103–4.

[69] Tanner, *Decrees*, vol. 1, p. 85.

[70] Kelly, *Dictionary*, p. 46, numbers this Pope Felix III, as does the *Annuario Pontificio*, p. 8. A number of historians number him Felix II, because the previous Felix II (355–65) was an antipope. In this and in all other cases, for clarity I have followed Kelly's numeration.

[71] For a military account of the period, see Ferrill, *Fall*, pp. 152–69.

3 The Popes in the Early Middle Ages

[1] For an interesting treatment of this period, see Jeffrey Richards, *The Popes and the Papacy in the Early Middle Ages: 476–752*, London: Routledge & Kegan Paul, 1979.

[2] Krautheimer, *Rome*, p. 52. For this whole period, see pp. 32–58.

[3] Richards, *Popes*, p. 295ff.

[4] For the Lateran in the fifth century, see Krautheimer, *Rome*, pp. 54–8.

[5] See Richards, *Popes*, pp. 287–323 for an account of the expansion of papal government.

[6] For a map of the central Italian estates in the mid-fifth century, see Cornell and Matthews, *Atlas of the Roman World*, p. 200, and for a detailed account of the patrimonial administration, see Richards, *Popes*, pp. 307–22.

[7] Bernhard Schimmelpfenning, *The Papacy*, New York: Columbia University Press, English trans., 1992, p. 50.

[8] Richards, *Popes*, pp. 62–5.

[9] Felix III, *Letter* I, 10, quoted in Herbert Jedin and John J. Dolan (eds), *History of the Church*, London: Burns and Oates, English trans., 1980, vol. 2, p. 616.

[10] See Richards, *Popes*, p. 21–2.

[11] Quoted in C. Kirch and L. Ueding, *Enchiridion fontium historiae ecclesiasticae antiquae*, Fribourg: Benzinger, 1960, eighth edition, 959. My own translation.

[12] Gelasius I, quoted in Richards, *Popes*, p. 22.

[13] Walter Ullmann, *The Growth of Papal Government in the Middle Ages: A study in the ideological relation of clerical to lay power*, London: Methuen, second edition, 1962, p. 2. See also Brian Tierney, *The Crisis of Church and State, 1050–1300*, Englewood Cliffs, NJ: Prentice-Hall, 1964, pp. 3, 7–11.

[14] Kenneth Stevenson, *Eucharist and Offering*, New York: Pueblo Publishing Company, 1986, p. 96.

[15] Kelly, *Dictionary*, p. 51.

[16] For this period, see Judith Herrin, *The Formation of Christendom*, London: Fontana Press, 1989. For the papacy, see Geoffrey Barraclough, *The Medieval Papacy*, London: Thames and Hudson, 1968.

[17] As well as Richards' *Popes*, see also his *Consul of God: The Life and Times of Gregory the Great*, London: Routledge and Kegan Paul, 1980.

[18] Richards, *Popes*, p. 16–17.

[19] Richards, *Consul*, p. 19.

[20] Jean Delumeau, *Catholicism between Luther and Voltaire: A New View of the Counter-Reformation*, London: Burns and Oates, English trans., 1977, pp. 159–61.

[21] Anton Wessels, *Europe: Was It Ever Really Christian? The interaction between gospel and culture*, London: SCM Press, English trans., 1994.

[22] See Eleanor Shipley Duckett, *The Gateway to the Middle Ages: Italy*, Ann Arbor: University of Michigan Press, 1961.

[23] Richards, *Popes*, pp. 293–5.

[24] Gregory of Tours, *The History of the Franks*, trans. with an introduction by Lewis Thorpe, London: Penguin, 1974, pp. 235–6.

[25] Christopher Hibbert, *Rome: The Biography of a City*, Harmondsworth: Viking, 1985, p. 74.

[26] For a description of the state of the city throughout this period, see Krautheimer, *Rome*, pp. 62–9.

[27] Richards, *Consul*, p. 25.

[28] The best treatment of his spirituality is still Cuthbert Butler's *Western Mysticism: The Teaching of SS Augustine, Gregory and Bernard on Contemplation and the Contemplative Life*, London: Constable and Company, 1922. See also Bernard McGinn, *The Growth of Mysticism: Gregory the Great through the 12th Century*, vol. II of *The Presence of God*, New York: Crossroad, 1996, pp. 34–79. See also G. R. Evans, *The Thought of Gregory the Great*, Cambridge: Cambridge University Press, 1986.

[29] Jonas of Bobbio, *The Life of Saint Columbanus*, translated by Dana Carleton Munro, Philadelphia: Department of History, University of Pennsylvania, 1895. See also Katharine Scherman, *The Flowering of Ireland: Saints, Scholars and Kings*, Boston: Little, Brown and Company, 1981, pp. 174–201.

[30] The writing of the *Liber Pontificalis* was resumed under Honorius I. See Davis, *Pontiffs*, pp. 64–92. This volume of Davis takes the *Liber Pontificalis* up to Pope Constantine (708–15).

[31] Venerable Bede, *A History of the English Church and People*, Book 2, chap 1. See translation by Leo Shirley-Price, Harmondsworth: Penguin, 1965, pp. 99–100.

[32] For an excellent overall survey, see Richard Fletcher, *The Conversion of Europe: From Paganism to Christianity, 371–1386 AD*, London: Fontana, 1998.

[33] For details see Diesner, *Great Migration*, pp. 90–123.

[34] See R. P. C. Hanson, *Saint Patrick: His Origins and Career*, Oxford: Oxford University Press, 1968, and *The Life and Writings of the Historical Saint Patrick*, New York: Seabury Press, 1983.

[35] Hanson, *Life and Writings*, p. 12.

[36] J. Leclercq et al., *The Spirituality of the Middle Ages*, (vol. II of *A History of Christian Spirituality*), New York: Seabury Press, English trans., 1968, pp. 42–3.

[37] Gregory II to Charles Martel, December 722, trans. in C. H. Talbot, *The Anglo-Saxon Missionaries in Germany*, London: Sheed and Ward, 1954, p. 74.

[38] Gregory II to Boniface, 22 November 726, trans. in Talbot, *Anglo-Saxon*, p. 81.

[39] Talbot, *Anglo-Saxon*, pp. xiv–xv.

[40] Judith Herrin, in *Formation*, pp. 250–90, discusses the issue of imperial disunity.

[41] See Bernard F. Reilly, *The Medieval Spains*, Cambridge: Cambridge University Press, 1993, pp. 17–50 for the Visgothic kingdom, and pp. 51ff. for Islam in Spain.

[42] Here, for once, I have not followed the dating of Kelly, *Dictionary*, but that of the *Annuario Pontifico*.

[43] Quoted in Jalland, *Church*, p. 363.

[44] See Richards, *Popes*, p. 208.

[45] For iconaclasm, see J. M. Hussey, *The Orthodox Church in the Byzantine Empire*, Oxford: Clarendon Press, 1986, pp. 30–68. See also Judith Herrin, *Women in Purple. Rulers of Medieval Byzantium*, London: Weidenfeld and Nicolson, 2001.

[46] Herrin, *Formation*, p. 343. For the context, see pp. 307–43.

[47] Peter Partner, *The Lands of St Peter: The Papal State in the Middle Ages and the Early Renaissance*, London: Eyre Methuen, 1972.

[48] Thomas F. X. Noble, *The Republic of St Peter: The birth of the Papal State, 680–825*, Philadelphia: University of Pennsylvania Press, 1984.

[49] The second volume of Davis' English translation of the *Liber Pontificalis, The Lives of the Eighth-Century Popes* (Liverpool University Press, 1992), begins with Gregory II, pp. 3–16.

[50] Noble, *Republic*, p. 48.

[51] See Heinrich Fichtenau, *The Carolingian Empire: The Age of Charlemange*, Oxford: Basil Blackwell, English trans., 1957.

[52] For the text, see Barry, *Readings*, vol. 1, pp. 235–40. For discussion of the *Donation*, see Herrin, *Formation*, pp. 385–7; Noble, *Republic*, pp. 134–7; and Ullmann, *Growth*, pp. 74–86.

[53] *Donation of Constantine*, in Barry, *Readings*, vol. 1, pp. 237–9.

[54] See Jalland, *Church*, pp. 376–8.

[55] Reginald L. Poole, *Lectures on the History of the Papal Chancery down to the time of Innocent III*, Cambridge: Cambridge University Press, 1915, p. 26.

[56] Herrin, *Formation*, pp. 385–9.

[57] Herrin, *Formation*, pp. 386–7.

[58] See Lewis Thorpe (ed.), *Two Lives of Charlemagne*, London: Penguin, 1969. See also Peter Munz, *Life in the Age of Charlemagne*, New York: G. P. Putnam's Sons, 1969.

[59] Fichtenau, *Carolingian Empire*, pp. 62–6.

[60] This is probably the same person as Notker the Stammerer, whose life of Charlemagne, *De Carolo Magno*, is translated in Thorpe, *Two Lives*.

4 Through the *Saeculum Obscurum*—The Dark Age

[1] For the general context, see Geoffrey Barraclough, *The Crucible of Europe: The ninth and tenth centuries in European history*, London: Thames and Hudson, 1976; Christopher Brooke, *Europe in the Central Middle Ages, 962–1154*, London: Longman, second edition, 1987; and Heinrich Fichtenau, *Living in the Tenth Century: Mentalities and Social Orders*, Chicago: University of Chicago Press, English trans., 1991. See also Eleanor Shipley Duckett's splendid *Life and Death in the Tenth Century*, Ann Arbor: University of Michigan Press, 1971.

[2] See Geoffrey Barraclough, *The Origins of Modern Germany*, Oxford: Oxford University Press, second edition, 1947; Friedrich Heer, *The Holy Roman Empire*, London: Phoenix, English trans., 1968, pp. 1–50; and Timothy Reuter, *Germany in the Early Middle Ages, c.800–1056*, London: Longman, 1991.

[3] See Marc Bloch, *Feudal Society*, Chicago: University of Chicago Press, English trans., 1961, two vols; and F. L. Ganshof, *Feudalism*, London: Longmans, English trans., 1952.

[4] Johannes Brondsted, *The Vikings*, London: Penguin, English trans., 1965; Michael Hasloch Kirkby, *The Vikings*, Oxford: Phaidon, 1977; and David M. Wilson (ed.), *The Northern World: The history and heritage of Northern Europe, AD 400–1100*, London: Thames and Hudson, 1980.

[5] 'Saracen' was a generic term for Arab Muslim raiders and pirates.

[6] Duckett, *Life and Death*, pp. 3–12.

[7] Quoted in Duckett, *Life and Death*, p. 12.

[8] Krautheimer, *Rome*, pp. 117–20.

[9] Theodore quoted in Jalland, *Church*, p. 379.

[10] Quoted in Jalland, *Church*, pp. 379–80.

[11] Jalland, *Church*, p. 378.

[12] Francis Dvornik, *Photian and Byzantine Ecclesiastical Studies*, Aldershot: Variorum Reprints, 1974, pp. vi, 19, 21.

[13] For Photius' views on the role of Peter, see Meyendorff, *Primacy*, pp. 72–3.

[14] John VIII quoted in Duckett, *Life and Death*, pp. 3–4.

[15] For this period, see Horace K. Mann, *The Lives of the Popes in the Early Middle Ages*, London: Kegan Paul, 1902–32. For a very readable account of the period, see E. R. Chamberlin, *The Bad Popes*, New York: Dorset Press, 1969, pp. 19–74.

[16] Louis Duchesne, *The Beginnings of the Temporal Sovereignty of the Popes*, reprint of the 1908 edition, New York: Burt Franklin, 1972, pp. 198–9.

[17] As a result of the sheer profusion of imperial candidates, I have not referred to any of them as 'emperor' and have simply used their real titles.

[18] Duchesne, *Beginnings*, p. 199.

[19] Duchesne, *Beginnings*, p. 209.

[20] Duchesne, *Beginnings*, p. 209.

[21] Liutprand's name is variously spelt. His works can be found in PL, vol. 136, col. 789ff. They have been translated by F. A. Wright (trans.), *The Works of Liutprand of Cremona*, London: George Routledge, 1930. For Liutprand's works' see also vol. 41 of the *Scriptores rerum Germanicarum in usum scholarum*, a supplement of the *Monumenta Germaniae Historica* (MGH). There is also a translation of his important work the *Relatio de legatione Constantinopolitana*, by Brian Scott, London: Bristol Classical Press, 1993.

[22] Liutprand, *Historia Gestorum Regum et Imperatorum, sive Antapodsis*, 2, 48, PL, vol. 136, col. 828. My own translation. Another translation can be found in Wright, *Works*, pp. 92–3.

[23] See Kelly, *Dictionary*, pp. 329–30, for a brief and cautious essay on this question. See especially Alain Boureau, *The Myth of Pope Joan*, Chicago: University of Chicago Press, English trans., 2001. See also Emily Hope. See also Emily Hope, *The Legend of Pope Joan*, Carlton, Vic.: Sisters Publishing, 1983; Joan Morris, *Pope John VIII—An English Woman: Alias Pope Joan*, London: Vrai Pubishing, 1985; and Peter Stanford, *The She Pope: A Quest for the Truth Behind the Mystery of Pope Joan*, London: Heinemann, 1998.

[24] Liutprand, *Liber de rebus gestis Ottonis Magni Imperatoris* (The Chronicle of Otto's Reign), chap. 4. Latin text in PL, vol. 136, cols 899–900. See Wright, *Works*, p. 217.

[25] Liutprand, *Liber de Rebus Gestis Ottonis*, chap. 10. Latin text in PL, vol. 136, cols 903–4. My translation. For the Synod, see Wright, *Works*, pp. 221–7.

[26] Liutprand, *Liber de Rebus Gestis Ottonis*, chap. 19. Latin text in PL, vol. 135, cols 908–9. See Wright, *Works*, p. 231.

[27] For a brief biography and an English translation of all extant letters of Gerbert, see Harriet Pratt Lattin, *The Letters of Gerbert with his papal privileges as Sylvester II*, New York: Columbia University Press, 1959.

[28] Glaber's *Histories*, chap. 46, translation in Chamberlin, *Bad Popes*, p. 67. For Glaber's complete works, see J. France (ed.), *Rodulfus Glaber Opera*, Oxford University Press, 1989. Like Kelly, *Dictionary*, I have used the word 'style' to describe the change of papal names from baptism to pontifical title.

[29] For an interesting discussion of papal resignations, see Patrick Granfield, *The Papacy in Transition*, Dublin: Gill and Macmillan, 1981, pp. 152–7.

[30] For a history of Byzantine views on the primacy from a Western perspective, see Francis Dvornik, *Byzantium and the Roman Primacy*, New York: Fordham University Press, 1966. For an Eastern Orthodox perspective on the papal reform movement, see Aristeides Papadakis, *The Christian East and the Rise of the Papacy*, Crestwood, NY: St Vladimir's Seminary Press, 1994, pp. 17–67. For the Byzantine ecclesiastical context, see Hussey, *Orthodox*, pp. 124–83.

[31] Dvornik, *Photian and Byzantine*, pp. xxii, 158.

[32] Dvornik, *Photian and Byzantine*, pp. xxii, 162.

[33] Dvornik, *Photian and Byzantine*, pp. xxii, 165.

[34] Dvornik, *Photian and Byzantine*, pp. xxii, 167.

[35] Dvornik, *Photian and Byzantine*, pp. xxii, 168.

5 The Medieval Papacy at Its Height

[1] See Colin Morris, *The Papal Monarchy: The Christian Church from 1050 to 1250*, Oxford: Clarendon Press, 1989; I. S. Robinson, *The Papacy, 1073–1198: Continuity and Innovation*, Cambridge: Cambridge University Press, 1990; and Gerd Tellenbach, *The Church in Western Europe from the Tenth to the Early Twelfth Century*, Cambridge: Cambridge University Press, English trans., 1993. For the city of Rome itself in this period, see Krautheimer, *Rome*, pp. 161–202.

[2] C. H. Haskins, *The Renaissance of the Twelfth Century*, Cambridge, Mass: Harvard University Press, 1927; and Christopher Brooke, *The Twelfth Century Renaissance*, London: Thames and Hudson, 1969.

[3] Albert Mirgeler, *Mutations of Western Christianity*, London: Burns and Oates, English trans., 1964, pp. 92–4.

[4] There are a large number of books, written mainly from a politico-legal perspective, on the struggle between papacy and empire, but little from a theological perspective. See Walter Ullmann, *Medieval Papalism* and the *Growth of Papal Government in the Middle Ages*. See also Brian Tierney, *Crisis of Church and State*; and John A. Watt, *The Theory of Papal Monarchy in the Thirteenth Century: The Contribution of the Canonists*, London: Burns and Oates, 1965.

[5] Tierney, *Crisis*, pp. 24–5.

[6] Friedrich Heer, *The Medieval World: Europe from 1100 to 1350*, London: Weidenfeld and Nicholson, English trans., 1962, p. 323–5.

[7] See Edmund Campion, 'Priesthood in the Middle Ages', in Gerald P. Gleeson (ed.), *Priesthood: The Hard Questions*, Sydney: E. J. Dwyer and the Catholic Institute of Sydney, 1993, pp. 21–30.

[8] Canon 6 of the synod, quoted in Tierney, *Crisis*, p. 43.

[9] Quoted in Tanner, *Decrees*, I, pp. 87–8.

[10] Humbert of Silva Candida, Libri III *Adversus Simoniacos*, quoted in Tierney, *Crisis*, p. 40.

[11] Peter Damiani, *Letter to King Henry IV*, quoted in Tierney, *Crisis*, p. 38.

[12] Quoted in Tierney, *Crisis*, p. 43.

[13] For the development of the College of Cardinals, see Robinson, *Papacy*, pp. 33–120.

[14] Wido of Ferrara, *De Schismate Hildebrandi*, quoted in Morris, *Papal Monarchy*, p. 109.

[15] Gregory VII, *Registers*, Book I, 15. See Ephraim Emerton, *The Correspondence of Pope Gregory VII: Selected Letters from the Registrum*, New York: W. W. Norton and Company, 1969, p. 11.

[16] Morris, *Papal Monarchy*, p. 110.

[17] Uta Ranke-Heinemann, *Eunuchs for the Kingdom of Heaven: The Catholic Church and Sexuality*, Harmondsworth: Penguin, English trans., 1990, pp. 107–16.

[18] Prohibition of lay investiture, November 1078, in Tierney, *Crisis*, p. 52.

[19] For the text of the *Dictatus*, see Tierney, *Crisis*, pp. 49–50.

[20] Papadakis, *Christian East*, pp. 54–7.

[21] *Dictatus*, 22, in Tierney, *Crisis*, p. 50.

[22] Humbert of Silva Candida, Libri III *Adversus Simoniacos*, in Tierney, *Crisis*, pp. 41–2.

[23] Henry IV to Gregory, 1076, in Tierney, *Crisis*, p. 60.

[24] See, for instance, Morris, *Papal Monarchy*, pp. 109–33.

25 Matilda's lands were actually north of Tuscany. They extended south across the Po plain to the Apennines around the city of Moderna.

26 Guibert of Parma (Clement III) was elected at Brixen on 25 June 1080, enthroned in Rome in March 1084 and died in 1100.

27 The first two of these antipopes (Theoderic [1100–01] and Albert [1101]) had nothing to do with the empire, but Silvester IV (1105–11) and Gregory VIII (1118–21) were used by imperial interests.

28 Papadakis, *Christian East*, p. 46.

29 Tanner doubts the ecumenicity of this council in *Decrees*, vol. 1, p. 187.

30 Tanner, *Decrees*, vol. 1, p. 190.

31 Krautheimer, *Rome*, p. 161. For the period, see pp. 161–202.

32 Krautheimer, *Rome*, pp. 187–90.

33 See Kenneth Pennington, *Pope and Bishops: The Papal Monarchy in the Twelfth and Thirteenth Centuries*, Philadelphia: University of Pennsylvania Press, 1984, especially pp. 1–12.

34 Tierney, *Crisis*, pp. 97ff.

35 Huguccio of Pisa, *Summa Decretorum*, quoted in Robinson, *Papacy*, pp. 300–1.

36 For an account of the struggle, see Barraclough, *Origins*, pp. 167–246.

37 Kelly, *Dictionary*, pp. 166, 167. For an account of this struggle among the cardinals, see Robinson, *Papacy*, pp. 33–120.

38 In 1143, the people of Rome had risen against the powerful clans that had dominated the city for so long. They re-established a republic and demanded that the popes surrender their temporal sovereignty. This Eugene III refused to do.

39 Quoted in Tierney, *Crisis*, p. 100.

40 Lateran III, canon 1, in Tanner, *Decrees*, vol. 1, p. 211. See Robinson, *Papacy*, pp. 84–5, 89–90. Pope John Paul II, in his Apostolic Constitution, *Universi Dominici Gregis*, 22 February 1996 (for a text, see *Origins*, 7 March 1996, pp. 617–30), decreed that the requirement of a two-thirds majority could be set aside in the case of a difficult, long-running and contested election. The new rule is that the cardinals can, after a set time, vote to change the rules to elect by a simple majority. The rule change is in paragraph 75. No reason has been given for the change.

41 Jane Sayers, *Innocent III: Leader of Europe*, 1198–1216, London: Longman, 1994, p. 1.

42 For the range of views, see James M. Powell (ed.), *Innocent III: Vicar of Christ or Lord of the World?*, Washington, DC: Catholic University of America Press, second edition, 1994.

43 Tierney, *Crisis*, p. 131.

44 Quoted in Tierney, *Crisis*, p. 132.

45 Quoted in Papadakis, *Christian East*, p. 50.

46 Hussey, *Orthodox*, pp. 184–219; Papadakis, *Christian East*, pp. 199–238.

47 Quoted in John Julius Norwich, *Byzantium: The Decline and Fall*, London: Penguin, 1996, p. 184.

48 Edward Peters, *Torture*, Oxford: Basil Blackwell, 1985, p. 64.

49 Tanner, *Decrees*, I, p. 234.

50 Tanner, *Decrees*, I, pp. 230–71.

51 David Abulafia, *Frederick II: A Medieval Emperor*, London: Allen Lane, The Penguin Press, 1988.

52 Frederick II to the Kings of Christendom, 1246, in Tierney, *Crisis*, p. 146.

53 For the full story, see Steven Runciman, *The Sicilian Vespers: A History of the Mediterranean World in the Later Thirteenth Century*, Cambridge: Cambridge University Press, 1958.

54 Watt, *Theory*, pp. 107–33.

55 Hostiensis, *On Decretals*, 4.17.13, *Per Venerabilem* [no. 78], quoted in Tierney, *Crisis*, p. 156.

56 Watt, *Theory*, p. 79.

57 Watt, *Theory*, p. 79.

[58] Watt, *Theory*, p. 81.

[59] Watt, *Theory*, p. 95.

[60] Tanner, *Decrees*, I, pp. 314–18.

[61] Patrick Granfield, *The Papacy in Transition*, Dublin: Gill and Macmillan, 1981, pp. 152–7.

[62] For Aquinas' theory of the state, see Frederick Copleston, *A History of Philosophy: From Augustine to Scotus*, New York: Doubleday (Image Edition), 1983, vol. II, pp. 412–22. See also Tierney, *Crisis*, pp. 165–71.

[63] St Thomas Aquinas, *Summa Theologica*, I, Q 96, A 4. My own translation.

[64] Francis Oakley, 'Celestial Hierarchies Revisited: Walter Ullmann's Vision of Medieval Politics', *Past and Present*, 60 (1973), pp. 6–10.

[65] Victor Martin, *Les origines du Gallicanisme*, Paris: Bloud et Gay, 1939, vol. I, pp. 149–208.

[66] Tanner, *Decrees*, I, p. 255.

[67] Tierney, *Crisis*, p. 173. See pp. 172–92.

[68] For the text of *Clericis Laicos*, see Tierney, *Crisis*, pp. 175–6 and Barry, *Readings*, vol. I, pp. 464–5.

[69] Text in Tierney, *Crisis*, pp. 185–6.

[70] Boniface VIII, *Unam Sanctam*, in Barry, *Readings*, vol. 1, p. 466.

[71] *Unam Sanctam*, quoted in Barry, *Readings*, vol. 1, p. 467.

[72] T. S. R. Boase, *Boniface VIII*, London: Constable and Company, 1933, pp. 341–51.

[73] George Tavard, in Paul C. Empie and T. Austin Murphy (eds), *Papal Primacy and the Universal Church*, Minneapolis, Minn.: Augsburg Publishing House, 1974, p. 113. See pp. 105–19.

[74] Tavard, *Papal Primacy*, pp. 116–17.

[75] Pius XII (7 September 1955), quoted in Tavard, *Papal Primacy*, p. 115.

6 Avignon and the Great Western Schism

[1] G. Mollat, *The Popes at Avignon, 1305–1378*, New York: Harper and Row, 1965.

[2] Kelly, *Dictionary*, p. 211.

[3] Mollat, *Popes*, pp. xi–xii.

[4] Mollat, *Popes*, p. xvii.

[5] Ullmann, *Short History*, p. 282.

[6] Tanner, *Decrees*, vol. 1, pp. 336–401.

[7] Tanner, *Decrees*, vol. 1, pp. 337–8.

[8] Mollat, *Popes*, p. 14.

[9] Brian Tierney, *Origins of Papal Infallibility, 1150–1350: A Study on the Concepts of Infallibility, Sovereignty, and Tradition in the Middle Ages*, Leiden: Brill, 1972, pp. 115–30.

[10] For a summary treatment of Eckhart, see Jean Leclercq, Francois Vandenbroucke and Louis Bouyer, *The Spirituality of the Middle Ages*, New York: Seabury Press, English trans., 1968, pp. 379–88. For the context of medieval mysticism, see Bernard McGinn, *The Flowering of Mysticism: Men and Women in the New Mysticism*, New York: Crossroad, 1998. See also Richard Woods, *Eckhart's Way*, Wilmington, Del.: Michael Glazier, 1986.

[11] Dante, *The Divine Comedy: Hell*, trans. Dorothy L. Sayers, Harmondsworth: Penguin, 1949, p. 188. See also pp. 190–1 and the helpful notes on the text on pp. 192–3.

[12] Dante, *Divine Comedy*, trans. Sayers, p. 191.

[13] For his political ideas, see E. F. Jacob, *Essays in the Conciliar Epoch*, Manchester: Manchester University Press, second edition, 1953, pp. 85–105; Arthur Stephen McGrade, *The Political Thought of William of Ockham: Personal and Institutional Principles*, Cambridge: Cambridge University Press, 1974; John Kilcullen, 'Ockham's Political Writings', in P. V. Spade (ed.), *The Cambridge Companion to Ockham*, Cambridge: Cambridge University Press, 1999. For his ecclesiology, see John J. Ryan,

The Nature, Structure and Function of the Church in William of Ockham, Missoula, Mont.: Scholars Press, 1979; John Kilcullen, 'Ockham and Infallibility', *Journal of Religious History*, 16 (1991), pp. 387–409. See also William of Ockham, *A Short Discourse on Tyrannical Government*, ed. Arthur Stephen McGrade and trans. John Kilcullen, Cambridge: Cambridge University Press, 1992.

[14] Ockham, *Dialogus*, I, xii–xiii. See also Ryan, *Nature*, pp. 16–21.

[15] Jacob, *Essays*, p. 103.

[16] Johannes Nohl, *The Black Death: A Chronicle of the Plague Compiled from Contemporary Sources*, London: Unwin Books, 1961; David Herlihy, *The Black Death and the Transformation of the West*, Cambridge, Mass.: Harvard University Press, 1997. See also T. S. R. Boase, *Death in the Middle Ages: Mortality, Judgement and Remembrance*, London: Thames and Hudson, 1972. For the effect in painting, see Millard Meiss, *Painting in Florence and Siena after the Black Death: The Arts, Religion and Society in the Mid-Fourteenth Century*, Princeton: Princeton University Press, 1951.

[17] Diana Wood, *Clement VI: The Pontificate and Ideas of an Avignon Pope*, Cambridge: Cambridge University Press, 1989.

[18] Constance Head, *Imperial Twilight: The Palaeologos Dynasty and the Decline of Byzantium*, Chicago: Nelson-Hall, 1977, pp. 83–7.

[19] For Catherine, see Jean Leclercq et al., *Spirituality*, pp. 409–16.

[20] Walter Ullmann, *The Origins of the Great Schism*, London: Burns, Oates and Washbourne, 1948.

[21] Catherine of Siena to the three Italian cardinals, quoted in Barry, *Readings*, I, p. 477.

[22] August Franzen, 'The Council of Constance: Present State of the Problem', *Concilium*, VII, p. 19.

[23] K. A. Finke, quoted in Franzen, 'Council', p. 20.

[24] Quoted in Barraclough, *Medieval Papacy*, p. 158.

[25] Brian Tierney, *Foundations of the Conciliar Theory: The Contribution of the Medieval Canonists from Gratian to the Great Schism*, Cambridge: Cambridge University Press, 1955, p. 5.

[26] Tierney, *Conciliar Theory*, p. 239.

[27] Tierney, *Conciliar Theory*, pp. 96–153.

[28] Tierney, *Conciliar Theory*, pp. 130–1.

[29] Hostiensis, quoted in Tierney, *Conciliar Theory*, p. 149. My own [inelegant] translation.

[30] Tierney, *Conciliar Theory*, pp. 220–37.

[31] Tierney, *Conciliar Theory*, p. 225.

[32] Papadakis, *Christian East*, pp. 370–1.

[33] Franzen, 'Council', p. 22.

[34] Tanner, *Decrees*, vol. 1, pp. 401–3, where the text jumps from Vienne to Constance.

[35] Franzen, 'Council', p. 23.

[36] Tanner, *Decrees*, vol. 1, p. 403.

[37] Cuthbert Butler, *The Vatican Council 1869–1870*, London: Collins, new edition, 1962, pp. 28–9.

[38] Franzen, 'Council', p. 23.

[39] Phillip H. Strump, *The Reforms of the Council of Constance (1414–1418)*, Leiden: E. J. Brill, 1994; and John Hine Mundy and Kennerly M. Woody (eds), *The Council of Constance: The Unification of the Church*, New York: Columbia University Press, 1961.

[40] Richental, *Chronicle*, in Mundy and Woody, *Council*, pp. 84–190.

[41] Richental, *Chronicle*, in Mundy and Woody, *Council*, pp. 189–90.

[42] Strump, *Reforms*, p. xiii.

[43] Tanner, *Decrees*, vol. 1, pp. 417–18.

[44] Tanner, *Decrees*, vol. 1, pp. 408–10.

[45] Tanner, *Decrees*, vol. 1, p. 409.

[46] All quotations from *Haec Sancta* come from Tanner, *Decrees*, vol. 1, pp. 409–10.

[47] Tanner, *Decrees*, vol. 1, p. 438.

[48] Tanner, *Decrees*, vol. 1, p. 439.

[49] Tanner, *Decrees*, vol. 1, p. 443.

[50] Tanner, *Decrees*, vol. 1, p. 416.

[51] Joachim W. Stieber, *Pope Eugenius IV and the Council of Basel and the Secular and Ecclesiastical Authorities in the Empire: The Conflict over Supreme Authority and Power in the Church*, Leiden: E. J. Brill, 1978; and Anthony Black, *Council and Commune: The Conciliar Movement and the Council of Basel*, London: Burns and Oates, 1979. For Ferrara–Florence, see Joseph Gill's three books *The Council of Florence*, Cambridge: Cambridge University Press, 1959; *Personalities of the Council of Florence*, Oxford: Basil Blackwell, 1964; *Eugenius IV: Pope of Christian Union*, London: Burns and Oates, 1961.

[52] Tanner, *Decrees*, vol. 1, p. 353. For the *acta*, see pp. 455–513. For an account of the history of the council, see Stieber, *Eugenius*, pp. 10–57.

[53] Tanner, *Decrees*, vol. 1, p. 457.

[54] See Gill, *Eugenius IV*, pp. 39–97 for the pope's attitude to the council.

[55] Tanner, *Decrees*, vol. 1, p. 477.

[56] Stieber, *Eugenius*, pp. 27–8.

[57] Victor Martin, *Les Origines du Gallicanisme*, vol. II, pp. 293–324.

[58] Gill, *Council of Florence*, p. 349.

[59] For a discussion of this council from an Eastern perspective, see Papadakis, *Christian East*, pp. 379–408.

[60] Paul de Vooght, *Les pourvoirs du Concile et l'autorité du pape au Concile de Constance*, Paris: Les Editions du Cerf, 1965.

[61] Hans Küng, *Structures of the Church*, New York: Nelson, English trans., 1964; Francis Oakley, *Council over Pope? Towards a Provisional Ecclesiology*, New York: Herder and Herder, 1969.

[62] Herbert Jedin, *A History of the Council of Trent*, English trans., London: Thomas Nelson; vol. I, 1957 and vol. II, 1961. Bibliographic details of Finke and Franzen are already noted.

[63] I discuss the theological significance of conciliarism in *Papal Power*, pp. 212–15.

7 From the Renaissance to the French Revolution

[1] For an English translation of the *Commentarii*, see L. C. Gabel, *Memoirs of a Renaissance Pope*, New York: G. Putnam's Sons, 1960.

[2] Masson, *Companion*, p. 83. See also Hibbert, *Rome*, pp. 125–6.

[3] Michael Mallett, *The Borgias: The Rise and Fall of a Renaissance Dynasty*, London: The Bodley Head, 1969.

[4] Mallett, *Borgias*, p. 103.

[5] Masson, *Companion*, pp. 474–5.

[6] Christine Shaw, *Julius II: The Warrior Pope*, Oxford: Basil Blackwell, 1993.

[7] Nelson H. Minnich, *The Fifth Lateran Council (1512–1517): Studies on its Membership, Diplomacy and Proposals for Reform*, Aldershot: Variorum, 1993; see pp. ii and 59–197.

[8] Minnich, *Fifth Lateran*, pp. ii, 154.

[9] Hibbert, *Rome*, p. 141. For a more complete description of Rome in this whole period, see Peter Partner, *Renaissance Rome, 1500–1559: A Portrait of a Society*, Berkeley: University of California Press, 1976.

[10] Quoted in Hibbert, *Rome*, p. 141.

[11] Minnich, *Fifth Lateran*, pp. iv, 163–253.

[12] Minnich, *Fifth Lateran*, pp. iv, 192–8.

[13] Minnich, *Fifth Lateran*, pp. iv, 194.

[14] Quoted in Minnich, *Fifth Lateran*, pp. iv, 197.

[15] Minnich, *Fifth Lateran*, pp. v, 218–19.

[16] Tetzel, quoted in H. J. Hillerbrand, *The Reformation in Its Own Words*, London: SCM, 1964, pp. 41–3.

[17] Quoted in Hillerbrand, *Reformation*, p. 42.

[18] Text in Hillerbrand, *Reformation*, pp. 80–4.

[19] Ludwig von Pastor, *The History of the Popes from the Close of the Middle Ages*, London: Routledge and Kegan Paul, English trans., 1891–53, vol. IX, pp. 107–8.

[20] Quoted in Hibbert, *Rome*, p. 152.

[21] Described in Hibbert, *Rome*, pp. 153–2.

[22] There is, of course, a vast bibliography on this topic, but particularly helpful is A. G. Dickens, *The English Reformation*, London: B. T. Batsford, 1964. Jasper Ridley, *Henry VIII*, London: Constable, 1984, pp. 157–222, describes the 'King's great matter' from Henry's perspective. Eamon Duffy, *The Stripping of the Altars: Traditional Religion in England, 1400–1580*, New Haven: Yale University Press, 1992, presents an interesting and more optimistic perspective on the actual state of Catholicism in England before and during the Reformation. See also Christopher Haigh, *English Reformations: Religion, Politics and Society Under the Tudors*, Oxford: Clarendon Press, 1993, with its up-to-date bibliographical essay on pp. 335–42.

[23] See Dickens, *English Reformation*, pp. 107–8 for a discussion of this.

[24] The Latin tag does not make much sense in English. It is a pun on the pope's name and on the title *Pontifex Maximus*.

[25] Some of the best-known books on the Counter-Reformation are H. Outram Evennett (ed. John Bossy), *The Spirit of the Counter-Reformation*, Cambridge: Cambridge University Press, 1968; A. G. Dickens, *The Counter-Reformation*, London: Thames and Hudson, 1968; John C. Olin, *The Catholic Reformation, Savonarola to Ignatius Loyola: Reform in the Church, 1495–1540*, New York: Harper and Row, 1969; G. W. Searle, *The Counter Reformation*, London: University of London Press, 1974; Marvin R. O'Connell, *The Counter Reformation, 1559–1610*, New York: Harper and Row, 1974; Jean Delumeau, *Catholicism between Luther and Voltaire: A New View of the Counter-Reformation*, London: Burns and Oates, English trans., 1977; John C. Olin, *The Catholic Reformation: From Cardinal Ximines to the Council of Trent, 1495–1563*, New York: Fordham University Press, 1990; Nelson H. Minnich, *The Catholic Reformation: Council, Churchmen, Controversies*, Aldershot: Variorum, 1993; and R. Po-Chia Hsia, *The World of Catholic Renewal, 1540–1770*, Cambridge: Cambridge University Press, 1998. This last book has an excellent bibliography for this whole period.

[26] Barry, *Readings*, II, pp. 92ff.

[27] Barry, *Readings*, II, pp. 96ff.

[28] Meriol Trevor, *Apostle of Rome: A Life of St Philip Neri, 1515–1595*, London: Macmillan, 1966.

[29] In my view, the two books of James Brodrick, *The Origin of the Jesuits*, London: Longmans, Green, 1940, and *The Progress of the Jesuits, 1556–1597*, London: Longmans, Green, 1946, are still the best treatments in English.

[30] There are many biographies of Loyola, including James Brodrick's *Saint Ignatius Loyola: The Pilgrim Years*, London: Burns and Oates, 1956. One of the more interesting modern lives is W. W. Meissner, *Ignatius of Loyola: The Psychology of a Saint*, New Haven: Yale University Press, 1992.

[31] See P. Matheson, *Cardinal Contarini at Regensberg*, Oxford: Oxford University Press, 1972.

[32] Pastor, *History*, vol. 12, p. 506.

[33] See Lewis W. Spitz (ed.), *The Protestant Reformation*, Englewood Cliffs, N.J.: Prentice-Hall, 1966, pp. 57–8.

[34] Hubert Jedin, *A History of the Council of Trent*, London: Thomas Nelson, English trans., vol. I, 1957 and vol. II, 1961. There are two further untranslated volumes in German covering the second and third sessions.

[35] The Decrees of the Council can be found in Tanner, *Decrees*, vol. 2, pp. 660–799.

[36] Tanner, *Decrees*, vol. 2, p. 664.

[37] Tanner, *Decrees*, vol. 2, p. 665.

[38] Tanner, *Decrees*, vol. 2, p. 666.

[39] Tanner, *Decrees*, vol. 2, pp. 668–9.

[40] Tanner, *Decrees*, vol. 2, p. 670.

[41] Tanner, *Decrees*, vol. 2, p. 669.

[42] Tanner, *Decrees*, vol. 2, p. 697.

[43] William V. Hudon, *Marcello Cervini and Ecclesiastical Government in Tridentine Italy*, DeKalb: Northern Illinois University Press, 1992.

[44] Tanner, *Decrees*, vol. 2, p. 724.

[45] Hubert Jedin, *Papal Legate at the Council of Trent: Cardinal Seripando*, St Louis, Mo.: B. Herder, English trans., 1947, pp. 658–92.

[46] G. R. Elton, *Reformation Europe*, London: Collins–Fontana, 1967, p. 195.

[47] Delumeau, *Catholicism*, p. 9.

[48] See my discussion of this in 'The artistic landscape of Spanish mysticism', *St Mark's Review*, Spring 1999, pp. 3–7.

[49] Collins, *Landscape*, p. 4.

[50] John M. Headley and John B. Tomaro (eds), *San Carlo Borromeo: Church Reform and Ecclesiastical Politics in the Second Half of the Sixteenth Century*, Washington, DC: Folger Books, 1988.

[51] Hibbert, *Rome*, pp. 175–8.

[52] For a description of the curia prior to Vatican II reforms, see Peter Canisius van Lierde, *The Holy See at Work: How the Catholic Church is Governed*, London: Robert Hale, English trans., 1962, pp. 44–162.

[52a] See my *The Modern Inquisition,* New York: The Overlook Press, 2002, pp. 1–45 for a history of the Roman Inquisition and CDF, as well as an explanation of how it works today.

[53] James Brodrick, *Robert Bellarmine: Saint and Scholar*, London: Burns and Oates, 1961.

[54] Brodrick, *Bellarmine*, p. 265.

[55] Brodrick, *Bellarmine*, pp. 62–3.

[56] Brodrick, *Bellarmine*, p. 105.

[57] Quoted in Brodrick, *Bellarmine*, p. 257.

[58] O'Connell, *Counter Reformation*, p. 360.

[59] Jamin, quoted in Butler, *Vatican Council*, p. 32.

[60] Jamin, quoted in Butler, *Vatican Council*, p. 33.

[61] Erich Schenk, *Mozart and his Times*, London: Secker and Warburg, English trans., 1960, pp. 142–3.

[62] H. V. Morton, *A Traveller in Rome*, London: Methuen, 1957, p. 39. The bees were part of the family crest. See also Roger Thynne, *The Churches of Rome*, London: Kegan Paul, Trench, Trubner, 1924, pp. 387–445, especially pp. 394–5; Masson, *Companion*, pp. 507–40.

[63] For the whole rites controversy, see George Minamiki, *The Chinese Rites Controversy from Its Beginning to Modern Times*, Chicago: Loyola University Press, 1985. The fact that opposition to Chinese rites was quietly dropped by the Vatican in 1939 is significant.

[64] For this period, see Owen Chadwick, *The Popes and the European Revolution*, Oxford: Oxford University Press, 1981.

[65] Maurice Andrieux, *Daily Life in Papal Rome in the Eighteenth Century*, London: George Allen and Unwin, English trans. 1968, p. 191.

[66] E. E. Y. Hales, *Revolution and Papacy, 1769–1846*, Notre Dame, Ind.: University of Notre Dame Press, 1966, pp. 80–115; John McManners, *The French Revolution and the Church*, New York: Harper and Row, 1969.

[67] Tallyrand was excommunicated in 1792. Between 1792 and 1796 he was out of favour, but he was soon back as foreign minister. Partially reconciled with the church in 1801, he transferred his loyalties to Napoleon. Between 1809 and 1814 he was in disgrace, but attended the Congress of Vienna. He was reconciled with the church on his deathbed.

[68] E. E. Y. Hales, *Napoleon and the Pope: The Story of Napoleon and Pius VII*, London: Eyre and Spottiswoode, 1962, pp. 3–41.

8 The Nineteenth-Century Papacy

[1] E. E. Y. Hales, *Revolution and Papacy, 1769–1846*, Notre Dame, Ind.: University of Notre Dame Press, 1966; and *Napoleon and the Pope*. See also Adrien Dansette, *Religious History of Modern France*, Edinburgh: Nelson, English trans., 1961, vol. 1.

[1a] Probably the only biography of Consalvi in any language is John Martin Robinson, *Cardinal Consalvi 1757–1824*, London: The Bodley Head, 1987.

[2] Hales, *Revolution and Papacy*, p. 133. For the conclave, see pp. 130–8 and *Napoleon and the Pope*, pp. 15–41.

[3] Dansette, *History*, vol. 2, pp. 130–2.

[4] Hales, *Napoleon and the Pope*, pp. 55–79.

[5] Hales, *Napoleon and the Pope*, pp. 83–147.

[6] Hales, *Revolution and Papacy*, p. 197.

[7] Some parts of the archives were lost. For Propaganda, see N. Kowalsky and J. Metzler, *Inventory of the Historical Archives of the Sacred Congregation for the Evangelisation of Peoples, or 'De Propaganda Fide'*, Rome: Urbaniana Press, 1983, pp. 63, 67–8. It was at this time also that some of the archives of the Roman inquisition were lost.

[8] Hales, *Revolution and Papacy*, p. 234.

[9] Hales, *Revolution and Papacy*, pp. 247–9.

[10] Hales, *Revolution and Papacy*, pp. 212, 236.

[11] Hubert Jedin and John Dolan (eds), *History of the Catholic Church*, New York: Crossroad, 1981, vol. 7, pp. 85–6 and vol. 10, pp. 5–8.

[12] J. L. Talmon, *Romanticism and Revolt: Europe, 1815–1848*, London: Thames and Hudson, 1967. For romanticism, see pp. 135–65.

[13] Hans Maier, *Revolution and Church: The Early History of Christian Democracy, 1789–1901*, Notre Dame, Ind.: University of Notre Dame Press, English trans., 1969, pp. 142–65.

[14] Owen Chadwick, *A History of the Popes, 1830–1914*, Oxford: Oxford University Press, 1998.

[15] Kelly, *Dictionary*, p. 307.

[16] Colman J. Barry, (ed.), *Readings in Church History*, Westminster, Md: Newman Press, 1963, vol. III, pp. 37–44.

[17] Hales, *Revolution and Papacy*, p. 294.

[18] E. E. Y. Hales, *Pio Nono: A Study in European Politics and Religion in the Nineteenth Century*, London: Eyre and Spottiswoode, 1954.

[19] See Talmon, *Romanticism*, pp. 166–96.

[20] Frank J. Coppa, *Cardinal Giacomo Antonelli and Papal Politics in European Affairs*, Albany: State University of New York Press, 1990, pp. 57–72.

[21] Thomas A. Kselman, *Miracles and Prophecies in Nineteenth Century France*, New Brunswick: Rutgers University Press, 1983.

[22] Barry, *Readings*, III, pp. 70–4.

[23] See Damian McElrath, *The Syllabus of Pius IX: Some Reactions in England*, Louvain: Publications Universitaires de Louvain, 1964.

[24] For the results in Australia, for instance, see John Molony, *The Roman Mould of the Australian Catholic Church*, Carlton: Melbourne University Press, 1969.

[25] The best book is Cuthbert Butler's *The Vatican Council*. See also the problematic book by August Bernhard Hasler, *How the Pope Became Infallible: Pius IX and the Politics of Persuasion*, New York: Doubleday, English trans., 1981. This translation is a summary of the two-volume German original. There have been a number of recent books looking at the council from a theological perspective. See, especially, Luis M. Bermejo, *Infallibility on Trial: Church, Conciliarity and Communion*, Westminster, Md.: Christian Classics, 1992; Hermann J. Pottmeyer, *Towards a Papacy in Communion: Perspectives from Vatican Councils I & II*, New York: Crossroad, English trans., 1998.

[26] Wilfred Ward, *William George Ward and the Catholic Revival*, London: Macmillan, 1893, pp. 84, 116–17.

[27] Dansette, *Religious History*, vol. I, p. 282.

[28] Hales, *Pio Nono*, pp. 282–3.

[29] Quoted in Butler, *Council*, p. 44. See also Butler's *The Life and Times of Bishop Ullathorne: 1806–1889*, London: Burns, Oates and Washbourne, 1926, vol. II, pp. 40–79.

[30] Frederick J. Cwiekowski, *The English Bishops and the First Vatican Council*, Louvain: Publications Universitaires de Louvain, 1971.

[31] Butler, *Council*, p. 57. See also Butler, *Ullathorne*, vol. II, pp. 305–8.

[32] Hasler, *Infallible*, pp. 53–5.

[33] See Margaret O'Gara, *Triumph in Defeat: Infallibility, Vatican I and the French Minority Bishops*, Washington, DC: Catholic University of America Press, 1988.

[34] Butler, *Council*, p. 110. Originally there were seven volumes, and two more were added by Josef Hergenrother. There are French and English translations.

[35] Butler, *Council*, p. 110.

[36] For Strossmayer's diocese, see Remigium Ritzer and Pirminum Serfin, *Hierarchia Catholica Medii et Recentioris Aevi*, Parvia: Il Messagero di S. Antonia, 1978, vol. VIII, p. 153.

[37] Butler, *Council*, p. 149.

[38] Butler, *Council*, p. 139; Hales, *Pio Nono*, p. 305.

[39] Hales, *Pio Nono*, p. 307; Butler, *Council*, pp. 400–3.

[40] Ullathorne (14 December 1869) in Butler, *Council*, p. 141. Butler dates this letter 16 December; this is incorrect.

[41] Butler, *Council*, pp. 145, 146.

[42] Hasler, *Infallible*, pp. 70–2.

[43] Tanner, *Decrees*, vol. 2, pp. 804–16.

[44] Quoted in Butler, *Council*, p. 158.

[45] Tanner, *Decrees*, vol. 2, p. 807.

[46] John P. Boyle, 'The Ordinary Magisterium', *Heythrop Journal*, 20 (1979) and 21 (1980), pp. 380–98 and 14–29.

[47] Tanner, *Decrees*, vol. 2, p. 809.

[48] Tanner, *Decrees*, vol. 2, p. 809.

[49] Butler, *Council*, p. 188.

[50] Quoted in Butler, *Council*, p. 312.

[51] Quoted in Butler, *Council*, p. 309.

[52] Quoted in Butler, *Council*, p. 308.

[53] Butler, *Council*, p. 330.

[54] Butler, *Council*, p. 332.

[55] Butler, *Council*, p. 345.

[56] Tanner, *Decrees*, vol. 2, pp. 814–15.

[57] Quoted in Butler, *Council*, p. 352.

[58] Hasler, *Infallible*, pp. 96–9.

[59] Tanner, *Decrees*, vol. 2, p. 816.

[60] Kelly, *Dictionary*, p. 310.

[61] John Jay Hughes, *Absolutely Null and Utterly Void: The Papal Condemnation of Anglican Orders, 1896*, Washington, DC: Corpus Books, 1968.

[62] See John Molony, *The Worker Question: A New Historical Perspective on Rerum Novarum*, Melbourne: Collins Dove, 1991; Bruce Duncan, *The Church's Social Teaching: From Rerum Novarum to 1931*, Melbourne: Collins Dove, 1991, pp. 20–91.

[63] John McManners, *Church and State in France, 1870–1914*, London: SPCK, 1972. See also Dansette, *Modern France*, vol. II, especially chap. 2.

[64] Quoted in Dansette, *Modern France*, vol. 2, p. 32.

[65] Quoted in Dansette, *Modern France*, vol. 2, p. 33.

[66] Kelly, *Dictionary*, p. 312.

[67] Aubert in Jedin and Dolan, *History*, vol. 9, p. 386. For details of the conclave, see pp. 381–4.

[68] From the vast contemporary literature on modernism, I would recommend Gabriel Daly, *Transcendence and Immanence: A Study in Catholic Modernism and Integralism*, Oxford: Clarendon Press, 1980.

[69] The redactors of *Pascendi* were the Oblate priest P. J. Lemius, who dealt with the theoretical exposition, and Cardinal Joseph Calasanz Vives y Tuto, who drew up the practical part. For Lemius, see Daly, *Transcendance*, pp. 179–87, 232–4.

[70] For the text of *Pascendi*, see Barry, *Readings*, III, pp. 112–20.

[71] The oath is contained in the *Motu proprio, Sacrorum antistites* (1 September 1910). My own translation.

[72] David G. Schultenover, *A View from Rome: On the Eve of the Modernist Crisis*, New York: Fordham University Press, 1993, especially pp. 180–8.

[73] Daly, *Transcendence*, p. 218.

[74] Aubert, *History*, vol. 9, pp. 467–80, outlines the views of Emile Poulat in his *Integrisme et Catholicisme Integral: Un reseau sécret international antimoderniste: La Sapinière, 1909–1921*, Tournai–Paris: Desclée, 1969.

[75] Aubert, 'Modernist Crisis', p. 387.

9 Benedict XV to 1958

[1] David Thomson, *Europe Since Napoleon*, London: Longmans, Green and Company, 1957, p. 514.

[2] See Alberigo's essay 'The Authority of the Church in the Documents of Vatican I and Vatican II', in Leonard Swidler and Piet F. Fransen, *Authority in the Church and the Schillebeeckx Case*, New York: Crossroad, 1982, pp. 119–45.

[3] Alberigo in Swidler and Fransen, 'Authority', p. 131.

[4] See W. H. Peters, *The Life of Benedict XV*, Milwaukee: Bruce, 1959. See also John F. Pollard, *The Unknown Pope: Benedict XV (1914–22) and the Pursuit of Peace*, London: Geoffrey Chapman, 1999.

[5] Jedin and Dolan (eds), *History of the Church*, vol. X, p. 585. Dansette, *History*, vol. 2, p. 331 says that about 45 000 priests and members of religious orders of men and women were mobilised in France.

[6] Daly, *Transcendence*, p. 220–1.

[7] There is no adequate biography of Pius XI. See Anthony Rhodes, *The Vatican in the Age of the Dictators, 1922, 1945*, London: Hodder and Stoughton, 1973; and Robin Anderson, *Between the Wars: The Story of Pope Pius XI*, Chicago: Franciscan Herald Press, 1977.

[8] Stewart A. Stehlin, *Weimar and the Vatican, 1919–1933: German–Vatican Diplomatic Relations in the Interwar Years*, Princeton: Princeton University Press, 1983, pp. 81–4.

[9] Rhodes, *Vatican*, p. 19.

[10] Rhodes, *Vatican*, p. 27.

[11] For the lead-up, see Rhodes, *Vatican*, pp. 37–52.

[12] Richard L. Camp, *The Papal Ideology of Social Reform: A Study in Historical Development, 1878–1967*, Leiden: E. J. Brill, 1969, pp. 36–40.

[13] Rhodes, *Vatican*, pp. 142–9.

[14] See Klaus Scholder, *The Churches and the Third Reich*, London: SCM, two vols, English trans., 1987, 1988, vol. 1, p. 240; For a summary of the background and the actual negotiations, see John Cornwell, *Hitler's Pope: The Secret History of Pius XII*, London: Viking, 1999, pp. 116–56.

[15] Stehlin, *Weimar*, pp. 368–447.

[16] Owen Chadwick, 'Was Pius XII "Hitler's Pope"?', *The Tablet*, 25 September 1999, p. 1284.

[17] Von Bergen to the German Foreign Office, 4 January 1936; Rhodes, *Vatican*, p. 199.

[18] See Camp, *Papal Ideology*, pp. 47–76.

[19] Hansjakob Stehle, *The Eastern Politics of the Vatican, 1917–1979*, Athens, Ohio: Ohio University Press, English trans., 1981.

[20] Stehle, *Eastern Politics*, pp. 26–66.

[21] Stehle, *Eastern Politics*, pp. 79–111.

[22] Stehle, *Eastern Politics*, p. 121.

[23] Stehle, *Eastern Politics*, pp. 142–9.

[24] See Jacques Leclercq, *Thunder in the Distance*, New York: Sheed and Ward, English trans., 1958.

[25] Anne Fremantle, *The Papal Encyclicals in Their Historical Context*, New York: G. P. Putnam's Sons, 1956, p. 239.

[26] Quoted in Rhodes, *Vatican*, p. 339. Rhodes notes that the remark was quickly reported to Berlin by Ambassador Von Bergen.

[27] There are two early English biographies of Pius XII: Oscar Halecki, *Eugenio Pacelli: Pope of Peace*, New York: Creative Age Press, 1951; and Nazareno Padellaro, *Portrait of Pius XII*, London: Dent, 1956. Both are inadequate. Owen Chadwick's *Britain and the Vatican during the Second World War*, Cambridge: Cambridge University Press, 1986, is written from the perspective of Francis D'arcy Osborne, British minister to the Holy See. John Cornwell's *Hitler's Pope* helps us see Pius XII in a fuller theological and ecclesiastical perspective than previous works.

[28] Sources from the Vatican archives were edited by a team of scholars (including the American Jesuit Father Robert A. Graham) and published in French by the Vatican Press between 1965 and 1978. A more limited documentary source is Saul Friedlander's *Pius XII and the Third Reich: A Documentation*, New York: Alfred A. Knopf, 1966. Carlo Falconi's idiosyncratic *The Silence of Pius XII*, London: Faber, English trans., 1970, is helpful. Since the publication of Cornwell's *Hitler's Pope*, the Vatican has pushed ahead with a joint Jewish–Catholic team to study the material in the Vatican archives on World War II, although this team broke up in mid-2001 with the Jewish scholars on it criticising the secrecy of the Vatican. See also Rhodes, *Vatican*, pp. 337–52.

[29] A copy of his account can be found in Friedlander, *Pius XII*, pp. 126–8.

[30] Christopher R. Browning, 'The Decision Concerning the Final Solution', in Francois Furet (ed.), *Unanswered Questions: Nazi Germany and the Genocide of the Jews*, New York: Schoken Books, English trans., 1989, pp. 96–118.

[31] Raul Hilberg, 'The Bureaucracy of Annihilation', in Furet, *Unanswered Questions*, pp. 119–33.

[32] See text in Friedlander, *Pius XII*, p. 131.

[33] Falconi, *Silence*, pp. 85–98.

[34] Cornwell, *Hitler's Pope*, pp. 268–77.

[35] An English translation was published in 1929 in London by Sheed and Ward.

[36] Hervé Savon, *Johann Adam Möhler: The Father of Modern Theology*, Glen Rock, NJ: Paulist Press, English trans., 1966.

[37] Odo Casel, *The Mystery of Christian Worship*, London: Darton, Longman, Todd, 1962.

[38] Romano Guardini, *The Spirit of the Liturgy*, London: Sheed and Ward, 1930.

[39] English translation published by Herder of St Louis in 1958. See also Mersch's *The Whole Christ*, Milwaukee: Bruce, 1938.

[40] See Etienne Fouilloux, 'The Antepreparatory Phase', in Giuseppe Alberigo and Joseph A. Komonchak (eds), *History of Vatican II*, Maryknoll, NY: Orbis and Leuven: Peeters, 1995, vol. 1, pp. 63–6.

[41] Fouilloux, 'Antepreparatory Phase', p. 65, is doubtful about this, but Peter Hebblethwaite, *Paul VI: The First Modern Pope*, London: Harper Collins, 1993, p. 228, is surer that there was some connection between the two. It certainly seems plausible.

[42] Originally in Belgium, Le Saulchoir moved to Etoiles, a small suburb to the south of Paris in 1937.

[43] Fergus Kerr, 'French Theology', in David F. Ford (ed.), *The Modern Theologians: An Introduction to Christian Theology in the Twentieth Century*, Oxford: Blackwell, 1997, pp. 106–17.

[44] See my summary of Teilhard's views in *God's Earth: Religion as If Matter Really Mattered*, North Blackburn, Vic.: HarperCollins, 1995, pp. 129–31. See also Ursula King, *Spirit of Fire: The Life and Vision of Teilhard de Chardin*, Maryknoll, NY: Orbis, 1996.

[45] It was not published in French until 1955, or in English until 1959.

[46] Hebblethwaite, *Paul VI*, pp. 230–4.

[47] See *Index of Speeches by Pius XII*, published by the Vatican Polyglot Press in 1956.

10 The Council and Conciliar Popes

[1] For biography, see Meriol Trevor, *Pope John*, London: Macmillan, 1967, and Peter Hebblethwaite, *John XXIII: Pope of the Council*, London: Geoffrey Chapman, 1984. See also Giancarlo Zizola, *The Utopia of John XXIII*, Maryknoll, NY: Orbis, English trans., 1978; E. E. Y. Hales, *Pope John and His Revolution*, London: Eyre and Spottiswoode, 1965. For the council, see Alberigo and Komonchak (eds), *History*.

[2] As already indicated in Chapter 6, contemporary historical opinion would not be so sure about the illegitimacy of the Pisan popes. The Council of Constance took the first John XXIII seriously enough to depose him.

[3] As apostolic delegate, he had no strict diplomatic status because he was appointed not to the government of Turkey but to the Catholic community. Only papal nuncios are, strictly speaking, diplomats.

[4] Hebblethwaite, *John XXIII*, p. 225.

[5] Marella was plucked from relative obscurity, for prior to the Paris appointment he had been apostolic delegate to Australia, resident in Sydney, from 1948 to 1953.

[6] Trevor, *Pope John*, pp. 208–11.

[7] John XXIII, *Journal of a Soul*, London: Geoffrey Chapman, English trans., 1965.

[8] Stehle, *Eastern Politics*, pp. 300–13. See also Zizola, *Utopia*, pp. 122–50.

[9] Zizola, *Utopia*, pp. 151–64.

[10] Alberigo and Komonchak, *History*, vol. 1, p. 13; Zizola, *Utopia*, pp. 233–42; Hebblethwaite, *John XXIII*, pp. 306–9.

[11] Hebblethwaite, *John XXIII*, pp. 283, 307.

[12] Alberigo and Komonchak, *History of Vatican II*, vol. 1, p. 42.

[13] Hebblethwaite, *John XXIII*, p. 337.

[14] Zizola, *Utopia*, pp. 165–80.

[15] Alberigo and Komonchak, *History*, vol. 1, p. 55.

[16] Alberigo and Komonchak, *History*, vol. 1, p. 94.

[17] Alberigo and Komonchak, *History*, vol. 1, pp. 98–149.

[18] Alberigo and Komonchak, *History*, vol. 1, p. 132.

[19] Hans Küng, *The Council and Reunion*, London: Sheed and Ward, English trans., 1961.

[20] I have described the workings of Vatican II in detail in my *Mixed Blessings*, pp. 20–49.

[21] Quoted in Zizola, *Utopia*, pp. 258–9. Andrea Riccardi describes the opening of the council and the results of the pope's speech in Alberigo and Komonchak, *History*, vol. 2, pp. 1–26.

[22] Zizola, *Utopia*, p. 260.

[23] For a profile, see Alberigo and Komonchak, *History*, vol. 2, pp. 166–76.

[24] Xavier Rynne, *Letters from Vatican City: Vatican Council II (First Session): Background and Debates*, London: Faber and Faber, 1963. 'Xavier Rynne' was the pseudonym used by the American Redemptorist historian Father Francis Xavier Murphy. Alberigo and Komonchak, *History*, vol. 2, also covers the period.

[25] Alberigo and Komonchak, *History*, vol. 2, pp. 26–32.

[26] There is an interesting account of the pre-conciliar discussion of this matter in Alberigo and Komonchak, *History*, vol. 1, pp. 272–7.

[27] Hebblethwaite, *Paul VI*, pp. 318–32.

[28] Kelly, *Dictionary*, p. 323, states it was the fifth ballot; Hebblethwaite, *Paul VI*, p. 329, says the sixth. I have followed Hebblethwaite.

[29] Hebblethwaite, *Paul VI*, pp. 292–94, 301–2.

[30] Hebblethwaite, *Paul VI*, p. 331.

[31] Hebblethwaite, *Paul VI*, pp. 348–69; Xavier Rynne, *The Second Session*, London: Faber and Faber, 1964.

[32] For Bea's speech, see Rynne, *Second Session*, pp. 218–23.

[33] Rynne, *Second Session*, pp. 223–4.

[34] For the texts, see Tanner, *Decress*, vol. 2, pp. 820–43,843–9.

[35] Annibale Bugnini, *The Reform of the Liturgy, 1948–1974*, Collegeville: Liturgical Press, English trans., 1990.

[36] Xavier Rynne, *The Third Session*, London: Faber and Faber, 1964.

[37] Rynne, *Third Session*, pp. 238–45.

[38] For the text, see Tanner, *Decrees*, vol. 2, pp. 898–900.

[39] Hebblethwaite, *Paul VI*, pp. 384–401.

[40] Tanner, *Decrees*, vol. 2, pp. 849–98, 900–20.

[41] Hebblethwaite, *Paul VI*, p. 401.

[42] Xavier Rynne, *The Fourth Session*, London: Faber and Faber, 1966.

[43] Paul VI, opening address, quoted in Hebblethwaite, *Paul VI*, p. 432.

44 Tanner, *Decrees*, vol. 2, pp. 921–47.

45 Text in Tanner, *Decrees*, vol. 2, pp. 971–81.

46 Texts in Tanner, *Decrees*, vol. 2, pp. 947–68, 981–1001, 1011–42.

47 Text in Tanner, *Decrees*, vol. 2, pp. 1042–69.

48 Christian Duquoc in Giuseppe Alberigo (ed.), *The Reception of Vatican II*, Washington, DC: Catholic University of America Press, 1987, p. 298.

49 Text in Tanner, *Decrees*, vol. 2, pp. 1069–135.

50 See Austin Flannery (ed.), *Vatican Council II: The Conciliar and Post-conciliar Documents*, Dublin: Dominican Publications, 1975, and *Vatican II: More Post-conciliar Documents*, Grand Rapids, Mich.: William B. Eerdmans, 1982.

51 Text in Flannery, *Vatican Council II: The Conciliar and Post-Conciliar Documents*, pp. 508–14.

52 It is significant that the word 'dicastery' is originally intimately connected with the law and judgement. A 'dicast' was a judge or juryman in Ancient Greece, and a 'dicastery' refers to the courts in which he sat.

53 For the best contemporary account of the curia, see Thomas J. Reese, *Inside the Vatican: The Politics and Organization of the Catholic Church*, Cambridge, Mass.: Harvard University Press, 1996.

54 Quoted in Hebblethwaite, *Paul VI*, p. 456.

55 Giancarlo Zizola, 'Secretariats and Councils of the Roman Curia', in the Concilium entitled *The Roman Curia and the Communion of Churches*, New York: Seabury Press, 1979, p. 43.

56 Reese, *Inside the Vatican*, p. 109. Zizola, 'Secretariats and Councils', says that in 1978 there were 3146, so it clearly depends on whom you count. Reese's number probably reflects the number working directly in the congregations, councils, and tribunals, and Zizola's possibly the total staff of the Vatican.

57 Giuseppe Alberigo, 'Serving the Communion of Churches', in *Concilium*, 1979, pp. 24–25.

58 Pope Paul VI, *On Evangelisation in the Modern World*, Washington, DC: US Catholic Conference, English trans., 1976.

59 Hebblethwaite, *Paul VI*, p. 537.

60 Robert Blair Kaiser, *The Politics of Sex and Religion: A Case History in the Development of Doctrine, 1962–1985*, Kansas City: Leaven Press, 1985; Robert McClory, *Turning Point: The Inside Story of the Papal Birth Control Commission*, New York: Crossroad, 1995.

61 Kaiser, *Politics*, pp. 183–7.

62 Kaiser, *Politics*, p. 183. Hebblethwaite, *Paul IV*, pp. 469–74, notes that the key figures on the committee were Ottaviani, Pietro Parente (CDF assessor), the Jesuits John C. Ford, Stanislas de Lestapis and Marcellino Zalba, the Redemptorist Jan Visser and the Franciscan Ermenegeldo Lio.

63 Kaiser, *Politics*, p. 193.

64 Hebblethwaite, *Paul VI*, p. 533.

65 See Stehle, *Eastern Politics*, pp. 314–74.

66 Eric O. Hanson, *The Catholic Church in World Politics*, Princeton: Princeton University Press, 1987, pp. 216–17.

67 Hanson, *Catholic Church*, p. 217.

68 For an up-to-date account of Vatican finances, see Reese, *Inside the Vatican*, pp. 202–29.

69 Peter Hebblethwaite, *The Year of Three Popes*, London: Collins, 1978.

70 David A. Yallop, *In God's Name: An Investigation into the Murder of Pope John Paul I*, London: Corgi Books, 1985.

71 For Cody, see Charles Dahm, *Power and Authority in the Catholic Church: Cardinal Cody in Chicago*, Notre Dame: University of Notre Dame Press, 1981.

72 John Cornwell, *A Thief in the Night: The Death of Pope John Paul I*, London: Penguin, 1989.

11 Pope John Paul II

[1] The literature on John Paul II is vast. Among straight biographies I would mention Lord Longford, *Pope John Paul II. An Authorised Biography*, London: Michael Joseph, 1982; Michael Walsh, *John Paul II: A Biography*, London: Harper Collins, 1994; Tad Szulc, *Pope John Paul II: The Biography*, New York: Scribners, 1995 (this rather poor work claims to be the official biography); Jonathan Kwitney, *Man of the Century: The Life and Times of Pope John Paul II*, New York: Little, Brown, 1997. (There is some new and interesting information in Kwitney but his grasp of the theological and church background is weak.) George Weigel, *Witness to Hope: The Biography of Pope John Paul II*, London: HarperCollins, 1999. For comment on John Paul's internal role in the church, see Peter Hebblethwaite, *Introducing John Paul II: The Populist Pope*, London: Fount, 1982; David Willey, *God's Politician: John Paul at the Vatican*, London: Faber and Faber, 1992. For his philosophical/theological background see George H. Williams, *The Mind of John Paul II: Origins of His Thought and Action*, New York: Seabury, 1981; Kenneth L. Schmitz, *At the Center of the Human Drama: The Philosophical Anthropology of Karol Wojtyla/Pope John Paul II*, Washington, DC: Catholic University of America Press, 1993; John M. McDermott (ed.), *The Thought of Pope John Paul II: A Collection of Essays and Studies*, Rome: Editrice Pontificia Università Gregoriana, 1993; John Saward, *Christ is the Answer: The Christ-Centered Teaching of Pope John Paul II*, Edinburgh: T. and T. Clark, 1995. There are many other biographies and studies, such as that of Carl Bernstein and Marco Politi (*His Holiness*, New York: Doubleday, 1996), which are political in orientation and of varying quality. Much of the material in this chapter is a development and amplification of my 1986 essay on Pope John Paul in *Mixed Blessings*, pp. 154–76.

[2] Thomas Keneally, *Schindler's List*, Harmondsworth: Penguin, 1983, and the excellent film based on the book.

[3] The thesis has been published as *Faith According to Saint John of the Cross*, San Francisco: Ignatius, 1981. See also Gerald A. McCool's discussion in 'The Theology of John Paul II', in John M. McDermott, *Thought*, pp. 33–40.

[4] Robert F. Harvanek, 'The Philosophical Foundations of the Thought of John Paul II', in John M. McDermott, *Thought*, pp. 6–11. For Scheler's philosophy, see I. M. Bochenski, *Contemporary European Philosophy*, Berkeley: University of California Press, 1956, pp. 140–53.

[5] Walsh, *John Paul II*, p. 26.

[6] First published in Italian in 1977, an English translation was published by St Paul Publications in London in 1978.

[7] While Kwitney's book is interesting, it does tend to isolate John Paul and does not explain, as John Cornwell points out (*The Tablet*, 21 February 1998, pp. 253–4), how this modern champion of human rights in the secular sphere acts as an ecclesiastical dictator in the church.

[8] See my essay 'The Peripatetic Pope' in Hans Küng and Leonard Swidler (eds), *The Church in Anguish: Has the Vatican Betrayed Vatican II?* San Franscisco: Harper and Row, 1986, pp. 52–7.

[9] Collins in Küng and Swidler, *Anguish*, p. 52.

[10] Matthew Bunson (Ed), *2001 Our Sunday Visitor's Catholic Almanac*, Huntington, Ind.: Our Sunday Visitor Publishing Division, 2001, pp. 246-48. The statistics do not include approximately 135 shorter trips inside Italy.

[11] For a complete collection of the Pope's encyclicals, see J. Michael Miller, *The Encyclicals of John Paul II*, Huntington, Ind.: Our Sunday Visitor Books, 1997.

[12] *Redemptor Hominis*, English trans., Boston: Daughters of St Paul, 1979, para. 1 (p. 5).

[13] *Redemptor Hominis*, para. 15 (p. 29).

[14] *Sollicitudo Rei Socialis*, English trans, Homebush: St Paul Publications, 1988, para. 28 (p. 57). This whole paragraph develops his ideas on 'consumerism'.

[15] Walsh, *John Paul*, p. 272.

[16] *Un Unum Sint*, English trans., Homebush: Society of Saint Paul (para. 88), p. 99.

[17] Hermann J. Pottmeyer, *Towards a Papacy in Communion: Perspectives from Vatican Councils I & II*, New York: Herder/Crossroad, English trans., 1998; for the text of the Quinn lecture, see Phyllis Zagano and Terrence W. Tilley, *The Exercise of the Primacy: Continuing the Dialogue*, New York: Herder/Crossroad, 1997. See also John R. Quinn, *The Reform of the Papacy: The Costly Call to Christian Unity*, New York: Herder/Crossroad, 1999.

[18] The original, French-language edition was published in 1992, the official Latin text was published in 1994, and most English-speaking countries have had a 1994 approved English translation published.

[19] For a positive assessment of the 1985 Synod, see Xavier Rynne, *John Paul's Extraordinary Synod: A Collegial Achievement*, Wilmington, Del.: Michael Glazier, 1986. For a less sanguine view, see Peter Hebblethwaite, *Synod Extraordinary: The Inside Story of the Rome Synod, November–December 1985*, London: Darton, Longman and Todd, 1986.

[20] Reese, *Inside the Vatican*, p. 217.

[21] Since 1997 he has been president of the Pontifical Commission for the Vatican City State.

[22] Reese, *Inside the Vatican*, pp. 209–13. There is a fascinating amount of detail in this section about Vatican finances.

[23] Josef Ratzinger with Vittorio Messori, *The Ratzinger Report: An Exclusive Interview on the State of the Church*, San Francisco: Ignatius, 1985. It should be remembered that this is the report of an interview with a right-wing journalist, but there is little doubt that it accurately reflects the views of the cardinal of the CDF.

[24] Carl Bernstein and Marco Politi, *His Holiness*, pp. 487–506.

[25] Giancarlo Zizola, 'The Power of the Pope', *The Tablet*, 17 October 1998, p. 1353. In 1999 there were 180 nuncios. Here it need to be remembered that some nuncios cover several countries, e.g. the nuncio in New Zealand covers all countries of the Pacific, except Australia and Papua New Guinea.

[26] See Kenneth L. Woodward, *Making Saints: How the Catholic Church Determines Who Becomes a Saint and Who Doesn't, and Why*, New York: Simon and Schuster, 1990.

[27] Statistics from *2001 Catholic Alamanac*, p. 266.

[28] *2001 Catholic Almanac*, pp. 267–68.

[29] Bernard Häring, *My Witness for the Church*, Introduced and trans. by Leonard Swidler, New York: Paulist Press, 1992, pp. 90–188.

[30] Häring, *My Witness*, p. 94. For the sake of the record I should remind readers that at the time of writing my own book *Papal Power* was subject to examination by the CDF.

[31] Jean-Pierre Jossua, 'Jacques Pohier. A Theologian Destroyed', in Küng and Swidler, *Church in Anguish*, pp. 205–11.

[32] Anthony Kosnik et al. (eds), *Human Sexuality: New Directions in American Catholic Thought*, New York: Paulist Press, 1977.

[33] First published in Dutch in 1974. An English translation was published by Collins, London, 1979.

[34] For the whole case, see Ad Willems 'The Endless Case of Edward Schillebeeckx' in Küng and Swidler (eds), *The Church in Anguish*, pp. 212–22. See also Herwi Rikhof, 'Of Shadows and Substance: Analysis and Evaluation of the Documents in the Schillebeeckx Case', in Swidler and Fransen (eds), *Authority in the Church*, pp. 244–67. Schillebeeckx's book *Ministry: Leadership in the Community of Jesus Christ*, English trans., New York: Crossroad, 1981, led to the second investigation.

[35] Ladislas Orsy, 'Are Church Investigation Procedures Really Just?', *Doctrine and Life*, 48/8 (1998), pp. 465–6.

[36] See Jonathan Kwitny, *Man of the Century*, p. 668 and index references for each of the women's names; see Bernstein and Politi, *His Holiness*, pp. 129–47 for Tymieniecka.

[37] Kwitny, *Man of the Century*, pp. 154–7. Her views, at least as outlined by Kwitny, would have to be said to be 'untypical' of the views of most Western women, and probably of most contemporary Polish women as well.

[38] Karol Wojtyla, *Love and Responsibility*, London: Collins, 1981, p. 229. Wojtyla was a member of Paul VI's Birth Control Commission. His influence on the commission and on the later secret textual development of *Humanae Vitae* is hard to define.

[39] For a critical assessment of three of the major groups (Focolare, Communion and Liberation and the Neocatechuminate), see Gordon Urquhart, *The Pope's Armada: Unlocking the Secrets of Mysterious and Powerful New Sects in the Church*, London: Bantam, 1995.

[40] A critical account of Opus Dei can be found in Michael Walsh, *The Secret World of Opus Dei*, London: Grafton Books, 1989. See also Joan Estruch, *Saints and Sinners: Opus Dei and Its Paradoxes*, New York: Oxford University Press, English trans., 1995. The Opus also attracts half-baked and silly criticism based on poor research, such as Robert Hutchison's book *Their Kingdom Come: Inside the Secret World of Opus Dei*, New York: Doubleday, 1997.

[41] See *Code of Canon Law*, canons 294 to 297. It is important to note that it requires the permission of the local bishop to operate in a diocese, but once that is obtained the Opus has autonomy in most matters.

[42] *2001 Catholic Almanac*, p. 523.

[43] Much of the information available about the Opus comes from former members, such as Maria del Carmen Tapia's *Beyond the Threshold: A Life in Opus Dei*, New York: Continuum, 1997.

[44] *1999 Catholic Almanac*, p. 524.

[45] Statistics from the *HarperCollins Encyclopedia of Catholicism*, p. 341.

Conclusion

[1] I have discussed all of this in considerable detail in *Papal Power*, pp. 178–218. While there are a number of new points in this brief conclusion, my proposal for a detailed scenario for the future of the church is set out in the previous book.

[2] Giancarlo Zizola, 'The Power of the Pope', *The Tablet*, 17 October 1998, p. 1352.

[3] Giancarlo Zizola, 'The Power of the Pope', *The Tablet*, 31 October 1998, p. 1429.

Bibliography

Abulafia, David, *Frederick II: A Medieval Emperor*, London: Allen Lane, The Penguin Press, 1988.

Adam, Karl, *The Spirit of Catholicism*, London: Sheed and Ward, English trans., 1929.

Afanassief, Nicholas, 'The Church which Presides in Love', in John Meyendorff (ed.), *The Primacy of Peter*, pp. 91–143.

Alberigo, Giuseppe, 'Serving the Communion of Churches', *Concilium*, 1979, pp. 12–33.

——, 'The Authority of the Church in the Documents of Vatican I and Vatican II', in Leonard Swidler and Piet F. Fransen (eds), *Authority in the Church and the Schillebeeckx Case*, pp. 119–45.

——, *The Reception of Vatican II*, Washington, DC: Catholic University of America Press, 1987.

Alberigo, Giuseppe and Joseph Komonchak, *History of Vatican II*, Maryknoll: Orbis/Leuven: Peeters, 1995, vol. 1; and 1996, vol. 2.

Anderson, Robin, *Between the Wars: The Story of Pope Pius XI*, Chicago: Franciscan Herald Press, 1977.

Andrieux, Maurice, *Daily Life in Papal Rome in the Eighteenth Century*, London: George Allen and Unwin, 1968.

Annuario Pontificio, Libreria Editrice Vaticana, Vatican City, 1999.

Aubert, Roger, 'The Modernist Crisis', in Herbert Jedin and John J. Dolan (eds), *History of the Church*, vol. 9, pp. 420–80.

Augustine, Saint, *Concerning the City of God: Against the Pagans*, trans. Henry Bettenson, Harmondsworth: Penguin, 1972.

Barraclough, Geoffrey, *The Origins of Modern Germany*, Oxford: Basil Blackwell, 1947.

——, *The Medieval Papacy*, London: Thames and Hudson, 1968.

——, *The Crucible of Europe: The Ninth and Tenth Centuries in European History*, London: Thames and Hudson, 1976.

Barry, Colman J. (ed.), *Readings in Church History*, Westminster, Md: Newman Press, 1960–63, 3 vols.

Batiffol, Pierre, *Cathedra Petri: Etudes d'Histoire ancienne de l'Eglise*, Paris: Editions du Cerf, 1938.

Bede, *A History of the English Church and People*, trans. Leo Shirley-Price, revised by R. E. Latham, Harmondsworth: Penguin, 1965.

Bermejo, Luis M., *Infallibility on Trial: Church, Conciliarity and Communion*, Westminster, Md: Christian Classics, 1992.

Bernstein, Carl and Marco Politi, *His Holiness: John Paul II and the History of Our Time*, New York: Doubleday, 1996.

Black, Anthony, *Council and Commune: The Conciliar Movement and the Council of Basle*, London: Burns and Oates, 1979.

Bloch, Marc, *Feudal Society*, University of Chicago Press, English trans., 1961, 2 vols.

Boase, T. S. R., *Boniface VIII*, London: Constable and Company, 1933.

——, *Death in the Middle Ages: Mortality, Judgement and Remembrance*, London: Thames and Hudson, 1972.

Bochenski, I. M., *Contemporary European Philosophy*, Berkeley: University of California Press, 1956.

Boureau, Alain, *The Myth of Pope Joan,* Chicago: The University of Chicago Press, English trans., 2001. First published in French in 1988.

Boyle, John P., 'The Orinary Magisterium', *Heythrop Journal*, 20 (1979) and 21 (1980), pp. 380–98, 14–29.

Brodrick, James, *The Origin of the Jesuits*, London: Longmans, Green, 1940.

——, *The Progress of the Jesuits, 1556–1597*, London: Longmans, Green, 1946.

——, *Saint Ignatius Loyola: The Pilgrim Years*, London: Burns and Oates, 1956.

——, *Robert Bellarmine: Saint and Scholar*, London: Burns and Oates, 1961.

Brondsted, Johannes, *The Vikings*, London: Penguin, English trans., 1965.

Brooke, Christopher, *The Twelfth Century Renaissance*, London: Thames and Hudson, 1969.

——, *Europe in the Central Middle Ages: 962–1154*, London: Thames and Hudson, 1976.

Brown, Peter, *The World of Late Antiquity: From Marcus Aurelius to Muhammad*, London: Thames and Hudson, 1971.

Brown, Raymond E., *The Churches the Apostles Left Behind*, New York: Paulist Press, 1984.

Brown, Raymond E., et al., *Peter in the New Testament: A Collaborative Assessment by Protestant and Roman Catholic Scholars*, New York: Paulist Press, 1973.

Brown, Raymond E. and John P. Meier, *Antioch and Rome: New Testament Cradles of Catholic Christianity*, New York: Paulist Press, 1983.

Browning, Christopher R., 'The Decision concerning the Final Solution', in Francois Furet (ed.), *Unanswered Questions*, pp. 96–118.

Bugnini, Annibale, *The Reform of the Liturgy, 1948–1974*, Collegeville, Minn.: Liturgical Press, English trans., 1990.

Butler, Cuthbert, *Western Mysticism: The Teaching of SS Augustine, Gregory and Bernard on Contemplation and the Contemplative Life*, London: Constable, 1922.

——, *The Life and Times of Bishop Ullathorne, 1806–1889*, London: Burns, Oates and Washbourne, 1926, 2 vols.

——, *The Vatican Council, 1869–1870*, London: Longmans Green, 1930. Reprinted in 1962.

Callahan, William J. and David Higgs, *Church and Society in Catholic Europe of the Eighteenth Century*, Cambridge University Press, 1979.

Camp, Richard L., *The Papal Ideology of Social Reform: A Study in Historical Development, 1878–1967*, Leiden: E. J. Brill, 1969.

Campion, Edmund, 'Priesthood in the Middle Ages', in Gerald P. Gleeson (ed.), *Priesthood: The Hard Questions*, pp. 21–30.

Casel, Odo, *The Mystery of Chritian Worship*, London: Darton, Longman and Todd, English trans., 1962.

Catechism of the Catholic Church, English trans., St Paul Publications, Sydney, 1994.

Chadwick, Henry, *The Early Church*, Harmondsworth: Penguin, 1967.

Chadwick, Owen, *The Popes and the European Revolution*, Oxford University Press, 1981.

——, *Britain and the Vatican during the Second World War*, Cambridge University Press, 1986.

——, *A History of the Popes, 1830–1914*, Oxford University Press, 1998.

——, 'Was Pius XII "Hitler's Pope"?', *The Tablet*, 25 September 1999, p. 1284.

Chamberlin, E. R., *The Bad Popes*, New York: Dorset Press, 1986.

Claridge, Amanda, *Rome: An Oxford Archeological Guide*, Oxford University Press, 1998.

Clement of Rome, *First Letter to the Corinthians*, in J. B. Lightfoot, *The Apostolic Fathers*, pp. 13–41.

Collins, Paul, *Mixed Blessings: John Paul II and the Church of the Eighties*, Ringwood, Vic.: Penguin, 1986.

——, *God's Earth: Religion as if Matter Really Mattered*, Melbourne: HarperCollins, 1995.

——, *Papal Power: A Proposal for Change in Catholicism's Third Millennium*, North Blackburn, Vic.: HarperCollins, 1998.

——, 'The Peripatetic Pope', in Hans Küng and Leonard Swidler (eds), *The Church in Anguish*, pp. 52–7.

——, 'The Artistic Landscape of Spanish Mysticism', *St Mark's Review*, Spring 1999, pp. 3–7.

——, *The Modern Inquisition,* New York: The Overlook Press, 2002.

Connolly, Richard Hugh, 'The So-Called Egyptian Church Order and Derived Documents', in J. Armitage Robinson (ed.), *Cambridge Texts and Studies*, viii, 4, pp. 1–169.

Copleston, Frederick, *A History of Philosophy: From Augustine to Scotus*, New York: Doubleday, 1983, vol. 2.

Coppa, Frank J., *Cardinal Giacomo Antonelli and Papal Politics in European Affairs*, Albany: State University of New York Press, 1990.

Cornell, Tom and John Matthews, *Atlas of the Roman World*, Oxford: Phaidon, 1982.

Cornwell, John, *A Thief in the Night: The Mysterious Death of John Paul I*, London: Penguin, 1989.

——, *Hitler's Pope: The Secret History of Pius XII*, London: Viking, 1999.

Cross, F. L. and E. A. Livingstone (eds), *The Oxford Dictionary of the Christian Church*, third edition, Oxford University Press, 1997.

Cullmann, Oscar, *Peter: Disciple, Apostle, Martyr*, Philadelphia: Westminster, English trans., 1953.

Cwiekowski, Frederick J., *The English Bishops and the First Vatican Council*, Louvain: Publications Universitaires de Louvain, 1971.

——, *The Beginnings of the Church*, Dublin: Gill and Macmillan, 1988.

Cyprian, *The Unity of the Catholic Church*, (trans. Maurice Bévenot in *Ancient Christian Writers* series), Westminster, Md: Newman Press, 1957.

Dahm, Charles, *Power and Authority in the Catholic Church: Cardinal Cody in Chicago*, Notre Dame, Ind.: University of Notre Dame Press, 1981.

Daly, Gabriel, *Transcendence and Immanence: A Study in Catholic Modernism and Integralism*, Oxford: Clarendon Press, 1980.

Dansette, Adrien, *Religious History of Modern France*, Edinburgh–London: Nelson, 1961, 2 vols.

Dante, *The Divine Comedy: Hell*, trans. Dorothy L. Sayers, Harmondsworth: Penguin, 1949.

Davis, Raymond, *The Book of Pontiffs* (English trans. of *Liber Pontificalis*), Liverpool University Press, 1989.

——, *The Lives of the Eighth Century Popes*, vol. 2 of English trans. of *Liber Pontificalis*, Liverpool University Press, 1992.

———, *The Lives of the Ninth Century Popes*, vol. 3 of English trans. of *Liber Pontificalis*, Liverpool University Press, 1995.

Dawson, Christopher, *The Making of Europe*, London: Sheed and Ward, 1932.

de Vooght, Paul, *Les pourvoirs du Concile et l'autorité du pape au Concile de Constance*, Paris: Les Editions du Cerf, 1965.

Delumeau, Jean, *Catholicism between Luther and Voltaire: A New View of the Counter Reformation*, London: Burns and Oates, English trans., 1977.

Dickens, A. G., *The English Reformation*, London: B. T. Batsford, 1964.

———, *The Counter Reformation*, London: Thames and Hudson, 1968.

Diesner, Hans-Joachim, *The Great Migration: The Movement of Peoples across Europe, AD 300–700*, London: Orbis Publishing, 1982.

Duchesne, Louis, *The Beginnings of the Temporal Sovereignty of the Popes, A.D. 754–1073*, London: Kegan, Paul, Trench, Trubner; English trans., 1908.

———, *The Early History of the Church from Its Foundation to the End of the Fifth Century*, London: John Murray, English trans., 1909–24, 3 vols.

Duckett, Eleanor Shipley, *The Gateway to the Middle Ages: Italy*, Ann Arbor: University of Michigan Press, 1961.

———, *Death and Life in the Tenth Century*, Ann Arbor: University of Michigan Press, 1967.

Duffy, Eamon, *The Stripping of the Altars: Traditional Religion in England, 1400–1580*, New Haven: Yale University Press, 1992.

Duncan, Bruce, *The Church's Social Teaching: From Rerum Novarum to 1931*, Melbourne: Collins Dove, 1991.

Duquoc, Christian, 'Clerical Reform', in Giuseppe Alberigo (ed.), *The Reception of Vatican II*, pp. 297–308.

Dvornik, Francis, *The Photian Schism: History and Legend*, Cambridge University Press, 1948.

———, *Byzantium and the Roman Primacy*, New York: Fordham University Press, 1966.

———, *Photian and Byzantine Ecclesiastical Studies*, Aldershot: Variorum Reprints, 1974.

Elton, G. R., *Reformation Europe*, London: Collins/Fontana, 1967.

Emerton, Ephraim, *The Correspondence of Pope Gregory VII: Selected Letters from the Registrum*, New York: W. W. Norton, 1969.

Empie, Paul C. and T. Austin Murphy, *Papal Primacy and the Universal Church*, Minneapolis, Minn.: Augsburg Publishing, 1974.

Eno, Robert B., *The Rise of the Papacy*, Wilmington, Del.: Michael Glazier, 1990.

Estruch, Joan, *Saints and Sinners: Opus Dei and Its Paradoxes*, New York: Oxford University Press, English trans., 1995.

Eusebius, *The History of the Church, from Christ to Constantine*, trans. G. A. Williamson, London: Penguin, 1989.

Evans, G. R., *The Thought of Gregory the Great*, Cambridge University Press, 1986.

Evennett, H. Outram, *The Spirit of the Counter Reformation*, ed. John Bossy, Cambridge University Press, 1968.

Falconi, Carlo, *The Silence of Pius XII*, London: Faber, English trans., 1970.

Fasola, Umberto M., *Traces on Stone: Peter and Paul in Rome*, Rome: Vision Editrice, 1980.

Ferrill, Arther, *The Fall of the Roman Empire: The Military Explanation*, London: Thames and Hudson, 1983.

Fichtenau, Heinrich, *The Carolingian Empire: The Age of Charlemagne*, New York: Harper and Row, 1964.

——, *Living in the Tenth Century: Mentalities and Social Orders*, University of Chicago, English trans., 1991.

Flannery, Austin (ed.), *Vatican Council II: The Conciliar and Post-Conciliar Documents*, Dublin: Dominican Publications, 1975.

——, *Vatican II: More Post-Conciliar Documents*, Grand Rapids, Mich.: William B. Eerdmans, 1982.

Fletcher, Richard, *The Conversion of Europe: From Paganism to Christianity, 371–1386 AD*, London: Fontana, 1998.

Fouilloux, Etienne, 'The Antepreparatory Phase: the Slow Emergence from Inertia (January 1959–October 1962)', in Giuseppe Alberigo and Joseph Komonchak (eds), *History of Vatican II*, vol. 1, pp. 55–166.

Ford, David F. (ed.), *The Modern Theologians: An Introduction to Christian Theology in the Twentieth Century*, Oxford: Basil Blackwell, 1997.

Foy, Felician A. and Rose M. Avato (eds), *1999 'Our Sunday Visitor' Catholic Almanac*, Huntington, Ind.: Our Sunday Visitor, 1998.

Franzen, August, 'The Council of Constance: Present State of the Problem', *Concilium*, VII, pp. 17–37.

Fremantle, Anne, *The Papal Encyclicals in Their Historical Context*, New York: G. P. Putnam's Sons, 1956.

Frend, W. H. C., *The Donatist Church: A Movement of Protest in North Africa*, Oxford: Clarendon Press, 1952.

——, *The Early Church: From the Beginnings to 461*, London: SCM Press, 1986.

Friedlander, Saul, *Pius XII and the Third Reich: A Documentation*, New York: Alfred A. Knopf, 1966.

Furet, Francois (ed.), *Unanswered Questions: Nazi Germany and the Genocide of the Jews*, New York: Schoken Books, English trans., 1989.

Gabel, L. C., *Memoirs of a Renaissance Pope*, New York, G. Putnam's Sons, 1960.

Ganshof, F. L., *Feudalism*, London: Longmans, English trans., 1952.

Gerbert of Aurillac, *Letters*, in Harriet Pratt Lattin, *The Letters of Gerbert, with his Papal Privileges as Sylvester II*, New York: Columbia University Press, 1959.

Gill, Joseph, *The Council of Florence*, Cambridge University Press, 1959.

——, *Eugenius IV: Pope of Christian Union*, London: Burns and Oates, 1961.

——, *Personalities of the Council of Florence*, Oxford: Basil Blackwell, 1964.

Glaber, Rodulfus, *Opera,* ed. J. France, Oxford University Press, 1989.

Gleeson, Gerald P. (ed.), *Priesthood: The Hard Questions*, Sydney: E. J. Dwyer and the Catholic Institute of Sydney, 1993.

Granfield, Patrick, *The Papacy in Transition*, Dublin: Gill and Macmillan, 1981.

Greenslade, S. L., *Early Latin Theology*, London: SCM, 1956.

Gregory of Tours, *The History of the Franks*, translated by Lewis Thorpe, London: Penguin, 1983.

Grillmeier, Aloys, *Christ in Christian Tradition: From the Apostolic Age to Chalcedon (451)*, London: A. W. Mobray, 1965.

Guardini, Romano, *The Spirit of the Liturgy*, London: Sheed and Ward, English trans., 1930.

Haigh, Christopher, *English Reformations: Religion, Politics and Society under the Tudors*, Oxford: Clarendon Press, 1993.

Halecki, Oscar, *Eugenio Pacelli: Pope of Peace*, New York: Creative Age Press, 1951.

Hales, E. E. Y., *Pio Nono: A Study in European Politics and Religion in the Nineteenth Century*, London: Eyre and Spottiswoode, 1954.

——, *Napoleon and the Pope: The Story of Napoleon and Pius VII*, London: Eyre and Spottiswoode, 1962.

——, *Pope John and His Revolution*, London: Eyre and Spottiswoode, 1965.

——, *Revolution and Papacy, 1769–1846*, Notre Dame, Ind.: University of Notre Dame Press, 1966.

Hanson, Eric O., *The Catholic Church in World Politics*, Princeton University Press, 1987.

Hanson, R. P. C., *Saint Patrick: His Origins and Career*, Oxford University Press, 1968.

——, *The Life and Writings of the Historical Saint Patrick*, New York: Seabury Press, 1983.

Häring, Bernard, *My Witness for the Church*, intro. and trans. Leonard Swidler, New York: Paulist Press, 1992.

Harvanek, Robert F., 'The Philosophical Foundations of the Thought of John Paul II', in John M. McDermott (ed.), *The Thought of Pope John Paul II*, pp. 1–21.

Haskins, C. H., *The Renaissance of the Twelfth Century*, Cambridge, Mass.: Harvard University Press, 1927.

Hasler, August Bernhard, *How the Pope Became Infallible: Pius IX and the Politics of Persuasion*, New York: Doubleday, 1981.

Head, Constance, *Imperial Twilight: The Palaeologos Dynasty and the Decline of Byzantium*, Chicago: Nelson-Hall, 1977.

Headley, John M. and John B. Tomaro (eds), *San Carlo Borromeo and Church Reform and Ecclesiastical Politics in the Second Half of the Sixteenth Century*, Washington, DC: Folger Books, 1988.

Hebblethwaite, Peter, *The Year of Three Popes*, London: Collins, 1978.

———, *Introducing John Paul II: The Populist Pope*, London: Fount, 1982.

———, *John XXIII: Pope of the Council*, London: Geoffrey Chapman, 1984.

———, *Synod Extraordinary: The Inside Story of the Rome Synod, November–December 1985*, London: Darton, Longman and Todd, 1986.

———, *Paul VI: The First Modern Pope*, London: HarperCollins, 1993.

———, *The Next Pope: An Inquiry*, London: HarperCollins Religious, 1995.

Heer, Friedrich, *The Medieval World: Europe from 1100 to 1350*, London: Weidenfeld and Nicolson, 1962.

———, *The Holy Roman Empire*, London: Weidenfeld and Nicolson, 1967.

Herlihy, David, *The Black Death and the Transformation of the West*, Cambridge, Mass.: Harvard University Press, 1997.

Herrin, Judith, *The Formation of Christendom*, London: Fontana, 1989.

———, *Women in Purple. Rulers of Medieval Byzantium,* London: Weidenfeld and Nicolson, 2001.

Hibbert, Christopher, *Rome: The Biography of a City*, Harmondsworth: Viking, 1985.

Hilberg, Raul, 'The Bureaucracy of Annihilation', in François Furet (ed.), *Unanswered Questions*, pp. 119–33.

Hillerbrand, H. J., *The Reformation in Its Own Words*, London: SCM Press, 1964.

Hope, Emily, *The Legend of Pope Joan*, Carlton, Vic.: Sisters Publishing, 1983.

Hsia, R. Po-chia, *The World of Catholic Renewal, 1540–1770*, Cambridge University Press, 1998.

Hudon, William V., *Marcello Cervini and Ecclesiastical Government in Tridentine Italy*, DeKalb: Northern Illinois University Press, 1992.

Hughes, John Jay, *Absolutely Null and Utterly Void: The Papal Condemnation of Anglican Orders*, 1896, Washington, DC: Corpus Books, 1968.

Hughes, Philip, *A Popular History of the Catholic Church*, London: Burns and Oates, 1939.

Huizing, Peter and Knut Walf (eds), *Concilium: The Roman Curia and the Communion of Churches*, New York: Seabury Press, 1979.

Hussey, J. M., *The Orthodox Church in the Byzantine Empire*, Oxford: Clarendon Press, 1986.

Hutchison, Robert, *Their Kingdom Come: Inside the Secret World of Opus Dei*, New York: Doubleday, 1997.

Jacob, E. F., *Essays in the Conciliar Epoch*, Manchester University Press, 1953.

Jalland, Trevor Gervase, *The Church and the Papacy: A Historical Study*, London: SPCK, 1944.

Jasper, R. C. D. and G. J. Cuming, *Prayers of the Eucharist: Early and Reformed*, New York: Oxford University Press, 1980.

Jedin, Herbert, *Papal Legate at the Council of Trent: Cardinal Seripando*, St Louis, Mo: B. Herder, 1947.

——, *A History of the Council of Trent*, London: Thomas Nelson, 1957, vol. 1 and 1961, vol. 2.

Jedin, Herbert and John J. Dolan (eds), *History of the Church: The Imperial Church from Constantine to the Middle Ages*, New York: Crossroad, 1981, vol. 2.

——, *History of the Church: The Church between Revolution and Restoration*, New York: Crossroad, 1981, vol. 7.

——, *History of the Church: The Church in the Industrial Age*, New York: Crossroad, 1981, vol. 9.

——, *History of the Church: The Church in the Modern Age*, New York: Crossroad, 1981, vol. 10.

John XXIII, *Journal of a Soul*, introduced by Loris Capovilla, London: Geoffrey Chapman, English trans., 1965.

John Paul II, *Redemptor Hominis*, Boston: Daughters of St Paul, English trans., 1979.

——, *Sollicitudo Rei Socialis*, Sydney: St Paul Publications, English trans., 1988.

——, *Ut Unum Sint*, Sydney: Society of St Paul, English trans., 1995.

Jonas of Bobbio, *The life of Saint Columban*, trans. Dana Carleton Munro, Philadelphia: Department of History of University of Pennsylvania, 1895.

Jossua, Jean-Pierre, 'Jacques Pohier: a Theologian Destroyed', in Hans Küng and Leonard Swidler (eds), *The Church in Anguish*, pp. 205–11.

Kaiser, Robert Blair, *The Politics of Sex and Religion: A Case History in the Development of Doctrine, 1962–1985*, Kansas City: Leaven Press, 1985.

Kasemann, Ernst, *New Testament Questions of Today*, London: SCM Press, 1969.

Kelly, J. N. D., *Early Christian Doctrines*, London: A. and C. Black, 1968.

——, *The Oxford Dictionary of Popes*, Oxford University Press, 1986.

Keneally, Thomas, *Schindler's List*, Harmondsworth: Penguin, 1983.

Kerr, Fergus, 'French Theology: Yves Congar and Henri de Lubac', in David F. Ford (ed.), *The Modern Theologians*, pp. 105–17.

Kesich, Veselin, 'Peter's Primacy in the New Testament and the Early Tradition', in John Meyendorff (ed.), *The Primacy of Peter*, pp. 44–57.

Kilcullen, John, 'Ockham's Political Writings', in P. V. Spade (ed.), *The Cambridge Companion to Ockham*.

——, 'Ockham and Infallibility', *Journal of Religious History*, 16 (1991), pp. 387–409.

King, Ursula, *Spirit of Fire: The Life and Vision of Teilhard de Chardin*, Maryknoll: Orbis, 1996.

Kirch, C. and L. Ueding, *Enchiridion fontium historiae ecclesiasticae antiquae*, Freiburg: Benzinger, 1960.

Kirkby, Michael Haslock, *The Vikings*, Oxford: Phaidon, English trans., 1977.

Kosnik, Anthony, et al. (eds), *Human Sexuality: New Directions in American Catholic Thought*, New York: Paulist Press, 1977.

Kowalsky, N. and J. Metzler, *Inventory of the Historical Archives of the Sacred Congregation for the Evangelisation of Peoples, or 'De Propaganda Fide'*, Rome: Urbaniana Press, 1983.

Krautheimer, Richard, *Rome: Profile of a City, 312–1308*, Princeton University Press, 1980.

Kselman, Thomas A., *Miracles and Prophecies in Nineteenth Century France*, New Brunswick, NJ.: Rutgers University Press, 1983.

Küng, Hans, *The Council and Reunion*, London: Sheed and Ward, English trans., 1961.

——, *Structures of the Church*, New York: Nelson, English trans., 1964.

Küng, Hans and Leonard Swidler (eds), *The Church in Anguish: Has the Vatican Betrayed Vatican II?*, San Francisco: Harper and Row, 1986.

Kwitney, Jonathan, *Man of the Century: The Life and Times of Pope John Paul II*, New York: Little, Brown and Co., 1997.

La Piana, George, 'The Roman Church at the End of the Second Century', *Harvard Theological Review*, 18 (1925), pp. 201–77.

Leclercq, Jacques, *Thunder in the Distance*, New York: Sheed and Ward, English trans., 1958.

Leclercq, Jean, et al., *The Spirituality of the Middle Ages*, vol. 2 of *A History of Christian Spirituality*, New York: Seabury Press, 1968.

Lierde, Peter Canisius van, *The Holy See at Work: How the Catholic Church is Governed*, London: Robert Hale, English trans., 1962.

Lightfoot, J. B. (ed. J. R. Hamer), *The Apostolic Fathers*, Grand Rapids, Mich.: Baker Book House, 1974.

Liutprand of Cremona, *Relatio de Legatione Constantinopolitana*, trans. Brian Scott, Bristol: Bristol Classic Press, 1993.

——, *The Works of Liutprand of Cremona*, trans. F. A. Wright, London: George Routledge and Sons, 1930.

Longford, Lord, *Pope John Paul II: An Authorised Biography*, London: Michael Joseph, 1982.

McBrien, Richard (ed.), *The HarperCollins Encyclopedia of Catholicism*, New York: HarperCollins, 1995.

McClory, Robert, *Turning Point: The Inside Story of the Papal Birth Control Commission*, New York: Crossroad, 1995.

——, *Power and the Papacy: The People and Politics behind the Doctrine of Infallibility*, Liguori, Mo: Triumph, 1997.

McCool, Gerard A., 'The Theology of John Paul II', in John M. McDermott (ed.), *The Thought of John Paul II*, pp. 29–53.

McDermott, John M. (ed.), *The Thought of Pope John Paul II: A Collection of Essays and Studies*, Rome: Editrice Pontificia Università Gregoriana, 1993.

McElrath, Damian, *The Syllabus of Pius IX: Some Reactions in England*, Louvain: Publications Universitaires de Louvain, 1964.

McGinn, Bernard, *The Foundations of Mysticism: Origins to the Fifth Century*, vol. 1 of *The Presence of God: A History of Christian Mysticism*, New York: Crossroad, 1995.

——, *The Growth of Mysticism: Gregory the Great through the 12th Century*, vol. 2 of *The Presence of God: A History of Christian Mysticism*, New York: Crossroad, 1996.

——, *The Flowering of Mysticism: Men and Women in the New Mysticism—1200–1350*, vol. 3 of *The Presence of God: A History of Christian Mysticism*, New York: Crossroad, 1998.

McGrade, Arthur Stephen, *The Political Thought of William of Ockham: Personal and Institutional Principles*, Cambridge University Press, 1974.

McLynn, Neil B., *Ambrose of Milan: Church and Court in a Christian Capital*, Berkeley: University of California Press, 1994.

McManners, John, *The French Revolution and the Church*, London: SPCK, 1969.

——, *Church and State in France, 1870–1914*, London: SPCK, 1972.

Maier, Hans, *Revolution and Church: The Early History of Christian Democracy, 1789–1901*, Notre Dame, Ind.: University of Notre Dame Press, English trans., 1969.

Mallett, Michael, *The Borgias: The Rise and Fall of a Renaissance Dynasty*, London: The Bodley Head, 1969.

Mann, Horace K., *The Lives of the Popes in the Early Middle Ages*, London: Kegan Paul, Trench, Trubner, 1902–32.

Martin, Victor, *Les origines du Gallicanisme*, Paris: Bloud et Gay, 1939, vol. 1.

Masson, Georgina, *The Companion Guide to Rome*, London: Fontana, 1972.

Matheson, P., *Cardinal Contarini at Regensberg*, Oxford University Press, 1972.

Meier, John P., *Matthew*, Wilmington, Del.: Michael Glazier, 1980.

Meiss, Millard, *Painting in Florence and Siena after the Black Death: The Arts, Religion and Society in the Mid-Fourteenth Century*, Princeton University Press, 1951.

Meissner, W. W., *Ignatius of Loyola: The Psychology of a Saint*, New Haven: Yale University Press, 1992.

Mersch, Emile, *The Whole Christ*, Milwaukee: Bruce, English trans., 1938.

——, *The Theology of the Mystical Body*, St Louis: Herder, English trans., 1958.

Meyendorff, John (ed.), *The Primacy of Peter: Essays in Ecclesiology and the Early Church*, Crestwood, NY: St Vladimir's Seminary Press, 1992.

Migne, Jacques Paul, *Patrologiae cursus completus: Series Latina*, Paris: Garnier, 1844–91.

Miller, J. Michael (ed.), *The Encyclicals of John Paul II*, Huntington, Ind.: Our Sunday Visitor Books, 1997.

Minamiki, George, *The Chinese Rites Controversy from Its Beginning to Modern Times*, Chicago: Loyola University Press, 1985.

Minnich, Nelson H., *The Fifth Lateran Council (1512–1517): Studies on Its Membership, Diplomacy and Proposals for Reform*, Aldershot: Variorum, 1993.

———, *The Catholic Reformation: Council, Churchmen, Controversies*, Aldershot: Variorum, 1993.

Minns, Denis, *Irenaeus,* London: Geoffrey Chapman, 1994.

Mirgeler, Albert, *Mutations of Western Christianity*, London: Burns and Oates, English trans., 1964.

Modras, Ronald, *The Catholic Church and Anti-Semitism in Poland, 1933–1939*, Chur, Switzerland: Harwood Academic Publishers, 1994.

Mollat, G., *The Popes at Avignon, 1305–1378*, New York: Harper and Row, 1965.

Molony, John, *The Roman Mould of the Australian Catholic Church*, Melbourne University Press, 1969.

———, *The Worker Question: A New Historical Perspective on Rerum Novarum*, Melbourne: Collins Dove, 1991.

Morris, Colin, *The Papal Monarchy: The Christian Church from 1050 to 1250*, Oxford: Clarendon Press, 1989.

Morris, Joan, *Pope John VIII—An English Woman: Alias Pope Joan*, London: Vrai Publications, 1985.

Morton, H. V., *A Traveller in Rome*, London: Methuen, 1957.

Mundy, John Hine and Kennerley M. Woody (eds), *The Council of Constance: The Unification of the Church,* New York: Columbia University Press, 1961.

Munz, Peter, *Life in the Age of Charlemagne*, New York: G. P. Putnam's Sons, 1969.

Murphy-O'Connor, Jerome, *The Holy Land: An Archaeological Guide from the Earliest Times to 1700*, Oxford University Press, 1986.

Murray, John, *The Epistle to the Romans: The English Text with Introduction, Exposition and Notes*, Grand Rapids, Mich.: Wm. B. Eerdmans, one-volume edition, 1968.

Noble, Thomas F. X., *The Republic of Saint Peter: The Birth of the Papal State, 680–825*, Philadelphia: University of Pennsylvania Press, 1984.

Nohl, Johannes, *The Black Death: A Chronicle of the Plague, Compiled from Contemporary Sources*, London: Unwin Books, 1961.

Nolan, Louis, *The Basilica of San Clemente in Rome*, Rome: Vatican Polyglot Press, 1934.

Norwich, John Julius, *Byzantium: The Early Centuries*, London: Penguin, 1988.

———, *Byzantium: The Apogee*, London: Penguin, 1991.

———, *Byzantium: The Decline and Fall*, London: Penguin, 1996.

Oakley, Francis, *Council over Pope? Towards a Provisional Ecclesiology*, New York: Herder and Herder, 1969.

——, 'Celestial Hierarchies Revisited: Walter Ullmann's Vision of Medieval Politics', *Past and Present*, 60 (1973).

O'Connell, Marvin R., *The Counter Reformation, 1559–1610*, New York: Harper and Row, 1974.

O'Connor, Daniel Wm, *Peter in Rome: The Literary, Liturgical and Archaeological Evidence*, New York: Columbia University Press, 1969.

O'Gara, Margaret, *Triumph in Defeat: Infallibility, Vatican I and the French Minority Bishops*, Washington, DC: Catholic University of America Press, 1988.

Olin, John C., *The Catholic Reformation: Savonarola to Ignatius Loyola—Reform in the Church, 1495–1540*, New York: Harper and Row, 1969.

——, *The Catholic Reformation: From Cardinal Ximines to the Council of Trent, 1495–1563*, New York: Fordham University Press, 1990.

Orsy, Ladislas, 'Are Church Investigation Procedures Really Just?' *Doctrine and Life*, 48 (1998), pp. 453–66.

Osborne, Kenan B., *Priesthood: A History of the Ordained Ministry in the Roman Catholic Church*, New York: Paulist Press, 1988.

Padellaro, Nazareno, *Portrait of Pius XII*, London: J. M. Dent, English trans., 1956.

Papadakis, Aristeides, *The Christian East and the Rise of the Papacy: The Church, 1071–1453 A.D.*, Crestwood, NY: St Vladimir's Press, 1994.

Partner, Peter, *The Lands of Saint Peter: The Papal State in the Middle Ages and the Early Renaissance*, London: Eyre Methuen, 1972.

——, *Renaissance Rome, 1500–1559: A Portrait of a Society*, Berkeley: University of California Press, 1976.

Pastor, Ludwig von, *The History of the Popes from the Close of the Middle Ages*, London: Routledge and Kegan Paul, English trans., 1891–1953, 40 vols.

Paul VI, *On Evangelisation in the Modern World*, Washington, DC: US Catholic Conference, English trans., 1976.

Pennington, Kenneth, *Popes and Bishops: The Papal Monarchy in the Twelfth and Thirteenth Centuries*, Philadelphia: University of Pennsylvania Press, 1984.

Peters, Edward, *Torture*, Oxford: Basil Blackwell, 1985.

Peters, W. H., *The Life of Benedict XV*, Milwaukee: Bruce, 1959.

Pollard, John F., *The Unknown Pope: Benedict XV (1914–22) and the Pursuit of Peace*, London: Geoffrey Chapman, 1999.

Poole, Reginald L., *Lectures on the History of the Papal Chancery down to the Time of Innocent III*, Cambridge University Press, 1915.

Pottmeyer, Hermann J., *Towards a Papacy in Communion: Perspectives from Vatican Council I & II*, New York: Herder/Crossroad, 1998.

Poulat, Emile, *Integrisme et Catholicisme integral: Un reseau secret international anti-moderniste; La Sapinière, 1909–1921*, Tournai–Paris: Desclée, 1969.

Powell, James M. (ed.), *Innocent III: Vicar of Christ or Lord of the World?*, Washington, DC: Catholic University of America Press, 1994.

Quinn, John R., *The Exercise of the Primacy and the Costly Call to Unity*, New York: Herder/Crossroad, 1999.

Rahner, Karl, *Foundations of Christian Faith: An Introduction to the Idea of Christianity*, New York: Seabury Press, English trans., 1978.

Ranke-Heinemann, Uta, *Eunuchs for the Kingdom of Heaven: The Catholic Church and Sexuality*, Harmondsworth: Penguin, English trans., 1990.

Ratzinger, Josef with Vittorio Messori, *The Ratzinger Report: An Exclusive Interview on the State of the Church*, San Francisco: Ignatius, 1985.

Reese, Thomas J., *Inside the Vatican: The Politics and Organization of the Catholic Church*, Cambridge, Mass.: Harvard University Press, 1996.

Reilly, Bernard F., *The Medieval Spains*, Cambridge University Press, 1993.

Reuter, Timothy, *Germany in the Early Middle Ages, 800–1056*, London: Longman, 1991.

Rhodes, Anthony, *The Vatican in the Age of the Dictators, 1922–1945*, London: Hodder and Stoughton, 1973.

Richards, Jeffrey, *The Popes and Papacy in the Early Middle Ages, 476–752*, London: Routledge and Kegan Paul, 1979.

——, *Consul of God: The Life and Times of Gregory the Great*, London: Routledge and Kegan Paul, 1980.

Ridley, Jasper, *Henry VIII*, London: Constable, 1984.

Rikhof, Herwi, 'Of Shadows and Substance: Analysis and Evaluation of the Documents in the Schillebeeckx Case', in Leonard Swidler and Piet F. Fransen (eds), *Authority in the Church and the Schillebeeckx Case*, pp. 244–67.

Ritzer, Remegium and Pirminum Serfin, *Hierarchia Catholica Medii et Recentioris Aevi*, Parvia: Il Messagero di D. Antonia, 1978, vol. VIII.

Robinson, I. S., *The Papacy, 1073–1189: Continuity and Innovation*, Cambridge University Press, 1990.

Robinson, J. Armitage, *Texts and Studies: Contributions to Biblical and Patristic Literature*, Cambridge University Press, 1916.

Robinson, John Martin, *Cardinal Consalvi 1757–1824,* London: The Bodley Head, 1987.

Runciman, Steven, *The Sicilian Vespers: A History of the Mediterranean World in the Later Thirteenth Century*, Cambridge University Press, 1958.

Ryan, John J., *The Nature, Structure and Function of the Church in William of Ockham*, Missoula, Mont.: Scholars Press, 1979.

Rynne, Xavier, *Letters from Vatican City: Vatican Council II (First Session): Background and Debates*, London: Faber, 1963.

———, *The Second Session: The Debates and Decrees of Vatican II, September 29 to December 4, 1963*, London: Faber, 1964.

———, *The Third Session: Debates and Decrees of Vatican Council II, September 14 to November 21, 1964*, London: Faber, 1965.

———, *The Fourth Session: The Debates and Decrees of Vatican Council II, September 14 to December 8, 1965*, London: Faber, 1966.

———, *John Paul's Extraordinary Synod: A Collegial Achievement*, Wilmington, Del.: Michael Glazier, 1986.

Savon, Hervé, *Johann Adam Mohler: The Father of Modern Theology*, Glen Rock, NJ: Paulist Press, English trans., 1966.

Saward, John, *Christ is the Answer: The Christ-centered Teaching of Pope John Paul II*, Edinburgh: T. and T. Clark, 1995.

Sayers, Jane, *Innocent III: Leader of Europe, 1198–1216*, London: Longmans, 1994.

Schenk, Erich, *Mozart and his Times*, London: Secker and Warburg, English trans., 1960.

Scherman, Katherine, *The Flowering of Ireland: Saints, Scholars and Kings*, Boston: Little, Brown and Co., 1981.

Schillebeeckx, Edward, *Jesus: An Experiment in Christology*, London: Collins, English trans., 1979.

———, *Ministry: Leadership in the Community of Jesus Christ*, English trans., New York: Crossroad, 1981.

Schimmelpfenning, Bernhard, *The Papacy*, New York: Columbia University Press, English trans., 1992.

Schmitz, Kenneth L., *At the Center of the Human Drama: The Philosophical Anthropology of Karol Wojtyla / Pope John Paul II*, Washington, DC: Catholic University of America Press, 1993.

Scholder, Klaus, *The Churches and the Third Reich*, London: SCM Press, English trans., 1987, vol. 1 and 1988, vol. 2.

Schultenover, David G., *A View from Rome: On the Eve of the Modernist Crisis*, New York: Fordham University Press, 1993.

Searle, G. W., *The Counter Reformation*, London: University of London Press, 1974.

Sellers, R. V., *The Council of Chalcedon: A Historical and Doctrinal Survey*, London: SPCK, 1961.

Shaw, Christine, *Julius II: The Warrior Pope*, Oxford: Basil Blackwell, 1993.

Smith, Denis Mack, *Italy: A Modern History*, Ann Arbor: University of Michigan Press, 1969.

Sordi, Marta, *The Christians and the Roman Empire*, London: Croom Helm, 1983.

Spade, P. V. (ed.), *The Cambridge Companion to Ockham*, Cambridge University Press, 1999.

Spitz, Lewis W. (ed.), *The Protestant Reformation*, Englewood Cliffs, NJ: Prentice-Hall, 1966.

Stanford, Peter, *The She-Pope: A Quest for the Truth Behind the Mystery of Pope Joan*, London: Heinemann, 1998.

Stehle, Hansjacob, *Eastern Politics of the Vatican, 1917–1979*, Athens: Ohio University Press, English trans., 1981.

Stehlin, Stewart A., *Weimar and the Vatican, 1919–1933: German–Vatican Diplomatic Relations in the Interwar Years*, Princeton University Press, 1983.

Steiber, Joachim W., *Pope Eugenius IV and the Council of Basel and the Secular and Ecclesiastical Authorities in the Empire: The Conflict over Supreme Authority and Power in the Church*, Leiden: E. J. Brill, 1978.

Steinmann, Jean, *Saint Jerome*, London: Geoffrey Chapman, 1959.

Stevenson, J., *A New Eusebius: Documents Illustrative of the History of the Church to A.D. 337*, London: SPCK, 1957.

Stevenson, Kenneth, *Eucharist and Offering*, New York: Pueblo Publishing, 1986.

Strump, Phillip H., *The Reforms of the Council of Constance (1414–1418)*, Leiden: E. J. Brill, 1994.

Swidler, Leonard and Piet F. Fransen (eds), *Authority in the Church and the Schillebeeckx Case*, New York: Crossroad, 1982.

Szulc, Tad, *Pope John Paul II: The Biography*, New York: Scribners, 1995.

Talbot, C. H., *The Anglo-Saxon Missionaries in Germany*, London: Sheed and Ward, 1954.

Talmon, J. L., *Romanticism and Revolt: Europe, 1815–1848*, London: Thames and Hudson, 1967.

Tanner, Norman P., *Decrees of the Ecumenical Councils*, London: Sheed and Ward, 1990, 2 vols.

Tapia, Maria del Carmen, *Beyond the Threshold: A Life in Opus Dei*, New York: Continuum, 1997.

Teilhard de Chardin, Pierre, *The Phenomenon of Man*, London: William Collins, English trans., 1959.

Tellenbach, Gerd, *The Church in Western Europe from the Tenth to the Early Twelfth Century*, Cambridge University Press, English trans., 1993.

Thomson, David, *Europe since Napoleon*, London: Longmans, Green and Company, 1957.

Thorpe, Lewis (ed.), *Two Lives of Charlemagne*, London: Penguin, 1969.

Thynne, Roger, *The Churches of Rome*, London: Kegan Paul, Trench, Trubner, 1924.

Tierney, Brian, *Foundations of the Conciliar Theory: The Contribution of the Medieval Canonists, from Gratian to the Great Schism*, Cambridge University Press, 1955.

——, *The Crisis of Church and State, 1050–1300*, Englewood Cliffs, NJ: Prentice-Hall, 1964.

——, *Origins of Papal Infallibility, 1150–1350: A Study on the Concepts of Infallibility, Sovereignty and Tradition in the Middle Ages*, Leiden: E. J. Brill, 1972.

Tillard, J. M. R., *The Bishop of Rome*, Wilmington, Del.: Michael Glazier, English trans., 1983.

Torjesen, Karen Jo, *When Women Were Priests*, Harper San Francisco, 1993.

Toynbee, Jocelyn and John Ward Perkins, *The Shrine of St Peter and the Vatican Excavations*, New York: Pantheon Books, 1957.

Trevor, Meriol, *Apostle of Rome: A Life of St Philip Neri, 1515–1595*, London: Macmillan, 1966.

——, *Pope John*, London: Macmillan, 1967.

Ullmann, Walter, *The Origins of the Great Schism*, London: Burns, Oates and Washbourne, 1948.

——, *Medieval Papalism: The Political Theories of the Medieval Canonists*, London: Methuen, 1949.

——, *The Growth of Papal Government in the Middle Ages: A Study in the Ideological Relations of Clerical to Lay Power*, London: Methuen, second edition, 1962.

——, *A Short History of the Papacy in the Middle Ages*, London: Methuen, 1972.

Urquhart, Gordon, *The Pope's Armada: Unlocking the Secrets of Mysterious and Powerful New Sects in the Church*, London: Bantam, 1995.

Vogt, Josef, *The Decline of Rome: The Metamorphosis of Ancient Civilization*, London: George Weidenfeld and Nicolson, English trans., 1967.

Walsh, J. E., *The Bones of Saint Peter*, Garden City, NY: Doubleday, 1982.

Walsh, Michael, *The Secret World of Opus Dei*, London: Grafton Books, 1989.

——, *John Paul II: A Biography*, London: HarperCollins, 1994.

Ward, Wilfred, *William George Ward and the Catholic Revival*, London: Macmillan, 1893.

Watt, John A., *The Theory of Papal Monarchy in the Thirteenth Century: The Contribution of the Canonists*, London: Burns and Oates, 1965.

Weigel, George, *Witness to Hope: The Biography of Pope John Paul II*, London: HarperCollins, 1999.

Wessels, Anton, *Europe: Was It Ever Really Christian? The Interaction between Gospel and Culture*, London: SCM Press, English trans., 1994.

Willems, Ad, 'The Endless Case of Edward Schillebeeckx', in Hans Küng and Leonard Swidler (eds), *The Church in Anguish*, pp. 212–22.

William of Ockham, *A Letter to the Friars Minor and Other Writings*, ed. Arthur Stephen McGrade and John Kilcullen, Cambridge University Press, 1995.

——, *A Short Discourse on Tyrannical Government*, ed. Arthur Stephen McGrade and trans. John Kilcullen, Cambridge University Press, 1992.

Williams, George H., *The Mind of John Paul II: Origins of His Thought and Action*, New York: Seabury Press, 1981.

Willey, David, *God's Politician: John Paul at the Vatican*, London: Faber and Faber, 1992.

Wilson, David M. (ed.), *The Northern World: The History and Heritage of Northern Europe, AD 400–1100*, London: Thames and Hudson, 1980.

Wojtyla, Karol, *A Sign of Contradiction*, London: St Paul Publications, 1978.

——, *The Acting Person*, Boston: Reidel, 1979.

——, *Love and Responsibility*, London: Collins, 1981.

——, *Faith According to Saint John of the Cross*, San Francisco: Ignatius, 1981.

Woodward, Kenneth L., *Making Saints: How the Catholic Church Determines Who Becomes a Saint and Who Doesn't, and Why*, New York: Simon and Schuster, 1990.

Wood, Diana, *Clement VI: The Pontificate and Ideas of an Avignon Pope*, Cambridge University Press, 1989.

Woods, Richard, *Eckhart's Way*, Wilmington, Del.: Michael Glazier, 1986.

Yallop, David, *In God's Name: An Investigation into the Murder of Pope John Paul I*, London: Corgi Books, 1985.

Zagano, Phyllis and Terrence W. Tilley (eds), *The Exercise of the Primacy: Continuing the Dialogue*, New York: Herder/Crossroad, 1998.

Zizola, Giancarlo, *The Utopia of John XXIII*, Maryknoll: Orbis, 1978.

——, 'Secretariats and Councils of the Roman Curia', in Peter Huizing and Knut Walf (eds), *Concilium: The Roman Curia and the Communion of Churches*, New York: Seabury Press, 1979, pp. 42–6.

——, 'The Power of the Pope', *The Tablet*, 17 October 1998, pp. 1352–3.

index

Names of individual popes are listed under 'popes'.

387